NORTH STAR
of Herschel Island

- Canada's Arctic Tall Ship -

The true story of the last Canadian sailing ship involved in Canada's Arctic fur trade. A vessel who played a part in Canadian Arctic Sovereignty, Sail-Training, Searching for Mermaids and International Goodwill Relations for Canada.

Produced by:

FriesenPress
Suite 300 – 852 Fort Street
Victoria, BC, Canada V8W 1H8

www.friesenpress.com

Distributed to the trade by The Ingram Book Company

For Sheila Claire, with all my love

With Thanks to:

Research for a book of this type draws upon hundreds of written sources, as well as movies, slides, websites and the memories of many people. With special thanks to - in no particular order: Margaret and Lyle Hawkins, Mary Carpenter Frost, Eddie Gruben, Susie Kivik, Patsy Gruben, Maureen Gruben, Martin Goodliffe (special thank you for putting me up in Yellowknife), Diane (Carpenter) Goodliffe, Ian Kirby, Joey Carpenter, Bill Pringle, Chuck Arnold, Bob Knight, Sven Johansson, Hohns family, Janie Jones at Mangilaluk School in Tuktoyaktuk, Lee Wark, Tiffany Thiem at CBC North in Yellowknife, Peter Thomson, Doug Hankin, Elvis Wolki, Dick Hill, P.J. Usher, Robin Weber at the NWT Archives, Merle Carpenter, John Bockstoce, Chris Payne, Adelia and Kathleen at the ICRC Library, Len Pearson, Murray Boy, Chuck Davidge, Jim Scott, Ernest Pokiak, Geddes Wolki, Bridget Wolki, Mrs Agnes Carpenter, my mother – Mary Young, Janet & John Hannam, Eleanor MacDonald, Lawrie & Susan Masterman, Keith & Chris Masterman, Chris & Brian Masterman, Derek Masterman, Jack & Theresa Masterman, Rick Gonder, the Inuvialuit Resource Center, the Prince of Wales Heritage Museum, Beverly Garven at the Inuvik Public Library, the Greater Victoria Public Library, the Hunter's Bed & Breakfast in Tuktoyaktuk (a special thank you for your hospitality), my father, Hugh MacDonald, the Maritime Museum of British Columbia and a special thanks to Ken and his staff at Aviva Coffee on Cook Street who allowed me countless hours of Internet usage and always kept my teacup full.

Photograph credits are listed with each photo, however, we have received hundreds of images over the last decade and a half and unfortunately, in some cases due to computer crashes, I have lost the name of the contributor and I apologise for that. A big thank you to all who have contributed to this project. To see more photographs of the ship please visit her website at www. northstarofherschelisland.com or find her page on FaceBook.

Perhaps the worst storm that North Star of Herschel Island was ever in occurred on Agnes Carpenter's honeymoon voyage. The year was 1956 and Fred and Susie were a little late in getting away from the Delta. The trip to Baillie Island was a nightmare with huge wind and waves but after a short lay-over the brother and sister decided to push on for Sachs despite the unsettled weather rather than risk being iced in for the winter short of their goal. Agnes recalls the night when as a teenaged bride, leaving her family behind for the first time she found herself alone in the pilothouse watching the waves with her husband and sister-in-law lashed to the top of the deck-house. "There was a big west wind. We were out in the open of the Beaufort Sea. We were crossing the middle of the ocean. One or two schooners went down that night. Everybody was out all night. I was scared. There was a big black wall of water, it was like the parting of the seas and there was black ice all around too. There was just myself aboard and Susie Sidney and Fred. They were brother and sister and they were piloting the boat. They were steering from atop the pilothouse. There was a gyro-compass there - a huge one - on top of the deckhouse. We would take soundings. The most important thing was the current. Fred would navigate by the stars. During the storm Fred and Susie were lashed to the top of the deckhouse for 36 hours, that's how long it took us that time from Baillie Island to Banks Island. The storm started at night, right after we left Tuk. I was in the pilothouse and was just seeing big black water. The waves were as high as, higher than the mast was - 75 feet, 60 feet. The waves were all around us."

Agnes knew of the ship's past and the storms that she had been in. North Star, known as the Queen of the Banksland fleet - a ship known throughout the Arctic for her adventures, strength and beauty. Still, the ship rolled, dipping forty degrees from side to side as waves hit the bow and then broke over the two helmsman sitting twenty feet off of the water. With silent prayers, Agnes held on through the night and 36 hours after giving her wedding vows, she heard the engine wind down, felt the waves lessen and saw land around her as the two tired navigators wove the ship through the sand bars outside her new home of Sachs Harbour.

Table of Contents

Foreword

In 1996 my wife and two daughters purchased and moved aboard the Arctic fur trading ship North Star of Herschel Island. We had been watching the ship for some time but knew nothing of her long and storied career in the Arctic, only that she looked like a very strong seaboat and that she resembled another ship that I had had the privilege of being the captain of on the Great Lakes, STV Pathfinder. North Star's owner was Sven Johansson who had formed the Discovery Dance Troupe in Victoria, B.C. My first time aboard North Star I sat with Sven in the old cargo hold that he had converted into a salon that was absolutely crammed with books, a record player, tv screen and a video player. Most of the material on display was to do with his great interest in dance. A water hose ran out to the boat from a dock ashore and he had pirated a t.v. cable from a marina ashore that ran a submarine cable out to the ship. I asked more about the ship and her adventures. Slowly he began to recount some of the things that North Star had done in the Arctic and a few photos were brought out, showing the ship under a different rig and crewed by Inuvialuit, many wearing caribou skins and fur parkas.

Sven had lived aboard for over thirty years and the ship had sat at anchor and also tethered ashore with numerous cables and lines for over five years. A thick growth of kelp and weeds clung to her hull. We were very interested in purchasing her and to raise our family aboard but Sven had no intention of selling and there were at least a dozen other people who had expressed interest in purchasing her. One day we were on our way back from looking at other boats up-island when we saw Sven walking down the street. We stopped the car and jokingly asked once again when he was going to sell North Star to us. This time he agreed and before he could change his mind we signed a contract and laid down a deposit.

We helped Sven to move ashore and found a dock for the ship, a rare find in the crowded harbour. The day to move the ship came and we were ferried out to the ship in his small skiff. The engine slowly came to life. We had heard that morning that our new dock space, which is a prime commodity in Victoria, was also being coveted by another vessel and mentioned this to

Sven. When Sven heard that the vessel was the SV Thane, owned by Len Pearson, another Arctic sailor whom he had known for years, everything went into top speed. Apparently there was a friendly rivalry between the two and Sven recognized that Len had a good chance at getting to the dock before us.

Lines were cast off and the ship slowly began to swing to her stern anchor, a storm kedge weighing three hundred pounds. The kedge line was run forward to the capstan on the main deck and we laid into the capstan bars with all of our strength. The anchor would not budge. Time began to pass. We took turns scanning the harbour for Thane. Sven laid aft and pulled his Swede knife out. The kedge line was cut and and buoyed and we were underway. Sven turned to the wheel and grabbed the king spoke. The wheel was seized. After years of lying at anchor the shaft to the worm-gear steering had corroded onto the rudder indicator making steering almost impossible. This, plus what must have been several tons of growth to the hull, rudder and propeller and North Star was not happy travelling under her own steam. A horrible screeching sound came with every effort at the large oak wheel. Inch by inch he managed to coax the helm to turn. His coat came off and sweat streamed off him in buckets. We worked our way over and hailed the Johnston Street Bridge. Traffic stopped and the big blue bridge rose allowing us to pass under. We turned to and came alongside the knuckle of the dock where a head spring was passed and made fast so that we could swing into our berth outside of the burned out shell of a building that would later rise Phoenix-like into a trendy restaurant.

The ship drew a crowd, something that we would soon grow used to at almost every port we took her to. Part of it was the massive amount of rigging that she carried and part of it was the sound of her GM353 air cooled diesel - a screaming Jimmy - that could not be ignored. The ship is full of character, proudly carrying the scars of her hard work in the Arctic. It wasn't long before we began to meet a steady stream of people who recognized her from up North. The first was an Inuit man who made his living carving soapstone for some of the local galleries. He had seen the ship in Tuktoyaytuk and now sat on the field astern of the ship day after day carving beautiful soapstone sculptures that he sold daily to the shops on the tourist strip. One day he was working more slowly than ever. He had a photocopy from a book of a frog leaping, its legs fully outstretched. He was laughing and asked us if we had ever heard of a more ridiculous thing. One of the galleries had commissioned him to carve a frog for one of their customers. Apparently frogs are a popular thing among collectors. "Have you ever heard of a more ridiculous thing?" he asked us. "An Eskimo carving a frog! I have never even seen a frog. We don't have them in the Arctic!" He carried on with his work and we began to go through North Star, emptying lockers and cleaning everywhere before moving our own gear aboard.

As mentioned, the ship had sat at anchor for many years and for the last twenty years, Sven had been batching aboard. There was an incredible amount of gear aboard that we had to move off and we ended up filling a dumpster with most of it. For instance, in the lazarette under the pilothouse there were cases and cases of pickled meat. Some of it was char, reindeer, caribou, jams and jellies. Most of it had turned and many of the jars had split open leaving an incredible mess and stench everywhere. There was evidence of rats and aloft, there were many birds' nests in the sails including ones with eggs that had long ago been abandoned and had been cracked open by crows. Otter scat was on the decks.

After cleaning this out, Sven called to say that he also had a storage room full of gear that went with the boat. When he had been up North, Sven had shipped down all kinds of things off of other ships and from his time working with the reindeer herds. We hired a truck and removed all of the items, enough to fill a small museum and carried on with our sorting. Sailors are a self-sufficient breed and in the North parts are hard to come by. We recognized how useful many of these items would be if we were in a secluded place, far from the big centres but had to judge what we could reasonably store and what we had to let go.

A few weeks later we learned that he had another store of things that we should get. He said that he had left them in an area in an abandoned field near where the ship had been anchored. We rowed over and looked around but didn't find what he had described. Next time we met up he drew us a treasure map. As an Arctic man, Sven had dug a hole and left a cache of things that he could not find room for. When we returned, we did a little digging. Here was a separate set of rigging, fine woods, jerry cans, food, oars, spare porthole glass and storm windows. There were slides and negatives, lying in the dirt, many of them now ruined but some that could be saved. Our skiff was loaded right up to the railing and we sculled slowly back, hoping that no waves would swamp us.

It was around this time that we truly began to recognize the historic significance of the ship. We had not just purchased a boat, but a floating museum and a living treasure of the Canadian Arctic fur trade.

With all of our gear aboard we decided to scrape the paint off of the ship and to see what shape all of the wood was in. The ship had never been down to bare wood since her birth in 1935 and we were astounded at the quality of her construction. We found that the hull, built of quarter-sawn edge grain fir was as tight as could be. There were no knots but a few Dutchman splices had been laid in where damage had occurred. In many places there were huge balloons of water between the paint and the hull and without removing it, the vessel could soon be at risk of rot. Besides, we were curious as to what condition everything was in. On deck we scraped down the hatches and found huge, sturdy bronze fastenings buried beneath almost an inch of thick white paint. The first owners and later Sven had preserved the hull by painting her every year, but we took pounds and pounds of paint off of her and allowed the wood to breathe and dry so that we could re-coat her.

We spent the first spring and summer scraping the hull down. In one place we found that part of the gunwhales had been repaired with a piece of bone as it was probably more easily found high above the tree line than a small piece of wood. Many of the sails were cut down and we began the process of patching what we could and scrubbing off years of mould, nests and other stains. She was ours though and a conscious decision was made to maintain whatever we could and bring the ship back to her former glory.

We were given some good advice by the owner of the old mission ship, Columbia III, who recommended that we only start what we could finish that season and no matter what, to get out to sea at least once each year so that our efforts would be rewarded with memories over the long winter ahead. Our goal was to take the ship to the first ever Saltwater Music festival to be held in Sidney BC. This festival was organised by Pat Thompson and Tony Latimer who lived aboard their pinky schooner Forbes and Cameron. We worked sunrise to sunset cleaning and painting. I took a hacksaw and carefully cut through the four bolts holding the steering gear to the rudder indicator so that the helm could turn easily.

The day dawned on our first trip. The engine fired up and we cast off. We had arranged to 'buddy boat' with another vessel who had made the trip out and around Trial Island, a manned lighthouse off of Victoria and then through the shoal infested waters of Baynes Channel leading up the strait to Sidney by the Sea. Our two vessels exited the harbour and our buddy leaned on the throttle and disappeared over the horizon. We were alone. Smoke began to pour from our engine room and when I looked down I could see that our transmission was glowing red. We reduced our rpm's and carried on, slowly and very noisily rolling our way up the channel. A pilot whale surfaced abeam us which we took as a portent of good luck. The voyage took most of the day as we had to stop and let the engine cool down many times. There wasn't enough wind to sail and so we drifted with the tide.

When we finally entered the narrow cut to Sidney it felt as though we had been at sea for months. There was a definite feeling of pride on all of our part as we threaded our way through the channel. We had assumed that we would be mooring on the first set of docks as the marina was quite crowded. Instead, we were directed to carry on down past row after row of shiny, fibreglass yachts. The size of the ship and her rigging, coupled with our 'screamin' Jimmy' drew quite a crowd. Many boat owners stood on the ends of their vessels and smiled bravely at us as we inched past their spotless, expensive yachts. In many cases we were only a foot or so off of them as I needed enough room to round up and into our space. Glancing around at the beautiful marina with the hundreds of boats, the well manicured grounds and the baskets of flowers hanging off of every piling I was so happy that we had carried on despite the transmission problems. Cranking the wheel hard over, I edged forward enough so that the stern could swing around and into our allotted space. I gently rocked the vessel astern and the large crowd ashore all broke into applause. Please, I thought. It's not the first time that I have docked a large square-rigger. Once our lines were secure ashore and the applause had stopped, a man ashore asked how I had managed to do that. It was the most incredible thing that he had ever seen. My stunned look back at him caused him to point forward to our jib-boom, the spar that stretches fifteen feet off our bowsprit. Hanging jauntily from the end of it was one of the hanging flower baskets. In manoeuvring the ship back and forth North Star had managed to snag herself a proper bouquet! It was one of many surprises that she was to hold for us in the coming years.

This book is the result of fifteen years of listening to stories from visitors to the ship including many of Fred Carpenter's children and grandchildren. North Star of Herschel Island is the last of the sailing ships involved in Canada's Arctic fur trade and a floating reminder of a very important part of Canadian history. Her story spans time from the primitive north to modern days; from searching for mermaids to surveying the controversial Alaska/British Columbia boundary and for her work in securing and representing Canadian Arctic Sovereignty.

This manuscript has taken years to write, in part because her Inuit history was mainly passed down in the oral tradition and therefore required extra effort to fact check from primary resources all of the interesting stories that I had been told. A trip to the High Arctic to interview Inuit and Inuvialuit elders as well as to see North Star's old stomping grounds first hand rounded out the research. I want to thank my daughters Maida and Isabel and most of all my wife, Sheila Claire, for their patience in putting up with living aboard a small ship with the large amount of books, photos and ephemera that I acquired during my research.

This is North Star of Herschel Island's story, the history of a ship that all Canadians can take pride in.

A Note To The Reader:

In researching this book I came across numerous names to describe the original inhabitants of our Canadian North. The term Eskimo is no longer used to describe Canada's Arctic First Nations' People, except perhaps by themselves, amongst themselves. When Eddie Gruben, a ninety-three year old fur trader from Tuktoyaktuk visited North Star of Herschel Island in 2010, he shook hands with one of my daughters and said, "You know what you are doing? You're shaking hands with a full-blooded Eskimo!" Eddie is not one for political correctness though he means no offence, however in this book I will try my best to be and hope not to offend any readers from any culture. I have left all quotes intact allowing the speakers to describe themselves in whatever terms they feel comfortable doing. To that end, I offer some modern definitions and explanations of names for people that I will be using, who all used to be called by those from outside of the Arctic, as Eskimo.

"The Inuvialuit - often referred to as the MacKenzie Delta Inuit, (or) the Inuvialuit as they now call themselves, inhabit the northwestern Arctic coast from Alaska to Avvaq. Nineteenth century records reveal that the indigenous population was divided among five subgroups, the largest of which was the Kittegaryumiut. Archaeological investigations in the territory of the Kittegaryumiut demonstrate that these ancestors of today's Inuvialuit maintained a uniform, rich, and distinctive culture from the fourteenth to the nineteenth centuries."[1]

"The forebears of the Inuvialuit shared their economy, their technology and their culture with the North Alaskan Inupiat, with whom they mixed and traded from early times and who were part of the inter-continental trade network of the Bering Strait. The predecessors of today's Inuvialuit also crossed to Banks Island to trade with the Copper Inuit. As well, trading between North American Indians and Karngmalit, an Inuvialuit group centered in Paulatuuq, occurred before the advent of non-Inuit traders. Goods found in the MacKenzie Delta that could have been from inter-Native trades include metals, dentalium shells, and Russian trade beads. Dentalium shells in particular were rare and highly prized, and were obtained by the Inuit only through trade.

Although the indigenous population of the MacKenzie Delta area numbered between an estimated 2,000 and 4,000 in the nineteenth century, a series of epidemics decimated the group. By 1910 only a few score survived, and they were deeply affected culturally and linguistically by the Alaskan Inupiat who had immigrated into the area during the boom times for whaling, 1889 to 1908 and with whom they inter-married."[2]

"Eskimo is the Indian (most likely Montagnais or Naskapi) name for the northern aboriginals. It was the designation originally used by whites because a Jesuit in 1611 had heard Indians refer to the northers as Eskimantsiks, a derogatory term meaning "eaters of raw flesh". Inuit, the more contemporary term, simply means 'people'. (Inuk is the singular of Inuit).Canada's 25,000 Inuit are divided into eight tribal groups: Labrador, Ungava, Igulik, Caribou, Netsilk, Copper and Western Arctic. They speak a common language, Inuktitut, which has six dialects. Dwellers in the western Arctic have in recent years coined a new word, Inuvialuit, to distinguish themselves from other Inuit. Those who live in Northern Quebec (Ungava) are 'Taqramuit' (people of the shadow); they call the aboriginal citizens of Labrador 'Siqinirmiut',' (people of the sun, which rises in their land first)."[3]

Dr W.E. Taylor Jr. adds an interesting perspective to the name-calling in the north. "I should stop here for a moment to explain something of the origin of the word 'Eskimo'. It is an English corruption, of a French corruption, of a Cree Indian word meaning, approximately, 'eaters of raw flesh'. And the Eskimos, who held the Indian in no higher regard, called him 'adlit' or louse egg, but refer to themselves with laconic pride as 'Inuit', the people."[4]

FOREIGNERS ARRIVING

"European explorers, arriving in Inuit lands in the 1500s, called the Inuit 'Eskimos'. That was a name used by neighbouring Indians, not by the Inuit themselves. Historians once thought that Eskimo meant 'eaters of raw flesh', but current scholars think the name probably refers to snowshoes."[5]

"The earliest outsiders to the Inuit world were the Vikings, sailors from Iceland and Norway, who established a settlement on Greenland in A.D. 985. The Vikings called the Inuit skraelings, meaning 'rough people' or 'savages' because they thought they were very frightening. This was because they were hunters and carried their tools - harpoons, spears and bows - with them all the time"[6]

"The word Inuit means 'the people' or the 'human beings' in the Inuktitiut language, and traditionally the Inuit considered all other races to be mixtures of human beings with either animals or demons."[7]

"The Inuvialuit belong to the Inuit culture. The Inuit culture developed over thousands of years. It is speculated that the ancestors of the present day Inuit arrived in North America 6,000 to 12,000 years ago, depending on which source you cite. It is also commonly accepted that the Inuit people crossed the Bering Sea from Siberia to Alaska."[8]

"A group of early explorers who crossed the Arctic returned home claiming that the Eskimo regarded the white man as inferior. To support this they quoted the Eskimo word 'Inuvialuit'- the name we use for our people, meaning 'the real man'. It does not mean that we think we are superior. It is simply used as an expression to describe the whole Eskimo family as one... man, woman and child."[9]

In 1978 the Canadian Broadcasting Company commissioned a show called The Northerners that focused on the people of the Canadian Western Arctic. The hosts of the show were warned to only refer to the First Nations people as Inuit or Inuvialuit. The E word was banned. Much to the hosts' chagrin, in interview after interview the Innu called themselves Eskimos. As a result, the eight one hour shows were never aired.

The politically correct discussion continues to this day. In November 2011, Conservative MP David Anderson of Cypress Hills Grassland, Saskatchewan used the word Eskimo on his website. This kicked up quite a hornet's nest on Capital Hill. One person who came to Anderson's defence was one of the original owner's of North Star of Herschel Island, Fred Carpenter's daughters, Mary Frost. Here is her letter to the editor of the Ottawa Citizen newspaper:

"ESKIMO is not a racist slur. And, Conservative MP David Anderson of Cypress Hills Grasslands, Saskatchewan is not a racist for using this word on his website.

ESKIMO, as our eminent Prime Minister Stephen Harper recently said about hockey, "to some extent it's a generational thing." I am a 68-year old Canadian woman from Canada's Western Arctic. I grew up being called, "Eskimo." I accepted being called, "Eskimo." My Inuivialuk parents, Ajgaliaq and Gahyupdoin, accepted being called, "Eskimo." So, Eskimo for me is not a racist slur.

I am also a Residential School Survivor. Painful. The first book published in 1949 by The Church of England was titled, "SERVICE BOOK OF THE WESTERN ESKIMOS," translated by "...the able assistance of Eskimo Catechists." I accept that and have come to appreciate the effort and the bridge building which came at a brutal high price. I lost my birthright to my parents, my clan, and my Inuvialuit way of life, Inuvialuktun, my shamanic roots, and my beloved siblings. My residential school experience brought me into close contact with the Fort McPherson and Arctic Red River Loucheux, who now call themselves, Gwich'in. The Loucheux called us, "Husky-mo." That was an insult. I did not accept that term but my parents informed me that Eskimos have husky dogs and that it's okay to be called, "Husky-mo." Being me, Tungoyuq Illoak, I did not, and will never accept "Husky-Mo." I accept, "Eskimo."

It was not the white people who labelled my people, The Inuvialuit ("The Real People"), "Eskimo." It was one of the various tribes attributed to this label. Tribes in Canada were practical people. These Indians saw my ancestors eating raw meat and being precise spoken, "Eskimo"– Raw-meat eaters" - was born. I accept that. My clan, the Inuvialuit of the Western Arctic, still eat raw meat. Yum!

Ottawa of the sixties did not have Members of Parliament or Urban Inuit living there who considered ESKIMO a racist slur. However, there were two white bureaucrats, Paul Lumsden and Victor Valentine who decided to enlighten Parliament Hill and the entire federal bureaucracy. Every time the word, Eskimo, appeared anywhere, these two men would write back and state authoritatively that the Eskimo called themselves, "Inuit." Paul Lumsden married my cousin, Mabel Pokiak, Canada's first Eskimo registered nurse from Tuktoyaktuk and Vic Valentine became an Anthropology Professor at Carleton University.

In 1977, at the Inuit Circumpolar Conference in Alaska, the Inuit politicians passed a resolution to change ESKIMO to INUIT. I accept that too. That was our original name for us to each other. But, Eskimo is not a racist slur. In my world travels, I have discovered a wonderful benevolence to ESKIMO. That precise name is always met with: smiles followed by: You rub noses? Igloos? Blubber? Polar Bears? International goodwill at its best!"[10]

The labels or "name-calling" goes both ways. If Eskimo was seen as being a derogatory term then the Inuit had one for the white foreigners in the North. Kabloona - a term for white people - has been interpreted by some as meaning 'big eyebrows'. de Poncins has another take on it. "The word Kabloona means 'white man'. It sometimes carries a scarcely concealed tone of contempt, like 'greaser' or 'gringo', and with some justification. The Eskimos who use it are seal-hunting tribesmen from the very northern edge of Canada, and they certainly endure the most brutal living conditions of any people on earth. They call themselves Inuit - 'men - pre-eminently.' Those who have not been contaminated and degraded by civilization deserve the name. They are hunters supreme, relics of an earlier age of man than the one we know."[11] "What should these foreigners be called? First there is the problem of origins. We cannot say "white men", because some were black. Europeans is not accurate, because eventually some were African or Asian, and after several hundred years many were Canadian or American. Some of them lived all their lives among native people and cannot be called 'strangers' or 'newcomers'. Words like Euro-Canadian and non-native are clumsy; in fact any term we choose will be open to debate. Let us settle for foreigner, in the sense of people who are born - as most still are - outside the north."[12]

Thrasher in his memoir, Skid-Row Eskimo, has the last word. "Listen to the North Wind. It has come to take us away. The name, Inuvialuit, will only be heard in the wind. The land will still be there, the moon will shine, the Northern Lights will still be bright, and the Midnight Sun will still be seen. But we will be gone forever..."[13]

Chapter 1
Fred Carpenter and the Wolkis

In order to appreciate the contribution of North Star to Canadian Arctic History we look back to the year 1908 when Fred Carpenter was born near Tuktoyaktuk. Fred's mother, a full-blooded Inuvialuit was named Divana. In those days Inuit generally went by one name only. Fred's father was John Carpenter who had anglicized his name from Charpentier when he immigrated to the United States from France. When he arrived in the Arctic he was an American working aboard a whaling ship that over-wintered at Sachs Harbour.

John Charpentier hailed from France and had moved to San Francisco to find work. How he came to find himself aboard a whaling ship bound for the Arctic Ocean is a mystery, though the consensus is that he was just as likely to have been shanghaied as to have volunteered to sign aboard. It was common practice in sea-ports around the world, that when more crew were needed for a voyage that a pressgang of men would scour the streets and bars in order to either 'doctor their drinks' as the sea-shanty goes or to knock them out with a black-jack. In either case, the new crew member would often not awaken until the ship was at sea and from there the freshly minted sailor soon learned a new trade, whether he liked it or not. A less romantic route that Charpentier may have taken was simply to have signed aboard ship in order to have an adventure and earn a wage. In either case he wound up aboard a whaling ship that anchored at Herschel Island. Fred's third wife, Agnes, believes that Fred, Susie and John's father, was an engineer on Captain Pedersen's Patterson which is another likely story.

Once in this new environment he would have met up with the local First Nations. There was a symbiotic relationship between the Inuit, the LaCheux Indians and the whalers. The whalers hailed from ports all over the world but were often ill-prepared for the cold of a Canadian Arctic winter. They hired the local Inuit to sew clothes for them and to bring them fresh meat - caribou, bear, seal and musk-ox in return for white man's food - tea, coffee, flour, sugar and with guns, knives and other riches from the South. It was common for the whalers to seek companionship from the Inuit women and even to move in with them for the winter. As a result, there were many half-breed children born and in most cases, once spring came the whalers left and never returned.

When the ship arrived at Herschel Island to over-winter, John, like most of his crew-mates found it more desirable to move in with an Inuit beauty than to continue share living space with his fellow whalers. "When the whalers came around, my mother went around with a white man. Inuit had nothing then, no whiteman. Young girls - you know girls. The whalers would take the women away from the Inuit men. They made children. Myself, Fred Carpenter, Jim Wolki and Susie Sidney. We are the whiteman's children. You know, they made kids. They would leave them and find another wife. Like they weren't married. That is how it happened. I am an illegitimate child. You know, no father. That is what they called us, even though we do have fathers."[1]

"They were mainly freetraders and trappers who married native wives and settled down to create their dynasties bearing the names Lyall, Firth, Joss, Carpenter, Ford, Ruben, Steen, Klengenberg, and several others. Such marriages were successful partly because the Inuit, unlike whites, have never had any serious concerns about racial mixing, and there have been few examples of the complex relationships involving Indians and Métis. By and large, it has been an Inuit tradition to accept any Kabloona who wants to become one of them and proves it by living in the Inuit way and perhaps marrying an Inuk. 'Living the Inuit Way' is, of course, an extremely difficult initiation for a white man to pass."[2]

When the whaling ship left Herschel Island for her return trip to San Francisco John Carpenter elected to stay behind. He and Divana had another son, named John Junior and two daughters, Susie and Mary. Jim Lambert is a former RCMP officer based in the Arctic. He recalls that "The whalers that were wintering over got dog teams and went up the coast. John went over as far as the Anderson River. They were known as the Anderson River people. They stayed there more than one winter."

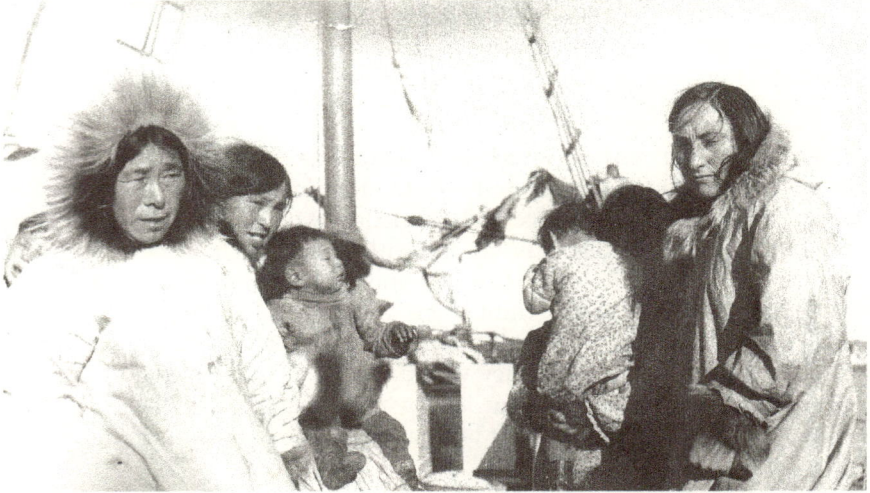

Divana, (Fred and Susie's mother), on far left and Susie on far right. Note Divana's facial tattoos. Photo taken aboard North Star on summer voyage.

When the children were quite young John proposed to Divana that he wanted to take the boys with him to Alaska and then to the United States to live. Divana refused to give up both boys as she needed the help of at least one of them and so John took John Junior and Mary leaving Susie and Fred to stay with their mother. In their retirement years Fred went to California to visit his brother, John. Fred recalls that, "we not recognise anymore. We played together forty years ago. California was good all right but I don't know that kind of life. I stay with my own family in the north country."

Fred Carpenter at home in Sachs Harbour in mid-1950's.

Reports of Herschel Island at that time were of a rough, frontier-style community with drinking, fighting and debauchery. Fred helped to provide for Divana and his grandmother as best as a child could, though it would have been up to Divana to do most of the hunting. There is a report that Fred mainly used a small bow and arrow to take down small birds like ptarmigan to give to her. "Fred was supporting a widowed mother by hunting with a bow and arrow when he was 13. In 1932 he came to Banks Island and settled for a year near Liot Point, on the west coast. In those days, one who went to Banks Island one summer could not leave until the next, for there was no radio, no mail, no planes."[3] There is no doubt that he, like every young lad in the community, would have been introduced to hunting and been expected to help provide for his family and the community at large. "It was different then. They didn't have guns or anything, so they used sling shots to kill birds, bows and arrows for food. They didn't have regular clothing so they had fur clothing - caribou and they used sinew from the caribou's hind leg to make thread for sewing and needles out of the bone." adds Fred's daughter, Diane Carpenter.

The noise, threats and language of life around Herschel Island all got to be too much for young Fred and so when he was about twelve years old he ran away from home and hid in a snowbank. He stayed in there for days before he was found by a white couple who had heard him crying. They took him home and cared for him as their own. From them, he learned to speak English. "My Dad was very industrious. He didn't speak too much English, but learned it on his own but also he ran off from his grandparents when he was twelve years old 'cause he was nervous and everyone was feuding and having fights and he got kind of nervous and took off and went into a snowbank to keep warm. There was these two white people, I guess they heard him, so they picked him up and he sort of grew up a little bit with them and learned the language from them. Then he just made what he could of himself." When some time had passed Fred returned to Divana and his grandmother to help them and provide for them but for the most part he continued to live with the English white people until he was in his late teens. Fred moved around between his grandparent's house, Divana's and the English parents. "I was only a little boy when the explorer Stefansson came to my mother's place, to that sod house my grandparents owned in the Tuk area. We were all sitting on the floor eating. Stefansson said to me, "Your mom and dad are Eskimo, how come you have blue eyes? I can tell you are a little bit white man." And he grabbed me and had me sit on his knees,"[4] recalled Fred Carpenter later in life.

As a side note it is interesting that while Stefansson has been revered in books for many years as the ultimate Arctic explorer, he did not make a very good impression with all of the Northerners when he first arrived. Most notably was James and Fred's father, Fritz Wolki , who was a tough man, a hard man who suffered no fools. Having started before the mast on a whaling ship, he eventually had his own command and had a reputation as an honest man whose experience in the North was not often equalled. When he swallowed the anchor and moved ashore he kept a schooner named Rosie H. and for many years operated a trading post at Horton River.

His assessment of Vhiljmar Steffanson, whom he was happy to sell provisions to for the expedition at exorbitant prices is classic. Wolki's comments were harsh: "A college professor who carries books in his sledge where a sensible man carries grub. Say, did you ever shake hands with him? He's got a hand as soft as a woman's! I don't believe that fellow ever did a real day's work in his life. I'll eat my shirt if he ever comes back."[5] Of course Stefansson made it and there are no reports that Wolki dined on shirt.

Stefansson is recognized as an Arctic hero for all of the exploring that he ended up doing, though like Sir Edmund Hilary and Tenzing Norgay, it is unlikely that he would have survived without the help of the Inuit. In history there is often a prejudice in the white man's interest. Fred Carpenter's meeting with the explorer was before Stefansson had started to map this island which the Eskimos called Igasuk. Billy Banksland was Stefansson's guide for five years. It took the two men two or three years to map Igasuk. They went by dog team, but they walked every foot of the island, all along the shore and into the river beds, and they measured every step. If Stefansson got tired, Billy walked ahead of the dog team. They also measured the island across. Stefansson said, 'Without Billy Banksland, the dogs and I would starve to death, but as long as Billy has one shot left, I know I will live.' Stefansson called this island Banksland. The maps call it Banks Island."[6] adds Fred Carpenter

Too often the only impression that we get of a person is that of their deeds. These were 'hard' people, for sure but in order to get through some of their adventures they must have had an optimistic spirit as well as a sense of humour. For instance, when a stranger arrived in camp Billy Banksland used to like to don a polar bear skin and then sneak up behind them and give them a real bear hug! When the person looked down and saw the polar bear feet or the paws around him his reaction would give everyone a laugh and from then on he was initiated into the joke.

While in his teen years Fred met and married his first love, Lucy Wolki, whose brothers Jim and Fred were his friends. Their father, who had the harsh opinion of Stefansson, was Fritz and their mother was Pisuktaok. Lucy and Fred had three children: Frank, Andy and Agnes. The family lived on the trapping ground, sleeping in double walled tents or icehouses depending on the season. During the summer they travelled to Herschel Island aboard Fred Wolki's Blue Fox, another Arctic schooner.

Fred had no time for the prejudices that were still rampant between the Inuit and the LaCheux First Nations. His son, Stanley, recalls that "he took in an Indian boy who was being prejudiced against. He took him out on the trapline and taught him how to trap." Stanley also recounts that his father was tough, but fair. "I used to go up to shoot pool at the D.O.T. You could go the long way around or cut through the dump. That's where there were polar bears, sometimes. He caught me coming from the dump and whipped me." Stan also remembers Fred taking out his children and anyone else who wanted to go out in the bay on North Star, just for fun.

When Lucy died, Agnes was given to his sister, Susie, to raise. Sharing children was a very common practice in the Inuvialuit culture. A family that had no children or who wanted a son or daughter might be given one by another family member. In this way all children are wanted and loved and within the community there are many parents and grandparents who feel connected to the next generations. As well, Fred may have thought that due to Agnes's age that she might have been too hard to care for by himself out on the trapline. When Lucy died, Fred married Ada Gruben. They had six children: Margaret Rose, Henry (who died in his first year), Mary Elizabeth, Noah Henry, Joseph (Joey) - he has no middle name so gave himself 'The" and John Willie.

When Ada died from tuberculosis Fred married Agnes Peffer, daughter of Jake and Ethel from Aklavik and they had eight children, though one died at birth. George William, Stanley, Diane, Brenda, Marilyn, Linda, Fred Junior and Thomas.

Perhaps it's true that one's first love is the strongest. Later in life, when Fred was hospitalized in a coma Mary Carpenter Frost was sitting across Fred's bed from his third wife, Agnes. "I poked him, he kept repeating Lucy's name, I slapped his face and yelled at him, "WHAT ABOUT ADA GRUBEN, MY MOTHER?" Agnes just laughed and told me "to calm down, that your dad doesn't know what he is saying."

In 1931, a 23 year old Hudson's Bay accountant named Richard Bonnycastle set out to visit all of the HBC posts in the Canadian Western Arctic. He travelled mainly with dog sled, meaning that he rode some of the time but mainly ran alongside of the sled since it was so heavily laden with stores and furs. The image of the sled driver always on the back, perhaps cracking a whip, is not always what happened. If there was no trail or the snow was deep then the driver had to walk ahead of the team to break trail. 1931 was a bad year for most of the posts and Bonnycastle was horrified to find out how much credit had been extended to the trappers. Their debts were any-where from $5,000 to over $35,000 dollars and many of them were asking for more credit since they had had a bad year of trapping. In his diary he calls them many names and is disgusted with the conditions that he finds many of the trading posts in. At one stop he found that the one room home where the trader and his wife and their six boys were living was dominated by the rotting head of a beluga whale which seemed to be their main source of food. On top of all of the debts he also found that the stock of goods that the HBC posts had was far too great and that the managers were still ordering more. One family offered him a fresh salmon but declined to share in it since they preferred the canned food. One ray of light came when he stopped at Horton River. "Fred Carpenter, his wife and baby were occupying a house belonging to Pat Wyant. Roddy and his family were also staying there. Edward's family came in and out and with Sigrid, who is a perfect brat, they made the place a bedlam. Fred Carpenter is a good lad and trapped 93 foxes this winter. Rolled in on the floor and glad to do so."[7]

In his spare time Fred enjoyed playing the violin and was often the musical entertainment at parties. There are pictures of him playing at the annual Christmas and New Years parties at the Department of Transport building in Sachs Harbour and at the Mounties headquarters on Banksland. He would be called out to play when the ships rendezvoused each year at Herschel Island or later, Aklavik. A self-taught musician, Fred would haul out his violin at parties and family gatherings and play music so that everyone would dance. "Crazy story. Peter Sidney, my dad's brother-in-law one time he sat on it - on the fiddle - and broke it! It was an expensive violin that in the '30's he paid $1,200 for that. A lot of money! ", recalls Dianne Carpenter. Fred adds, "I used to play all right. Somebody sit on my fiddle. They broke it up and I never fix it. I quit playing for a long time then. Maybe I'm crazy about it," he laughs. "I can tune it up myself. Somebody learned my step-father, Jim Cockney, he play the fiddle. He's like my brother, married my mother. We sent the fiddle to Edmonton after it broke. He, Jim, loved to play. I love to see him happy like that."

"Fred moved down the west coast and settled north of Cape Kellett on Blue Fox harbour. Then he returned to the mainland, not coming back to Banks Island until 1937. That year he established the settlement at Sachs Harbour, named for the ship Mary Sachs of the Canadian Arctic Expedition of 1913."[8]

Another of Fred's hobbies was playing poker, something that his mother enjoyed as well. Fred was always up for a game and enjoyed the gambling side of the action as much as the cards. He and many of the other Bankslanders were notorious for their poker games when ashore in Tuktoyaktuk, Herschel Island or Aklavik, or to pass the time at sea aboard North Star, often betting large amounts that would draw a crowd. "He tried his best at everything and he became a good trapper and he loved to play poker. They would play with foxes at that time - him and his friends would get together. My Dad got tired of winning so what he would do - once he won the pile of foxes he would give them back to the peoples and say, 'Let's play again!' Just to have more time to play," adds Diane.

Fred was a shrewd businessman and knew how to get to get the top dollar for his fur catch. When he and his third wife, Agnes, opened their store on Banks Island it was more out of recognition that this was a necessary service rather than a profit making one, though they did quite well with the store. Fred had the business sense as did Agnes, who had grown up working around her father's and uncle's store in Aklavik. Since they were ordering supplies to be picked up with North Star and later by an annual barge, they had to anticipate what the needs of their household as well as the whole community would be a year hence. "Fred couldn't read or write but I had been raised by a merchant. I had to do all of the ordering - barge orders. Order everything a year ahead of time" says Agnes.

Former RCMP Constable Cal Alexander remembers Fred as a "tall, slender man, not of typical Inuit stature or having their facial features. He was almost freckle-faced and his sister, Susie, had the same skin coloration. On top of that, one of his children was red-haired!" Cal had heard, most likely incorrectly, that "the story was that Fred's father was a Fiji Islander who had wintered over at Herschel Island. He would have been a whaler." It would be easy to make this assumption considering Fred's large freckles and skin colour. There are gravestones at Herschel Island and in many other places in the Western Arctic of Fiji and Hawaiian Islanders who either signed aboard or who were shanghaied by American and British whalers. The skill of the South Pacific whalers was very established and so these men were highly valued aboard whaling ships.

Fred's status as the leader of Sachs Harbour is legion. He was a good man who took an interest in his community and tried to help others. Diane Carpenter sums up her father this way. "He always tried everything. When he bought the schooner he wanted to use it for a good purpose. He knew in Tuk there was not too much food and some people - well there wasn't a variety of food - he went to Banks Island I think in the 1930's or somewhere around that time - they would go there in the summertime and then come back to the mainland - back and forth and then they decided they would stay there because there was an abundance of livelihood - food, good water there and they could make money off of the land. So that's what he did. He made sure they had a little store so that they could make sure the community - that they had food - and he had the schooner for transportation and he was a good trapper. My dad was a survivor. He did what it took to survive."

Fred Carpenter was born on October 1908 and died April 14th, 1984.

Fred Wolki

Fred Wolki was born in Teller Alaska in the early 1900s. His mother was Pisuktaok and was an Inupiat Inuk. Fred's father was Fritz Wolki, a German/ Swiss whaler. Fritz and Pisuktaok had two sons, Fred and Jim, and a daughter named Lucy all of whom are part of North Star's early history.

Fred gained his sea legs when he signed on with the Canadian Arctic Expedition from December 1917 until February 1918. The leader of this leg of the expedition was Storkersen. Storkersen felt that Fred was too young to carry on when the expedition became stuck in the ice with no break in sight and so he ordered Wolki back with a support team that was led by Castel. Fred was paid forty-five dollars a month while on the expedition with a bonus of five dollars a day when the team was travelling on ice. When he joined the support team he was given another bonus of seventy-five dollars, a tidy sum in the early 1900s, especially for a teenager! When Fred made it back to Barter Island with Castel, he continued to work in some capacity for the team.

Six years later, in 1924 Fred signed aboard the schooner Maid of Orleans that was skippered by Christian Klengenberg. Henry Larsen and fellow RCMP Constable MacDonald were travelling aboard as well. When the ship was caught in a storm MacDonald was lost overboard. As the storm raged on "Bror Wiik remained on deck with Fred Wolkie, the son of a German whaling skipper, who was at the helm,"[9] recalls Larsen of the RCMP's St. Roch.

In 1929, Fred took his family to trap on Banks Island. He had learned of the riches of this island while working with the Canadian Arctic Expedition and heard of trapping methods when speaking with the crew of the Polar Bear. The family made camp on the west coast of Banks Island, at Blue Fox Harbour. There he met and married Fred Carpenter's sister, Susie. "Fred's wife Susie was from Aklavik and they had a son, Roy." recalls David Berhardt interviewed in Kugluktuk.

Fred, Susie and son Roy on vacation in Vancouver.

Fred died at a relatively young age from tuberculosis. After his death his widow Susie married Peter Sidney. Fred Carpenter teamed up with Fred Wolki's brother, Jim, and began to run trap lines. They became known for their superior dog teams that they spent a lot of time and money on in order to have the best ones, as well as becoming two of the top fur trappers in the Canadian north.

An example of the tough lives that these men led happened during the winter of 1933/34, a couple of years before North Star arrived in the North, when Jim Wolki and his family became iced in at Banks Island. Their food was running out and things looked bleak for surviving another winter. In the late summer they loaded up their schooner Omingmuk and tried to force their way through the thin leads out in to the Beaufort Sea. Their boat was laden down with a year's worth of trapped fur as well as their dogs, tents, family and friends. They pushed Omingmuk as hard as they dared and made it about thirty miles before facing a completely frozen ocean. They could sit alongside the ice pack and hope for another lead to open but doing that meant that they might be frozen in thirty miles from shore for the winter. While they hoped that Omingmuk would be forced up and on to the ice, there was a very real risk that their boat could be splintered like a matchstick when the pack moved in. They turned and carefully threaded their way back to Banksland.

With the ship back at Sea Otter Harbour, they waited for the ice to clear but a big westerly wind rose up and pushed the sea ice into the harbour. Their fate was sealed for that year as there was no way that that amount of ice would clear again this late in the season. "There was nothing else to do than put on a good face to our misfortunes and take the challenge, a very tough one."[10] recalled Jim in his memoir, The Toughest Year of My Life.

With no tea, tobacco, sugar or other taniktut - white man's grub - and running very low on shells for their rifles, the family reverted back to their traditional diet of seal, owl and even occasionally, fox. By the end of December the whole family was losing faith that they would get through the next six or seven months. With dogs to feed and ammunition running short they had many mouths to feed and no easy way to do it. A decision was made to attempt an overland trip to the Hudson's Bay Post at Lettie Harbour at Paulatuk. This was a very dangerous proposition as it required stable ice conditions in crossing the strait to the harbour as well as the dangers from polar bear or becoming lost or disoriented in a storm. The biggest danger is that far from land the ocean is still running under the ice, causing it to move, buckle or even break up.

Jim Wolki with wife Bessie and children, Aklavik, 1940.

Jim told his wife, Bessie, of his intentions and while she did not agree with the plan she knew that if anyone could survive this adventure it would be her husband. Paul Adams agreed to go along and Ol Andreasen stayed behind with Bessie and the children.

The trip across provided many challenges and sometimes for days they were snowed in waiting for the weather to clear. There was not much food for the dogs or the men and so they could not push along as hard as they wished to. When they got to the other side they met up with Bertrand Pokiak who gave them some supplies and pointed them in the right direction to the post. Later they meet Einard Jansen, one of the white trappers and he gave them some help - "This he added would be a token of gratitude and acknowledgement to Fritz Wolki, my father, who years ago had treated him so well along with his partner, Carl Patterson, at Horton River."[11]

Out in the wilderness, with no sign of other people, the days turned into weeks and the two men were anxious to get to the trading post. One day they came across some sled tracks and followed these. "They were my brother Fred and my brother-in-law Fred Carpenter. The world is small indeed, of all the Inuit we could have encountered, it had to be my two brothers."[12]

After getting to the trading post, they exchanged their white fox pelts for supplies. They loaded so much onto the sled that it was to prove a challenge to get back, but Wolki knew that if they were snowed in again for another year, that he would not want to make this overland trip again.

Returning to the camp after months away Wolki was scared to look in case his family had starved to death in his absence. "Thanks to God, all the members of the families were not only alive, but in good health. The only thing that had kept them alive was the foxes and Old Adam had made sure that there would always be enough for them all. They lived on fox meat, they were lighted (their stoves were lit) with fox fat. Foxes were the only and the ultimate element and agent of their survival."[13] "Old Adam had not stayed idle in our absence, and visiting his traps he had got close to four hundred white fox."[14]

The following July they set out again on Umigmak and made it to the Delta where they were able to trade their fur and also to pick up a motor for their schooner. The motor had been sitting in storage waiting for their arrival for almost two years. "The years to follow brought me many good trapping seasons and good crops. Many more times, Fred Carpenter as my partner and myself, went to Banks Island and shared the hazards of fur trappers."[15]

After years of being friends, brothers-in-law and trappers together the two men spoke of building a big sailing ship that could handle both of their families rather than continue to use the aging Blue Fox and Omingmuk. That ship, North Star, would become a reality in 1935.

Chapter 2
C. T. Pedersen

Captain Christian Theodore Pedersen was a whaling captain and was considered by many to be the foremost expert in Arctic navigation. As Captain of the whaling ship Herman he spent many seasons in the western Arctic taking whales and built up a reputation among the Native people as being a kind and fair man who treated them well. He would often take on Inuit crew as seasonal workers. He also hired other Inuit to supply his ship's larder with fresh meat and hired the local women to sew proper Arctic skin clothing for himself and his crew.

Theodore Pedersen was born in Sandefjord, Norway about 1877. He went to sea as a very young teenager in the position of deck boy on a large sailing barque carrying a load of lumber from the St. Lawrence River to Dublin, Ireland.

Captain C.T. Pedersen who brought the schooners north.

He began his Arctic career as an apprentice seaman and harpooner, 'before the mast' aboard the steam barque whaler, Fearless (ex Elida), in 1893 that ended up wintering at Herschel Island in 1894. The young man took to the hard work of life aboard a whaling ship and quickly saw the enormous profits that could be made by someone who knew the waters and the First Nations people. Pedersen spent a little over a decade with this ship, slowly working his way up through the chain of command while learning seamanship, ice-piloting and navigation. In 1908 he was able to get his own command, the whaling schooner Challenge, which he took back up to the Arctic where he over-wintered at Point Barrow, Alaska. "When someone first saw a whale, the Captain (Pedersen) would pay them too....with a gold watch. The Captain would tell them, the first ones sees a whale shall have a watch. At that time a watch was so valuable it was big money. They would say to each other that they saw him first and take the watch because the watch those days was so high price."[1]

The whalers initially were interested in the whales for their oil which was used in everything from street lights to make-up but a secondary market for baleen quickly became their primary focus. Baleen, the brush-like filters in Bowhead and other non-toothed whales mouths, is a very strong, flexible material that was used for things such as buggy whips and in women's' corsets. Like every other ocean that white people have entered, the Western Arctic's whale population was soon decimated and the majority of whale ships left to look for other areas to hunt.

Captain Pedersen, the ice master, manouvers his ship, Patterson, through the ice to trade at Herschel Island.

He saw the void that the whalers had left since the Inuit had grown used to having access to 'white man's food' as well as tools, knives and perhaps most importantly, his ability to carry up from San Francisco fairly large boats to sell or trade. Pedersen stayed on in the Arctic and turned his sights onto the growing demand for fur. "Later on, when the whalers were gone, Captain Pedersen started coming around and he was hauling stuff down there. That's before anyone ever come down by these rivers with boats. Only by the coast Captain Pedersen would bring stuff and food."[2] In 1911 he gave up the Challenge and with his profits from whaling he purchased his first ship, the schooner Elvira. Just two years later, in 1913, Pedersen got caught in pack ice off of Alaska and Elvira was crushed and sank. Having lost everything Pedersen went looking for a job and was hired by the San Francisco trading business, H. Liebes Company. He took command of their ship, Herman, and hired one of his former deck-hands from Elvira, George Washington Porter, a half-breed European/Eskimo. H. Liebes Company operated fur trading posts throughout the Beaufort Sea area, trading with the Eskimo for fur in exchange for food, tools and small boats. Pedersen spent the next eight seasons making the run between San Francisco and the Arctic and built up his already good reputation with the fur trappers, both Native and White, as being a fair man to deal with. "Pedersen was well liked by everybody. He was fair. He gave them good prices," recalls Agnes Carpenter.

In 1923, after many years of providing a reliable service to the traders and turning profits for H. Liebes and Company, Pedersen asked for and was denied a pay raise. Liebes was upset with him since the previous year Pedersen had diverted Herman to the Siberian Coast in order to rescue the explorer, Bartlett, who was stranded there. Liebes felt that this had cost the company $13,000. Pedersen quit in disgust, again taking George Washington Porter with him. Able to now purchase another ship, Pedersen bought the 261 ton three-masted, lumber schooner Nanuk and formed his own company, the Northern Whaling and Trading Company to go into head to head competition with Liebes. In his first season Pedersen found himself in a neck and neck race with his former command, Herman, as they entered the ice. Both ships looked as though they would be caught and trapped but Pedersen saw a lead and followed it into open water, quickly leaving Herman astern. His crew were in awe of him as he went aloft to watch for ice-leads and ended up staying in the crow's-nest for 24 hours navigating the ship through the ice.

At the first port that Nanuk entered Pedersen purchased every fur offered, some nine hundred pelts and some blue fox pelts, leaving just two pelts for the next ship. The crew had just finished stowing the valuable cargo and was busy packing them when a look-out shouted that a trading schooner had hove into view. "I had been in the crows-nest 24 hours, working through ice, to St. Lawrence Island to grab the winter's catch of furs. I had heard (on the wireless) that a trader from Nome had chartered a schooner to beat us across. The minute we tied up, I started buying white foxes. After I cleaned up all the skins held by the Eskimos, I (bought) all the skins in the native stores. I was up in the attic when the little Nome schooner arrived after working ice for a week. (He) got only two white fox skins and he paid a fancy price for them. I picked up about 925 white fox skins and over 40 blue foxes, many polar bear skins, and all their hair seals."[3] Pedersen had gone 72 hours without sleep or rest. He continued with this strategy and by the end of that season H. Liebes and Company was bankrupt. The Canadian Government's law also caught up with Liebes which effectively sounded their death knell. On the 20th of March new orders came from Ottawa in an effort to protect the hunting grounds of the Canadian indigenous people. The beginning of the order reads:

Whereas the Commissioner of Dominio Parks, who is administering the NorthWest games act, has reported that a number of foreign trappers propose going into Banks Island, NorthWest Territories this year for a period of three years, for the purpose of trapping in that territory;

And whereas the difficulties of police control of this Territory prohibit proper supervision to prevent the illegal slaughter of game there;

And whereas this is confirmed by the Commissioner of the Royal Canadian Mounted Police who also advises that the hunting ground in the Arctic should be preserved for the native Eskimos.

A further setback and adventure for Pedersen occurred the following season. "In 1924, his trading schooner Nanuk was pirated by Russian Cossacks off the Siberian coast. He was held prisoner for several days before being released but lost his $20,000 cargo of trade goods."[4]

It was not all clear sailing for the Northern Whaling and Trading Company now, though. The Canadian Government had been watching with growing concern foreign vessels entering Canadian waters and trading with no Customs duties or Canadian laws respected. The Canadian Government sent two RCMP officers to Herschel Island to enforce this law. Previously ships of all flags, including Pedersen's American ships, would sail unhindered as far east as Baillie Island, trading with Canadian trappers and then turning back to the USA without declaring any of their business. The law, which had been on the books but never enforced, now required all foreign ships to stop at Herschel Island, land all of their trading goods and then pay duty on them. In order to comply with the Canadian government Pedersen then formed a subsidiary of the Northern Whaling and Trading Company and so the CanAlaska Trading Company was born. An office was set up in Vancouver, B.C. and two Canadian ships were hired, Nigalik and Emma. Pedersen's business strategy was to sail Nanuk to Herschel Island, off-load and pay duty on his trade goods and then load them aboard the two Canadian ships who were then legally allowed to remain and trade into other Canadian ports.

Quite often an RCMP officer would stay aboard the ship to make sure that Canadian laws were followed.

In 1924, as his business continued to grow, he built a bonded warehouse and in 1925 a trading post at Herschel Island right across from the Hudson's Bay Company which quickly became a landmark and a meeting place for trappers in the Western Arctic. It is still standing today. Sarah Meeyok recalls meeting the culturally diverse crew of Pedersen's ship. "There was lots of people there coming to Pedersen's store. My grandparents had a good friend. Someone from Pedersen's boat. Me, I didn't know and was so scared of a man that always looking at me and smiling a lot. He eyes were just white. He served us while I was sitting between my grandparents. When he was out of sight I asked 'why is it they put black soot on him?' He never put soot on him, my granddad told me, he was born like that. We went to go have supper with a colour guy on Pedersen's boat and I thought they put black soot on him! Maybe he come because he had job on Pedersen's boat. When I first saw him I was very scared of him. Then, after I knew him, I wasn't scared anymore. We would buy sugar , tea. All those were down at Pedersen's store. The penny were big as five cents."[5]

Patterson, who carried supplies and 'schoo-ners' north for trade with the Inuvialuit.

Pedersen's business was going so well that he needed a larger ship to transport the trade goods from California as well as to take back all of the fur. He sold Nanuk in 1925 and purchased the much larger Patterson, a 580 ton former survey vessel. The barquentine was already 43 years old and required a complete refit for Arctic service. Captain Pedersen and the Patterson

27

became famous in the Arctic as their arrival each season meant the beginning of trading and the availability of everything from fresh fruit to appliances and tools that would make life in the Arctic easier. The Patterson was large enough that in addition to regular trade goods, Pedersen was able to load on deck and hanging outboard, large boats that he would sell or trade to the Inuit. One of the most famous of these was North Star.

"Captain Pedersen, he was a white man. He was always handing freight for the ships. White man food. He would bring them by the ocean. When he bring the boats, they were like little toy boats, he just lined them up on the ships and brought them like that. They would be quite a lot of them on his big ship. And when he reached Herschel Island, he would unload them there. He would work with them toy boats. The North Star and these other boats were big boats, you know. The boat would hang on the big ship on the sides. I don't remember how much they cost. The ones that Captain Pedersen brought were very strong ones, the ones that went to Sachs Harbour and that, travelled by ocean all the time. And the ones that came later on, they bring them by the Delta. The ones that Captain Pedersen brought to Qikiqtaqruk were strong ones. That time people always get stuff from Qikiqtaqruk, long ago. By boats, all the way by ocean."[6] "Every year he carried several schooners on the deck of his ship the Patterson, offloading most of them at Herschel Island off the coast of the Yukon. On two trips he brought food and medicine to the starving and sick residents of Point Barrow, Alaska. His wife, a registered nurse, travelled with him, assisting the natives."[7]

Persis Gruben remembers how her father purchased North Star's sister-ship, Reindeer, paying for her in fur. "For the first year, and considering the limited knowledge we had of the Island, and a limited range in trap lines, it had been a success. The trappers were satisfied and happy. One needed only to take a look at all the furs hanging and swinging in the sun at the mercy of the wind, to know that it was worth a small fortune. Dad had set up his mind to pay Captain Pedersen as quickly as possible for the acquisition of the 'Reindeer'. He had been told by Captain Pedersen that furs, any kind of furs were as good as cash. As a trader he was well known and respected by all Inuit along the Arctic Coast, for his fairness and the quality of goods he did bring to the North. His knowledge of the North and of navigation in the treacherous water and ice of the Arctic ranked him as one of the best skippers who travelled North."[8]

"Pedersen carried a lot of debt for the trappers, so he may have allowed his best customers to pay off their debt for the boats over time," says historian and Arctic adventurer, John Bockstoce. Pedersen's giving credit to trappers was a calculated risk on his part, but with his experience in the North, he had learned which trappers he could trust. He was also aware of the cycles of good fur years and bad and so could make an educated guess as to how many furs an experienced trapper could be expected to bring in. When Jim

Wolki and Fred Carpenter ordered North Star, probably the most expensive private vessel to be brought into the Arctic Ocean, it was done on credit. Pedersen purchased the boat and then re-sold her to Wolki and Carpenter upon delivery in the Arctic.

"Two of the more successful traders who had been whalers were Captains Pedersen and Klengenburg. Among other things, they sold schooners to the Bankslanders. Fred Carpenter's North Star, with its inside furnishings of mahogany, was purchased from Captain Pedersen"[9]

It should be noted that some of the independent traders took time to make fair deals with the native people. For example, Captain Pedersen enjoyed a good reputation among the Inuit, and he had no need to go beyond Herschel Island. He established a trading centre that flourished in competition with the Hudson's Bay Company until the Depression of the 1930's and the rapid decline in the price of white fox. Pedersen left, never to return; the Hudson's Bay Company also pulled out; and that was the end of Herschel Island as a hub of commerce."[10]

Each year Pedersen would work Patterson up to Herschel Island and then make the return trip to San Francisco. In 1931 the ship was caught in the ice and the pressure squeezed the old, wooden hull onto the ice where she was left stranded for fifteen days until he could break her free and escape back to California.

The HBC and CanAlaska became bitter rivals, undercutting each other on prices and creating a sellers' market for fur. Many people felt that one of Pedersen's greatest contributions to the traders was that merely by his presence he was able to keep the Hudson's Bay Company's prices in check. He also brought in goods from the United States that the HBC did not have ready access to.

"Mrs Petersen (sp) usually sailed with him. A motherly influence who frowned on alcohol in any form, she was a good influence. She could be seen knitting contentedly at any time aboard, while Cap hastened to sell his wares and get back around Point Barrow again before the ice caught him."[11]

As the Great Depression effects began to be felt in the Arctic a decision had to be made over the CanAlaska's future. The HBC had met CanAlaska's presence by creating more trading posts around the coast. Pedersen wanted to do the same and tried in vain to convince his business partners to no avail. The final play of the two rivals chess game came when the HBC opened up a post in Tuktoyaktuk. Pedersen followed suit. He had been thinking of retiring and selling out to the HBC but by opening the post in Tuktoyaktuk the value of his company rose since by buying him out the HBC would be rid of his pesky competition. CanAlaska sold out to the Hudson's Bay Company in 1936. He also sold them the Nigalik for $10,000 and after twenty-one consecutive voyages north, left the Arctic forever. He had apparently strained his heart while moving 804 sacks of coal to the beach by himself at Herschel Island, no doubt a personal challenge for the tough ice-master since there would have been crew aboard to do this.

His ship, Patterson, under her new owners, was driven ashore and wrecked at Cape Fairweather, Gulf of Alaska, on December 11th, 1938.

Patterson wrecked at Cape Fairweather.

Pedersen and his wife retired to Pacifica, California and started a mail-order fur trading business for polar bear skins out of Russia. He also tried his hand at mink ranching and he and his wife regularly entertained visitors from the Arctic. He kept in touch with his old friend Henry Larsen and even sent him a photograph of his wife, feeding a hummingbird by hand in their huge backyard garden. "It's quite a change from ice-pilot and fur trader to feeding hummingbirds," he wrote.

He often said that his goal was to live to be one hundred. At 92 years of age Pedersen and his community were aware that two men had escaped from a nearby prison. There were many sightings of the convicts and some teenaged girls even helped to hide them, fooled into thinking that the police were unfairly chasing them. On June 24th, 1969 the escapees broke into the Pedersen's home.

"The Captain met his end in 1969 under terrifying circumstances. Two young convicts escaped from jail in nearby San Bruno and broke into the Pedersen house. The couple, who had gone to bed, were savagely beaten, evidently in an attempt to find out where they kept their money. A neighbor called the police, who arrived in force. With the help of trained dogs, they apprehended the culprits under the house. The Captain and his seventy-four year old wife were put in an ambulance, but he died en route to hospital. His wife's skull was fractured, but she survived."[12]

His ashes were scattered over the Pacific Ocean.

Chapter 3
Herschel Island

North Star of Herschel Island was originally named North Star and like all of the ships delivered by Pedersen the port of Herschel Island was added below her name. Herschel Island was North Star's first port of call however after that she mainly stayed at Sachs Harbour on Banks Island but for years made an annual voyage to Herschel Island in order that the Bankslanders (as they are so called) could trade their fur for provisions, tools and equipment. Herschel Island has an incredible history and in order to fully appreciate what the Bankslanders aboard North Star of Herschel Island were a part of, it is important to get a taste of what life at Herschel Island in the years before and during North Star's annual migration was like.

By 1936, when North Star was delivered to the Arctic, the infamous trading grounds of Herschel Island and trading via schooners to there was drawing to a close. The Wolkis, Pokiaks, Grubens, Carpenters and so many other Bankslanders and Delta Inuvialuit had grown up with the trading model of sailing to Herschel Island each summer to exchange their winter's catch of fur for the goods that they needed to get through the following winter now voyaged mainly to Delta ports.

The Inuit call Herschel Island Qikiqtaruk, which is the Inuvialuit word for 'the island'. Herschel Island lies 200 miles above the Arctic Circle. Pauline Cove on the south shore of Herschel Island is the only deepwater cove between Point Barrow and the MacKenzie Delta. It has depths of up to 3 fathoms and is protected by a 1/3 of a mile sandspit, making it a good deep water harbour for vessels of all sizes. The island is only five miles wide and about eight miles long but can be seen from far at sea as it rises to a height of six hundred feet. It lies about 5,000 miles from San Francisco, where North Star of Herschel Island was built.

To look at Herschel Island on a chart or map it is impossible to fathom how difficult it was to get there. For years, the American and Russian sailors had hunted in only the Western Beaufort Sea, trying to keep their ships safe from the ice pack and hoping to be able to find a lead out or safe harbour should winter come early. It was only when this area was overharvested that ships slowly began to move in, though not without tragedy. "This body of water has been cursed by sailors since Frobisher's expedition in 1576. Its shores are decorated with the skeletons of wrecked ships and lost men, the ships of nations that sought a new east-west waterway here. Dozens of explorers have hurled their vessels at the ice barrier, during the last four centuries, some driven on by the lure of discovery, others simply eager to plant their country's flag at the top of the new world. Few returned from the adventure; most left their ships, many their lives. Caught and crushed in the drifting ice were ships like Perry's Fury, Ross' Victory, Franklin's Terror, McClure's Investigator. Sometimes the ocean literally consumed the ships, sometimes they were abandoned, to be plundered by the Eskimos..."[1]

The first 'foreigners' to arrive and winter over at Herschel Island were the whalers who came in search of the Bowhead whale. Having plundered the stock of whales on the Eastern seaboard of North America and the Eastern Arctic, they found the mother lode when they arrived in the waters just west of Herschel Island. The general belief was that there were no whales in the western Arctic but in 1889 the whaling ship Grampus took a gamble and headed up and around Point Barrow. Here there were thousands of whales, enough to fill thousands and thousands of barrels of oil and to supply the seemingly endless need for baleen that was used primarily for making women's corsets as well as umbrellas and buggy whips. Grampus spent the season filling her holds and returned to San Francisco having taken twenty-two Bowheads. One large Bowhead whale of one hundred tons might produce a ton of baleen which sold for about five dollars a pound or about ten thousand dollars. Her arrival back in the United States set off a gold rush and whaling ships from around the world set off to fill their holds from the western Canadian Arctic.

The whaling fleet at Herschel Island in the late 1800s.

The whalers decimated the Bowhead population in the Arctic, something that has never recovered. They left their mark in other ways as well. The Inuit and the Indians had developed a taste for and reliance upon the 'white man' for a source of trade income. While they were disgusted with the waste of the whalers' practice, they appreciated that their lives in many ways had become easier. Prior to the whalers' arrival, the Inuit were a nomadic society, moving with the seasons in order to follow the rhythms of the animals that provided them with food and clothing. They were always on the move, either following the caribou migration, finding polar bears on the tundra or collecting eggs when the great flocks of snow geese arrived each spring. The whalers introduced a lifestyle where they only had to provide fresh meat and they could have different food or materials to make their lives easier. "Then the whalers came. To the Eskimos they were fascinating and infinitely rich. Their ships were laden with treasure. The whalers needed hundreds of tons of meat to feed their crews. They paid for it with trade goods, with useful articles such as guns, pots, knives, and hatchets, but also with less essential items such as chewing gum, suspenders, cigars, canned milk and often, despite official interdicts, with liquor."[2]

Roughly a century ago, Herschel Island was, according to whom you wish to believe:

'an out post of civilization' - Vilhjalmur Stefansson

'the Sodom of the Arctic'...'inhabited by demons of debauchery and cruelty' - Nome newspaper, 1905

'a thriving Arctic metropolis' Captain Henry Larsen of the RCMP St. Roch

... but the 'scenes of riotous drunkenness and lust which this island has witnessed have probably never been surpassed.' - Reverend C.E. Whittaker

"I prefer not to mention the many and queer tales I heard during my sojourn" at Herschel Island. Roald Amundsen

"It was a place where rather staid New England ladies attended opera performances and minstrel shows, and their husbands who tended to be 'corpulent and their hair thin' (Roald Amundsen) played whist and drank port. And to a nine year old Eskimo boy who saw it for the first time it was: 'Herschel! The great big town' (Nuligak). Whatever their views, it is hard to argue with the Reverend I.O. Stringer, later Bishop of the Yukon, that this was a community like none other that ever existed in Canada.'

For a decade, from 1894 to 1905, Herschel Island was the whaling center of the Western Arctic and when whaling declined it became the hub of the extensive fur trade of this region. Henry Larsen spent his first winter at Herschel in 1924 and loved it: 'there was never a dull moment'. That year the Royal Canadian Mounted Police bought some of the old whalers' buildings and made Herschel its subdivision headquarters. In an unofficial way, Herschel had become the 'capital' of the Western Arctic."[3]

John Herschel by Jula Margaret Cameron, April 1867.

In 1826, John Franklin and his men descended the Mackenzie in two open boats, then turned west to explore the unknown coast. Franklin reached the island on 17 July and named it Herschel after the famous scientific family. There has always been some debate of whether it was named solely after Sir John Frederick William Herschel, a famous British astronomer and chemist, and son of the equally famous Sir William Herschel, who discovered the planet Uranus and became Astronomer-Royal to King George 111. "... the Seven Year's war persuaded a nineteen year old military oboist named William Herschel to turn from carnage to the cosmos and sail for England. There he set music aside and began to study the stars. Within a decade Herschel was producing Newtonian (mirror) telescopes without peer. He discovered Uranus, which doubled the diameter of the known solar system and garnered a grant from the King. With money in hand, Herschel sought a foundry to cast a thirty-six inch mirror with three times the light gathering ability of previous mirrors. When all refused he decided to cast it himself.

After constructing a circular mold from densely packed horse manure in his basement, Herschel fired up the furnace and proceeded with the pour. The mold cracked. When he tried again, the furnace cracked, sending a fiery stream of molten metal flooding across the floor - and Herschel abandoned the casting business.

A few years later, the King's foundry finally produced a forty-eight inch mirror for Herschel's new reflecting telescope. When the king invited the archbishop of Canterbury to the dedication, he reversed their usual roles, telling the archbishop, 'Come my Lord Bishop, I will show you the way to Heaven.'"[5] The planet that was later named Uranus by Herschel was originally named by Herschel "Georgium Sedis (George's Star) in honour of the King. In return, George III granted him a pension of 200 pounds per annum with the only requirement being to live near Windsor and to show the Royal Family the heavens at their pleasure."[6] Sir John Frederick's sister Caroline, was also a skilled mathematician who joined her brother and became his assistant. She became the first woman to ever publish a scientific paper and discovered eight comets. Sir John Frederick's son, also a Sir John, carried on the family tradition and was considered one of the most pre-eminent scientists of his time. "Upon his death he was buried in Westminster Abbey next to Sir Isaac Newton, indicating the outstanding esteem in which he was held."[4] Charles Darwin was later laid to rest between them.

Many Eskimos lived on Herschel Island and others frequently visited it, for 'it abounds with deer (caribou) and its surrounding waters afford plenty of fish'. Franklin noted its harbour, the only one along this coast; 'one of the finest harbours in all the Arctic,' as Stefansson described it later.

In order to reach the safe harbour of Pauline Cove the whaling ships would edge their ships into the shallow waters between the mainland and the ice that was grounded offshore. The vessels would often drag their keels on the bottom earning the whaling ships the nicknames of 'mud pilots'. Once they arrived at Pauline Cove the crew would come ashore for a break to await the emptying of the ice to the east of Herschel Island, which then signalled the time for the short whale hunt. Philip H. Godsell was an author, fur trader and an inspecting officer for the Hudson's Bay Company. He spent many years in the Arctic and describes what the arrival of the whaling crews looked like. "The arrival of the whaling fleet was the signal for a Bacchanalian orgy that is still remembered by older Eskimos. Down the gang-planks of a score of vessels surged a polyglot horde of mixed humanity till the beach was overrun with a drunken mob of dark-visaged Kanakas, bearded Russians, ebony-faced Negroes, sallow Portuguese and slant-eyed Orientals, leavened with lean Yankees, and even the occasional professional man or titled Englishman in search of adventure. Rum, black as molasses and fiery as fire(!), flowed like water, Soon every Eskimo from nine to ninety was staggering around drunk as a lord, howling, shouting and raising bedlam, while cinnamon-cheeked belles, caught in the hairy arms of sodden brutes, disappeared into the depths of dank fo'c'sles."[7]

The whalers who set up camp at Pauline Cove at Herschel Island came from all over the world but were primarily from the United States. At times it seemed that the island was either owned by the USA or was simply an ungoverned spit of land where lawlessness prevailed. Not only were Canadian laws and values being ignored, there was the large matter of foreign vessels importing trade goods into Canada and not paying customs dues on them. Prior to 1903 when the North West Mounted Police established its first detachment at Herschel Island, the Inuit were at the mercy of the whalers, who brought in barrels of rum and came ashore looking for women. When the news reached San Francisco that a police detachment had finally been established on Herschel Island, a local newspaper carried the story and added the hope that the small force of two men was adequate to "cope with the demons of debauchery and cruelty who walk on two legs and call themselves white.' Any laws or rules on Herschel Island had until this time been handled by the ship's Captains.

In 1892 the Reverend I.O. Stringer, later archbishop of the Arctic, visited Herschel Island and he observed that there were American flags everywhere, but not a British or Canadian one to be seen. And then he remarked, 'I don't suppose the British or Canadian governments will interfere, as they do not seem to take enough interest in the North to care.' The Hudson's Bay Company viewed the whalers of Herschel Island as unwelcome competition. They reported the untaxed goods entering Canada with the whalers. The Canadian Government was slow to respond but in 1903 two members of the NorthWest Mounted Police (later known as the Royal NorthWest Mounted Police, 1904-1919 and then as the Royal Canadian Mounted Police, 1919-present) were sent to the island.[8] The role of the police was not only to enforce Canadian criminal laws and custom's duties on Herschel Island but also to represent Canadian sovereignty on the Yukon. The two NorthWest Mounted Police would have certainly had their work cut out for them.

"The whalers also engaged in the lucrative business of trading with the Inuit, and it was this competition that the Hudson's Bay Company thought unfair. Some of the traders, not content to wait at Herschel Island for the Inuit to come to them, moved gradually east to Baillie Island and Tuktoyaktuk. Finally, after protests from Hudson's Bay people, a Customs House was established on Herschel Island and duty was demanded from the whalers on their cargoes of trade goods."[9]

The entrance of the whalers into the Inuvialuit hunters' lives not only changed their annual schedule of travelling and hunting but changed the way that they viewed the actual killing of animals. With the whalers seemingly insatiable demand for meat, the Inuit began to kill animals in large numbers, rather than just for what they needed. They also shifted from using every part of the animal, an act of respect for the animal that had given its life in order for them to survive, to just taking what the whalers wanted and leaving the rest of the carcass. Prior to the whalers arrival into Inuit life, "hunting for food was the main reason for an Eskimo man's existence. It was more than just the food that was needed to survive; it was a spiritual compulsion to outwit the game. When a native hunter killed a caribou or a whale he would hold a brief ceremony to thank the animal's spirits. Spirituality among natives and hunters is deeply embedded, something white men and missionaries have difficulty understanding."[10] In the early 1900s the western Arctic's whale population had been decimated by the whalers. In fact, the impact of the whalers on the environment can still be felt today. Whole herds of caribou were slaughtered in order to feed the whaling crews, as were seals, swans, geese and ducks. "On the average, each ship required at least 10,000 pounds of meat per season. In some years, nearly 200,000 pounds of meat, mainly caribou, were brought to the ships, and this consisted primarily of saddles and haunches."[11]

This waste of food and disrespect for the animal was a source of friction between the whale-men and the Inuit. The whalers were primarily interested in the heads of the Bowhead whales for this is where they collected the baleen that was needed for women's' corsets and umbrellas. On average, a Bowhead whale weighs 3,000 pounds and has foot thick blubber full of oil. It has about 500 baleen and in the early 1920's this was selling for seven dollars a pound. The head also held the greatest collection of oil that was used for lighting lamps and stoves. The rest of the body was left to float away, often ashore where the Inuit would cache the meat if they got to it before it began to rot. Sarah Meyook recalls hearing of the scavenging after the whalers. "They found a Bowhead whale and we had some of the muktuk from there. Because even for years, the dead whale never spoils. That's why you still could eat it well. The blubber is like this thick. Even if the gulls pick or crack it, it never spoil. And if the dead whale stays on land and of the skin is not cracked it never spoils. It's not like Beluga whales."[12]

Very soon the whalers were no longer interested in the oil, for rendering the fat took too much time that could be better invested in harvesting more baleen, which had a stronger market value.

The rotting whale meat may have triggered the large population growth of scavengers such as the Arctic white fox which coincidentally had just become a much sought after commodity. "Later, the trappers learned to train the foxes to come to the carcasses so that they could be trapped. The Nunatagmuits make a practice of feeding these foxes each autumn scattering seal carcasses here and there about the section of the country in which they intend to trap. The foxes soon become accustomed to finding these lying promiscuously about, and when the traps are later concealed cunningly near the bait they flounder unsuspectingly into them, to decorate later on the neck or gown of some young lady thousands of miles away."[13] In the book about the culture of the Inuit, Inuvialuit Pitqusiit, the authors explain that the "traders made visits to us exchanging things such as flour, tea, tobacco and other goods for the furs we brought them. Our people did not immediately take to trapping because we were not accustomed to the wastage involved."[14]

The degree of increased activity in the Western Arctic provided the impetus for building an R.C.M.P. patrol ship as until now the RCMP were forced to beg passage aboard local schooners. "At this time the Government of Canada was expressing its sovereignty over the northern lands. The RCMP vessel St Roch was launched in 1928 as a supply ship for the isolated Royal Canadian Mounted Police (RCMP) throughout the Arctic. These outposts enforced Canadian law among Inuit and monitored foreign whaling and trading expeditions. Many families still lived on the land, coming to the trading posts only when they wanted to exchange furs for tools and food such as flour, sugar and tea. Others had begun to gather around settlements that had been established by various trading companies where they worked in a cash economy for the traders and the RCMP. The government found it easier to administer people who had settled in one place and encouraged the growth of these settlements."[15]

The RCMP was also tasked with keeping track of the First Nations Canadians in the north and the concept of issuing tags or discs was given to them to implement. "With the Inuit, one of the difficulties was identification. The first policeman to deal with them found they had no family names - only individual names. This problem was solved by giving each one a metal disc stamped with the letter E (for east) or W (for west) and a number. Some Inuit and a few whites were outraged by this depersonalization. Gordon Robertson felt, however, that numbering Inuit was not much different from the social insurance numbers of all Canadians."[16]

Tom Thrasher, whose father piloted the schooner Our Lady of Lourdes, was a sailor from one of the San Francisco sailing ships. "My grandfather was from San Francisco, he was Portuguese. Got a job with the whaling ships out of San Francisco. Them days they hunt whale for oil and baleen, big money ah. So my granddad was Captain of one of those ships, so they froze in at Herschel Island and my grandmother, I guess she sewed his clothes you know for the winter, made him winter clothes and in the end he lived with her. My granddad is a Portuguese, real dark, real nigger. He didn't marry my grandmom, he shacked up with her, that's where my dad comes from. The ship he captained was named Thrasher, Thrasher. And my granddad's last name was Walker. My dad should have been named Billy Kimiksana Walker, my name should be Walker. But when the white people came into Herschel Island they taken down census ah, your name where you came from, whatever. My granddad by that time sailed back down to San Francisco and he never came back, so my grandmother grew him up. So they were taken the census, the government from Ottawa. Taking the census, numbering people now, ah. And my Dad his only name was Billy Kimiksana. But white-man had to put an English name on you somehow, so they ask questions and the only question that they got like his dad was Captain of the boat Thrasher. Thrasher, that's all they said his dad was captain of the boat Thrasher was all the answer they gave him about my granddad so they called him Billy Thrasher (chuckle) named after that ship....so we are named after a ship".[17]

Whale meat is an important part of the Inuit diet and each year a hunt was organised in the Western Arctic as far as Herschel Island. North Star was used by Fred Carpenter for many seasons in whaling, mainly for beluga. Larger whales are more difficult to come by and are considered more of a delicacy. The muktuk or flesh from a Blue Whale is much coveted. Up until the early 1900s the standard way of preserving muktuk was to put it into 'pokes' or bags made from seal skin and then filled with seal oil. It was a rarity and a delicacy since so much work would have to go into killing a whale. When Pedersen showed up each year on the trading ship Patterson he would always have many pokes of Blue Whale muktuk to trade for fur.

"Pedersen sold not only white man goods but also bowhead whale muktuk in seal containers (pokes) and reindeer furs which Inuvialuit especially liked." Kathleen Hansen was told the following story by her father: "My dad always gets everything at Captain Pedersen's. Even muktuk in a poke. They say Ole Andreasen's wife, when Captain Pedersen started to unload, she would watch for it because they wanted to eat blue whale's muktuk. They would watch on the shore. They said that day they were going to unload them. While being on the shore, Ole Andreason's wife, Atugyuk was her name, she tried to be the first to get some. So she picked five pokes."[18]

Repeating history, the foreigners unfortunately introduced alcohol to the western Arctic First Nations as a trade item, a disastrous choice that changed Inuit life forever. "Unlike their east-coast counterparts, the western whalers distributed large quantities of liquor to the local population and participated in such uninhibited sexual orgies that a disgusted witness described Herschel as " a paradise of those who reject all restraint upon appetite and all responsibility for conduct; when a dozen ships and five or six hundred men of their crews wintered here, and scoured the coasts for Eskimo women. I do not think it is extravagant to say that the scenes of riotous drunkenness and lust which this island has witnessed have rarely been surpassed.' Another observer noted that "when girls were not obtainable, wives were enticed away from their husbands, or men induced to rent out their wives.'"[19] "There were drinking bouts almost every day," Nuligak recalled. Henry Larsen, the famous captain of the RCMP ship St Roch, who spent years in that region, said many whalers 'moved in with Eskimo women, and a period of wenching and home-brewing followed that is still remembered in the North."......A report to the Canadian government states that there were 15 huts ashore, warmly insulated and heated and 'used in winter by officers..... ...who nearly all keep a woman'.[20] One observer noted that with liquor as the medium of exchange, the whaler-traders pressured the Inuit to 'rent out' their wives in trade for booze. One missionary remarked, "The greatest shock I ever experienced was the many white or black children of Eskimo mothers."[21]

Inuit woman with seal skin poke at Herschel Island, 1925.

Throughout the age of the Northern fur trade there were many constants besides the cold in the winter and the mosquitoes in the summer. One of these was the way that each Hudson's Bay Post was set up. A very early form of customer control that is ingenious in how effective it was. "The inside walls of the HBC stores were unpainted and there was no attempt at decoration except for the Coleman lamps and dog chains suspended from the ceiling. Merchandise was divided into three categories: provisions (flour, cornmeal, jam, baking powder, sugar, tobacco, tea, candles and matches); dry goods (canvas and duffel, tartan shawls, mirrors, toys, yard goods and the utilitarian panties known as 'joy-killer bloomers'); and hardware (rifles, ammunition, files, traps, knives, pots, pans, hand-powered sewing machines, and coal oil or kerosene.) These basic stock lists were gradually expanded to include accordions, axes, blankets, ostrich-feather boas, beads, boots, buttons, belts, tailor-made cigarettes, dresses, gingham, harmonicas, hats, mitts, needles, fish and mosquito netting, paints, perfumes, prepared and canned foods, snowshoes, soap, spectacles, sweaters, tents, toboggan boards, towels, tools, twine and waders. Since few customers could read, colours were important in arranging the displays: five pound tins of HBC tobacco were bright red, while the cheaper Ogden's brand came in light green; red-label tea was stronger than the green-label tea; red boxes held 12-gauge Imperial shotgun shells while blue boxes were used for Dominion shells, yellow boxes for the cartridges, and so on."[22]

The disparity in values between the Inuit and the whalers sometimes caused conflict and there are many reports of Inuit and whalers fighting. The Inuit have a very strict moral code and are very sensitive to being dealt with in a disrespectful way. They are also the stewards of the land and while they were hunting for the whalers, they were aware of how big an impact the reduction in caribou herds or seal pods would have upon future generations. When whalers went ashore to hunt for themselves and were seen as overkilling of the caribou herds fights would sometimes break out. "A ship was sunk by some Ungava Inuit because its crew killed too many caribou, which were very scarce then. The captain and half his crew from a wrecked ship were killed by Ungava Inuit for trying to kidnap women."[23] The whalers were not always prepared for the Innu ingenuity. Some Inuit women were able to outsmart a crew of whalers after they had been kidnapped by them, "At Kuuvik near Richmond Gulf some whalers terrorized the Inuit until the women promised to make mitts for them. They made special mitts with no thumb piece, and tied them tightly around the whalers' wrists. The whalers were then helpless and their guns were taken away."[24]

These were rough times. It was the era of the 'bully-boy mates' aboard whaling ships who would enforce ships' rules with their fists or guns. The crew were often uneducated criminals who had signed aboard in order to get away from the law or who had been shanghaied to work aboard at petty wages, often for years at a time. Frenchy Chartrand, an Arctic old-timer recalls, "That was in the days of old Bill Seymour, when Cap Pedersen was only a cabin boy. That was something! Herschel Island was full of whale carcasses, anchors, harpoons; and all day long you could hear the cat-o'nine-tails whistling on deck. As soon as a man said anything, they strung him up the masts by his thumbs, and you'd better not ask how he happened to be dead when they untied him. ..Those days are over. You don't find men like that any more. Compared to them we're a lot of cream-puffs."[25] The crews of these ships were a mixed lot of Europeans, Africans, Japanese, Chinese, Arabs and men from all over the South Seas. The Inuit of Bering Strait in Alaska were expert whale hunters, and had learned the European way as employees of the whaling fleet. Some of them moved to the MacKenzie Delta with their families and became known as 'Masinkers'."[26]

"The crews were a motley lot and their reasons for going north diverse. Some joined voyage after voyage because they liked the life, they liked the work, and they liked the North. When whaling declined, many of these men remained in the North as traders or trappers. They often married Eskimo women and their descendants still live in Alaska and the western Canadian Arctic."[27] "While many whalers were perhaps wild and depraved, Nuligak in his reminiscences remembers them more as friends than as fiends. The whalers' knew a hundred different ways of amusing themselves. They had different kinds of musical instruments...White men and Inuit played games together, as well as hunting side by side. We played baseball and wrestled. We danced in the Eskimo fashion to the sound of many drums."[28]

Nuligak aboard schooner Omingmuk at Tuk, 1948. Photo by Hunt.

One of the positive things that the whalers brought to the Inuit was the idea of offering credit, rewarding hard work and honesty. The whalers recognized that they had trade goods that the Inuit wanted and that if they grub-staked a family to go and hunt for them, then the family would be more than likely to return and repay their investment so that they could acquire more of the white mans' goods. As the whalers' began to get to know the Inuit there was often a trust built so that the whalers could hand over goods such as quality rifles, axes and even whaleboats knowing that these would be used to pay back the debt. In many ways they ended up treating the Inuit as equals which was a refreshing way for the Inuit to do business.

As the demand for baleen dropped and fashions changed, just as suddenly as the whaling ships had arrived in the Inuit lives, they were gone. In 1932 the RCMP moved most of its operations to Aklavik. A few years later, in 1938, the Hudson's Bay Company moved its operations to Tuktoyaktuk. Ted Pedersen had made his last forays into the Arctic with his delivery of North Star. In

1938, the RCMP permanently closed its Herschel Island operation, returning years later only to breed their dogs. "When Henry Larsen on the return
trip through the NorthWest Passage (aboard St. Roch), in 1944 stopped at
Herschel, the place which he had known as a young man 'as a thriving Arctic
metropolis' was 'completely deserted....not a soul was to be seen'.[29]

These were hard, hard times for the Inuit. The whalers had left, leaving many
of the population diseased and now dependant upon white man's goods
which they had incorporated into their daily lives. Many moved in from their
camps and set up homes in the Delta, mainly around Tuktoyaktuk, where
the HBC still kept a post and where they could still be able to trade some
fur for essentials. Many of the newer generation had never learned to hunt
without rifles or steel traps and so were unable to provide for their families
without being able to acquire these at the HBC. This new generation had
also been raised with a taste for western goods such as tea, tobacco, sugar
and flour.

Not only did the whalers decimate the whale and caribou population and
then leave after the Inuit had come to rely upon them for a source of western
goods, they left something far worse in their wake. The crew from points all
over the world brought with them their diseases, something that the Inuit
had no immunity to. Measles, flu and smallpox tore through the Inuit communities in the early 1900s. Out of a population of 2,000 MacKenzie Inuit,
only 130 survived. On top of that, syphilis and consumption spread through
every village. There were funerals every day and the Inuit were buried all over
Herschel Island in shallow graves, due to the permafrost. In recent years, due
to erosion and climate change, many of these graves have been heaved up to
the surface. From a strong, thriving people, within twenty years of the whalers
arrival over ninety percent of the local Inuit died. With the population
decimated, other Eskimos moved into the MacKenzie Delta region. These
were people from St. Lawrence Island, from inland Alaska (Nunatagmiut),
from the Seward Peninsula (Kinugmiut), from Siberia (Chukchi and Yuit).
All of these races mixed together and with the whalers to the point that in
1905 Roald Amundsen observed that "a pure Eskimo is exceedingly rare."
By 1934, said Diamond Jenness, 'not more than fifteen MacKenzie Natives
could claim descent from the original population.'

The whalers departure and the flu epidemic left the battered ranks of Inuit
to re-group. Just when things seemed most dour the fashion industry again
played a card in their favour. Baleen for corsets was out. Fur was in. A huge
demand for fur in Europe and North America meant that the Inuit could
continue trading with the foreigners. "The European fur market had no
limits. There were never enough furs arriving at posts to satisfy the demands
in Moscow, Leningrad, London and Paris."[30]

The trading of goods for fur had been sparked by a Danish man named
Christian Klengenberg who had been given temporary command of a small

supply vessel named Olga. He was ordered to stay within sight of the larger ship, Charles Hanson, and was given only two weeks food as a precaution in case he decided to steal the valuable ship. As it turned out, the vessels became caught in fog and Klengenberg disappeared with the Olga. Most speculated that he had sailed her out of the Arctic and down to the South Seas in order to sell her.

In the mean time Roald Amundsen arrived aboard his Gjoa, finishing his voyage of the NorthWest Passage. The winter set in and Klengenberg and Olga were missing. It wasn't hard to imagine the small ship being crushed and sunk. When the following summer dawned Vilhjalmur Steffanson arrived for his first expedition to the Arctic. He had hardly settled when Klengenberg sailed Olga back in. What he had actually done was to voyage east on a pet plan to meet up with a race of people that he had heard lived in the middle of the Arctic and had never been seen the outside world. And that is just what he did.

The race that he had 'discovered' was the Cogmollocks and they had happily traded their furs for copper pots, cheap knives and other trinkets. The men at Herschel Island took all of this in, particularly Steffanson, however the bigger problem was that Klengenberg had sailed with a crew of nine and returned with only five of them. His story of having to shoot one in self defense and another had died of scurvy while two others had fallen through the ice was backed up by the remaining crew. That story might have held except that in the middle of the night Klengenberg took his wife and children aboard a whale boat and sailed for Alaska, far from the long reach of the R.C.M.P. After he was over the horizon his crew told a different story, that of murder and men being marooned on ice floes. Years later, in a San Francisco court, Klengenberg was acquitted of all charges.

Meanwhile, in May of 1910, Steffanson tracked down the Cogmollocks and wrote articles about them that appeared in papers all over the world. He described some of the Eskimos as having blonde hair and blue eyes. He also wrote about how they would trade small copper and steel items for their white fox pelts and other pelts. Many traders now headed to Herschel Island and the surrounding area to trade with the local people for fur. The first Hudson's Bay company ship to arrive was Ruby, skippered by Captain Cottle. Alaskan traders such as "Cogmollock Pete, Otto Binder, Carroll, Peter Gruben, D'Arcy Arden and Pete Norberg"[31] also set up camps.

The Alaskan Eskimos began to move down to Herschel Island and the Delta, filling the void left by the deceased. Trapping for muskrat in the Delta as well as fox became very profitable, but the big ticket item was the white fox and the much more rare, blue fox. White fox were particularly coveted since they could be died any colour. Trappers now began to spend their winters running their trap-lines and then travelling by schooner to Herschel Island to trade with the Hudson's Bay Company, Liedes until its demise or Pedersen's

CanAlaska Company. Even though North America was in the throes of the Great Depression, many of the Inuit trappers were making money hand over fist. The pelt of a common red fox, in 1938 for example, brought the Eskimo about $15 worth of merchandise at the trading post, (or approximately half the retail market price in Vancouver, British Columbia).

Money rarely changed hands in the Canadian Western Arctic at this time. It was all about what a pelt could be traded for. "A white fox could trade for about three boxes of twenty rifle shells in each box, or ten yards of calico for his wife's sewing or twenty-five pounds of flour and a pound of tea or tallow to boot. A cross fox - so named for its red and black fur, with the black areas forming what is considered a cross on the animal's shoulders and spine - traded for some $60. Each silver fox, actually having black fur mixed with white, meant the equivalent of about $75 Canadian to its captor and retailed for double that amount. A mounted white fox would carry a retail price of at least $150. On average, for every hundred white foxes one blue or platinum fox would be born. They bought about $120 worth of Hudson's Bay Company's goods for the Inuit hunter or trapper and retailed for $300 Canadian in Vancouver."[32]

"The Bay sold millions of beaver pelts to European milliners at a great profit. When the beaver market died in 1854, The Bay closed several posts leaving the local natives with unsold pelts and nowhere to trade. The company posts moved to areas where fox was more plentiful, and told the Eskimos to forget caribou and trap foxes. They encouraged them to live close to a trading post, get rich and trade for white man's food. At this point, natives' health started to deteriorate as they bought only sweet and salty foods and colas to drink, and ate less of their traditional country food which is laden with nourishment. Combined with liquor and less activity, the change from proud itinerant Eskimo to sedentary Inuit had begun."[33]"In those days the only things the Bay bought were seal skins and fox pelts. We were paid in tokens. When we brought skins in they put out the tokens, and when we bought something they took them away. The tokens weren't real money but they put them down to show us how much we had to spend, how much our furs were worth. There were big tokens and small ones and when we bought something they took the big ones away and replaced them with small ones. That was before people knew anything about money and when we saw tokens with the number 100 on them, we thought they must really be worth a lot. They were probably only one dollar."[34]

Not only were tokens used but also glass beads, the different sizes or colours, mainly red and green, denoting different values. The uses of chits, Hudson Bay tokens or beads were used in many HBC trading posts but at Herschel Island and later at Aklavik the standard currency was fox pelts. A trapper would put down a pelt and point to the goods he wanted. The trader would then indicate how many more he needed or how much of something else he could get. "The Company does not use the coin of the realm in these remote parts. It has its own trade tokens with a fox's mask graven on them."[35]Even today, beachcombers can find trading beads scattered over the land.

For the HBC and CanAlaska traders, life at the posts could often be extremely boring. Days or even weeks would go by without anyone arriving to trade. When a trapper did arrive, trading would not commence until after a cup of tea and exchange of news. This would be followed by the serious business of trading at the unheated store. As mentioned, the stores were kept unheated to encourage the trappers to not get too comfortable and to get back out on the trapline. George Burnham describes the process: "The trapper would pull the first white fox out of a sack and lay it across the counter. He would select some item, such as four pounds of tea, and Charlie (the manager) would indicate on the skin how much was used for the tea or how much was left. Another selection would be made and when goods had been purchased to the full value of the skin, Charlie would pull the skin over to our side of the counter and drop it onto the floor. Out would come another pelt and the trading was resumed. The fox skins were not put in the sack "willy-nilly", no indeed the best skin was always at the bottom and others laid on top so that the poorest skin was always the first to be traded. Thus, the trapper felt that the more he could squeeze on a poor skin, the more he would be able to get on better skins."[36]

"A trader would extend credit to an individual trapper, supplying him with the provisions he needed, on condition that the trapper would bring all his furs back to the same trader. The 'jawbone' system, based on credit and debt, probably had more dislocating effects on fur production than any trading method used up to that point. By labelling some trappers as 'better risks' than others for credit, this system emphasized new distinctions between people. A good trapper was pleased to have a large 'jawbone,' but it also put him in debt to a particular trader. Such arrangements gave the trader more power than the trapper to decide what furs should be trapped. This imbalance increased as trappers became increasingly dependent on consumer goods which they could acquire only by trapping whichever furs were bringing good prices that year."[37]

Teddy Pedersen, son of C.T., and the man who launched North Star in 1936.

Ted Pedersen Jr. remembers that when he and his father would arrive aboard Patterson they would start by passing out candy and gum to the children and cigars to the men. "There were so many of them you could barely move, all talking, joking and laughing for about a half hour. Then one of the Eskimos would sneak down and pass my dad a bag with some fur in it. My dad would look at it and shake it and then say, 'maybe fourteen dollars' and then they'd talk awhile. Here would be Eskimo after Eskimo, some with five or ten or maybe a hundred, and that would be going on constantly until all the fur was gone. You'd give them a slip and they would go to the main cargo hatch and the men would get it for them. Guns, traps, ammunition, flour, hard-tack."

One of the reasons that the Inuit liked to trade with Pedersen was that he kept track of what they wanted in exchange for their fur. He would bring in their very favourite type of tea called Silver Fox, as well as a very thick jam that he imported from New Zealand. In a clever marketing scheme that is still much in use by many businesses today, Pedersen would hand out calendars to all of the trappers. The calendar was on a half-sheet of card-stock and on the edge it read, "To Our Arctic Friends, it'll pay you to owe your fox skins to Captain Pedersen. Receive the highest prices for them. He will carry a big supplies of groceries, hardware, tobacco, dry goods, ammunition & so forth and sell you these at lowest prices."

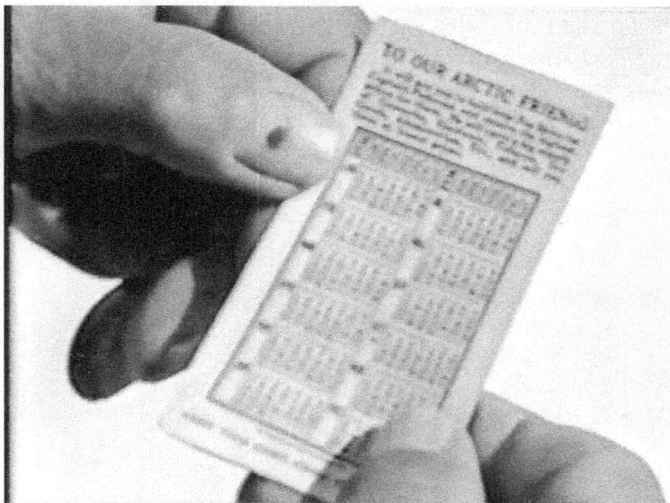

**Teddy Pedersen with calendar that his father
would give to his customers each year.**

Liebes and Company and later the CanAlaska Company and the Hudson's Bay Company kept on expanding their stock of things for the trappers to trade for. What began as simple things like flour, tea, tobacco, bolts of cloth, and for a real luxury, apples and oranges made way for record players and the LP's of music (both kinds, country and western), Western style clothing, and even dolls (with white skin, of course), that had their own wardrobes to trade for. Rather than just trading for and living with the necessities of life, the traders had introduced the idea of conspicuous consumption. This brought on the concept of personal ownership, something that was never part of the Inuit's past. Belongings, until this point, had more of a communal feel to them. Now that a trapper had traded his fur for a coveted object, it became his and not his neighbours.

"Neither the Indian nor the Inuk was a commercial fur hunter before the white man came. They hunted for food and for skins to keep them warm or to use in building shelters and boats. Bones and teeth might be useful weapons or tools. A small surplus became largely symbolic trade goods exchanged between family groups or tribal bands. The white man turned the killing of animals into a highly organised industry, the price of furs set by the laws of supply and demand in far-off London or Paris."[38]

The big societal change was that very quickly, and after centuries, the Inuit were no longer a nomadic people. They had become trappers first and hunters second and stayed within range of the trading post so that they could continue to acquire store bought food and clothing. The risk that the

Inuit were taking was huge. If demand for furs dropped they would be stuck with the pelts and nothing to eat and there are accounts of families arriving at a trading post with a sled piled high with furs, only to find it abandoned. "As trapping grew more profitable, trappers found they could increasingly afford to neglect hunting and fishing to devote their time primarily to catching fur bearers, though when prices fell or animals grew short in supply, they found their specialized adaptation imperiled. But hunting and fishing have never been entirely abandoned."[39]

12.1 Eskimo Identification tag.

The party and holiday atmosphere at Herschel Island was something that both the traders and the trapping families looked forward to. Families would leave with their schooners from Banksland as soon as the ice was cleared out. Other families would travel by walking as far as they could and then meeting up with boats at points along the way. Sometimes people were charged for their passage, though it might be taken in barter for work on the boat to make her ready for sea or for a promise of fur from the coming season. There are reports of trappers putting their sledges on the ice and if it was windy, rigging up a canvas like a sail and then letting the wind drive them along with their dogs keeping pace. In any case, once they arrived at Pauline Cove, vessels would be rafted together. Tents would be put up on deck as all of the bunks below would be spoken for. Other people would camp ashore. In the 24 hour daylight, the activity never stopped. There were dances, drumming, feasts, card games, wrestling and other Eskimo games like leg wrestling and blanket toss.

Traditional blanket toss game.

"We entered the harbour, Pauline Cove, where many ships, schooners and boats had preceded us. Three big ships were anchored in deep sea, among them the Bay-Chimo, the Hudson Bay cargo ship. Many schooners were near the shore and tied together, a ladder fixed on the first one in line to climb aboard. After that one could easily go from one to another."[40] There was always a festival feeling when the first boats came in, and it didn't take long for bad moods to be washed away with booze. There were trappers from hundreds of miles around all sitting around there waiting for the boats to get in so they could trade their catches and pick up their orders, and damn near every one of them made sure of getting a full twelve bottle liquor ration. There was one hell of a drunk."[41]

With the incredible profits being made in the white fox trade, many orders were made for schooners. "The white fox trade was centered in two communities in the western Arctic, in Aklavik and Herschel. In the 1920s, the price paid for the white fox was twenty times more than it was less than a decade ago, many trappers made huge profits. This new prosperity has led to the establishment of a fleet of schooners belonging to the premises. In 1924, there were at least 39 of those expensive boats based in Aklavik."[42]

"That's where people used to go for tobacco, supply of tobacco for the winter I guess, and tea. That's all they need that time around there, tobacco and tea. As long as they got tobacco and tea they were well off."[43] (Laughter)

"Yeah! When we get out to Qikiqtatruk (Herschel Island) with Ole Andreasen's boat named Ann Olga. When we arrived Pedersen's big ship used to arrive. We would tie our schooner right next to Pedersen's. Those black people used to play music right on the deck of Pedersen's store. There was fur clothes for sale. Outer parkas and women shoes made by Inuit. Just beautiful work done by fingers."[44]

Schooners at Herschel Island in the 1930's.

Not only were the schooners an effective means to transport goods and to trapping, but they were a symbol of success. Possession of a schooner meant that you were someone important. One such owner was known as Nuligak Inuvialuit. In his book "I, Nuligak" he writes, "this summer of 1926, I had finally a schooner! It was brand new, built in the year, and was named Bonnie Belle. It measured 40 feet long, with an engine heavy duty 'Francisco Standard ten horses. It worked perfectly. " "The 60 motor schooners belonging to "Nunatagmiut Eskimos" (as Godsell called all Inuvialuit) are a clue that for many people, prosperity remained high or even achieved new heights in the new years after the whaling boom. The schooners were two masted and 12 to 15 metres (40-50 feet) long with powerful gas engines. They replaced the earlier sail-driven whale boats after 1912 and cost about $6,000 each, a considerable fortune ninety years ago. According to one observer, the average standard of living for Inuvialuit during the early 20th century was higher than that of many working-class southern Canadians."

It was the fur trade that supported this prosperity. The Inuvialuit had been involved in trading furs since 1850, but before the whaling years, it had not dominated their lives. The shift to an economy that depended more and more on trapping was also encouraged by a sharp rise in the price of furs. Between 1915 and 1919, the price of white fox in the Western Arctic rose from $2.50 to $50.00 a pelt, marten from $2.50 to $55, mink from $1 to $20 and muskrat from 40 cents to $1.50

"Most (trappers and traders) continued to winter on Banks Island, where they grew affluent on the white fox trade. The schooner fleet continued to grow during the 1930's and '40s. By 1936, 41 trappers or fully forty percent of all Inuvialuit trappers in the western Arctic had trapped on the island for at least one season. Two of the best trappers, Fred Carpenter and Jim Wolki, got together and bought a 17 metre (57 foot) schooner they called North Star. Named for Natkusiak's boat, which had since been lost, it was the biggest and finest schooner ever brought into the western Arctic. For 26 years it was the "flagship" of the Banksland fleet. It cost $35,000 at the time, or about $300,000 in modern funds. In 1935-36, another trapper was able to afford a year-long holiday with his family in San Francisco and Vancouver."[45]

Fred Carpenter and Jim Wolkie were not only excellent trappers but also shrewd businessmen. They could shop their prime furs around between the two competing companies in order to trade for the highest fur prices and the best goods. They could also order a myriad of supplies with their profits from either company and negotiate the price for same. In dealing with Pedersen, Carpenter may have recognized many similarities with himself. Both were hard men with many years spent out in the elements and had no patience for dishonesty or game playing. When the time came for Carpenter and Wolkie to order a ship of their own, they went to Pedersen.

"With this type of economic inducement, some Inuvialuit were even able to step into economic roles previously occupied only by whites. They were not just hunters and trappers; some were now traders and entrepreneurs as well.

Beginning in 1910 and picking up momentum after 1920, a string of trading posts was opened in the Mackenzie Delta and along the western Arctic coast. About fifty posts were opened before 1945, by the Hudson's Bay Company, the CanAlaska Trading Company and other smaller companies and independent traders. Most lasted no more than a decade. At least eight were owned and operated by Inuvialuit; Inuvialuit schooner captains were also active in trading."[46]

The competition between the HBC and Pedersen allowed the trappers to go from one to the other to try and get the best price. Both companies tried to be the first to arrive each season so that they could trade for the most fur. Ted Pedersen was the acknowledged expert in working the ice and the three masted Patterson was in an annual race with the HBC ship's to get to Pauline Cove and set up the 'store'. Both companies had warehouses ashore where they could trade as well as from the decks of their ships. Eddie Gruben remembers meeting Captain Pedersen many times and at one time travelled aboard Patterson as she shifted berths at Herschel Island. "Jimmy Jacobson recalls being at Herschel Island in the '30's when "Captain Pedersen used to bring a lot of beer by wooden barrels, big wooden barrels! Rum and they buy them by the cases, white people only. People bring their furs, Captain Pedersen put up the price, trying to get all the Eskimo's fur.

Finally I was about thirteen years old when I came back with my dad. Bonnycastle (of the HBC) got so mad! Dad sold his furs for fifty dollars each to Captain Pedersen. When they got drunk, Bonnycastle - who was a big Hudson's Bay man, gave my dad a black eye! I never forget it. They were fur crazy that time!"[47] In 1926 Nuligak aboard Bonnie Belle sailed from Aklavik to Herschel Island. "The HBC ship, an iron boat was in. Captain Pedersen was there too, and a whole fleet of little schooners, with people coming to sell furs and buy provisions. The price of fox was high: forty, fifty dollars a pelt. We sold and bought and then loaded the Bonnie Belle brim-full with our purchases."[48]

The children looked forward to the candy. "Only later at Qikiqtaqruk (Herschel Island) there was some candies that were hard to break. We used to play with them and stretch them. They would get long because they were hard to break! We held them with our teeth. They were so big and good candies at the time. We used to see who would break them first with Peter Joe and them. They (the candies) were kind of rough ones and (they were) very good ones. At the time they were good, not like now." "Some of them came from somewhere," recalls Dora Malegana (and my favourite quote in all of this research). Several of Fred Carpenter's daughters confided in me that one of their young lives' greatest pleasures was sneaking into North Star's lazarette on the voyage home to sneak some of the toffee-like candy. They made sure to reach down and take it from the bottom so that it looked undisturbed but like any parent, I am sure that the Fred and his wife recognised the tell-tale sticky fingers and cheeks.

"Also, there was pickles in wooden barrels then. When (the container was) empty we would use it for making sour dough. They were very good! Also, we would use the butter containers, those large cans. Long ago, they were all wooden boxes or containers, not papers. Also there was rice and no potatoes or bananas, no other fresh stuff. Only rice, raisins and raw apples to cook. They was lots of raw fruits then, they would come in wooden boxes too."[49]

One season, after the Patterson was in and had started trading the Hudson's Bay ship hove into view. Pedersen kept on trading as fast as he could to try and secure as many furs as possible before his competition dropped anchor. When hours had passed and the BayChimo was still outside the harbour, word was passed that she had run hard aground on one of the many sand-bars around Herschel Island. For days she sat there while Pedersen kept on trading and filling the Patterson's massive cargo hold with fur. Finally, a request was made by the HBC for Pedersen to tow BayChimo off the bar. Pedersen sent word back that he would do it for sixty white foxes, a huge sum, which the HBC refused. The next day the weather began to turn and the locals predicted a big westerly gale, one that would push BayChimo further up onto the reef. HBC accepted Pedersen's offer and he had them off the reef before the storm hit. The delay in paying Pedersen had cost the HBC much more than sixty pelts as they had missed out on days of trading and in the end had to swallow their pride.

Just as quickly as the white fox had come into fashion, it began to decline. In the mid 1920's there were some trappers earning over $10,000 a year, a veritable fortune in those days. Fox pelts were selling for upwards of fifty dollars each. By the beginning of the thirties they had dropped in price to only a few dollars each.

"As in other regions, the late 1930's brought the demise of the Hudson's Bay Company's major competitors, as well as a decline in the independents. The subsequent decade however, brought resurgence in the muskrat trade, which by this time was more than ever the staple fur of the region."[50]

Even though the price for fox was not reliable, the trapping lifestyle and the desire for Southern luxuries had taken hold. Many people moved into the Canadian Western Arctic from Alaska and made permanent homes in Aklavik, Tuktoyaktuk and Banks Island. Suddenly there was more competition between the trappers, which was again another cultural shift for the traditional Innu way of life.

The introduction of rifles meant that the Inuit were able to shoot more game which caused a noticeable decline in many species. As the next generations grew up the tradition of killing only what you needed seemed to be waning, which would have a negative effect on the future livelihood of the community's' well-being. "The steel traps were having their effect too. The white fox, much in demand for coats by rich women all over the world, was at its peak in the winter months. It's coat was thickest and whitest then, so traders encouraged the Eskimos to set their traplines during the coldest months of the year. But, traditionally, winter had been a time for seal hunting. It was then that the Eskimos obtained their winter meat, as well as the skins that were so important for tents and clothing. Winter had also been a time for getting together with the community, for singing and listening to the stories that made up the cherished culture."[52]

In the end it was the whim of fashion thousands of miles away that determined whether a family would survive the coming winter or conversely, had enough to purchase a schooner or take a vacation south. This new lifestyle, after centuries of leading a nomadic existence, now coupled with the allure of white man's food, brand new rifles and other luxuries was the situation that Carpenter and Wolki found themselves in aboard North Star.

"After World War 1 the price of fox furs went up to between $30 and $70. A blue fox fur could bring two or three times as much, and even muskrat skins were worth a dollar each during the 1920's. The high prices between 1920 and 1930 meant that if a trapper took 300 foxes (easily possible during the peak year of the fox cycle), he could earn from $9,000 to $18,000. This was at a time when most Canadians earned only $1,000 a year or less. The price of store goods was much lower than it is nowadays, even in the Arctic. Although the trapper could earn a lot of money, it meant hard work in very cold weather for him, and his wife and daughters might have their hands badly marked from cleaning hundreds of skins."[53] It also meant, as mentioned, less time with the community, less time for dancing, story-telling and other traditional pastimes.

After the departure of the whalers, the trappers, traders and the RCMP post, Herschel Island was left mainly abandoned. In the 1950's it was used by the RCMP once again, but this time as an area for dog breeding. In 1987, after the completion of the Inuvialuit Final Agreement of 1984, the island became Herschel Island Territorial Park. It is managed jointly by the Inuvialuit and the Yukon Government. Cruise ships visit regularly and when conditions are right, tourists are taken ashore in excursion boats. A couple of the old buildings are standing and there is even a mudhouse. Outside, an Inuvialuit man dressed in caribou skin and fur will let you take his photograph for a fee.

"The Eskimos' economy changed from one of subsistence - relying totally on themselves for all essentials - to one of money or trade. Unable to feed themselves on seal, whale, caribou and walrus, the Eskimos were turning more and more to food purchased at the trading post. They were no longer self-reliant. Somehow, the outsiders had taken charge."[54]

Chapter 4

Geo. W. Kneass – Boat Builder

Captain Pedersen was known as the man who could bring in the 'Arctic Schooners' for the Inuit and the boat yard that he hired in San Francisco was just as famous for building them. Kneass Shipyards was to California what Burrard shipyards; the builder of many ships including the RCMP's St Roch was to British Columbia. Pedersen's favourite boatyard was owned and operated by a man named George Washington Kneass. San Francisco was the Patterson's home port and Ted Pedersen delivered the work order from Herschel Island to Kneass. Ted Pederson had been supplying small Arctic ready vessels to the Inuit for many years. He ordered these from the Kneass shipyard, perhaps the best in the business along the Pacific Coast.

Geo. W. Kneass.

George Washington Kneass was born in Yolo County, California in 1859. Not much is known of his parents or if his lineage contained shipwrights, other than that his parents had immigrated to the United States from Wales. They encouraged their son to learn a trade and so G.W. started in the boatbuilding business as an apprentice to a well known boatbuilder in San Francisco named Martin Vice. When his apprenticeship of five years ended, Vice took Kneass on as a full partner. The old man and the young man built on Vice's solid reputation for constructing very seaworthy ships, made to order to the buyer's specific needs. Vice had operated his relatively large shipyard for many years quite successfully. When Martin Vice passed away, G.W. Kneass carried on the business, but now under the banner Geo.W. Kneass Boat Builder - Steam Launches A Specialty. By the early 1890's, Kneass had expanded his business to two shipyards, specializing in vessels under seventy feet. Business was booming and Kneass enjoyed a reputation for his quality work and fast delivery.

**Geo. W. Kneass Boat Builders where North Star
and many other Arctic ships were built.**

Kneass Shipyards employed fifty people and they built boats up to seventy feet as well as vapour launches, pleasure boats, coffee lighters and rowboats. "George Washington Kneass was a strong willed, competitive boat builder whose versatility was evident on signs at his post turn of the century shop: yawls, dinghies, gigs, steam and gasoline launches, metallic life-boats, whitehalls, salmon, surf, sail and rowboats. He moved houses and sold flagpoles also."[1] The coffee lighters were small boats specifically designed for carrying coffee from shore out to deep water ships. Kneass sold these lighters to Guatemala, Central America, and Santa Cruz, New Mexico. Kneass also had built by 1891 over forty sealing boats for the English and American Fleets and the shipyard also built all of the small boats for the battle-ship Monterey.

In 1898 and in the early 1900s the Kneass Shipyards were rocked by one fire after another. There were at least four serious fires recorded, the last being in 1915. The wood that Kneass was using for his craft was all first growth, dried and quarter sawn. With a lot of this stock ruined each time, along with the iron machines which were in many cases rendered useless, Kneass had to keep re-building and keep producing boats in order to hold off bankruptcy. It is a sign of his strong character and work ethic that he was able to do so. Kneass kept on with his business until his death on March 3, 1923. He was 64. One of his obituaries described his shops as being "fully equipped with saws, planers, and other machinery, all run by steam, where he builds all kinds of boats." An unsubstantiated rumour that kept on popping up in my research was that Kneass drank himself to death and that his wife was so upset at the stressors of the boatyard that she went down and burned all of the boat plans.

The Kneass Shipyard continued though, now being run by his brother Webster L. Kneass and his son, George W. Kneass Junior. These were the men who took Ted Pedersen's order for the North Star.

At around the time that they received the order for North Star Kneass Shipyard was turning out all kinds of vessels and by their resume they seemed to have taken pride in being able to fill somewhat eccentric orders. They built Taku, an 80 footer for the Coast & Geodetic Survey; cargo lighters for Vladivostok during the Russian-Japanese War, lighters for South Sea and Hawaiian Island companies; shallow draft boats with tunnel sterns for use on the Armoor River in China; a flat bottomed boat powered with a Ford engine for a mining concern away in the interior of Venezuela; a flat-bottomed craft powered with an airplane engine that drew only three and a half inches and could make 35 knots as well as a luxury schooner of fifty-five feet named Rejoice."[2] Kneass also built the well-known eighteen foot salmon boat, Pacific, in which Bernard Gilboy crossed 7,000 miles of the Pacific Ocean alone in 1883, the first person in the world to accomplish such a feat. Gilboy's adventures that he had recorded in his logbook were later edited and released by John Barr Tompkins entitled A Voyage of Pleasure. This non-stop solo voyage in a small boat was an incredible feat and speaks to the abilities of Gilboy and the strength of the Kneass' Pacific however his family 'never thought much of the voyage at that time. Bernard was away at sea so much. "He was not a family man", as the published log says. He once came home and 'injured' his house,"[3] whatever that means!

North Star of Herschel Island was an idea that must have been conceived over numerous conversations amongst the western Canadian fur trappers over the years. Certainly there would have been talks between Fred and Jim Wolki and Fred Carpenter over what would be the ultimate 'schooner' for use in the fur trade in those dangerous waters. The Kneass Shipyards had built many "Arctic schooners" before and knew how to ice strengthen the hull and what lines the ship would need to stay safe should she be caught in ice. What made this order special was the sheer size of North Star as well as the attention to detail that was being asked of them. Carpenter and Wolki were making a statement with this ship. She was to be the Queen of the Arctic.

Fred Carpenter's wife, Agnes, proudly and correctly states that, "North Star was built out of good wood." The three and a half inch square ribs were steamed and bent and set up every twelve inches for the length of the 57 foot hull. Massive three and a half inch quarter sawn, edged grain Douglas fir planks were steamed and fitted to the ribs. More strengthening was added to the bow. A layer of Stockholm ship's tar was coated on the hull from six inches at amidships to two feet at the bow, down and over what would be the draft of the ship. On top of this, Irish ship's felt was laid, a material that allows the hull to flex and is impervious to rot. This felt also helps to hold the caulking in place as the vessel twists in heavy weather at sea or as the wood contracts or expands with temperature changes. Many of the first wooden ships that voyaged to the Arctic sank as their hulls contracted with the cold, allowing the caulking to spill out and the icy water to flow in. A second layer of Stockholm tar was coated on top of the Irish ship's felt and it was on top of this that a second hull of ironbark, one of the hardest woods in the world, was secured with copper nails.

Agnes Carpenter remembers her husband telling her that "the two Freds" had designed the ship up and then placed their order with Captain Pedersen for delivery the following year. Over time, the original sketches that were sent down to the Kneass boatyards have all been lost, probably through fire, though her original blueprints are still aboard.

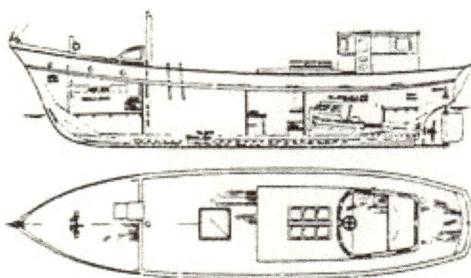

North Star's blueprints.

Another Kneass ship, Our Lady of Lourdes, held many similarities with North Star, ideas that may have been employed in designing North Star.

For instance, the shape of the hull, designed as Pedersen had promised the Brothers in the construction of Our Lady, so that the ship would be pushed out of the ice and not be crushed. That, and a full outer hull of ironbark, wood that is often just used on the bow of vessels to protect the hull from ice or other obstructions. The anthropologist Diamond Jenness saw the steam whaler Belvedere near Herschel in 1914 and although she had battered the Arctic ice for 20 years the 'ironbark showed scarcely a scratch." He described ironbark as "an incredibly hard wood."

North Star of Herschel Island in dry-dock. Note the round-ness of her hull to allow her to be squeezed out of the ice.

The freeboard of the ship - the height of the vessel from waterline to gun-whale capping rail and the height of the bulwarks to keep people, dogs and cargo safe from breaking waves is another similarity between the two vessels. Pictures of North Star loaded with her passengers and their belongings show that they would often extend these bulwarks with extra wood in order to keep their cargo safe.

North Star was designed with a 'clipper bow' which cuts through the water like a knife. Our Lady of Lourdes and the other Kneass built Arctic 'schooners' had bluff bows and the hull is much beamier right through to the transom. The clipper bow was a design feature that Jim Wolki had demanded and it was this bow that first caught North Star's second owner, Sven Johansson, to envision her as a fully-rigged sailing ship.

North Star at the Kneass Boat Building yard with her clipper bow.

While the ship was being built, Fred telegraphed down to Kneass that North Star must be fitted with an Atlas gasoline engine. "I know that engine, I've worked on that engine and I know how to fix it" he said. The news back was not encouraging. Atlas was no longer building the engines and there were none available. Carpenter was adamant however and Kneass and the Atlas Company managed to find bits and pieces and parts of the engine and it was cobbled together, becoming the last gasoline engine of this size that the famous Atlas Company ever built. To start this two ton, thirty-five horse-power engine with three cylinders required a mighty push on a steel bar inserted in large holes in the flywheel. The holes were designed so that the bar would slip out as the wheel turned. The engine didn't have spark plugs, using instead a series of contacts which would make and break according to the cycle of the engine. This is where the term 'make and break' comes from.

Atlas engine block aboard Fox. North Star's was the last make-and-break engine made by the Company.

North Star's transom was constructed of mahogany, another exotic hard-wood and one that had apparently never been seen before in the western Arctic. The vessel's living areas were fitted out with more mahogany. Up forward, the focsle had bunks either side, a small wood or coal stove and a table running down the middle. Forward of that were two anchor chain bins and then more storage in the crash lockers right in the bow.

Abaft the focs'le was the cargo hold. This deep and wide space would be filled after fur trading with all of the orders from other families that Fred and Jim had received. The Captain's Cabin was also fitted out in mahogany. The pilothouse was built into the ship in San Francisco. At that time, it was stan-dard practice to build this structure once the boat arrived out of found wood or while the Patterson was underway but both Carpenter and Kneass wanted a proper job done. This pilothouse was large enough that it would accom-modate a whole family's living quarters for the season. Under the deckhouse, a lazarette area provided storage as well as bunks for three crew. There was a bucket abaft the deckhouse for use as a head.

North Star was the epitome of excellence for boatbuilding of that era. The extra touches that Kneass used showed this to be the highlight of his career and he must have been very proud of her.

North Star at San Francisco, 1935.

In 2008, Geo. W. Kneass's grand daughter Katrina Kneass toured the ship in Victoria. She remembered being aboard her when North Star was first being laid up and had memories of her father and her uncle working along-side to finish the ship. Katrina was blind since birth but the ship had made such an impression upon her as a child, that along with her guide dog, she was able to show herself around, touching the bulkheads that she had last touched when both she and North Star were young. Miss Kneass passed away shortly after her visit to the ship. Katrina's brother Mark has collected a family history of his family's boatyard. He is more famously known as Saint Germaine. He and his followers believe that he is a reincarnation of an alien who has inhabited our planet for 500,000 years in different guises including that of Plato, Merlin, Francis Bacon and Christopher Columbus.

Kneass Shipyards finally closed their doors in 1970, though they built their last boat in 1965. If you look up Kneass Boat Works on the Internet you will be taken to the website of a Kneass descendant who now uses the company name to sell her art.

Chapter 5

Peterhead Schooners

North Star, Our Lady of Lourdes, Omingmuk and dozens of others were collectively known as 'schooners' or 'Eskimo schooners', 'Arctic schooners', or in many cases, 'Peterheads'. Many of the first vessels to enter the Western Arctic were legitimate schooners, vessels carrying two or more masts with the main mast being the tallest and the ship rigged in a fore and aft fashion. When the Inuit heard these ships referred to as schooners they began to collectively use this word to mean sailboat. Most of these boats were built in San Francisco, California or Vancouver, British Columbia. This liberal use of the word schooner was also noted at the same time on Canada's East Coast by a British sailor who had made the trans-Atlantic passage in his single-masted sloop. "St. John's is one of the few ports of the world where sail is still very much alive, practically all the local carrying trade being done by water in schooners from thirty to two hundred tons. This is the sole rig, in so much so that the word schooner has become synonymous with sailing vessel, and Emmanuel (a sloop) was often spoken of as 'that little schooner.'[1]

In Canada's Eastern Arctic a similar language event was occurring. Strong, seaworthy sailing ships that had been built in Peterhead, Scotland were arriving aboard the large whaling ships. These were sold to, traded for or given to the Inuit as a reward for their work over a winter, usually in supplying fresh meat or doing other sorts of chores for the ships' crews. These vessels, despite the differences in rig or shape began to be collectively known as Peterheads. Over time, this word made its way into the Western Inuit vernacular, though in the West it seems to have not mattered if the ship was built in Scotland, only if it was a trading ship of some substantial size with a pilothouse aft and a roundish frame, much like North Star of Herschel Island. I suspect that the RCMP may have been instrumental in introducing this word as their members transferred between different Arctic bases and also as they ended up owning and operating many of them.

In the early 1900s a Hudson's Bay trader described how he kept his journal in the rugged interior of such a boat. "Some was written in a tiny wooden cabin in the bows of our little Peterhead schooner, which was dignified by the name of the focs'le, where my eiderdown sleeping bag shared the small surface of planking with the serpentine coils of the anchor chain."[1A] "In addition to the wooden whaleboats and the MacKenzie schooners which had reached the Inuit by way of the whaling fleets, the Hudson's Bay Company in the 1920's and 1930's brought Scottish Peterhead fishing boats to the Inuit of the Eastern Arctic."[2]

The Peterheads or Arctic Schooners were workboats, crammed full of all of the owner's possessions as well as all the worldly goods of anyone who sailed with him. It is incredible to see how much gear could be loaded into the boats. "When all these materials have been brought on board there followed the procession of wives, children and grandmothers of the crew - and, of course, the inevitable mother-in-law. The dogs are got aboard last. They scuffle, howl and whine like a roomful of unmanageable children and are evidently uneasy at the rocking of the boat in the aftermath of the last storm. When the incoming ocean swell meets the current at the river mouth a small boat dances like a nutshell. While the dogs, distressed by the tossing boat huddle together in a ball, the women fly apart in all directions and bend over the gunwhale with faces as gray as chalk."[3] Photos of these ships, including North Star, often show a vessel loaded right down to her gunwhales, with only inches separating the cargo from the sea. While aboard the RCMP ship Nascopie, Cecil Bradbury described loading the vessels they took North with them. "We had to take a supply of....kindling.....because there was no wood where we were going. We also carried Peterhead boats, forty foot sailing boats, long and sturdy, used for daily business or moving camp. They were made in Peterhead Scotland. The Inuit used them in addition to kayaks for hunting walrus. As well we carried twenty-eight foot trap boats."[4]

Charles Gillham was an American scientist working in the Canadian North in the late 1930's and early '40's and made many trips via 'Eskimo schooner' or Peterhead. He describes one that he doesn't name, operated coincidentally by a man named Fred. "The craft was the Mission's boat run by an Eskimo named Fred. It was the usual Eskimo schooner, about 45 feet long and powered with a two lunger heavy duty motor. All below deck was one cabin, and the ceiling was too low to walk upright beneath it. A low rail about eighteen inches high ran about the deck and there were two masts. A cockpit to the aft held the steering wheel, and directly behind it was a soap box on which the steersman might sit and guide the craft of the Church upriver. All along both sides of the upper deck were sled dogs chained to the railing. They numbered something over thirty. It was impossible to walk on deck and keep from stepping on one or more. As they are surly beasts, it was a fine idea not to attempt a promenade."

Ledyard describes the shift from building the boats in their namesake port to Canadian boatyards. "The type of boat used in the northern waters is known as a Peterhead. Originally made in Peterhead, Scotland, the boats were brought over by the Hudson's Bay Company for use in trading. For years they have been built in the Canadian Maritimes. These sturdy boats used in the Canadian Central Arctic are usually 40 to 45 feet long, with a beam of from 9 to 12 feet, and will draw three to six feet of water depending on the load. The larger Peterheads could carry up to fifteen tons of freight. Mainsail and jib are used when winds are favourable, but if the Eskimo has been fortunate with fox pelts he will ignore the fair winds and burn expensive gasoline by the drum. This seems to give him a greater prestige. Old-style, slow-speed, single or twin cylinder, heavy-duty engines were the favourites of most Eskimos. A monkey-wrench, file, and hammer were the only tools necessary to keep them running."[5]

Sven Johansson recalls that when he was working in the Canadian Western Arctic that "there were two kinds of schooners. The first were ones built in Canada in Winnipeg and sent by rail and then by river down to the Arctic and the second were those that came around Alaska on the deck of trading ships."

Prior to the arrival of the small whale-boats and Peterheads, the Inuit relied mainly upon umiaks. These are boats thirty feet or more in length built of walrus skin stretched over frames. The beauty of these craft are that not only are they waterproof, due to the amazing sewing abilities of their builders, but that they flex with the waves and can ride over small ice bergy-bits without causing any damage. (Bergy bits are chunks of ice-bergs about the same size as a standard refrigerator. Another type of dangerous ice is called a growler. These are chunks of ice that only present about one meter or three feet out of the water. As they melt, the trapped air underneath escapes and some-times makes a growling sound like an animal, hence their name.) Umiaks are also able to carry a lot of cargo and have served the Inuit faithfully for hun-dreds of years. "In 1906-07 a good many of the Eskimos owned whale-boats purchased from the ships. These boats are about 28 feet or 30 feet long, will carry a ton of freight and sail beautifully, but they are fragile, difficult to keep in repair and not very seaworthy when heavily loaded. The big Eskimo skin-boat called umiak is for most purposes far better." "They left behind wooden boats; some with motors, others with sails. They were given to the Inuvialuit as a reward for loyal service, or in trade for fur. Those who owned the boats became very successful and respected hunters. Those same people, because they spent considerable time with the trappers and whalers, usually spoke English. Over time, these hunters gained much influence. They became a new kind of leader for our people. As time passed, the boats, and the influ-ence they represented, were handed down from father to son."[6]

One of the many jobs tasked to the RCMP was to stop people from heading out into the Arctic Ocean with unseaworthy boats and risking their lives.

Sometimes this resulted in a change of citizenship as Alaskan Eskimo arrived in Canadian waters in waterlogged schooners hoping to trade up to Banks Island. "They come here with a boat, lotsa people from Letty Harbour, they get stuck there..... So they got stuck,... Lots a them went to, these guys the Greens, like Jessie and Johny Green, they get stuck at Letty Harbour. Their boat is not worth going to Banksland, that white-man (RCMP) stopped it. It was kind a old boat for crossing long ways. They never go back to Alaska. People, lots of them try to go to Banksland but they didn't make it. ... You know when they have some old boat, that RCMP too long ago they can't allow to make them go with rough boat. Old one anyway for crossing is long ways. From Booth Island when you start crossing, its long ways."[7]

The vessels were lived aboard for several months at a time. People found a place to sleep wherever they could, often lying aboard the cargo. When the boats made it to port families would pitch tents on deck or ashore beside the schooners. On North Star, the Carpenter and other Bankslander children would leave Sachs Harbour at the beginning of the sailing season in late July and would sleep on top of the bales of fur in the cargo hold. Margaret Carpenter recalls stacks and stacks of polar bear skins, white fox pelts by the hundreds as well as marten, wolverine and caribou. When we moved aboard North Star we still found small bits of fur that had lodged itself into the corners of the bulwarks and ship's sides.

Upon arrival on the mainland, North Star's furs would be moved to a warehouse for sorting and the family would often share a communal bed in the cargo hold. Father Bern Will Brown visited the ship in Aklavik by dog team and noted that with all of the fur off of North Star and with plenty of room the whole family still shared a bed under a pile of caribou skins.

Once the fur had been sold, the winter's supplies would be loaded aboard. The hold would fill with gunny sacks of coffee, tea, beans, flour, and other dry goods. These would become the make-shift mattresses for some of the children on their way back home to Sachs Harbour.

Travelling by schooner was perhaps the most significant change in the Inuvialuit's hunting history. After centuries of nomadic living, following game to be trapped as each season presented itself; the hunter was now a trapper and a trader and required a vessel to transport his catch of furs to market. "The boats changed the way that our people had traditionally hunted. Men were now able to easily travel great distances to hunt. Individual hunters were able to haul in enough game to satisfy the needs of the people in the few small camps remaining after the many sicknesses."[8]

The desire to own a schooner was very big for many of the Inuvialuit. The schooner owners had more prestige within the community and they were also able to travel whenever ice allowed them. Without a schooner, a family could be stuck on a remote island such as Banks or Baillie for years.

Sometimes the schooner owners charged for a passage or took it in furs or in labour of getting the boat ready for sea. Those that did not have enough money to purchase a schooner sometimes tried to barter for them. "A schooner captain, who gave people passage to and from the coast, organized the hunt, men and women in his group sharing the meat, oil and muktuk that they cooperatively produced."[9]

The Ledyards were a missionary family who were working in the Arctic to spread the word of God. They recognized early on that they would need a schooner in order to do this and they eventually found one that was in need of a lot of work. The Eskimo did not want cash for the boat as he knew that trading for material goods would be better for him in the long run. The Ledyards made a deal that in exchange for the Peterhead they would trade him a new canoe, outboard engine, and a rifle. Once the transaction was finished they realised that in order to get the boat running they would have to acquire all of the repair materials including a lot of caulking compound which were ordered by radio to be picked up in Churchill. "It had not been in the water for six years. It was so dry we could see daylight through all the seams on the side where the sun had been the brightest during the years it was on the beach. Just after the last trip our Eskimo friend, Shevikkata, had taken the four-cylinder Fordson tractor engine (converted to marine use) all apart and had never reassembled it. Parts were scattered all over the engine room, but he assured us everything was there."[10]

With the value of boats so high, Sarah Meyook remembers that one time an Inuit named Anaqttuk had a nice boat that had a sail and an engine. "Long ago when I could remember, the whaleboats had no engine on them. But Anaqtuq had put an engine on his boat and the people were so surprised that they thought they'd seen or heard something strange for them because they never knew anything about engine on boats before. They always called the small boats 'whaleboats' long ago. They just travelled with rowboats and sails, that is how. And so these Annik and them just had a daughter. Anaqtuk asked them if he could buy their little daughter with his whaleboat. Annik said, 'Maybe we might not have a daughter again.' Before that he had tried to adopt from Sugayaluk with a boat with engine. That was how it was."[11]

The Ledyards work on their new Peterhead was typical of the work that the Inuit put into theirs such as North Star. The work list that they encountered in reviving their schooner who had been beached for a half-dozen years with the engine in pieces is remarkably similar to the project that Sven Johansson took on when he purchased North Star.

"While Cliff scraped the old caulking out of the seams, I put the old engine together. I had never seen one just like it. The block was upside down just as it had been left six years before. Although the Eskimo had thoughtfully oiled all the parts, the jigsaw puzzle was surely a mess. ..By the middle of the afternoon we were ready to try our completed puzzle. The engine fired on the first turn!"[12]

They faced a steep learning curve as they headed out to sea. "None of us had ever run a boat of this size before. By the time it started to float, we three were out on it ready to take the boat to deep water to wait for daylight. We started the engine, cast off the ropes, and pushed the drive lever forward. Only one thing was wrong - there was no slow speed! The engine, turning at a fast idle, took us through the foggy night far too fast, and soon we were working our way through pans of ice. When we came to a deep spot, not knowing just how far we were from shore, we dropped the anchor."[13]

The mayhem of heading out into the Arctic Ocean in fog aboard a Peterhead stuck in full forward was indicative of the way the boats often found themselves. For instance, with up to four or five families aboard, plus each of their worldly possessions, sledges and dogs, there was not much room for moving around. North Star's galley was in the focs'le where one of the women typically did all of the cooking. Most food was prepared pre-voyage as cooking in such a small space was not a popular undertaking. Bags and bags of bannock were the norm and on deck there was dry meat hanging from the rails for anyone to take a slash off of if they were hungry. All over the boat, out of reach of the chained dogs hung food for the long voyage to Herschel Island and Aklavik. "....my Mom, we stay two nights sometimes, she make drymeat, she hang them on top the boat. She used to hang the meat there, boy! ...... they buy things from Herschel Island, Bankslanders."[14] "Cook in the house, cook in the boat. They had wood stove right in the boat. They had oven stove, big iron stove with oven. When it's too hot they cook, you know them Primus stove, one burner."[15] Aboard another Arctic schooner the author describes the scene. "The boat was jammed with sledges, weapons, kitchenware, decayed seal and walrus meat for dog food and 'several bags of stinking fat ... ...partly for lighting purposes and partly for cooking during the winter.'[16]

Many of the schooners were operated under sail alone. The boats with engines were much sought after but until their arrival the Inuit became very good sailors. "We possessed then a little schooner, a sail boat, the Kusseriuoak, but we were less fortunate than Angik Ruben with his 'Nigek' and old Bennett Ningarsek with his 'Shamrock'. Those two schooners were propelled by gasoline engines and of course they outdistanced us very soon after our departure from Nanolreak (White Fish Station), enroute to Baillie, a matter of some two hundred miles to sail."[17] When the use of engines became commonplace the owners were more likely to operate their boats under power even when the wind was fair. Some people have perceived this as being a way of showing a higher status, being able to burn precious fuel when there was no need to.

"William Duval had an old boat powered by steam. It is said by some that on occasion the only fuel he had to use in the thing was seal oil and the smoke and stench from it would have given even the milder member of a pollution control committee unbearable nightmares."[18] The use of seal oil or other types of lubrication was not that uncommon. Charles Gillham was near the MacKenzie Delta one spring in the early 1940's when he came across "three Eskimos in their tiny rat canoes, heading out for the coast. They told me they had a whale boat left there from the year before, and were going after it. They said that they had gasoline but no motor oil for it and wanted to borrow or trade a bit from me. As I was very short myself, I let them have only a quart. It was not a tenth part of what they needed for their 300 mile trip. Three days later I looked down the river and saw them returning. Behind their boat, a blue fog hung over the water. It smelled to the high heaven. They were burning seal oil with the quart of the good stuff that I had given them, but the seal oil was about gone. I went through my outfit and added a half gallon of bacon grease and a three-pound pail of vegetable cooking fat. I saw them in Aklavik three weeks after, two hundred miles away."[19]

William 'Paddy' Gibson was considered an 'expert' on the Western Arctic Eskimos and after reviewing a manuscript by photographer Richard Nash Hourde about his experience making a voyage around the Delta in 1936 where he met up with North Star he noted that "since the utilisation of the gas engine the MacKenzie Eskimos are becoming very poor sailors. The young men really cannot handle sail at all. Trained by the American whalers, the older generation were skilled sailors in the strict meaning of the term. The first gas engines made their appearance among them in 1920. Nowadays, every schooner is equipped with one."[20]

Generally North Star and the other schooners return voyage to Sachs Harbour would see the flotilla gather off of Tuktoyaktuk and wait for a good weather window. Once this arrived they would head out together and drop anchor off of Tuft Point. They would lay on the hook, sometimes for days, sometimes for weeks, until the Captains felt confident that they could make McKinley Bay. Here, the dogs would be put ashore and the families might go hiking to pick berries or do some hunting. The next leg of the voyage was oftentimes the most dangerous as they had to sail through the shallow water off of Cape Dalhousie which could produce some frighteningly large standing waves. With a strong wind the ships could be tossed up onto the point and so the Captains again had to pick their weather carefully. This leg of the voyage would see the fleet anchor at Liverpool Bay and after another stop they would carry on up to Cape Parry where they would anchor before making the final push of one hundred and twenty miles to Nelson Head and then home. By climbing the cliffs at Cape Parry they could take a bearing on Nelson Head and judge the ice conditions before continuing. Fred Carpenter liked to time this last board of the voyage so that they would arrive at night and be guided by the lights on in some of the tents or houses as they drew closer to help him pilot the fleet home.

The overloaded schooners with families, tons of furs and all of their possessions would make quite a sight. Their arrival in port was noisy as the barking and howling of all of their dogs mixed with the calls of the Bankslanders as they saw family and friends for the first time in at least a year. Mary Evik Ruben describes the pandemonium. "They used to get enough foxes. Coloured fox, red fox, silver, all kinds a foxes. Then my Mom used to dry them up before July, we used to go to Baillie Island to bring them. My Dad sold everything then we got whole winter outfit. You know just like long ago Sachs Harbour people always buy their food for the winter, eh? Like that when my Dad got boat. We never short of anything. They get everything. We used to live so nice that time when my Dad got boat. We used to go to Baillie Island and we see lots a people there, Bankslanders. We used to meet them there July, they come back from Herschel Island from August, ready to go across there. They load their boat (North Star) with food. All Bankslanders go to Herschel Island. When they come back in August, they come back, their boat just load. You know, they have dogs too on top, just full with dogs! Well, that's the only dogs they travel with. Boy! Enough dogs used to be on top the boat! Sometimes they put their dogs inside their boat, so close their chain not to move around. Only with dogs they travel with that time. We used to meet lot's a people there, Baillie Island. Lot's of boats! Your grandfather Lennie, David Piqtuqan, David Anderson, Fred Bennett's parents, lot's a them from Sachs. Old Adam, Jim Wolki's, Frank, Fred Wolki, Angus parents, that time Angus and Noah they were so young, eh"[22]

Fred Carpenter was once asked how much cargo he carried aboard North Star. "Forty-four tons, sometimes maybe fifty-eight, I never count. Sometimes it took twenty tons coal, coal for the families, you know? We put twenty tons in bow of the schooner, inside there. On deck forty tons fuel, gas - twenty tons gas, maybe coal-oil - maybe ten tons. Seven families coal oil, you know - on deck, with thirty-five tons on deck sometimes. We get our load. Big boat, you know? Carry a lot of oil. Carried about fifty ton easy, that schooner. Fifty-seven feet long. Took seven families," he remembered.

Now with only North Star of Herschel Island left afloat many Inuvialuit elders have fond memories of their times out on the ocean, even though some of them were in rough weather and biting cold. Albert Elias has many schooner memories from his childhood. "A lot of the memories from my childhood were on travelling by schooner between Aklavik and Tuktoyaktuk and Sachs Harbour. I have a lot of memories of travelling with the schooners. These were amazing vessels, sturdy, very dependable and very limited equipment that they had. The compass and the barometer were about all they had for navigation. At that time there were no radios equipped with them so it took a lot of courage and ingenuity amongst the seamen and they were real amazing to watch. Men like them that operate these schooners, they were just natural seamen. I never forgot that."

Albert Elias remembers helping to get his father's boat, Fox, ready for the trip to the mainland. He recalled how the family and neighbours would pitch in to help paint the boat and his Dad would get the engine going. He described the sound of the engine as the best in the world when he was a child because it meant that soon they would be travelling again. "Sometimes Dad would hoist the sail. Dad had purchased the boat from an Inuvialuit leader who had did some business in the CanAlaska trading company in the Holman area in the 1930's and 1940's. His name was George Porter, who then had moved over to Gjoa Haven with David Tukhuk and his schooner and their families."

Fox at Sachs Harbour.

The Elias' Fox still sits ashore at Sachs Harbour and there is hope in the community that one day she might sail again, though with each passing year it seems less likely. Our Lady of Lourdes is mounted as a permanent display at Tuktoyaktuk. Most other schooners have been crushed in the ice, wrecked ashore or in the words of the late great Canadian songwriter Stan Rogers, 'hauled on the beach and forgotten'.

One of these, Nanuk II was vandalised and burned on the beach in Fort Franklin. She was built by Kneass and shipped up on Pedersen's Patterson and owned by James Wolki and later was inherited by Susie Sidney who was married to Jim's brother Fred Wolki. Susie owned at least two boats at the time.

The Omingmuk (which means musk-ox), originally based at Tuk and now broken up in storms was originally owned by James Wolki who also owned Nanuk 11 (Polar Bear). James Wolki had traded half interest in North Star to get Nanuk 11. Susie had been married to Fred. When Fred died, Susie inherited Nanuk 11. She traded Nanuk 11 to James for his 1/2 share in North Star.

Through wheeling and dealing in bad years Nanuk 11 was later owned by Stanley Peffer from Aklavik. Later, the Department of Indian and Northern Affairs purchased her from Peffer. After years of very hard service Sven Johansson purchased her for use in reindeer operation at Reindeer Station to transport the carcasses from the slaughter-house to market or storage. She was his first vessel in Canada. Years later he sold her back to the Department of Indian and Northern Affairs but kept the auto-pilot which he later installed on North Star. Nanuk was put into service on Great Bear Lake. Some children caused a fire which consumed her.

Chapter 6

The Original North Star & Arrival of the new North Star

The Original North Star

Carpenter and Wolki's new ship was to be named North Star, a tribute to the original North Star that plied their waters. The original North Star was owned by trapper Martin Andreasen and Ira Rank. Andreasen had heard from Norwegian explorer Amundsen that a small fortune could be made by a trader who could work his ship east and set up trade with the Coppermine River Inuit, a group who had been left virtually untouched by the other fur trading companies. Andreasen and his friend Joe Bernard, who owned the schooner Polar Bear "sailed to another part of the Arctic coast and is reputed to have made a profit of $150,000 from the furs he brought out."[1]

When the Arctic explorer Stefansson was looking for a solid boat in the spring of 1913, he had his eye on the original North Star. He wrote to the backers of the Canadian Arctic Expedition: "The North Star is of the same capacity as the Teddy Bear, but has a centre-board instead of a keel, and therefore draws only four feet of water as against six feet for the Teddy Bear... The North Star, according to the intention of her captain last summer, was going to winter in Liverpool Bay, just west of Cape Bathurst....Of the five ships wintering in the Arctic, two are from our point of view desirable - the Teddy Bear and the North Star. Each of these is for sale at $4,000 or possibly even less... I believe Mr. Rank has not the power to sell the North Star without the consent of Captain Andreason."[2]

© GSC / CGC
39644

The first North Star buried in ice at Bernard Harbour, May 1915.

Soon after, in the winter of 1913-1914, Stefansson purchased her from Captain Andreasen at Demarkation Point, Alaska, to replace the lost Karluk. Andreasen struck a hard bargain and the government ended up paying thirteen thousand dollars for the ten ton, forty foot, gasoline-powered schooner, a secondary gas workboat, as well as standard ship's tools and equipment. That summer, North Star was "caught by ice conditions as it sought to reach Nome from Herschel Island in August 1913, and wintered in Clarence Lagoon, some 10 miles east of 'Duffy' O'Connor's place at Demarkation Point."[3]

In the summer of 1915 Wilkins took North Star east to Bathurst Inlet to assist the Southern Party scientists, then crossed over to Banks Island and took the schooner as far up the west coast as the ice conditions permitted. North Star was hauled up on shore opposite Robillard Island. In the winter of 1915-1916 North Star became one of the camps used by the advance and hunting parties to further the next year's exploration. Stefansson's Inuit guide, Natkusiak, established another hunting camp nearby at the tip of Cape Prince Alfred. From there he hunted seals and polar bears and collected specimens for the expedition.

The Canadian Arctic Expedition was based in the western Arctic between 1914 and 1917. Their purpose was to explore the western Queen Elizabeth Islands. The expedition was headed up by Stefansson and it was his Alaskan Eskimo guide, Natkusiak, who purchased the North Star for use as a trapping and trading vessel in 1917. At the end of the Canadian Arctic Expedition in 1917, Stefansson gave the North Star and supplies to Natkusiak in lieu of $2,000 wages owing. He stayed on the island, trapping and trading for four years. He was grubstaked by Pedersen who had command of the Liebes and Company ship, Herman. Their plan was for Natkusiak to trap all winter and then be picked up by Pedersen the following summer. The weather was not in their favour and Pedersen was locked out of Banks Island for two years by severe ice. In 1919 he was able to get to the Masik River on Banks Island and pick up another trapping party who had taken several hundred furs. Word was passed to Pedersen that Natkusiak and the North Star would stay on the ice choked island and so he left them a cache of food at Cape Kellett. Pedersen and Herman pulled away from Banks Island with the plan once again of returning the following year. Once again the following two years left the sea around Banks Island chock-a-block with ice. It was another two years before Pedersen and the Herman made it back to Banks in order to re-supply Natkusiak and take back any fur that he had trapped! After four years of living off the land and trapping for Pedersen Natkusiak had had enough and breaking through a lead in the ice forced North Star out into the Beaufort Sea. Pedersen took North Star in tow and they headed for Baillie Island.

Natkusiak had spent four years (1917 to 1921) in northwest Banksland using the schooner as his base for fox trapping. According to the RCMP, North Star was "ice bound" on the west coast of Banks Island just south of Cape Prince Alfred for six years before being released.[4] The small ship was blocked in by ice, with no open leads, year after year. It is an incredible story of isolation and determination since, as he later proved, he could have taken his dog team and fled south, abandoning North Star. In an interview with Usher in 1971, Fred Carpenter recalled that Natkusiak and his team took about one thousand foxes between 1917 and 1921. In order to get supplies, Natkusiak took his dog team from North Star harbour where he was based, down to Nelson Head at the south end of Banksland and then incredibly made an ice crossing of the Amundsen Gulf in 1918/19 and perhaps 1919/20. This was in order to trade his fur for much needed supplies from Fritz Wolki's trading post. There is only one other recorded instance of such a crossing, and it has always been considered extremely hazardous due to the possibility of moving ice and open leads in Amundsen Gulf at any time during the winter."[5]

Some of the details of Natkusiak's time aboard North Star show the kind of ingenuity that the Inuvialuit later became renowned for. "According to Fred Carpenter, of Sachs Harbour, Natkusiak spent two years on the north of the island, by which time he had run out of shells and was making his own. Natkusiak was so low on ammunition that when shooting caribou he would wait as the herd passed and try and shoot when two caribou were lined up so that he could take two with one shell." His association with Banks Island was shown through his self identity as he soon after changed his name to Billy Banksland.

Natkusiak's story and the incredible amount of fur that he had taken spread throughout the Western Arctic. In the 1920's with the continuing shortage of white fox on the mainland, traders were seriously looking at outfitting seasoned trappers to head off to Banks Island. "The trappers received encouragement to go to Banks Island from several quarters. Many of those who lived on the coast heard about the island and its abundance of foxes from Natkusiak and from members of the crew of the Aklavik. Ole Andreasen, a trader at Atkinson Point who had once travelled on Banks Island with Stefansson, also encouraged them to go. In addition, he along with Captain Pedersen was willing to provide the outfits required."[6]

The Loss of the North Star

One of Natkusiak's family is Jimmy Memorana of Holman. He remembers when the family's schooner was lost. "North Star lost 1932 or 33. Big west wind coming, roll over, go into shore, wrecked bottom, had just put new engine on it, right to the bluff. In the winter Natkusiak took off the mast [pulled out with tackle from the cliff]. Some parts used for ice house."[7]

Natkusiak's daughter, Agnes Goose, of Holman, recalls information about the North Star: "When my Dad finished working for Stefansson, he got the North Star. It was an old ship and eventually was wrecked when I was about seven years old. I remember seeing it when the waves took the boat, so I ran into the house and was crying. Someone had been using the boat to get driftwood and hadn't anchored it properly. So when it got really stormy, the waves just took the ship [at Baillie Islands]."[8]

Elizabeth Banksland also remembers her husband Alex Banksland's story of the loss. As the schooner was blown away in the big west wind, they "couldn't do anything, just watching it drifting away." Alex described how Natkusiak told the others not to worry about trying to save the schooner, "Never mind, leave it, just let it go," he said, "I can't do anything more with it, just let it go, it's not a person."[9]

Agnes Goose also remembers her father then "married my mother Topsy Ikiuna. Her family was also working for Stefansson, and she and my Dad met up at Melville Island. After my Dad finished working for Stefansson, he lived on Banks Island and then moved to Baillie Island where they had a house". Billy and Topsy had six children and in 1939 they moved to Holman Island. Natkusiak died and was buried in Holman in 1947. A Peninsula in Victoria Island and a basalt rock formation on Holman Island are named in his honour.

The New North Star

North Star, later North Star of Herschel Island, a 57-foot wooden sloop, was ordered by Fred Carpenter and James (Jim) Wolki and built in San Francisco in 1935. She was transported to the North on Pedersen's boat, Patterson. With a hull shaped like a clipper ship, the new North Star served for many years as an Arctic supply ship, travelling to and from Banks Island.

"Fred Carpenter and Fred Wolki, they were the ones that made the blueprints, they drew the schooner. That was in 1933 or maybe '34," recalls retired trapper, Eddie Gruben. When Wolki and Carpenter spoke with Pedersen about their order for North Star, the three men walked around looking at various schooners and picked the best parts of each to be incorporated into the new ship. Pedersen had previously taken orders for 'schooners' usually based on length alone with perhaps one or two added features. In fact, on several occasions he had carried a schooner up aboard Patterson with no buyer in mind, knowing that someone would be interested. When the Pokiaks received Reindeer, they only knew that they needed a trading schooner and Pedersen even took no money for her but let them sail off on the understanding that they would pay him back at the end of the season or in seasons to come. This time practically every part of the new ship was discussed at length.

"Jim Wolki's sister I married, Lucy Wolki. We talking, him and me someday - 'You and me, we get a big boat called schooner. Maybe we have to go to Banksland. We get lots of fox, maybe get lucky. 'Sure we would Fred', that's what I think to myself. You and me buy a big boat so we can go to Banksland trapping. Maybe we make a living after this. After we get the big boat we start to load it up. We go to Captain Pedersen at CanAlaska trade. 'We need a big boat that can pass ice.' We ordered that boat, North Star. "We load 'em up after we buy it. We go to Banksland. We find a good harbour, Sachs Harbour."

North Star, as deck cargo aboard Patterson
enters the ice for the first time, 1936.

The keel was laid and the ship was finished and ready for shipping in 1935, however Pedersen had to wait until the summer thaw of 1936 to take her north. After rounding through the Aleutian Islands and travelling through Bering Strait, Patterson entered the Beaufort Sea and made for Herschel Island, the strong bluff bow of the Patterson breaking the ice until she could anchor in Pauline Cove at Herschel Island. Patterson had left San Francisco in the spring of 1936, burdened with a hold and deck cargo of trade goods for the Can-Alaska company to trade with. There would have been many special orders aboard for the Inuit who had become more aware of what their furs could be traded for and how their quality of life could change for the better. Strapped firmly aboard her starboard deck was a jewel of a ship, freshly painted and with a large pilothouse aft, North Star was heading for her new Arctic home.

Patterson with North Star aboard, arrives at Herschel Island, 1936.

It was still early in the season and there was ice all around. Back in San Francisco, North Star had been loaded aboard the Patterson with the luxury of a crane. Here, five hundred miles north of the Arctic Circle, there was no crane. In fact, there wasn't even a dock to moor at. The ship dropped anchor and the crew prepared to launch their precious cargo.

North Star in slings aboard Patterson.

North Star being lowered into ocean at Herschel Island, 1936.

Pedersen shifted tons of his ballast to the Patterson's starboard side, inducing a heel on her hull so that she was leaning her rails almost to the icy waters. In this precarious position the steam donkey engine was fired up. This was operated by Pederson's son, Ted Junior. A hook-block was seized to North Star's masthead and the line was then sent down to the donkey-engine. As North Star was drawn aloft, Ted Junior took up the slack from what the engine gave him. Since Pederson had heeled his ship over so far, North Star naturally swung out and was hanging in the precarious position just over the Patterson's railing, directly over the Arctic Ocean. The strain on the line holding 25 tons or more of North Star made a higher and higher pitched whine, like a violin string being wound too tight. Ted Junior had taken five turns around the donkey winch's drum, to ensure that North Star would not slip and go crashing down to be wrecked in the ocean, or to smash down onto the Patterson's railing, potentially sinking both ships.

The order came to lower North Star and Teddy eased up on the tension from the halyard. North Star didn't budge. With five wraps on the drum, there was so much friction that the line was held fast. In order to release one wrap, without losing the whole load, he had to use all of his considerable strength to maintain tension on the line while unwrapping one turn. There comes a point in this exercise where if you don't maintain absolute control of the halyard, it can quickly get away from you or rip your hand off if it gets caught in the bite. With Fred Carpenter and Jim Wolki watching from ashore and Ted Pederson watching from the quarterdeck while keeping an eye on his own ship and the dramatic heel that he had on her, Teddy slowly took one turn off of the winch. "He was a big strong guy" remembers Sven Johansson.

Now with four wraps on the drum, Teddy again was given the order to lower away. Still, North Star hung from her masthead halyard, perhaps looking reticent to enter her new home. Now with only four wraps on Pedersen again slowly took another turn off. North Star hung aloft. Waves were washing past the Patterson's rail. If the wind blew any large ice into the cove, they would have to wait until it cleared or risk damaging both ships. North Star refused to budge.

Any seaman will tell you that you never want to have less than three turns on a winch drum. This provides the minimal amount of tension to keep the load from slipping. Ted Pedersen walked forward on the steeply angled deck to speak with his son. Veins stood proud on his son's forearms. They both knew that in order to complete the launch, the younger Pederson would have to go to two wraps on the drum. Both father and son knew the imminent danger in doing this. One thing about life in the Arctic is that you must be self-reliant. There is no one to call on for help. You either rise to the occasion or you die.

"The really important thing is North Star was too heavy for any booms or derricks so you see how Captain Pedersen - he released and then he put the tackle right on the masthead and then he put North Star up past the height of the gunwales and then he heeled her over and then Teddy Pedersen, he was first mate, and he told me how he had taken five turns around the capstan and he was down to one line and he couldn't get it to slip so he took off another one and then it was down to two turns before they could let it slip," said Sven.

Teddy Junior once again slowly removed the wrap. With only two wraps on the drum now, the line began to pay out. The screech of it over the drum was almost deafening and the smell of the manila line heating up permeated the clean Arctic air. The line paid out faster and faster. Teddy was working hard to keep the launch in control. Captain Pedersen rushed to the rail, the cold water in the scuppers reaching up past his ankles as he fended North Star off of Patterson until her keel kissed the icy waters of the Arctic Ocean. A cheer went up from the crowd ashore. She was home. Bern Will Brown had a picture that he took of North Star being off-loaded from the Patterson. He sent it via helicopter to Sachs Harbour for Fred Carpenter but the helicopter crashed, killing everyone aboard and burning all of the mail and cargo.

Receipt from C.T. Pedersen to James Wolki and Fred Carpenter for sale of North Star, August 16th, 1936.

North Star was towed into shore with her small skiff. The water in the Arctic tends to drop off quite suddenly from shore and so they were able to manoeuvre her in close and then toss a line to her new owners. The RCMP was waiting to claim their customs dues. All around there was laughter as well as sighs of relief, now that the new ship was here and that she had been safely launched. The selling price was $23,000.00, a veritable fortune in 1936. To put this price in perspective, the Ford Motor Company was selling its Model 40A motor car that year for $500.00. First, the RCMP inspected Ted Pedersen's paperwork and accepted the Customs due for importing North Star for sale into Canada. The ship technically had been sold by the Kneass Brothers Boatbuilders to Ted Pedersen's CanAlaska Company. When the Canadian Government had their fee is when more paperwork should have been done to register North Star as a Canadian owned ship. Wolki and Carpenter didn't know about this as ships brought in by the CanAlaska Company and HBC were considered by the Inuit to be simple workboats. This would come back to complicate things when Fred and Susie ended up selling the ship many years later. The Registrar of shipping would be surprised to learn of North Star's existence in 1967 even though she had been in Canadian waters for her whole working life

In any case, the Customs dues were paid and then reports from the time say the four men leaned upon an old fuel drum and caught up on each others' news as Fred and Jim counted out the money in cash. The men were short of the full amount so they added a few pelts and put them atop the pile of cash. To this they dug deep and added some Hudson's Bay Company money to seal the deal. With handshakes all around, Wolki and Carpenter stepped aboard North Star for the first time. It was August 1936 and North Star of Herschel Island was ready to take on her first job. Fred Carpenter was once asked how he and Jim Wolki came up with the money in the 1930's. Some of it at seemed to have come from an inheritance from Lucy and Jim's mother. "I know," he said. "Even today money can't buy much. When you have one dollar - nothing. Now these days you can see one dollar, go up to the store, you lucky if you can find a candy. One candy. That money. Fritz Wolki trading outfit. His wife Eskimo - Rachel. My first wife got $30,000. Jim Wolki got $13,000 but he got the rest of it from his wife, he told me." Fred then sold Jim his boat, Numnik (Nanuk?). "Fred he said. I give my soul - what's left of my soul. I give him the boat - good size boat we call Numnik. 1926 (built), thirty-five feet long, make it forty feet. Big, wide one, you know? Sixteen horsepower, heavy-duty Atlas engine. We use it, too. After North Star he decide to sell it to somebody else."

After a quick tour of the empty hull Carpenter and Wolki moved to the engine room. The Atlas engine took up almost half the ship and weighed almost two tons. It had a large flywheel and three large cylinders. In order to start her one of the men rammed a slotted three foot handle onto the flywheel and began turning it. In order to build up enough pressure for the fuel to ignite he would turn the handle harder and harder. At the exact moment when the engine fired he pulled the handle off and stood back. In some models, if the handle wasn't disengaged from the engine it would continue to turn faster and faster and most likely fly off at high speed with enough force to take a hand or a head off. The hole was designed so that the bar would slip out as the wheel turned to save the engineer from potential injury.

In the late thirties American scientist Charles Gillham happened to tour North Star, whose ownership he attributed to the "Wilke" (sp) brothers. In speaking of boats he wrote in Raw North "...it is often possible to take in a big wad of cash, and as a result, the natives go in for boats. One belonging to the Wilke brothers cost, reputedly, $36,000. The name was the North Star and I went aboard once to look it over. On the wall of the cabin hung the latest model Winchester rifle, with the finest telescope sight fitted to it that money could buy. There were binoculars of the best make, and even a movie camera. Squatted around a table were the women of the family in their homemade fur parkas. They were eating boiled fish from a common bowl with their fingers. Their only implement was an oola (ulu), or a half-moon-shaped round-bladed knife, a direct descendant from the stone ones used a few generations back by their ancestors. The boiled fish were being eaten with gusto, first being dipped in high smelling seal oil. The finger sucking and smacking that went with the process hardly fitted in with the modern-ness of the boat."[10]

Before leaving aboard their new ship, the men loaded her up with all of the necessities to get their families through another winter. Sacks of oats, sugar, tea, cases of beans, meat and cases of ammunition, traps, stretchers, coal oil and gasoline made up part of their order. With the engine fired up they cast off their lines and headed towards Aklavik to provision up for the coming season and so that their friends and families could see the ship. North Star was the largest and most luxurious Inuit owned vessel ever built and they were justly proud of her. Crowds gathered to see the famous ship for the first time. All of the MacKenzie Delta knew about the ship and had been looking forward to see this, the largest and strongest of the trading schooners ever built. After provisioning in 1936, they headed north to Banks Island for their first year of trapping with North Star as the base camp. They arrived too late in the season to get her hauled ashore and so drew her in as close as they could and then ran anchors out ashore so that when the ice started to melt in the bay, that North Star would remain fast to the island. Fred Carpenter once shared that "in summer, around August, couldn't go across. Too much ice. And another schooner there. And Billy Banksland and David. The first year we stayed at Banksland with the North Star".

The following year, 1937, Wolki and Carpenter traded with North Star down to Tuktoyaktuk. Everyone came out to see the new ship, the largest and the grandest of the fleet and there were lots of congratulations in order. Perhaps because of all of the celebrations, the two men were late in getting away from the mainland. They took the preferred route up the coast of Baillie Island with the intention of crossing over to Banks Island but got caught in the ice.

The preferred route was to head northeast to Booth Island which was a significantly shorter open ocean crossing and then from there to follow the coastline of islands until they made Banks. It was a bad year for ice though and they ended up being frozen in at Booth. They had entered harbour and then watched in resignation as a big west wind came up, pushing the ocean ice into the bay, effectively sealing them in for the winter and once again forcing North Star to be frozen in over winter! "Yeah, that second year after we get North Star. Second year we froze in at Booth Island", must be 1937. That summer the ice never leave hardly, you know? All the way, the ice year is something like this year. And we start kind of late from Aklavik, and late in August and we can't make it come through. Nobody got across. Everybody stayed at Booth Island. A whole bunch. Just going that far. And main ice not right from the beach. Only about a couple of hundred yards in some places. And we go in the harbour there and that night, next day, supposed to be one load. And the wind switched, west wind right away. Before even the wind switched, ice started coming in. We tried to move to get to open water, just about, we got caught in the ice. Just made it in the harbour before it gets us. It pushed that all heavy ice right at the sand spit and the mainland. And they never left that, all fall. Breakup way out about 20 miles offshore,"[11] recalls Carpenter.

Some of the families took their dog teams and returned to Sachs Harbour for the winter, leaving Fred, his mother Divana and a handful of others to trap at Booth all winter. "Jim Cockney and Bertram (Pokiak) went back to Sachs Harbour. We unload our summers and winters supply stuff and before we go to North. That ways he came back with the dogs. Then they left the dogs behind too. Good thing he took the dogs. And soon the North Star can't move in ice, pushed right in. Soon as you get the snow come, he come by the land. Go to Sachs Harbour. Me and Jim Cockney and my mother was left behind."[12]

The ice in that area was noted by Captain Henry Larsen of the St. Roch when he made a trip by dog team to Banks Island in 1941 to be very difficult to work in. He noted "much heavy old ice. Some icebergs, over fifty feet high, pressed up against the shore."[13]

North Star of Herschel Island had arrived in the Canadian Western Arctic and became a much admired and respected ship due to her construction and the way she was operated. At age 91, former fur trapper Eddie Gruben who had travelled many seasons in her summed up the way that most Northerners felt and still feel about her.

"North Star. F*&%ing solid boat! I know that."[14]

Chapter 7

EARLY YEARS: Sachs Harbour/Banksland

Sachs Harbour on Banks Island was the home port of North Star of Herschel Island for over thirty years. The reason for this being her home lies in the history of the island and the abundance of fox as well as the other game there.

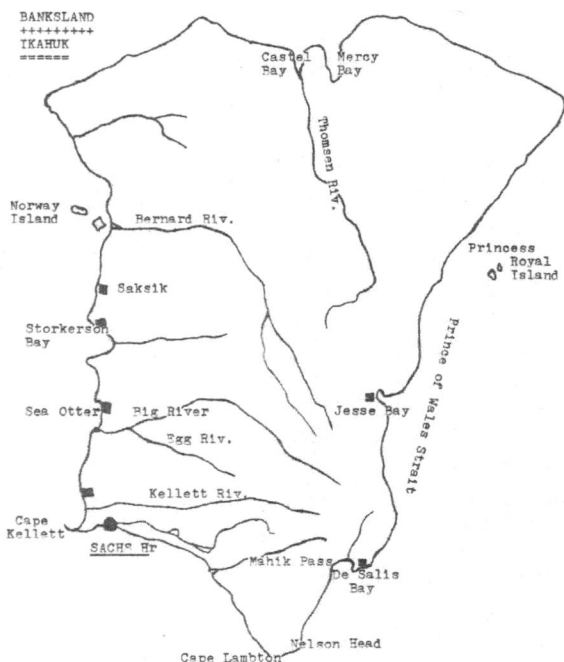

Banks Island or Banksland. Sachs Harbour is on SW corner.

Banks Island lies at the entrance to the fabled NorthWest Passage. A vessel must travel past its north or south shores in order to enter or exit the passage and it has stood witness to every eastbound attempt on the route. The island sits between 64 and 71 degrees north latitude and at 115 and 125 west longitude and is the most westerly of the Canadian Arctic archipelago. Banks Island is roughly the size of the province of New Brunswick and Usher notes that it is about twice the size of Vancouver Island, "being the fourth largest of the Arctic Islands after Baffin, Ellesmere and Victoria."[1] It is also home to the largest muskox herd in the world and the largest nesting population of snow geese in the western Arctic. It is Canada's fifth largest island and the 24th largest island in the world. Eskimos of the Thule culture lived on Banks Island 500 years ago, though the island seems to have gone uninhabited for centuries at a time. This is curious since Banks Island is rich in resources. "Banks Island is believed to be one of the first northern regions inhabited by humans. Archaeological remains here date back 3,400 years. Seventeen archaeological sites have been identified along the southern coast. The Inuvialuit name for the island is Ikaahuk, meaning a place to cross. This refers to that part of Banks Island closest to Victoria Island, where the Inuvialuit traditionally crossed Prince of Wales Strait."[3]

In 1820, the Sir William Edward Parry expedition in search of the NorthWest Passage named the island in honour of Sir Joseph Banks, president of the Royal Society in Britain who had encouraged the British Navy to resume its quest for the NorthWest Passage. From then on it became known as Banks Island though Robert McClure in the years 1850-54 found that on his charts it was marked as Baring Island. Sir Joseph Banks was an English botanist who sailed with Captain Cook aboard Endeavour from 1768-1771. One interesting part of Banks trivia is that Joseph Banks used some of his inherited wealth to provide financial support for many voyages including that of George Vancouver to the Pacific NW and to William Bligh's Bounty voyage that ultimately led to the infamous mutiny. He was also a very enthusiastic proponent of populating what would become Australia. The area that would eventually be New South Wales was initially to be called Banksia.

When McClure arrived with Investigator, one of two ships dispatched to find the lost Franklin expedition, the course of life on Banks Island changed dramatically for not only did he end up abandoning his ship full of all kinds of riches, he also built a fortified cache ashore at Mercy Bay that he filled with food, tools, clothing and equipment. Upon his exit the Inuit made good use of all of the wood, iron and copper that they could scavenge from Investigator, as well as whatever else they wanted from the Mercy Bay cache.

In 1913 the explorer, Vilhjalmur Steffanson, began the first scientific exploration of Banksland aboard the ship 'Mary Sachs'. Mary Sachs ran aground about seven miles west of the current town of Sachs Harbour. The ship, which had long since paid her dues and was well past her prime was hauled ashore and used as a base camp for the Canadian Arctic Expedition of 1914-17. The wreckage lies about ten km from Sachs Harbour, a tiny Hamlet that is surrounded by low hills and lots of rock. "There are, of course, no trees but small bushes, shrubs and wildflowers are common. The beauty of Banks Island clearly proves the Arctic coastal region is not a barren wasteland. Despite the harsh climate, the island is host to a rich variety of flora and fauna. One of the lushest islands in the Western Arctic, Banks Island in the summer looks like a prairie landscape, with gently rolling hills and endless sky."[4] In 1967, as part of the Canadian Centennial Project, several parts of the wreck of the Mary Sachs were built into a cairn overlooking the Hamlet to commemorate the founding of Sachs Harbour.

Sachs Harbour is the smallest Inuvialuit community, with a present population of approximately 100. In the early 1900s, Inuvialuit families from the mainland and from Victoria Island would go to Banks Island to trap arctic fox (Alopex lagopus). Permanent occupation began in 1929, and the trade in fox pelts was so lucrative that it led to the "Schooner Era, "when some of the natural wealth was used to acquire large vessels to transport furs to centres such as Aklavik. This was somewhat ironic since it coincided with the Great Depression being experienced in the 1930s by the rest of the North American continent. The lucrative white fox fur trade brought the most recent wave of settlement to Banks Island to trap the large number of white fox who live there. News of their success prompted a rush of trappers to the island from across the western Arctic. In 1930, the first permanent home in Sachs Harbour was built by Fred Carpenter. Year round habitation began in 1953."[5]

"The 1920's was a very prosperous time for many Inuvialuit. But a twenty-fold increase in the price of furs from the turn of the century meant that dramatic overharvesting of furbearing animals was beginning in the Delta. This overharvesting caused Inuvialuit families to seek out other areas to pursue fur harvesting. In 1926, trapping was mainly contained to the mainland coast and the season was very poor. The highest number of white fox taken by one trapper was only 62. There were 25 trappers working in the area. Many of the natives were talking of attempting the crossing to Banks Island, and the local police felt that if one schooner tried, others would follow. The schooners in the 1920's were very small and many had no engine. Many were not well kept. Local knowledge of the unpredictable weather, the fierce storms and the likelihood of hitting ice or becoming trapped in the ice must have weighed on Carpenter and Wolki's minds as they were thinking of what qualities their schooner, the future North Star, would have.[6] "Natkutsiak (aboard the original North Star) had led the first group of trappers, mostly Alaskan and Métis people, to Banks Island in 1916, and it became known as the best fox-trapping area. The first trappers on Banksland were August Mahik and Adolf Binder in 1916, and a year later Fred Wolki. Adam Inualthuyak was another active trapper at this time. The first Inuit trappers to winter at Sachs

Harbour were Bennett Nigasea, Kowitchuk Raddi, Jim Cockney, and much later Fred Carpenter who started the first store. Bessie Wolki has some justified pride in her family's long association with Banksland. " We were the first ones to get to Banks Island. Piqtuqan, Lennie and us. There was nobody there, nothing! Just old log house right there at Masik Pass. We wintered in it. Covered with moss. One winter at Mary Sachs, another winter at Masik Pass. Old timers, that what they say. Who went to Banks Island first? They were Inuvialuit! Inuvialuit!"

It was in the fall of 1928 when Adam Inoalayak and his son Paul sailed their schooner from Baillie Island in company with Lennie Inglangasak, David Pektkana and their boats and families. The three schooners set up camp at the deserted base of the Canadian Arctic Expedition at Mary Sachs, west of Sachs Harbour. The trappers set the stage for the white fox bonanza with each hunter taking about one hundred pelts. "The next year, the same men returned to trap. Inoalayak brought his son-in-law, Jim Wolki; Inglangasak brought Alex Stefansson and Pannigabluk (Stefansson's mother), while Pektukana brought a Copper Eskimo by the name of Nakitok, who had been his trapping partner for some years at Pearce Point. In addition, Allen Okpik, from the Delta, had purchased a schooner and outfit from Ole Andreasen at Atkinson Point, and he brought his family, including three grown sons, Owen, Colin and Hebert, to Banks Island. The Baillie Islanders got 200-500 foxes each, and the Okpik family got over 1,100 between them. Even though the price of white fox had tumbled by 40 percent that spring, they had gained a fortune. The reputation of the Island was established."[7] In 1938 another trapper and his wife got 1,300, probably a world record. They received only $15,000 in that year, though years earlier their catch would have been worth over $70,000.[8] Three Inuvialuit families sailed from Aklavik to Banks Island in 1929. They established the community of Sachs Harbour for the purpose of harvesting white fox and other furbearing animals. Sachs Harbour later became known as the white fox capital of the world for its large production of white fox pelts."[9] "The first Eskimo trapper to winter at our harbour (Sachs) was Bennett Nigaseq in 1932. In 1937, Raddi Kowitchuk was also there with Jim Cockney; so was Fred Carpenter."[10]

White foxes drying at Sachs Harbour on thousand dollar lines.

Persis Gruben remembers that 'when my Dad bought Qun'ngialuk we went to Banks Island in 1929. That was when we crossed. At the time they weren't crossing yet to Banks Island. Three boats crossed at that time. Piqtuqan's boat, Inualhuuyaq's boat and my dad's boat, Qun'ngialuk. Piqtuan's boat was named Eagle. Inualhuuuyaq's boat was named Ukpik. Three boats crossed at that time. We wintered at Mary Sachs. We unloaded our supplies, then went to Sachs Harbour, to the little harbour where they docked the boats. They left us behind with Inualhuuyaq because there were a lot of polar bears. When we first arrived we couldn't even play outside there were so many bears. Bears came from all directions."[11] "They called the place Mary Sachs. Long ago a boat was shipwrecked there. They brought the ship's stern to the land and used it as a house. It had round windows. They cut off the stern and boarded it up with lumber. Bears would go to it. There were two big engines in the sand. We used to play on them."[12]

Susie Sidney, widow of Fred Wolki and Peter Sidney and sister of Fred Carpenter remembers the hardships of living on the land at Sachs Harbour when it was first being settled. "People have come here (Sachs Harbour), a long time. They come by schooner in fall. They bring dog teams, sleds, coal, everything by schooner. They build frame tent, moss underneath to keep the dampness out, snow around the tent. On the trap line they build snow houses. All that time it is blowing cold. No insulation. In summer, people go back to the mainland. Next fall they come again, build a new tent. I first come up here in 1930, work around the camp, going back to the mainland all the time. In 1938 I started trapping. After my husband is dead I go trapping with Michael Amos, and with my little girl all wrapped up. Fred Carpenter is the first one to build a house here. I stay with him that time. I shoot polar bear in summer only. No law that time against shooting them in summer. I have arthritis now. I have it bad. It is good to live in a house - warm."[13]

With no trees to chop down for fuel the Inuvialuit of Sachs Harbour would scour the beaches for driftwood or pieces of wrecks to take back to their tents or frame houses to burn. "Sometimes we found a piece of wood about three feet long, and carried it home with pride. We also collected dwarf willow branches. Wood was only used to start the fire in the morning. Once we had it going we heaped on seal oil, mixed with ashes. This mixture threw out quite a lot of heat, but it had a nasty odour until we got used to it. Sometimes on their way home from the trap lines, the men brought coal that they had picked up. This was not in solid lumps; it was chips and dust and we had to use a lot of it to keep the house warm."[14]

With more trappers who had the luxury of owning their own schooners or the moxy to get aboard one wintering at Banks Island, the Delta trappers on the mainland noticed a reduction in the amount of white fox available to them. The Delta trappers felt that Banks Island was a breeding ground for white fox and so it should be off-limits to trapping. They were unable to prove this. A more popular theory as to why there were so many fox on Banks Island was that the island lies directly in the currents of the Beaufort Sea and as a result was a natural area for the carcasses of the whales that the whalers had left behind to wash up. The Inuit had been insulted and sickened by the waste that the whalers left when they only took the heads of the whales but now theorised that the whale carcasses that washed ashore on Banks Island had caused a huge spike in the fox population. Some trappers learned to set their traps all around a whale carcass and found that this was very successful. Unlike the Inuit, who used every part of the whale, the whalers were most interested in the baleen and the rest of the whale head, which stored the greatest amount of oil. In most cases, once a whale had been killed, the head would be severed and hauled on deck for rendering into oil and removal of the baleen while the body was cut free. These carcasses would wash ashore days or months later, providing an amazing amount of food for the foxes.

Another theory of why white fox runs were inconsistent year to year that was raised by the elders was that the white fox and the coloured foxes were very competitive and that as trappers caught the white fox, the coloured foxes took over the area, even moving into the white fox dens which made recovery of the white fox very difficult. This theory points to another example wherein man's interference with the natural order of things, had caused one species to appear to die out in certain areas.

As the rest of the western world fell into the Great Depression, the Inuvialuit were making comparative fortunes. The fashion designers of Paris, London, New York and Montreal had latched on to white fox as being the next trend and their decisions allowed Canada's Western Innu to survive. It is bizarre to think that these fashionistas on the other side of the globe became reliant upon the fifteen or twenty Inuvialuit trappers who provided them with the raw material to satisfy their demand.

In order to get to Banksland the mainland trappers of the Delta required sailing ships. As families with these boats began to bring in large hauls of white fox a great demand for 'schooners' began. The schooner era was underway. The Toronto Star newspaper reported at the time that "in 1924 the Eskimo fleet at Aklavik consisted of 39 schooners (19 of which had auxiliary power), 28 whale boats and two other vessels."[15] In the MacKenzie Delta region particularly, the first years of the trapping boom were exciting, and most people had a lot of money or credit at the stores. "In 1917 Natkutsiak bought the North Star, a 57-foot schooner, from the Canadian Arctic Expedition. In 1935 two other Inuit bought a new schooner which was delivered from San Francisco at a price of $25,000. This boat was also called North Star, and became the 'flag ship' of the Banks Island fleet. Altogether in 1926 the Delta region trappers had 39 schooners, 28 whaleboats and 2 sloops worth over $128,000 - about one-third of them with engines."[16] "In the 20s and 30s there were whale boats and schooners, most of them propelled by auxiliary motors. Then, each year for at least two months out of the year, from the end of July or the beginning of August til the end of September, in a normal year, schooners were travelling East and West."[17] "As soon as they got the opportunity and the means to buy and acquire some whale boats or schooners of respectable size, thirty to forty feet in length they did so in the 20s and 30s, the golden period of fur trade. It was not for pleasure nor for fun that they bought these schooners, but as a means of transportation to their trapping grounds, where they spent the winter in trapping and hunting. Returning in the summer to the big centers to trade, sell their furs and to buy their outfits for the next winter. As did their ancestors, they proved themselves good travellers and good sailors, and fearless in their battles against the elements, storms and ice, always resourceful and thorough. There again, a will to survive, a technique for survival, helped them to overcome all difficulties they encountered in their journeys."[18]

Persis Gruben recalls in her booklet, LIFE OF THE PIONEERS IN BANKS ISLAND 1928-1929, what it was like for the trapping families in the late 1920's. "The next day, the last sailing day, we left Masik River and followed the coast in search of a good place for wintering the schooners. This was important for us, as the ships would be the only means of transportation come next summer, and the only way to go back to the mainland. The schooners were securely fastened on the shore and we began unloading all the supplies and all our belongings. Right on top of the hill, some one hundred yards up stood a small house. Made apparently from the wheel house of the 'Sachs'. This was evident from the windows and portholes as well as from the doors, all coming from a ship. It had been built some ten to twelve years before, when Steffanson bought the schooner 'Challenger' from Crawford and partners in order to leave Banks Island for the south." Persis continues, "a suitable and safe place for wintering the schooners had to be found immediately. This was an urgent task to be accomplished right away, as the ocean had begun to freeze. So the men during the first days at Cape Kellet spent their time mooring and wintering the schooners in a small cove, probably Baur Harbour, three miles east of the Cape. The schooners were hauled up to the beach above the waterline, engines opened for quick inspection, doors tightly closed, etc.. all things requiring time and attention." "We visited and played in the sod houses built by the expedition of the Inuit trappers, Alaskan trappers, working for Captain Pedersen. A polar bear wandered into camp.." Old Adam followed him, and from the porch door fired and killed him. It didn't take much time to have it skinned and flensed, just a few minutes. Excitement over, we crowded around the carcass and admired his size, his fur etc. What a subject of conversation for we children." "All hunters and families then shared the same cache. We called it the seal house and good it proved to be, the former fuel tank of the Sachs. Of course the blubber and the smell of it was temptation enough for polar bears. Before cleaning them thoroughly and before stretching them in the sun, he spread them out in the snow for a free first cleaning job. Hungry foxes in search of food roamed almost every day around the houses stealing the leftovers. They were delighted to find something ready for them, blubber and small pieces of meat left on the fleshy side of the skins. A very convenient way to clean the skins and a good move on Dad's part. They did a good job and never mangled or tore the skins. Amazing isn't it?"[19]

The traders on the mainland recognized by the 1930's that the schooners making the round trip to Banksland were a good risk for investment. The HBC, Pedersen and private traders began to outfit the schooner crews with traps, rifles, ammunition, clothing and food on credit and at a good price on the understanding that the schooner owners would trade their furs back to them to repay their debts. Some of the schooner owners began to charge trappers up to five hundred dollars for the passage to Banksland or would take the passage back in a like amount of furs or for work on the boats. "Their (the trappers) hopes and expectations were set very high, much was at stake, in order to come here they were deep in debt to Pedersen and all the traders in the mainland. So far polar bears and foxes, if not plentiful were all the same numerous around our camp. This seemed to be good auger for farther inland and on the sea."[20]

Usher records that "there were two peak years of abundance during the first seven years of settlement, and those men who had trapped on the island for both of them made large amounts of money. For example, two of the best trappers (Fred Carpenter and Jim Wolki) obtained in partnership, a 57 foot schooner which they named North Star. She was one of the largest schooners ever brought into the country, and certainly the finest, and was for 26 years the 'flagship' of the Banksland fleet. Another trapper (Fred Wolki) took his family to spend the winter of 1935-36 in San Francisco and Vancouver. That he was able to live an entire year outside without overdrawing his credit is indicative of the wealth that some of the Banksland trappers were accumulating at this time."[21]

Mary and Alexandra Elias remember how bitterly cold it was at Sachs Harbour when they first over-wintered in 1941 after sailing in company with North Star aboard Nanuk. "We were in tents with ice blocks. We had a hard time keeping warm with the little coal we had, mixing it with seal blubber. Sometimes it was pretty cold. When we set the table for a meal, on the floor, we couldn't even see each other across the table..there was so much steam, but we stood it just the same."[22]

1944 is known as "the summer of no return" according to Mary and Alexandria Elias. "That summer on our way back from Tuktoyaktuk, all the schooners were stopped at Booth Island and consequently it was a poor winter for all. Some of us went hunting up the Horton River, "they say.

The summer of '46 was a tough one for sailors and most could not get to Tuk and so did their trading at Holman Island. As Edward Lennie remembers it, 1948-49, was the winter during which Sachs Harbour was crowded with five schooners stranded there. North Star, Reindeer, Umikmak, Fox and Nanuk. People were living in tents banked with ice blocks. The whole fleet was iced in and all of their fur was bundled in huge heaps near the beach. It seemed that all of their hard work and the money that they would receive from it would have to be put on hold for another year. They were also in need of groceries, traps, ammunition and many other things to get them through the following winter. Pooling their money together they decided to charter a plane to come in and drop off their supplies and pick up their fur. This had never been done before and due to the lack of radio contact from Sachs Harbour a group of them had to travel by dog team to Holman Island in order to set it up. This initial plane run was the harbinger of the end of the schooner era. If a plane could fly over the Beaufort Sea in two hours, a trip that could sometimes take weeks and be of great risk to the Bankslanders, then why bother with the expense and maintenance of a ship?

From then on many Bankslanders didn't see any advantages in this yearly costly migration. Navigation was risky, trapping only fair and the price of fur ridiculous, so a few families decided to stay on the mainland.[23]

Continuous occupation was acknowledged by the establishment of an RCMP post in 1953. Peter Esau, an Inuvialuit, was made Special Constable in '58 which was a source of pride and an acknowledgement of his and his peoples' strong morality. An Upper Air Station was built in 1954, and Fred Carpenter opened the first store in 1958. Today the Hamlet of Sachs Harbour is the headquarters of Aulavik National Park, but the meteorological station has been closed down. The anti-trapping movement and the decline of the fur industry have seriously affected this community. At present, limited tourist activity, sports hunts, and sporadic commercial harvests of the burgeoning muskox population provide the only nongovernmental employment.

"During the 1960's and as part of the negotiations with the federal government in respect to funding a school for the children of Sachs Harbour, the government insisted on meetings that required first that the Bankslanders form a Housing Association. This would require them to conform more and more to being controlled and regulated by the Southern Canadians and did not sit well with the Banksland or even the Inuvialuit culture. The Federal Government plan was to "bring the Eskimo into the twentieth century". "Seldom has there been mutual agreement about where things ought to go, and the Bankslanders have usually felt that the planners have not understood their concerns."[24] Nowhere was this more evident than when a city planner with the Department of Indian Affairs in Ottawa drew up a plan for organising and beautifying Sachs Harbour. "The original blueprint showed all existing details faithfully, including two locally owned schooners, (North

Star and Fox), which had been beached for some years. Next to these was the notation 'Eskimo schooners, haul away'. In their desire for orderliness, it apparently had not occurred to the responsible planners that these boats belonged to people who might have had other arrangements in mind."[25] One can only imagine how the poor machine operator sent by Ottawa would have been treated had he attempted to bulldoze the Carpenters' North Star or the Elias' Fox.

The blueprint also showed row after row of neat houses each with a boundary determining the property markings. Inuvialuit have always had a different view of the land and the sea. In this communal society, placing a fence between your neighbor and yourself would be both absurd and insulting."[26] In 1962, the Roman Catholic and Anglican churches began to visit the island.

An ice cellar was started in 1936; a sign that people were recognising that this was a place where they might wish to settle permanently. The cellar has been attributed to Fred Carpenter since he certainly enlarged it in years to come, but may have been a joint project with others wintering over.

Malcolm Macdonald in Canadian North writes, "These Eskimo's wealth varies with the fluctuations in the animal population of the north and in the prices of furs in the south. I was given the following example of a family who trapped on Banks Island and made a small fortune in a single season. An old Eskimo spent a winter there with his three sons. In the following June they arrived in Aklavik with 1,100 white fox skins. That year these skins were fetching forty-five dollars a piece. So the four men divided up almost $50,000 between them."[27]

The self-sufficiency and strong work ethic of Bankslanders is something that has been ingrained in them over the century since their ancestors started making the crossing from the Delta. It was a quality that was noted by National Geographic magazine when they ran a feature about the Hamlet in 1964. (At Sachs Harbour) there are no unemployment lines, and Sachs Harbour does not tolerate a drone. Sachs Harbour has a powerful attraction for those who enjoy living off the land. There is a spirit of independence and individuality here."[28]

Chapter 8

SACHS HARBOUR: DAILY LIFE & the RHYTHM OF SEASONS

When the Inuvialuit began to cross to Banksland they initially split into different areas so that each group would have their own well defined trapping zone. The schooners would arrive at Sachs Harbour and be hauled ashore and then the different groups would travel by dog team up to their own camps. For the first few years the northern trappers would travel by schooner right up to their camps, either at Sea Otter or Horton River but they soon learned that these areas are the last to be rid of the ice in the spring and stood a greater risk of being iced in year round. "The chief criterion has been accessibility by schooner. It was soon realised that to winter a schooner along the west coast, particularly at Sea Otter, was to risk being unable to clear the Island in the event of heavy ice conditions the following summer. It became the custom then to leave their schooners at Sachs and then to sledge their gear to their camp area and then to drag it back in the spring, often taking several trips."[1] It was imperative that the Bankslanders found a safe spot to winter their schooners, for if they were wrecked then they would be stuck on the island. "Jim Wolkie was there and also working. I think that he decided to come to Banksland that summer. Horton River, or the place where Patsy Wien had his house, offered no shelter to schooners, nor boats of any kind. Therefore, after unloading the ship, all the fleet took refuge in the mouth of the river between numerous sand bars. At night there was a terribly high tide and strong wind which looked as though it was going to wash the boats to shore and the shore to sea. No sand bars or land were to be seen and many of the dogs suffered, some from exposure to the cold water, others fighting amongst themselves, some even drowned. Fortunately all the schooners, being well anchored, rode throughout the storms without damage."[2] One year, North Star of Herschel Island, under Fred Carpenter, found herself in a small harbour near Cape Bathurst with another boat. They were frozen in for the winter. During that winter, unable to get home, they trapped fox and marten until break-up in the spring. The harbour is now marked on charts as North Star harbour.

If they could, they would pull North Star out of the harbour in the fall. This was a major test of seamanship and engineering. Using block and tackle and five ton manual winch on the running end, the vessels would be pulled out sideways. The tidal range is only about twelve inches, so is negligible.

Using drift logs, which are always smooth in the Arctic, as a ramp they would attach cables at the bow and stern. The logs would have freshly killed sealskins on them as a lubricant. With a log buried in the sand called the deadman holding the winch, they would commence pulling in the cables, through triple purchase blocks until the vessel began to slide up the ramp. They would walk the vessel up the ramp, pulling first on the bow cable, then on the stern cable, until the vessel literally wiggled into its resting place. If the job was very difficult they would double up the triple purchase blocks for greater mechanical advantage. These blocks are still aboard the ship and are massive enough they can be used as ballast! Boats and ships had to be hauled ashore before freeze-up or they would most likely be crushed by the winter ice or dragged away during break up in the spring, never to be seen again. Smaller boats could be hauled ashore bow first but ships such as the Arctic Fox, Reindeer or North Star were taken ashore and re-launched in this back breaking fashion In the spring, the vessels would be launched by the villagers standing with their backs to the vessel and then pushing against her until she moved down the skids and back into the ocean. This was a happy chore and pictures taken of the event show smiling faces as they encouraged the ships back into the ocean.

North Star was frozen in three or four winters. It may have been because the beach was the wrong configuration or perhaps they waited too long or there wasn't any driftwood to use as a ramp. Carpenter and Wolki also may have not had the proper cables and winches the first two winters. On at least two occasions they made the best of a bad situation and once iced in they turned to trapping wherever the ship was stuck.

In 1952, T.H. Manning and his crew began what was to be an adventure that would last two summers, that of attempting to circumnavigate Banks Island by canoe. He was helped along by many Bankslanders, particularly Fred Carpenter who opened up his house to him and provided him with food, gasoline and even got some of his family and neighbours involved, by helping to sledge by dog-team, the adventurers' gear from post to post. The story that resulted is quite an adventure but also allows us a peak at an outsider's impressions of Sachs Harbour and Fred Carpenter in the early fifties. Manning picks up the story.

The men of Sachs Harbour launching Reindeer by putting their backs to her. Fred Carpenter on far left. Photo credit Dr Hohn.

"We arrived at Sachs Harbour on June 21, and were hospitably received by Fred Carpenter and the other Banks Islanders. Next afternoon two of them took us across the harbour and a few miles along the coast by dog team. The ice was intersected by water-filled cracks and pools, and after a few miles it became too broken for safe sledging with the Alaskan hitch which the Banks Islanders use." (The Alaskan hitch is a method of harnessing sled dogs - running them in pairs in a straight line, the other most common method being the fan hitch.) "We were ferried to land over the 150-foot shore lead in a small canoe brought for the purpose. Later we learned that both men, with the dogs and sledges, had got into the water during the return trip, and that one of the dogs had been drowned. They gave us a meal and talked to us for a long time in Fred Carpenter's house, where we afterwards slept.

Jim Wolki and son.

Towards the end of the navigation season these people come up to Banks Island in boats of various sizes and degrees of seaworthiness, the largest being Carpenter's North Star. They spend the winter trapping foxes, and leave for Tuktoyaktuk as soon as the ice is gone. There were only four families there at the time of our visit, and as the island has a large fox population they were very well off in spite of the low price of fox-skins. The following afternoon two of the men gave us a lift on their sledges along the rotten coast ice on our way back to De Salis Bay, but large patches of open water forced them to stop after about six miles.

At the present time there are no Eskimo living permanently on Banks Island, but most years a party of about 20 mainland Eskimo from Tuktoyaktuk cross to Banks Island in September and remain until there is sufficient open water, usually in late July, for them to return with their catch of arctic foxes. There is obviously considerable white blood in many of these Eskimo-indeed, some are more than half white. Most of them can speak English, and can read and write. At Sachs Harbour Fred Carpenter, the leader of the group on Banks Island, has a comfortable frame house heated with diesel oil which he brings with his other supplies from Tuktoyaktuk in a 55-foot schooner, the North Star. The centre for this group while they are on Banks Island is now usually Sachs Harbour, although a few families may have winter camps farther north on the west coast, and in some years, also at De Salis Bay or farther up the east coast. However, none of those on Banks Island in 1952 had ever visited the north coast."[3]

Fourteen years later, in 1966, Jack Grainge was at Sachs Harbour. He described the people there as "proud to be working and self-reliant. David Nasogaluak, a successful hunter, told me about a welfare officer who had arrived the previous year. He called a meeting and told the people what he could do for them. However, they did not want welfare. They told him to leave. They considered assistance for old or sick people justifiable but not for healthy people. They were proud of their abilities to hunt and trap game, particularly the white and blue foxes that abounded on Banks Island, their island."[4] This Bankslander pride was a characteristic that defined these Inuvialuit and even though they were offered social assistance time and again they always turned it down. If a person could work, they did. Those that couldn't would be helped by the others and quite often when their working days were over they would retire to the Delta and an easier way of living. Usher provides perhaps the strongest comment on the people of Sachs Harbour. "A true pioneer people, they have maintained a way of life they value strongly, and have created a community they feel most suitable for raising their children. Although they visit the mainland frequently, and have relatives there, they disdain to live in what they perceive to be a society without economic opportunity, without adequate supplies of country food, no longer in control of its own destiny, and characterized by drunkenness, delinquency, brutality, poverty and aimlessness."[5]

North Star may have been owned by Carpenter and Wolki but as Inuit culture is seen as more communal, everyone who knew the men felt some ownership and pride towards her. This is understandable since she and the other schooners were their prime mode of transportation during the summer months as well as a way to transfer their own furs to market or to receive trade goods that they could order through the two owners. All of their quality of life would improve with keeping North Star seaworthy. There was no grumbling if help was needed to man the ship or haul her out or launch her. Since everyone benefited from her, everyone helped with her. Indeed, one of Carpenter and Wolki's motives in building such a large ship was that it would benefit the community at large.

When the Inuvialuit made winter camps they used driftwood and covered these with sod and then piled ice all over the structure for insulation. Even up until the 1950's they would cut windows into their homes and then cover these with the stretched and dried intestines of the bearded seal. Bertram Pokiak of Tuktuujaqtuup, writing in 1976 about the old days as related to him by his grandparents, mentions their traditional windows 'Where driftwood was available, sod houses were made. The sides were covered with mud and more logs were piled on top of the mud. The roof was then covered with sod. Each house had one window and it was made with the intestines of whales or bearded seals. They also used these intestines to make parka covers to use as raincoats.'[6] Paul Amos, who was born in 1912 and made many crossings with North Star recalls, "Well, we never had white man windows. Just the intestine from walrus and also bear's intestine and also the moose's intestine."[7] When Carpenter built his solid wood frame house he brought in glass for his windows. In fact, in order to conserve energy he used triple paned glass. When the government was setting up its own buildings they requisitioned triple paned glass but this was turned down. In many ways the Carpenter house was the most advanced on the island in terms of building strength, energy conservation and comfort. "Carpenter's triple pane windows surprised us. He said the extra pane made the house warmer. For many years the engineers in our office had been advocating triple pane windows for northern houses."[8] In May 1964, National Geographic magazine described Carpenter's home."Fred's frame house, set on oil drums embedded in the permafrost, is lined in the flooring and roof - as well as in the walls - with Fiberglas insulation. His first house was a tent, walled outside by ice blocks. Today ice bricks are seldom used, except as windbreaks around a door of a home."[9]

The homes in Sachs Harbour were heated by burning diesel but initially it was done by burning coal. There was a seam that they would mine on Banks Island with North Star on their way back from the Delta to load up with coal for the winter. "(On Banks Island) there are peat bogs and many open seams of coal. Fred Carpenter, who like the other Eskimos at Sachs Harbour, now uses fuel oil for heating, burned coal all one winter. When I asked him how it was he answered 'All right, I guess.' Then laughingly: 'But it worked best when I added seal blubber."[10] Fresh water was obtained by harvesting blocks of ice and then melting them as needed.

The old joke about a true salesman being one who could sell a freezer to an Eskimo would have fallen with a thud at Sachs Harbour. The Inuvialuit live on top of permafrost, a permanent layer of frozen ground. In 1936 an ice house was started at Sachs Harbour and when Fred Carpenter built his wood frame house he continued to expand the ice house. The name 'icehouse' is a bit of a misnomer as it is actually a vertical tunnel that burrows down below the permafrost and then branches out into horizontal tunnels, with each tunnel being used for different type of game such as seal, fish, caribou and bear. Additional tunnels are created for different families. Diane Carpenter describes their ice-house. "It was okay because its permafrost after about a foot down. One big hole and then you put geese on one area and caribou in another, musk-ox in an area, fish in an area. It was usually just for my Dad and his sons and then they had another two or three in Sachs. Everybody would share and just keep it clean.

Inuit hunter waiting by an aglu for a seal.

The Federal government continued to view Sachs Harbour as a seasonal camp rather than an established center but also recognised that the Bankslanders were doing well financially and were not only in little need of governmental assistance, but under Fred Carpenter's leadership did not want it. The idea of a permanent home was a new concept for the Inuvialuit who had always been a transient society, following the game that they needed and living off of the land. While Carpenter built a wooden home and his neighbours pondered the idea while living in sod houses, the majority of time was still spent in snow houses or double walled tents out on the trapline. Many of the Carpenter children have spoken about the harsh lifestyle when they were growing up. Agnes Carpenter, Fred's third wife, was once asked by a CBC reporter what part of living on Banksland was the most difficult to adjust to after having grown up in the comparably warm town of Aklavik. "The cold", she replied. "Yes, I would have to say getting used to the cold". I say uncharacteristically because the cold is an uncommon topic of conversation for the Inuvialuit. The prolific author Fred Breuhmer explains that "to survive successfully in the Arctic for millennia, the Inuit and their forebears evolved a culture perfectly adapted to cold. While we talk endlessly of weather (without their weather talk the British would be nearly muted), the Inuit with whom I lived for thirty years rarely did. So it was cold. Of course it was cold! What do you expect in the Arctic?"[12] Agnes Carpenter continues, "Fred had nine or more dogs at a time, nine dogs on his team. I had my own team. During the winter, we would stay out on the trail for one month at a time. We would sleep in double-walled tents and cook on a Swedish primus stove. We would have to order them, make a special order for them to come all the way from Sweden. We were always ordering them."

Susie and Roy Wolki on the trap line, Banks Island, 1930.

Susie Wolki travelling by dog team, Banks Island, 1935.

One result of being married three times was that Fred Carpenter sired seventeen children and there were always some of his offspring about. Many times one brood would be at Residential School in Aklavik while the older ones were at Sachs or off at college or university and the younger ones still at home. One time Joey Carpenter came home and was out on the land with his father. Joey had been getting into some trouble with following direction at school. They went by dogsled to the northern end of Banksland. Suddenly, Fred stopped and told Joey to head for land. His sister, Mary explains the life changing father/son moment that Joey then had." Usually Joey would do just the opposite but in this case, he listened and complied. Fred Carpenter waited until Joey was safely on land and he slowly, very slowly, took his dogsled and parked beside Joey. All of a sudden, a noise that would deafen Ottawans, pierced the air, the entire sea ice churned up and sunk. To this day, Joey tells this story with awe."

Fred loved his children and grandchildren. He was interested in how they perceived life at Banksland but would probably have been surprised as the leader of the community to learn that despite the Carpenter name status that his family were often treated with racism for not being full breed. Andy Carpenter says: "My Dad had a white father. It was a bit different growing up. We used to be called names and get beat up. But my Dad and Granddad taught us to try our best in everything we do. We lived a traditional life. I can speak Inuvialuktun. We wintered in Sachs Harbour to trap, and travelled in the summer by our schooner, the North Star, to pick up supplies in Aklavik.'"[13]

Diane Carpenter explains some of the family dynamics. "My Mom was younger than some of Dad's other children, but they were usually away in residential school. Mom and Dad were together but we mostly saw his older children. He had three older children. Once in awhile the second group of children would come up for a holiday and they stayed at my parent's place. It worked out okay. She had nine children, but one of them passed away. I still remember him. He was born a year before Linda and Linda was third youngest. They have a little grave in Sachs and it's real nice looking. A baby's grave, real cute. I still remember when he was born, '64 or something. When he was born he was put in a bread pan to keep him warm because he was quite small. They put him in the bread pan and they put him in the oven - a fuel stove oven to keep him warm. Still he was too young or too small 'til he passed away, but they put him in a nice grave." Dr Joseph Cramer of the government hospital in Inuvik said that it "is not uncommon for a mother to lose half her babies in infancy (due to diseases brought in by white people that the Eskimo have yet to be unsusceptible to). Death seems more taken for granted, however, more easily accepted than in western civilization."[14] In 1964, National Geographic magazine explained a difficult part of being an Inuvialuit at the time. "Children are precious to Eskimos; and they seem especially precious at Sachs Harbour. One reason is that when the child is six, he or she leaves home and goes to school at Inuvik. It is a public school; the children stay in hostels, one Catholic, the other Anglican. From the age of six, the child is home only in the summer. And as Florence Carpenter, wife of Frank, said: "A home is empty without a baby."[15]

Agnes Carpenter recalls how she instilled a love of reading into her children by ordering books up from the library. She filled their home with books on every subject. "I wanted them to know that there was a big world out there and that there was more to see than living on this island up in the Arctic."

The community of Sachs Harbour really began to come together in the 1950's when outlying villages moved into the area. The Department of Transport's arrival as well as the RCMP station rounded out the Hamlet. There was still no mistaking that they were living out in the wilderness all winter with lots of wildlife in the area. Fox could be seen darting in and around the homes and polar bears were a common sight. "There is nothing between us and the wilderness - so many animals close by. Every year polar bears come to our beach, sometimes right into the settlement, even though there are big lights on the road. You watch every time the dogs start barking. And you watch where your kids go to play; you don't leave the little ones out of sight. A hungry bear will attack anything alive. I watched a bear right outside the house trying to get at the pups in the corral. Another bear chased Peter Esau. Peter couldn't make it to his house and jumped on his skidoo. First the bear went after the skidoo, then it killed Peter's dog - ripped the stomach right open. Quite a few dogs have been killed in the past. It's pure luck we haven't lost any kids so far," remembers Agnes Carpenter."[16]

Life at Sachs Harbour changed quite a bit from when the DOT and the RCMP became entrenched in the Hamlet. Not only was there improved radio communication and regular flights, time was also made for community dances, movie nights and the big Christmas party to look forward to. Diane Carpenter remembers the freedom of walking around Sachs Harbour and going to visit neighbours. "I remember once we went to visit Mable Steffanson - that's Shirley Esau's mother-in-law - we went to Shirley and Peter Esau's place and I still remember Mable was showing us bloomers - it was kind of shocking but you never show too much emotion or people will get upset." Diane and her friends sat and tried to keep a straight face as Steffanson showed the young girls what women used to wear, quite a shock to them!

As the furs came in and were cleaned they would be hung on clothes line to bleach in the sun. "We used to always call those 'thousand dollar lines", remembers Diane.

In the early fifties construction began on the Dew Line site and many of the Bankslanders took jobs helping to construct it and stopped trapping as much. DEW line construction ended in 1957, and this reduced the number of jobs locally available to Eskimos. With the DOT and Weather Station firmly entrenched on Banks Island, their need for supplies brought in regular flights and ships. The Department of Transport also had a weather station for monitoring weather as well as forecasting. One method of doing this was to send a large weather balloon up with thermometers and other equipment. When these were later found deflated out on the land the Inuit hunters would bring them home. The women would then cut them up and use them for diapers and sheets for the babies. Fred Carpenter told Sven Johansson that in 1960 or 61 the government started sending in a supply ship every year to support the Upper Air Weather Station. The people got their supplies then, too. There was also an airlift every two months, then every two weeks, so the need for a trading schooner vanished. North Star and the other Arctic Schooners had gone from being essential to the Bankslanders to unnecessary.

Chapter 9

The RCMP Arrive on Banks Island

In 1953 North Star was in Tuktoyaktuk and Fred Carpenter was busy trading fur and purchasing their winter supplies. Fred and Lucy Carpenter's son, Andy Carpenter, struck up a conversation with an RCMP member named McDougal and found out that he was to be stationed at Sachs Harbour in a brand new detachment for the force. Arrangements had already been made for the RCMP officer's transportation aboard the Hudson's Bay Company ship, Fort Hearne, and so the two men parted.

"The H.B.C. Fort Hearne was making her first trip to Banks Island so the captain was rather nervous as he could see ice moving around the schooner," remembers Andy. The shallow water at Sachs Harbour was already choppy, making for a dangerous approach. "Coming along the sandspit outside the harbour the crew couldn't see anyone at the village; not knowing the entrance of the harbour the Captain kept on going as far as Cape Kellett and there of all places, building materials, outfits and gear were unloaded in a few hours...and goodbye to Constable D. McDougal."

Staying in his tent the Mountie didn't really know what to do next, until a schooner showed up, coming from the hunting grounds of the northern coast. It was North Star and McDougal was a happy man when he saw the Bankslanders coming ashore and ready to give him a hand. All things were brought to Sachs Harbour and a small cabin was built for the first winter 1953-54." If Fred Carpenter had decided to stay in the Delta or had left late and been iced in then "he would have been all alone on the island for a year! He was pretty happy to see us,"[1] remembered Andy Carpenter. Andy's sister, Diane, remembers the event. "One crazy thing - when the RCMP first came to Sachs - they put themselves on the other side of the bay from Sachs. So my Dad went over with his dogteam or his boat or something and he picked them up. He said, 'I don't think you can do anything from way over there. I think you should come over here and he made sure the RCMP was right across from my parent's place."

When the police first arrived at Herschel Island in 1903 their title was Northwest Mounted Police. This changed in 1904 to the Northwest Mounted Police, a title that lasted until 1919 at which point they took on the name that is still used today, Royal Canadian Mounted Police.

Since their arrival, the Mounties provided medical care to the people and helped them in many ways outside the line of duty. Amongst the Mounties stationed at Sachs we gathered a few names as they are remembered by the people: Bob Hunter, Phil Bibeau, Brian Dunn, George Wool, Stan Seltenrich, Bill Pringle, John Kaminski, Bob Knight, Paul Pertson, Bill Yakenishin, D. McDougal, and special Constable Peter Esau.

The Carpenters and the rest of the Bankslanders were happy to have the RCMP in their community since it took some of the work off of their own shoulders, particularly in paper work and in dealing with the government. The RCMP was helpful in explaining the Inuvialuit their rights as Canadian citizens. Crime had traditionally been handled by the leaders of the community themselves and one Bankslander recalled that when the RCMP arrived 'there was not much for them to do as we had no concept of breaking and entering as we were all related to each other and there was no real concept of private property.' "Even though there's no trouble, there's a sense of security knowing that the law's here and no one's going to mess with you," says Joey Carpenter, one of Andy's younger brothers.

In 1955 the DOT established a Meteorological Station at Sachs Harbour and the RCMP expanded their facilities and hired an Eskimo special constable, Peter Esau, from the Delta. Years later Fred and Lucy Carpenter's first son, Frank, joined the RCMP and was based in Aklavik. Frank was a well respected trapper but his sense of duty to the community - something that he no doubt inherited from his father, coupled with the unreliable prices for furs, helped make his decision. Diane Carpenter recalls that "when he died and the service was in Inuvik, the whole gym was filled. Imagine! It was neat. They had all RCMP's come from Yellowknife, all in their red serge and when we went to walk up into the gym; they were all saluting to us. They asked my Dad to be an RCMP, but he said, 'No, I have to be a leader.' He didn't want to offend anyone, but his son did become an RCMP."

Cal Alexander was based at Sachs Harbour and has many fond memories of helping Fred with his mainland orders. "I helped them order from the Eaton's catalogue. It came in on the HBC ship, the Fort Hope. Everyone else on the island was living in double wall tents with moss. Alexander had arrived right at the cusp of change when Carpenter had made the decision to spend the rest of his life at Sachs and so built a sturdy wood frame house while his friends and neighbours were still living in tents, deciding whether to stay or go.

In 1992 the detachment was shut down over budgetary concerns. It was re-opened in 2010, partially to help with the policing of the community but primarily "due to a need to guard Canada's Northern frontier as climate change heats up the International political landscape." For Andy Carpenter the reason that the RCMP returned was "to educate young people, facilitate community development and monitor a piece of Canada's border." The Mounties are stationed at the edge of the world as a symbol of Canada's claim to the North.'"[2]

One of Fred's many home movies show how the RCMP became part of the community very quickly. "The films also show RCMP officers wearing their yellow-striped pants and, often, plaid shirts. The Mounties are seen helping pull fishing boats ashore, or racing children for fun. "Every Canada Day was special," Joey Carpenter says. "They'd put on their red uniform and put up the Union Jack, sing, God Save the Queen."[3]

Chapter 10

Trapping methods, Fur Preparation & Banksland Food

"It is hunting that has moulded his physique and his character. Hunting is the center of his existence, and even his rudimentary religion is designed to help him achieve success in the chase. He is a hunter, the Inuk, first, last and all of the time, and anyone who wants to understand him must study him always as the hunter, the one who kills, in order to live."[1] There is no question that the Inuvialuit of the Western Arctic are hunters and trappers. They have been at it for centuries. It is in their blood. Prior to the arrival of foreigners they were hunting to survive, using whatever they could to bring down their prey from bows and arrows and spears to sharpened rocks and ingenious traps. When the economy changed to trapping for fur to be traded for material goods and food, they still needed to continue hunting in order to eat and to feed their dog teams. Until quite recently they continued to use the pelts for clothing and some continue to use parts of them for that, though the primary focus since North Star's time has been on hunting for food and trapping for fur for trading.

Fred's third wife, Agnes, spent many years on the trail, trapping and hunting. "We, Fred and I, would be out on the trap line for about a month at a time. This was before I had my children. After the children he would be gone two weeks, three weeks. The time goes because you are working every day. It was just me and the children. I found it very isolating. No mail. There was a weather station at the D.O.T., but that was about three miles away. I must say, it's a hard life. A hard, cold life and the biggest problem is getting used to the weather, the cold. We used to be on the trail from morning until night. It got really cold. Then we would pitch up a double tent and Fred would cook up the dogpot inside the tent and we would have to wait for it to be done to get warm, because all of the heat was going into the ten gallon pot and not into the tent. By the time you get the dogs fed and everything, it would be 11,

12 at night and then you'd get up at 6 or 7 - at the break of dawn just to start the routine all over again. Yes, I would say it was a hard, hard life."

Mrs Agnes Carpenter.

The author and Mrs Agnes Carpenter, 2010.

Charlie Gruben once recalled that "I stayed there ten years on Banksland. The less (least amount of) fox I got was 340. 1955 was the last time I was to Banks Island 'cause my wife worked too hard skinning foxes. Two years I got over 1500 hundred foxes and I sold them 34 dollars each straight through. And 12 bears on top of that. My wife got two and I got ten."[2]

Fred's grandson, Jason Goodliffe, was assigned to write a school report about famous Canadians. He chose his grandfather. He wrote that, "He used to stay on the trapline sometimes for a month without coming home. When he came back to the community it would be only for a short time, to rest and get more supplies. Traplines were usually situated about sixty miles out of the community. All winter he would trap, and when he came back into the community he would help my grandmother, Agnes Carpenter, in the store."[3] Some of the greatest changes in the early trapping pattern described previously came in the 1940s. During the years 1945-48, several trappers were running lines of 100 to 200 miles in length, with 600 or even 800 traps, and making trips of 10 to 14 days or more, much as is done today. A few of the best trappers were spending up to 75% of their time on the trail, making trips of 17 or 18 days."[4]

Geddes Wolki was a great friend of his uncle, Fred Carpenter. He liked to refer to him as Captain Carpenter since he made so many voyages on North Star and often it was Geddes who was the one at the helm. He was born in 1933 and after graduating from residential school in Aklavik he moved back to Sachs Harbour and lived with Fred and Agnes for over a year. "I trap lots, me. Over 5,000 in one year. I was 'High Man', he recalled in telephone interviews from Sachs in 2012. He continues, "I use dog team. Sometimes I stay out to set traps a month or more. I start to go home earlier when they're set. Then stay two weeks out and back home. My dad was Big Jim Wolki. He was one of the best trappers at Banks Island. He taught me. My Dadak, Fritz Wolki, he's got an Eskimo wife, Eewona, I hear she's good at sewing, a good sewer. Banks Island - that's the place that's got the most polar bears in Arctic. I don't hunt now but the boys here, when they get a bear, they give me fresh meat, even caribou. Good people, those Sachs Harbour people."

It was not just the fur-bearing animals that the trappers were after, for in order to survive they also had to hunt meat for themselves and for their dogs. When the ships arrived back on Banksland in the late fall the first order of business was to head out onto the newly formed ice and get seals, primarily for dog food but also for themselves. The men would head out onto the ice in the small rowboats or dinghies that each schooner carried or sometimes in canoes or skin covered boats. The goal for each hunter was to harvest at least twenty or thirty seals which would see them through until February. Agnes adds, "We would hunt seals with rifles to eat and also for dog food." Each seal makes several air holes or 'aglus' in the ice. The hunter will stand or lay beside an aglu with a large hook and then quickly try and snare the animal when it comes up to breathe. Fred Carpenter once related that he knew of several hunters who had foolishly tied the end of the seal-hook around their wrist or waist and then been dragged under by the hooked seal and drowned. "To hold a hooked seal, I have had to lie flat on the ice, my arms in the hole up to my armpits, as the seal goes round and round, Fred said."You hang on for dear life."[6]

"Corn meal is an important component of the dogs' diet at Sachs Harbour. It is customary to feed dogs a mixture of corn meal and seal which is mixed and cooked every night. About one hundred pounds of corn meal per dog per year is used and, as there are about 185 adult dogs in the settlement, it is estimated that about 18,500 lbs of cornmeal are imported annually. Corn meal is considered a desirable dog food because it is light and compact and therefore allows greater travelling mobility and can also be kept on the trap line from one year to the next without spoilage. Many Eskimos also feel that the dogs do not work as well on a diet of seal alone, and that a warm meal is desirable."[7] The seal hunt is the most common type of hunt, for the dogs are especially fond of seal meat and it is their main diet. "Once, however, not many years back, the Eskimos of Sachs Harbour lost 20 dogs. They were hunting seals in canoes, their four dog teams being in harness with their sleds anchored on ice. Suddenly the ice broke and the 20 dogs drifted out to sea before a strong offshore breeze. There was no way to save them. All the dogs were lost - all but one. A month later he raced into Sachs Harbour. But how he reached it no one knows."[8]

By late September or October the caribou herds would arrive and hunting parties went out to try and fill the icehouses with this, their primary source of protein as well as a source of clothing. Caribou hunting was a favourite activity for the Bankslanders. Fred Carpenter remembers, "Caribou, you shoot only when you need 'em but maybe two hundred and fifty or four hundred go by. Don't shoot that one - there's lots more behind. Lots more. You only shoot what you need. Don't shoot what you don't need. Then, in the future life, people have lots of game. No good for families in the future but if you listen to me, life in the future - life after we, still lots of game here. Sure enough, got lots yet - but too many musk-ox! Too many. You help me! Somebody kills more musk-ox, the more I like it."

As they were out on the land for so long the trappers would build snow-houses or igloos along the way. These could be re-used throughout the winter and provided markers to watch for. At the end of the trail some would build a wooden shed or hut where they might be out of the elements a little bit before turning around and following the trapline home. "Most trappers set out with six or seven dogs, a toboggan or basket sled and about 100 traps, although a few had 200 or 300. {..} Most of the line was set on the first trip and then extended with each additional trip. They would trap for about a week at a time and make about ten trips in a typical season.[9] Snow houses or igloos were much more common in the Eastern Canadian Arctic but on Banks Island the Inuvialuit also used them. A good snow house could last a season and was re-used all winter long until the spring thaw.

Cutting the door to the snowhouse by exiting it.

Some say that compared to a double-walled tent or a cabin the snowhouses were not as comfortable. "The snowhouses they did build were crude and uncomfortable. They had no sleeping platforms, even though it was recognised that the floor was the coldest part of the structure. The Bankslanders always used primus stoves inside their snow houses for heat and cooking, although when weather permitted they cooked their dog pots outdoors in order not to heat up the house too much. Still, there is little wonder that the interior soon became rather damp, and that after one or two nights the interior walls were completely iced over and impervious to air. Some trappers put up canvas next to the ceiling of the snow house to reduce the dripping."[10]

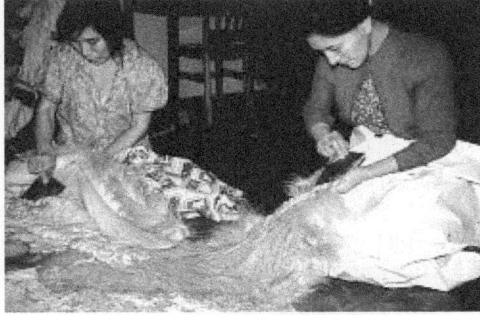

Flensing a polar bear skin.

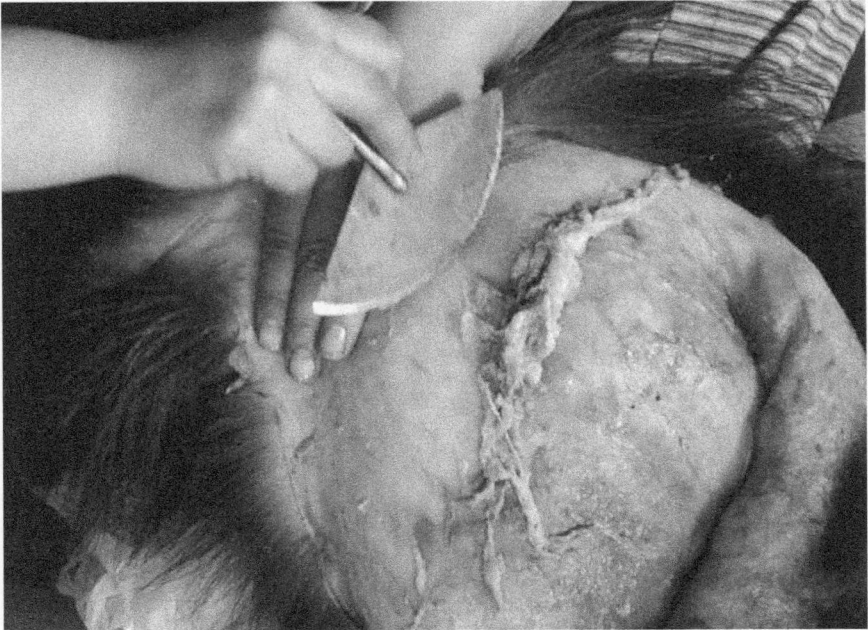

Close-up of flensing a bear with an ulu. Photo credit Trait d'Union.

Growing up on Banksland offered the children a different outlook on life and death. Watching their parents shoot and skin animals, helping in the flensing or fleshing of the skins and eating the meat and wearing the fur from them, gave the children a different perspective on killing or where their food comes from than perhaps a child growing up in the city might have. "I was old enough. I killed a polar bear with an axe. I think I chased it about an hour; it was a little bear, never grow. Mom and I went hauling wood. Here comes a polar bear towards us! When it stood up I picked up an axe from my sled. I chased it 'til I was pretty tired. I wanted it for a pet. Once in awhile he'd try and claw my hair. I asked my Mom to give me a rope. I want to put the bear on lace, so I can take out the bear in my sled, so I could have it for a pet. My mother kept repeating, 'Kill it! If you have a pet, you'll end up dying.' I hit the bear on the hind and it made a loud noise like bang. With the back of the axe I kept doing the same thing. Finally it stood up and I went right to the bear. I try hitting the bear on the head and I missed it. It almost bite me! The breathing of the bear was so close. He was just foaming all over his mouth. It was warm. As I got close to the house I killed it. I sat on top of the bear breathing hard myself. 'Haaah! Haaah! Haaah! Then I crushed its head." (laughter)[11]

Dead foxes that had been put in the ice house would be brought into the family living room to be thawed and then skinned as would seals, bears or any other game that had been killed. A not uncommon sight was to see the bloody skin of an animal being scraped of its fat with ulus by the women of the house while the father sat and watched and the children played around, maybe even sneaking a piece of rich fat from the skin. Mrs Anna E. Rokeby Thomas lived with an Inuit fox-trapping family one winter. She recalls that as the fox corpses came in to thaw out, that they would be hanging from the rafters. "They were hanging inside-out, in groups of six, from the ceiling of Milne's house. ..Their white, fluffy tails were the only beautiful thing about them , at that stage, for the limp, grey, nakedness above the tails was repulsive to look at. Even the tails became objectionable for they hung low enough to tickle our faces as we walked about. There was a heavy sweet odour from them. ..Sometimes I watched the women prepare them. They were their happiest when wielding an ulu and scraping every last bit of flesh and fat from the raw skin. I quite imagine they were dreaming of all the things the pelt could be exchanged for in the trade store. At regular intervals, a handful of the fat scraping reached their mouths and they ate it with apparent enjoyment. It was an understood fact that fox meat was unpalatable and they didn't eat it unless almost starving. But fat was always irresistible...even from a fox!"[12] The curious fox - curiosity killed the fox.

"There are several kinds of foxes in the Eskimo lands, but they belong to two species only: the red or common, and the Arctic fox, which between them show five or six colour phases. There is the Arctic or white fox, the most common, worth only two and a half francs. There is the silver fox, black with white tipped fur. Another variety is the cross fox, black with a white streak down the back. The blue fox is given the same name as the white one by the Eskimos. It is valued even less then the white. To my eyes this animal is lead grey with metallic glints. As to the superb black fox, the rarest of all, with fur as black as crow feathers, the Eskimos get 15 francs for it and the Company used to sell it for as much as 1,000 francs to the mandarins of the celestial empire."[14]

"While the men were away, the women skinned, stretched and dried the pelts."[15]

One of the reasons that the Banksland furs always fetched a good price had to do with how the pelts were prepared. Taken almost exclusively by traps meant that there were no gun shot holes in them. Then they would be cleaned of all of their bones and innards which were often stacked outside and often became part of a dog pot. The process of cutting out the fur is called casing. Once the fur is off it is put onto a stretching frame inside out until it dries, a process that takes two or three days. Each fur was then rubbed with cornmeal which scoured the fur clean. It got rid of the yellow stains that were primarily from the fox having dribbled some fat from an animal that it had eaten. The cornmeal was one way, other times white flour was used instead. After the furs were made as clean as could be the women would sew up any small tears in the pelt. Then all of the pelts would be strung on to a clothesline to bleach in the sun.

A child walks past a thousand dollar clothes line, Sachs Harbour, 1940s.

To clean the fat off of the furs the women would use their ulus, a crescent shaped knife that is perfect for this purpose. The ulu on Banks Island was once made of slate, it is now made from a section of a crosscut saw, ground to a sharp edge. A piece of copper is riveted onto the crescent-shaped blade, and a bone handle is affixed to the copper. The ulu can also be used in eating. Meat placed in the mouth is cut off with one downward stroke. "It's a safer stroke than the ones the Indians use", Angus Sherwood said. "Indians use an upward stroke and an Indian friend of mine once lost a piece of his nose as a result of a careless movement."

An ulu.

Only one side of the ulu is honed. The sharp edge is drawn over a knife blade to remove any bead that would furrow a hide. Some Eskimo women want their favourite ulu to be buried with them. An Eskimo woman with a sharp ulu may be able to flesh 16 fox pelts a day. But it is close, delicate work, one false move reducing the grade of the fur. Once a fox fur is fleshed, it is put on a stretcher and placed on overhead stringers in the kitchen to dry. When dry, it is hung like laundry on a clothesline and allowed to air outside for several days.[16] "Have you seen, if only in a picture, Neapolitans eating macaroni? It will give you an idea of the elegant way in which the Eskimos eat their blubber. Cut into long strips, they dangle it above the mouth which holds one end of the strip. Then with smacking lips, they bite on a portion and cut it so close to the mouth they seem in imminent danger of cutting their lips or nose. When I watched them I was always afraid a bit of nose might be sliced off."[17]

One of the biggest jobs assigned to the Inuvialuit women was 'fleshing' or 'flensing' polar bear skins. These huge skins that have a thick layer of fat would take two women about three hours to complete. Once flensed, the skins would be taken out and draped over North Star's or the other schooners" rigging to be aired out and dry. Later, the fur would be scrubbed with corn meal to get out any stains. One reason that the Bankslanders' catch of fur was always in high demand was due to the amount of work that the women did in preparing them.

Polar Bear and fox pelts drying in North Star's rigging.

The Inuvialuit of Banks Island would typically bring the frozen bodies of the trapped animals, primarily white fox, back to their homes at Sachs Harbour where they would be put in the ice house until time permitted the thawing and skinning of them in the warmth of the tent or home. Bern Will Brown recounts the story of Budgie - a man that he describes as 'one tough cookie' -a trapper whom he met who could not afford the extra weight of the fox bodies while he was out on the trap line and so came up with an unorthodox method of dealing with the frozen foxes. "The toughest part of trapping out on the Barrens, according to Budgie, was thawing the white fox he caught in traps. During the day he would be picking them up frozen stiff and carrying them in his dogsled till evening when he slept. As wood was scarce and the tent was heated for a very short time, the foxes wouldn't have time to thaw out. Once skinned, their fur would be as light as feathers, but carrying them, carcass and all, would add too much weight to his sled. There was only one solution: to take the frozen foxes into his sleeping bag with him at night and let the heat of his body thaw them so that they could be skinned in the morning. I could just imagine the difficulty of keeping oneself warm out on the Barrens in an unheated tent at forty below, without being surrounded with frozen fox carcasses."[19]

"Spring bear hunting trips are usually made in early May and last up to a fortnight. In both 1965 and 1966 each hunter travelled an average distance of about 190 miles, obtaining 0.7 bears the first year and none the second. ...There is always a chance of big winnings, since individuals have been known to return with five or more skins from a hunt."[20] "Cornered or wounded, an angry, charging bear makes a large but poor target for the rifleman. He twists like a tornado, and has a trick of sliding toward the attack on his chest, so that there is nothing to shoot at but his skull, and often the bullet will glance off. He does rear up when he closes in, though, for he kills, not with his teeth, but with his powerful paws. You have a split-second here, and it was at this instant that the old-time Eskimo hunter, not having a rifle, plunged his harpoon between the bear's shoulder blades, or, pressing his body close against the beast, thrust to the heart with his knife."[21] The polar bear is considered by many to be the most dangerous animal in the world. In Land of the Long Day, the author describes the great mammal. "Even in death the bear was a magnificent animal. Although small for a polar bear, he was some six feet from nose to tail. The long white fur was stained yellow in spots, smeared with the fat of the seals he had killed and eaten. The mighty jaws with twin rows of interlocking teeth could crush through bone as if it were paper. The paws were nine inches across the pad, five toes each tipped with an inch-long claw. Those teeth and claws had played havoc with our dogs, a number of whom now sat licking wounds, their blood mingling with that of their late foe. None had been killed, fortunately, although in a bear hunt, this is not an uncommon thing."[22] "The Inuit consider polar bears as sea mammals, a sensible notion considering that they eat mainly seals and are rarely found far from the sea coast. The most carnivorous of bears, and the largest of all terrestrial carnivores, the polar bear is a formidable creature. Adult males average about 450 kilos, up to a maximum of 700 kilos, and can reach lengths of almost four metres. They can run faster than a man and are excellent swimmers. Polar bears have been sighted swimming in open water 40 kilometres from the nearest land."[23] Not only were the animals used for food and clothing but also for design elements in some of the clothes. "On the top of my hood rim there is a little piece of white fur, which my grandmother insisted be there. We call it yurturuaq. It comes from the word yuq. When you make Jello it becomes jelled after awhile - that's the state of yurturuaq, or yuq. My grandmother described my parka hood as the bear's den, where the bear comes in and out. When the bear comes out of hibernation in the spring, it sits on top of its den for awhile and slowly 'jells'. It is an old notion from what we observe when bears come out of hibernation. So this is part of our design element that is indicated on this particular garment."[24]

Tracking a polar bear requires skill and patience and the best hunters have learned from their forefathers the most successful way of doing this. "Inventiveness and ingenuity, as well as the learned skills, the infinite patience of the true hunter, and their knowledge of animal behaviour helped them to survive."[25] Polar bears are often trapped, the chain being allowed to freeze deep in the ice so that the bear cannot drag the trap. A variation is to bury a gun in the ice, with the muzzle at the edge of a hole baited with seal blubber. The bear puts his head into the hole and pulls out the seal blubber, causing the gun to fire. "The Eskimos in the past sometimes used whalebone to kill a bear. The bone was bent into the shape of a U, tied with sinews, and then baited with seal blubber. In time, the sinew dissolved in the bear's stomach, the whalebone straightened, and the bear died an agonizing death."[26]

North Star hauled on the ice while the Carpenter's ready themselves for the trapline.

By July, the polar bears are hunting seals amid the broken ice, and the Eskimos can pursue them in their canoes. There are photographs of Fred Carpenter out in a canoe made of ugmuk or bearded seal skin, out beside a swimming bear. As Carpenter was in no need of meat at this time and the animal's skin was too rough at this time of the year it appears that Fred was just out enjoying the novelty of being able to course along beside the fast swimming bear. This scene speaks to the Inuvialuit's respect for the animals and their stewardship of nature. Bertram Pokiak, the patriarch of the famous Pokiak clan was a well known trapper at Banks and in the Delta. He was also a regular pilot aboard North Star and a good friend of Fred Carpenter's. His philosophy of environmental management and his rhythm with the land is descriptive of the Inuvialuit philosophy. "Whatever kind of food I wanted, if I wanted caribou I'd go up in the mountains; if I wanted coloured fox, I went up in the mountain; in the Delta I get mink, muskrat; but I never make a big trapper. I just get enough for my own use for the coming year. Next year the animals are going to be there anyway, that's my bank. The same way all over where I travelled."[27]

Geddes Wolki has lost track of how many polar bears he has taken in his hunting and trapping career. One time he and a partner were out hunting and set up their tents next to each other for the night. "Near morning the polar bear came and knocked the other guy's tent down. The guy screamed when he knocked tent. That bear was too hungry, was angry. He makes hissing sound. When I start to reach my hand to tent, he's smelling it. I could feel his big forehead. I try to slap him through the tent right there. The bone on his forehead was so hard. Later we tracked him down. I took two shots. I use a thirty-odd-six. Best gun for bears. Other guy uses a 22 - not strong enough. You need a thirty-odd-six."

Fred Carpenter recalls a close call with a polar bear when he was out on the ice. "One time I got scared all right," he recalls. "I was out on the ice. I got an ice boat, a good sized ice boat." Carpenter might have been clearing away the breathing holes that seals make. "I cut away the ice, cut away, cut away - nothing. I had two pups tied up behind me, with the mother in lead. My two pups, they make funny noise. Funny noise before I put the breach in. I looked up. Look at THE POLAR BEAR STANDING RIGHT BEHIND MY SLED! Behind my sled a polar bear standing right there. My poor little puppies holler and cry. One gets out. I let go of my lead. They want to go for the polar bear! I turn around, start to walk. I get my axe, my sled, my dog. Polar Bear standing up ten feet away. Mother help me, I'm going to die!" With no gun at the ready, Carpenter had to think fast. With only his axe and his lead dog he stood facing the bear. "I figured that I'd clap it in the head, figured out the right place in his head," he remembers. "I'm not even scared. He's going to harm me anyways in some way. Life and death I know. I watch it put its head down. I jump out on the ice, my dogs howling and crying. BOOM!

I hear somebody start to holler from the house over there. 'Heeeey. I save your life!' Jim Wolki. He shoot the polar bear in the head. That's how he saved my life. Everybody run down to come see me. I start to hit the bear in the head with the axe until I see blood come from his mouth. You hit him right there, you know? I hit him with back of axe, big heavy axe, seven pounds. Jim Wolki run down rather quick. I say, 'Good shot, Jim Wolki.' He says, 'You sit down, you can't miss anything.' Jim said he's watching me on the ice, chopping on the ice. He's watching and sees something move behind me. Polar bear - walking right behind me and I never look back."

Bessi and Jim Wolki, Fred and Agnes Carpenter.

Eddie Gruben is a retired trapper now living in a beautiful home overlooking the Beaufort Sea in Tuktoyaktuk. He sailed many times aboard North Star between Aklavik and Tuktoyaktuk to Herschel Island and Banks Island and trapped all over the Delta and Banks Island for many years. Above his chesterfield there is a photograph of him as a young man driving an impressive team of dogs. "See the dog team right there (in the photo). That's the dog team that made me a million bucks - believe it or not. I got over a thousand white foxes from here, from Tuk. From base camp here. I would go from here a hundred miles east and then I would go out on this land here - on the peninsula. Lots of ice. Lots of white fox. There was a thousand white foxes and I got over one hundred fifty or sixty coloured foxes. I got a whole bunch of martens too and all of my fur I shipped to Edmonton fur auction sales.

The name of the guy that I sold my fur to was Bill Lavine. When I sold my fur I got over two million bucks."

Eddie's great success in trapping is as legendary as Fred, Frank or Andy Carpenter or the Wolki brothers. At 92 years of age he told me some of the secret methods he used to be such a success out on the trail. We were sitting in his comfortable home overlooking the harbour at Tuktoyaktuk when he began to share some of the methods that brought him legendary success out on the trapline. "For bait, pretty sure you're going to use seal blubber. Sometimes caribou meat. Then you gotta use rotten 'timber' fish, so that the fox can smell it for long ways. And another thing I use. Only certain people that know that kind of tricks I know. And me, my trick was when I set a trap, like in the springtime after the sun comes out is I don't use bait of any kind! I harness my dogs in the snowbank and they pee all over the snowbank. And then their piss freeze and I pick up this piss in the morning and put it in the box in the back of my toboggan - my sled. I set my trap all day, maybe 150 traps all day. Setting trap I never used bait in the month of March. When I set my traps I put the big chunk of piss, look like snow, but it's piss. North right here and West is here and you put the piss between North and West. You set your trap right here and you put a chunk of snowblock about this high. Even at night, when the moon is bright, you could see the snowblock long ways. They see that block, but the first thing they go for is the piss. They go there to piss on it. Mating time, ah. Holy man. I'm the only one that know about that. Watching the fox all of my life. I was a trapper, eh? I watched all of this. That's where I learned how to be a good trapper. You gotta watch the animals. You have to learn. Lot's of trappers my age - they're nothing. I learned this when you're going to set a trap. Take some loose snow and mix it together. Bound them together - put that in the grave. Set your trap. Lotta times, there's somebody beside me. They set their traps. I set my traps. After about a week, maybe two weeks, come back. That guys trap is hanging in the air, but I never tell them why. You gotta mix sugar snow and you turn it to ice to hold the trap. Oh, I know so much about trapping. I make a million bucks, just by trapping. I know so much, even the fishing. Mind you, I'm not bragging right now. It's just like when I go hunting , everything comes to me. I don't know why."

Eddie Gruben in his trapping days.

"To set his trap the Eskimo hunter digs a small hole in the snow, just deep enough to put the trap below the level of the surrounding snow. Then the steel jaws are covered lightly with snow and this is scraped down to match the blanket. A chip of meat or morsel of blubber is placed near the trap for bait. Soon a hungry fox is on the scene and quickly caught in the trap. .....Ordinarily, the Eskimo trapper sets out anywhere from a hundred to three hundred traps, spaced five hundred yards or so apart, covering a total distance of fifty to one hundred miles. It may take him two weeks to make the round of his trap line, and he builds igloos all along the route so that he can travel in comfort, and, if he's a wise Inuk at all, he takes time out to do some real hunting on the way - for bear, caribou, Arctic hare - and to fish in the lakes."[28] "Traps set near dead animals are put on the west side, because foxes usually approach from downwind and will step on the trap before reaching the meat. The fact that winds prevail from the east makes it easy to predict the direction from which they will approach, because they pick up the scent from downwind. Little caution is necessary while walking around setting the traps, except that the Eskimo does not step downwind of the set. In addition to using old carcasses for bait, a trapper may carry some frozen stomach contents of caribou, and perhaps some meat. The frozen guts are usually carried and can be chopped off with a large knife. The bait is scattered just upwind (east or northeast) of the set so that the fox, reaching for it, will step on the pan of the trap. Baited traps are usually placed on or near some conspicuous landmark, such as a mound."[29]

**Frank Carpenter's thousand dollar clothes line
at Sachs. Photo credit Bob Knight.**

Another prey for the Inuvialuit was the owl. Owl meat provided a change of diet for the families and their feathers were used for decorative work. Fred Carpenter once said, "You see owls in different places. Old saying says, ' Owls make noise, they're calling for others: there's lots to eat.' Like, you know, happy. Says other time - there's no mice and owls are quiet because there's nothing to eat. That's funny? They're calling for others. Maybe not true. Everybody I guess wants to make noise once in a while (laughing)."[30]

Fred Carpenter was in tune with the Banksland environment. He knew that the foxes which he based his livelihood on ate a steady of mice, as do owls. When the owls were making a lot of noise he could count on it being a good fox year. After a year where there was a lot of rain and the mice were washed out of their holes then there would be a lower catch of fox.

Owls were also a source of food for the Inuvialuit. One hunter told the Oblate Priest, Father Le Meur, that "white owls are common on the island, and one day I got as much as seventy. The meat - white meat - is delicious. They also provided us with a source of fat, a good substitute for butter."[31]

Loon were another source of protein for the hunters and their families. Lily Lipscombe was interviewed by the Yukon North Slop Cultural Resources survey and had this to say. "And the tuullik (loon), on the other hand, it's eatable. It's really good, it got real strong taste to it, mind you. But what they use to do is, they use to skin it, because it got such pretty feathers on it, they skin it and they make little bags for their ulus. One year my Mom even made me a short jacket with all the feathers, just from the back of the necks. A jacket for Christmas. They're really, really pretty."[32]

One of Fred Carpenter and Jim Wolki's fellow trappers was Charlie Gruben. Gruben was a young boy when he caught his first fox and he proudly ran it over to the trading post to see what he could get for it. "One time, first time I got a funny fox. I went over there, I took it to Jack Ilavinik at Liebes Store at Kitigaaryuit. He gave me a brand new Winchester .22, two cartons of shells, flour and groceries and stuff like that. I got rich with one fox! He did that on purpose because that was the first fox I get."[33]

"The Bankslanders always prepared their furs with considerable care, and accordingly tended to receive prices well above the average tariff. Their yearly outfits were also more costly than the average, amounting to a minimum of $3 to $5K per family. Coal and gasoline were major expenses as were capital goods such as rifles, traps, canvas, ammunition and dog feed. The annual purchase of groceries included not only staples such as flour, lard, sugar and tea but tinned fruits and vegetables as well. Moreover, the Bankslanders in most years could afford additional durable goods such as washing machines, sewing machines, phonographs, radios, watches and cameras. A few of the best trappers were also able to afford new schooners, costing $10,000 to $15,000. Usually the trappers required credit for part of their outfit (...)Very little cash circulated locally; most transactions being on paper or in kind."[34]

Cal Alexander was an RCMP officer at Sachs Harbour and he recalls Fred Carpenter's status as a trapper there. "Fred was the Patriarch of Banksland, He was the driving force behind fox trapping in Banksland. One full trapping season, I saw Fred, Frank and Andy all with 1,000 fox pelts each. In 1954 I started out at Sachs Harbour and lived with Fred Carpenter for awhile. Andy Carpenter and I were about the same age and hit it off right away. I travelled his trap line with him. He taught me how to survive in the Arctic. North Star was impressive - a good boat. In July '54, North Star rendez-voused with the Fox and left to go and re-supply with foodstuffs at Aklavik and Tuk, next thing we know they're coming back over the horizon. They had taken a walrus, which was highly unusual for the area. He must have come down on an ice floe. North Star was bobbing in the waves, there were ropes around the walrus's mid-section. There is an old 16mm film that Fred shot of this event. The walrus is lashed to North Star's transom and then it seems that the whole town turned out and hauled the huge animal ashore. Everyone seemed to take a turn standing on top of it or touching the long, white tusks."

Albert Elias is another Banksland trapper. "How long a trapping line? Me and my dad, it was about sixty miles plus some more. At the end of each line - most hunters would get to the end of their lines and then a couple of miles from the end would tack some short lines on for a short day line to get to your base camp. You're looking at ten days, two weeks on the trapline. The longest I was out was 22 days out. But the land is there, you know, and we survived storms, rocks. You use everything to survive. We would have 9, 10, 11 dogs. Sometimes I miss the dogs. When you have them for so long, they get in your mind all the time. They're still in my mind. I keep a dog still. If you don't have it (a sense of humour), it's kind of scary eh? Being out on the trapline." When Sven Johansson left the Arctic he sold his dogteam to some members of Sachs Harbour. It was a sad parting as the dogs are such an important part of a Northerners life, even more so at that time. In 1978, he returned to Sachs Harbour to be interviewed for a documentary. There were many Inuvialuit friends there to meet Sven but none made as big an impression on him as one of his old sled dogs, King, who recognised Sven right away and came over to him. Sven was obviously touched by this but was quick to point out that in the North the dogs were not pets but working animals. "It was this …group, composed of recent Alaskan Inuit immigrants and so-called MacKenzie Delta half-breeds, that became the trapping elite of the Western Canadian Arctic. Usher has described them in these terms: ""(They) proved the most flexible in mobility of residence, and the most versatile in resource exploitation…They had learned or retained skills both in caribou hunting and in sea-mammal hunting. They were already the best white fox trappers…Trapping was, for them, no longer a side line: it was a way of life, to which all other activities were adjusted. They were keen traders, and many had obtained large schooners with auxiliary power. (Extensive sea) travel…was common in summer…In winter they traveled with equal facility over land or sea."[35]

Unlike solid land (hunting on ice), it is a permeable surface through which he may pass rapidly and disastrously. Not only is the surface on which the Eskimo may spend one-fourth of his life constantly moving, it also lacks the gross complexity of most other geographic zones. The visual cues are small, consisting of subtle changes in the colour of the ice, of small patches of snow which reveal wind direction and force, of water texture and slight indications of tidal changes and currents. Even these minimal cues may be obscured by fog, snow, wind, rain, glare, darkness, and low level contrasts that camouflage the animal as well."[36]

"Contrary to stereotypes of eating only meat, the Inuvialuit enjoyed picking berries and roots as well as the leaves of some plants. Sarah Meyook recalls 'we would pick berries too and rhubarbs also other green leafs. They made fruit with them after boiling them in a big boil, they put sugar also flour.' Dora Malegna remembers 'Cloud berries, black berries and blue ones, only these kinds. Also, roots from the ground, the ones the mouse store for winter. We had so much fun doing things like that with my mom and my two aunties Annie and Mary March."[37]

It is a myth that Inuit only ate meat and blubber. As Sarah Meyook and Dora Malegna recalled, berry picking was a popular pastime and provided a good source of vitamins. Ernie Comerford who spent six years in Nunavut and twenty-two in the Northwest Territories adds, "Some flowering plants have leaves and stems that can be eaten like a salad, or they can be used to make soup or to flavour stews. Other plants have roots that can be used the same way and lichen can be boiled to make a digestible food that is nutritious. Also, there are edible puffballs and mushrooms, not to mention edible species of seaweed."[38]

That being said, if no plant-based food had been put aside the Inuit could still get all of their vitamins from hunting. An article published on-line in the October, 2004 issue of Discover magazine by Patricia Gadsby explains that, "vitamin A, which is oil-soluble, is also plentiful in the oils of cold-water fishes and sea mammals as well as in the animals' livers, where fat is processed. These dietary staples also provide vitamin D, another oil-soluble vitamin. Meanwhile, organ meats in the traditional Inuit diet were a good source of Vitamin C if eaten raw (cooking would have essentially destroyed the vitamin.) These meats included raw caribou liver and seal brain. Raw kelp also provided a good supply of vitamin C. "Still higher levels, "writes Ms Gadsby, "were found in whale skin and muktuk - whale skin with its underlying blubber. Indeed, Sue Munro of the geography department of North Toronto Collegiate points out that muktuk of the narwhal, on an ounce-per-ounce basis, contains more vitamin C than lemons do."[39] While the smell of muktuk is quite pungent and to many off-putting, the taste is much milder. The experience is described as being similar to being initiated into eating blue cheese.

The Eskimo used to hunt only what he needed - bear, seal, caribou. The little foxes - Tirganiak - he despised. In the old days the Copper Eskimo hardly recognized the existence of the fox. If he met one on the trail he might risk an arrow on him, just to try his skill, but never because he wanted the animal. Fox meat makes poor eating, and fox fur is too frail for anything but baby clothes.

But fashionable women in Paris and New York did not share the Inuk's contempt for the fox. They regarded Tiriganiak's silvery fur as a perfect complement to their gleaming shoulders. What women want, men will get, and so the white man came to the Arctic after foxes and dinned into the Eskimo's ear the value of fox pelts.

'Do you want a rifle, eh, Inuk? Ammunition? Then go and get us foxes, plenty of foxes. Plenty of foxes.

The Eskimo wanted the white man's rifle, steel knife, fish net, boat. So he went after foxes. And soon he found he was so busy getting the miserable little animals that he had no time left in which to hunt for real meat - for bear and caribou."[41]

"Them days the big thing was white fox, white fox was big money then, that's how come some of these Eskimos were like millionaire with white foxes - they don't get a hundred they get hundreds (laughter) Yah, in a season ah. Sachs Harbour was great for that. Biggest trapper there was Frank Carpenter. One year I heard he made $75,000 with fox. One year, fox alone - probably about eight hundred. That's a lot of foxes for one man but you know he had big boys, too ah. Frank Carpenter, the guy who retired from the cops, he was their oldest son, he had quite a few big boys. And then he had a store too ah - getting all the foxes. (laughter)"[42] It appears that Tom has mixed up parts of Fred and Franks' lives here, though both men were highly regarded trappers.

"In general, it is fair to say that the Eskimo must perform in an arena which has many high-level constraints on behaviour and which offers little guiding information. Penalties for mistakes are prompt and drastic. Death in cold water is measured in minutes because of the accelerated heat loss in water as compared with air. The Eskimo concern with orientation and sequence, their unusual mechanical abilities, inventiveness, navigational skills, their ethological and anatomical knowledge, and the structure of language itself, represent an intellectual adaptation with a neuro-physiological base and important social and genetic correlates."[43]

"The very best trapping seasons on the Island have produced harvests of 7,000 to over 11,000 foxes, including those lost or subsequently destroyed in traps. ...remarkable in view of the small number of trappers involved. It is true that these trappers have expended more than the usual effort to obtain foxes. Every year, thousands of traps are set along hundreds of miles of tra-plines over an area as much as 10,000 square miles."[44]

"When seals could not be found, Nuliajuk, a sea spirit would be consulted. It is said that when Nuliajuk was mad, she would drive all the seals away from their usual breathing holes and on to others. Nuliajuk is the boss of all seals and other sea mammals. My father said this half -woman/half -fish would only be angry for some reason. Perhaps we did not perform all the spiritual practices required of us when we hunted. Both my father and brother-in-law always knew just what to do. Because each of them was an angakkup (shaman), they would consult with Nuliajuk through their helping spirits and make peace with Naliajuk. Then in the coming days there would be seals again in the area where we used to live. My father used to say that we must always show respect to the animals. He said that if you make fun of the animals, they will eventually pay you back."[45]

Another animal that is very common on Banksland is the lemming - a regular dinner for the fox. The story of lemmings killing themselves by jumping off cliffs does not hold water for Fred Carpenter. He has a different theory.

Lemmings are good swimmers and when they leave Banks Island, according to Fred, "it is not to commit suicide but to find new food supplies on the mainland, a 70 mile swim away. Fred who has lived for years on the Arctic coast , has seen lemmings swim in from the ocean."[46]

"At one time the Eskimos considered the white fox worthless and used it as a towel to wipe their greasy hands upon. At the time of my visit, however, they were getting as much as forty and fifty dollars apiece for these pelts. It had been a 'good white fox year' along the coast and quite a number of Eskimos and their families had trapped as many as two and three hundred of these little animals and sold them to the traders for an average price of about thirty-five dollars apiece, enabling them to purchase motor schooners, high powered rifles, gramophones and even cameras."[47]

In 1989 Mary Carpenter Frost made a presentation in Calgary, Alberta at the UNESCO Culture Conference on the topic of Inuit Cultural Survival in the Face of Change. "The Inuvialuit today still live in harmony with nature. Our relationship to the land is spiritual. It is on the land that we gain a sense of achievement and identity from our traditional economy of hunting, trapping, and fishing. The land and the people are one. Without this relationship, we would not have survived. Vince Steen is a trapper from Tuktoyaktuk and when I asked him to explain his identity and Inuit culture, he answered, "To the Inuvialuit, land is life. Without our land, and the way of life it has always provided, we can no longer exist as people. If the relationship is destroyed, we too are destroyed."[48]

The decade ending in 1960 showed a record of 400,000 arctic foxes having been taken with a total value of over five million dollars, with prices ranging from eight dollars to twenty four dollars each. The winter of 1954/55 was the best ever with a total catch of 81, 783 foxes. Buliard in his book, <u>INUK</u>, ends the conversation about trapping with his observation of how the desires of foreigners for fox pelts may have given the Inuit some material goods but robbed them of their culture. "He ceased to be a hunter in many cases, and became a trapper, a slave to the little foxes he despised."[50]

BESSIE FROM BANKSLAND

1. Bessie came back to Banksland
She was looking for a husband who was looking for a wife
She wore her hair in a beesnest pouf, tight dress above her knees
She lighted up a filter tip and said, 'Who'll Marry Me?
Oh me, sweet me'

2. 'I have been to school and learned to be a perfect wife
Put flowers on the table and lead a dainty life
I've learned to iron shirts and sheets and cook electronically
And I have learned to dance with a man so he'll have to marry me
Oh me, sweet me'

3. She glanced around Sachs Harbour at all the single males
Her eye fell on a handsome lad, his name was Bobby Bales
Said Bob, 'It's true I need a wife and you can dance with me
But you won't lead a dainty life if you marry me -
Not if you marry me'

4. 'You will cut up dry fish and I'll not scrape the skins
You will flour foxes and pack the water in,
You will sew my parka and you will boil my tea
And you will harness up the dogs, if you marry me
Yes, if you marry me'

5. 'Well, I'll not cut up dry fish and you will scrape the skins
And I'll not flour foxes and pack the water in,
I can't sew a parka and I don't like boiled tea
And I'm scared to hell of your husky dogs so you can't marry me
Oh me, sweet me'

6. Bessie went away from Banksland, she went down to Inuvik where
Two years more or less had passed 'til Bobby saw her there
She said, 'I lead a dainty life with a man from DOT (MOT)
But he has got an outside wife so he can't marry me
Oh me, poor me.'[51]

Chapter 11
The Sachs Harbour Store

The Hudson's Bay company had for years been in an elaborate chess match with the other trading companies such as Liebes and CanAlaska as well as the individual traders who showed up each season. As different parts of the western Arctic became popular with the Inuvialuit or G'wichin they would see if cutting down on their travelling time to Herschel Island or Aklavik was worth the investment of opening and operating a remote post. The incredible fur runs that the Bankslanders brought in would seem to justify an HBC post there, however, until the 1950's the Bankslanders seemed to have no complaint in crossing over to the Delta since it was a time for them to meet up with family and friends, dance, gamble and have a vacation. There was also the problem of how to stock such a post, since the Bankslanders made enormous purchases in comparison to other communities, partly because they could, but mostly since they were buying for at least a year in advance.

The Department of Northern Affairs also investigated opening a store on Banks Island but could not justify the expense. At Department meetings Fred Carpenter's name was knocked around as a likely person to run such a private venture. He was known as a smart businessman, a hard worker and a man who commanded enough respect from his fellow trappers that a remote business such as this could run relatively smoothly. The Department of Northern Affairs contacted Agnes and Fred in 1957 and they travelled to Aklavik to take a short course and exam on how to run such a venture and in 1958 were granted an official trading license. "Fred and I got the first trading license to make it legal. That way we could trade for furs and other trappers wouldn't have to go all the way to Aklavik," recalls Agnes.

The store allowed trappers to trade with the Carpenters year round, so that budgeting wasn't as much of a problem. It also either spelled the end or recognised the end of the schooner days since there was no longer a fleet of fur laden schooners needing to make the crossing. The Fox and North Star were the last two to make the trip. Fred had become acquainted with a representative at Edmonton Fur Auction Sales in the early fifties and had been sending some parcels of furs directly to him. This had been at the suggestion of RCMP officers Cal Alexander and Jim Lambert who had seen a way for the local trappers to cut out the middle man and deal with the big fur brokers themselves. The Bankslanders were able to make more money and Edmonton Fur Auction Sales were guaranteed the most sought after white fox pelts in the world.

When Edmonton Fur Auction Sales heard about Fred and Agnes Carpenter's trading post they provided some revenue so that the Carpenter's could carry a large inventory of trade goods in their store. The Carpenters were also able to buy in bulk which saved them even more money

Diane Carpenter remembers her father's store. "His store was excellent. He would take furs or a lot of time people would just go on credit. She also remembers what a great treat it was to have a father owning the only store for hundreds of miles - and one that had candy and chocolate! "Whenever I would camp out at one of my friends I'd go to my Dad and say "Dad, I'm going to camp out and so I'd like to get some chocolates and I'd get a box about this big and I'd go there and I'd point at the chocolate and he'd put them in! Oh God!! (Laughter)" Albert Elias was also a frequent visitor to the store. "Fred's store - Oh yeah, I go in there. He used credit. He knew people would bring their furs to him. People have to eat. He had the basics for food, plus hunting and trapping equipment."

**North Star and Fox at Sachs Harbour with Fred
and Agnes' store in foreground.**

Sue Kovik recalls, "I can remember going to his store there. Get groceries in that little store. All on credit.' The Carpenters would supply the community with basic grocery supplies as well as stretchers for furs, ammunition and other needs in return for fur. Fred and Agnes knew which trappers would be able to pay off their tab with fur by the season's end and by watching the market carefully through radio reports were able to give a fair price for the collected furs and still be able to turn a profit when they transported them on North Star to the mainland in the summer. As the acknowledged leader of Sachs Harbour and the co-owner of the trading post, Fred Carpenter also kept track of how quickly people were using up their winter supplies. The Inuvialuit characteristic of being self-sufficient was ingrained into Fred but he sometimes had to remind people that they had to use their supplies prudently. If they ran out of something and the trading post was out of it, then the neighbours would soon be borrowing from others and putting a dent in their supplies. He even kept track of how much oil people were burning to heat and cook with and was known for telling people to turn their heat down all of the time so that the community wouldn't run short of oil. Joey Carpenter explains that "there was no law, no police and you had to have law and order over people, 'cause if somebody just turned up the heat too much then you're going to run out of resources, say, by April. Boat can't leave Sachs until July, so what these people doing after they run out in order for them to live, they go bum something off other families. So everybody short of everything. Some guy has to say, 'Look, be careful.' If my Dad or somebody like him didn't clamp down on people, it was dire consequences. You know, generosity can only go so far. You know, if I have to help you, then it can get to the point where I am suffering. So, consequently, lots of bad feelings start coming out and pretty soon it affects the whole community."

Fred Carpenter in his store.

One story of some famous customers' runs in contrast to the picture of the store only catering to Inuvialuit. The trading post was used mainly by the residents of Banksland, the trappers who were out on the land and who wanted a quick return for their work rather than holding out for the summer trade on the mainland or dealing with the brokers in the east. Banksland fur was becoming very famous and was known world-wide as the place to purchase prime fur. Occasionally orders would come in by telegram or later by phone from people wanting to purchase fur directly from the island. Mary Carpenter remembers two of the most famous orders that she received while at home at Sachs Harbour. "Our most famous customer - I picked up the phone one day

"Do you know who I am?"

"Of course," I said, "Who wouldn't?"

It was Bette Davis and she wanted to buy 25 prime foxes

She said "You know where to send them."

Another time the Empress of Iran - she sent us a huge box of jewellery. We didn't know what to do with them so we cut them apart and made dog collars. The jewels all fell out, all over the island. Some day some archaeologist is going to wonder where all of these stones came from!" (laughter)

We had so much. Agnes would say to anyone who came over, "Just take what you want". I don't blame them for taking them. Who wouldn't?

Another time a contact phoned from Buckingham, Palace for Princess Margaret for a lot of white fox pelts. You can see pictures of her wearing these gorgeous shawls of white fox - Fred Carpenter's white fox!" Mary's sister, Margaret Hawkins, remembers orders coming in from Canadian movie star, Mary Pickford, and screen legend, Marlene Dietrich. "They really were the most famous furs in the world at the time. Everybody wanted them. It's because the people at Sachs Harbour were very careful about cleaning and preparing them," she adds.

Agnes Carpenter was perhaps the hardest working person at the trading post. As the only member of the team with store experience and as the only one who could type, much less read and write she was kept busy taking orders, making orders, keeping inventory as well as working with the furs. "At the trading post store we would value the fur and then think of what it's worth. We sort of had to guess at what we thought the furs would bring but we pretty much knew what prices they were fetching. We would trade goods for the fur or sometimes money. Mostly goods like hardware and food. We would tell them how much they had to spend and then they would trade for that amount in goods. We had to keep the trading post stocked and so we were always making orders. We would order one year in advance and all of the orders had to be typed out which was my job. I would be typing for many days!"

In every trade, the old trappers lament was remembered: 'When prices are low, who gets skinned worse, the fox or the trapper?"

Chapter 12
Readying North Star for Sea & Loading

In the spring the schooners would be launched. To do this, the whole village would turn out and put their back to the boat, brace their feet on the ground, and then push her into the ocean. To put that into perspective, the ships ranged from five tons to North Star's twenty-two tons! Each ship was launched in turn and then was made fast to the shore while the wood took up, or swelled, and then were ready to be loaded with fur. In the last few years of the 'schooner days', the local Department of Transport tractor was put into use to simply push the ships in. The launches were always made after the risk of ice coming into the harbour was diminished. Some years, this never happened and so the people and the ships had to make it through another year fending for themselves. In the self published Banksland Story a description is made of watching ice clear from the harbour. "Have you seen the ice-pack moving away in the spring? The icefield has been there frigid for 7-8 months, then a few leads widen up and suddenly the fantastic mass is on its way, and there is the wide, open sea. In a few hours the ocean is free and the shipping season seems to be at hand. Then the icefields follow the laws of the arctic currents and high winds. There you witness the indomitable power of nature."[1] Persis Gruben adds, "Progressively the ice began to melt, to move in and out from the shore 'til the pack ice finally disappeared in the horizon. Alex and Dad then pushed the Reindeer into the water and left it there in the shallow water for a few days. During the winter and the spring the planks had opened a little bit and needed only a few days before it would be seaworthy again. When the schooner was made ready he began loading all the furs and all our belongings and we sailed to Masik Pass, Sachs Harbour now being deserted. When we arrived at Masik Pass the whole population of Banksland was there. The Adams, the Pirtokranas and the Allens were all there. The Ookpik had suffered some damages but they were all repaired for our arrival. We were told that the mast of the Ookpik had been broken then, but it had also been repaired. Upon our landing Dad had tied up along the

Ookpik and we could easily visit without going ashore, only needing to step from schooner to schooner."[2]

Innu standing on Banksland shore next to North Star, waiting for ice to retreat.

Persis Gruben remembers the launchings. "Lennie Inglangasuk's father, Kuugaatchiaq he would lean back his back on ground and push the boat up with his legs. Lift the boat up and all, they all put skids on the boat - the people that he was working with."[3]

"July was devoted chiefly to working on the schooners. They were caulked and perhaps painted, then winched off the beach into the shore lead. After the engines were put into working order, the boats were loaded. Everything was put on board: dogs, travelling and camping equipment, traps, meat, the winter's fox catch, even the canvas and lumber from the tents, because there was no guarantee they would return to the same spot the next year. Now they only had to wait for the ice to disperse and allow them unhindered passage to the mainland shore."[4] "Working at the furs and pelts and at the schooners, repairing, painting and overhauling the motors took most of our time. But to break the monotony and the routine of our days, a sort of relaxation in one way was organised - hunting trips."[5]

Once the ship was caulked, painted, and launched the Inuvialuit of Sachs Harbour had to wait for the ice to clear the harbour before they could set out for Herschel Island or the MacKenzie Delta. With the ship ready, the fur cleaned and bundled and the islanders more than ready to head out and meet up with their family and friends as well as get fresh groceries and supplies, sometimes the wind would hold the ice in place as the summer turned to fall. Dr Hohn recalls waiting to board North Star at Sachs Harbour one year. "Launching didn't mean we were free to go. There was open water for about a mile offshore, but beyond that the ice was still unbroken. Every day we'd climb the nearest of the coast hills behind the settlement and examine the lay of the open water. Seeing the whales on the 19th of July was a good sign, as it indicated open water to the south of us, for it seemed unlikely that the whales would swim long distances under ice."[6]

North Star pushing through the ice. She often lead the flotilla of Banksland vessels due to her size and strength.

North Star heading out of harbour with ice all around. Note hunter on bow with rifle.

Sometimes, North Star would be used to try and break through the ice but as Banks Island lies directly in the path of the current and the westerly winds, the ice build-up would sometimes be beyond an actual icebreaker's capabilities. "Steffanson records landfast ice extending down 120 feet at Banks Island, where it is initially piled by strong west winds with high tides, and is grounded solidly in spring and summer when there are east and southeast winds with low tides."[7] Joey Carpenter remembers those days, "In the spring we would go to Tuktoyaktuk and stay for the summer. No one wanted to stay on Banks all year."

Loading dogs aboard North Star.

After all of the fur was loaded into the cargo hold, the rest of the gear including sleds, clothes, lumber, tents and all of the food for the voyage was packed on deck. Then the loading of the dogs began. One by one they were carried up the gangplank by the ruff of their necks and their tails. Each dog had to have to be chained in its own spot as they often fought and so this process could take hours. North Star regularly loaded over fifty dogs and the one wolf. "On North Star we would load up everything we had, dogs and all, at least fifty dogs", recalls Joey Carpenter. "As soon as trapping season was over and days began to get longer and warmer, we all moved to the small harbour, where stood frozen in snow and ice, our three schooners. There again, in a new surrounding we continued to work at our own leisure and pace. It was not time for relaxation and rest yet, much had to be done before the break-up. Men and women spent hours every day, checking furs: polar bear, white fox and seals, cleaning them, a thorough cleaning and scrubbing, then setting them on a line to be bleached by the sun and wind. Mother spent countless hours sewing seal skins."[8]

North Star packing sled on top of pilothouse.

When Cal Alexander was an RCMP member stationed at Sachs Harbour between he spent a lot of time with Fred Carpenter and considered Andy Carpenter to be a very good friend. He remembers how Fred doted on North Star in order to keep her in top shape. "She was sure a sound boat with a gas engine and she was maintained really well. They looked after her really well, scraped her, painted her, caulked her, they recognized her value. They couldn't live their lifestyle without that boat. She was not just used for 3 months and then put away and forgotten."

The Captains would watch the weather and when conditions looked safe, would make a break from Sachs Harbour to Baillie Island. If the weather was still fair they would then continue on to Tuktoyaktuk, Aklavik, or in the early years, Herschel Island. If the weather looked unsettled, the vessels would anchor at Baillie Island and wait it out. The Inuvialuit have tremendous respect for the dangers of the ocean and over the years many ships had been lost in storms, crushed in ice or damaged in rough weather.

Fred Carpenter and Geddes Wolki on top of North Star's pilothouse.

Aboard North Star navigational duties were shared between Fred Carpenter, Jim Wolki when he was aboard in the early years and a series of pilots or steersman including Geddes Wolki, Peter Sidney, Susie Sidney and Michael Amos. Quite often, Bertram Pokiak was the engineer. A lot of the navigation was based on dead-reckoning, that is, using clues from the sea, waves and landmarks to determine positions. Compasses are unreliable in the Arctic due to the high magnetism. For some time Fred Carpenter had a gyro-compass mounted on top of the deckhouse but reports also suggest that he had a very strong instinct about direction and mainly used his own intuition to guide the ship. Some anthropologists have suggested that the Inuit have a different sense of space and time and that this creates their unique navigational abilities. As a renowned navigator, and with the biggest ship, Carpenter would lead the flotilla of schooners back and forth across the Beaufort Sea each year. Another advantage to having North Star lead the way was that sometimes the shallow harbours were still frozen over when they made port. "I remember once in the schooner and the harbour was kind of frozen over. Ice thick enough to walk on. The North Star broke the ice so the other boats could go in." Sometimes North Star and other schooners would lash themselves side by each and then drive at full speed into the ice to break their way into port. "...look at how the land joins the sea, as Inuit would. Inuit do not make maps and instead rely upon their memories as well as oral traditions to inform them about how space fits over the horizon. The most memorable things were first seen and then heard, not measured by specific times or distances."[9] The author, Jonathan Waterman was making a single-handed attempt to kayak and walk the NorthWest Passage and commented on the Innu's navigation skills. "The anthropologist Edmund Carpenter believes that Inuit perceive space more from auditory cues than from the visual and measured cues that we apply to geography. While Kabloona eyes pinpoint a place specifically within a space and next to a background, Inuit ears can perceive sound coming from any direction. More precisely, Carpenter believes that Kabloona sensory traditions mirror the first sentence of Aristotle's Metaphysics, telling us that sight, not sound is 'above all others.' Our traditions continue with the Bible's 'Seeing is Believing' and on to modern physics measuring light waves. Yet the parts of our brains that process sound or intuition are little used - unlike those of traditional Inuit."[10]

Life aboard during the crossing was a time for relaxing after the hard work of trapping and then readying North Star for sea. It was the highlight of the year to get away from the island and travel out on the ocean. Many people have dropped down to visit North Star over the last fifteen years or so and they all have memories of good times had aboard while the ship was sailing in the Arctic Ocean. "As I sat on deck that evening I felt content and happy. Later I went down to bed and fell asleep listening to the sounds of the schooner swishing through the water."[11]

Food was prepared before leaving so that only minimal cooking was done aboard. The galley was set up in the focs'le of North Star, an iron cookstove with a table running fore and aft that could seat a half dozen people easily. "Them days, it (food) would just be hanging on the outside on the rail. There'd be caribou dry meat, maybe some muktuk, but the muktuk would always be in barrels, there'd be whale dry meat, all kinds of good stuff like that. Just help yourself. The galley was the focs'le. Everybody sorta took turns with the cooking. I wasn't the cook. No, no. I just didn't want to bother with it," recalls Agnes Carpenter. Ernest Pokiak remembers travelling on North Star during the summers of his childhood. "My Dad Bertram and Fred were very good friends and to each other. We ate mostly country food, keep in mind during that period we were still pretty nomadic people. We ate a lot of caribou meat, seal, bearded seal (ugyuk) oil fermented to taste for dip and some times dry meat was made from ugyuk meat, ptarmigan, snow geese (wavies) goose eggs in the early spring. Staples were flour, lard tea, coffee, sugar, rice, dried Klim and Macintosh toffee which was rationed. All food items were managed to last, absolutely no waste of anything.

Fred, his wife Ada, and Bertram Pokiak reading Beaver magazine. Note Fred's chair on top of pilothouse.

In regards to dining at the North Star, we ate as family. The bow of the North Star was not big enough to hold 18 to 20 of us at one time. Fred Carpenter usually ate with us tho'. At the time his wife Ada was in the hospital in Aklavik." "Another spring meal that we had was a soup made from caribou bone legs. We had eaten the marrow during the winter and had saved the bones until spring. We pounded them with rocks to break them up and boiled them in a big pot to get every last bit of goodness from them. After the broth cooled we had an inch or two of fat on top to eat with our sourdough bread. The caribou hooves were also made into a tasty soup. We skinned and boiled them until they were falling apart. Then we took them off the stove to cool, removed the toe-nails, added onions, rice and dehydrated vegetables and simmered the broth again. This may sound offensive because of the toe-nails, but it tasted good."[12] "On North Star all of the cooking was done in the focs'le on a coal stove made out of cast iron. Everyone used to eat there too." Albert Elias adds, "we had bunks in the center part and next to the engine room there were more quarters for people to sleep in there. We would take all of the family when we went. All of Fred's older sons and daughters would be there. Others would sleep right in the pilothouse and in the area under the pilothouse. Fred used to sleep in the pilothouse or next to the engine." Albert Elias found that there was always plenty of food that had been prepared for the crossings. "Mostly sleep in the focs'le, pilothouse, cargo room. Pretty well all the food was prepared already. Traditional food, hanging by the ship there, help yourself, lots of bannock, tea and you're okay for the day."

Crashing through the waves of the Beaufort Sea in the often overloaded North Star with hatches open for ventilation the ship's bilges would have to be pumped out regularly. Seas would slosh aboard and find their way down the air vents or skylights. When any wooden ship is worked hard the hull and deck sometimes twists a little under the incredible strains put upon her. A dribble here and there soon adds up. When the motor is running a certain amount of water is let in naturally at the stuffing box where the propeller shaft exits the ship to help keep it cool, so a close eye is always kept on the bilge to see how much water has collected. Joey Carpenter remembers many shifts of doing this, even when he was a young lad. "There were two places, up on top and down below where you would pump out the water, eh? Get tired. Big muscles."

In July of 1986 anthropologist and Arctic explorer John Bockstoce was in Sachs Harbour. He describes it as being "one of the cleanest, neatest, and most "pulled together" northern villages I had ever seen. ...I would guess that two hundred people lived there, most of whom were active trappers and hunters. A group of Eskimos from Tuktoyaktuk had colonised the island in 1925, when the price of white fox pelts was soaring. They built their own houses, trapped all winter, then sailed back to the mainland in their boats on a fifteen-hundred-mile round-trip voyage to trade at Herschel Island or Aklavik. Each time they left Banks Island on one of these trading expeditions they took all their possessions, including their dogs, with them - because they could never be sure in any year whether the sea ice might block their return. In that case they would simply make camp wherever the trapping seemed good, repeat the annual cycle, and then try again for Banks Island the following autumn. "The loading of the dogs was quite a game - hardly any of them would walk the gangplank, so we simply hauled them up by the chains fixed to their tight collars. I feared this would break their necks but it seems they can take it. The wolf was a more awkward proposition. First a long chain was manipulated around his neck and this was held tight by a man on each side, then he was knocked on the head with a piece of two-by-four till he was pretty groggy and a muzzle slipped on. After that he was no more of a problem than the dogs."[13] Hohn later noted that getting the dogs ashore whenever the ship stopped was much easier as they would simply toss them into the sea and let them swim the short distance to land.

In walking around town Bockstoce and his wife, Romain, noticed "near the beach, up on blocks, was the little motorized "schooner" Fox. A beamy cargo sloop, like all the fur trade "schooners," and only about forty feet long, it had been one of the vessels making the annual voyage between Banks Island and the mainland trading centers (the North Star, now owned by Sven, was another). It had now become an artefact symbolizing the community's pride in their self-reliance and competence."[14]

In his voyage aboard North Star in 1953, the ornithologist Dr E.O. Hohn described his initial impression of life aboard. "The North Star carried quite a crew. There was Fred Carpenter, one of his sons of about 20, a teen-aged daughter and a little boy. The Carpenters slept in the bunks of the cabin forward of the engine. Pat Herschel, a bachelor of about my age, and I had our sleeping bags on the cabin floor. The pilot house accommodated another married couple and their little girl, while the forepart of the hold adjoining the forecastle, which was kitchen and messroom, held Bertram Pokiak, his wife, two teen-aged daughters and five younger children. On top of 18 people we had 50 sled dogs chained on deck and a captive wolf, kept for breeding with the dogs...as well as two sleds tied to the railing, and sacks full of fox traps."[15]

Wolkie and Carpenter's business idea was to use the ship to travel into remote areas to set their trap lines and to hunt. They also loaded North Star's cargo hold up with trade goods purchased from the CanAlaska Company and the HBC and set out to trade with the hunters of the western Arctic. Margaret Carpenter Hawkins remembers these voyages very well. "My father would load up with everything that people had ordered from him as well as all of the things that he knew that others would need. The cargo hold was filled right to the top with big bags of tea, coffee, flour, oats and all of the other food. On deck we had barrels of gasoline and other fuel. My whole family would come along. The Wolki's slept in the focs'le and my parents had the Captain's cabin and Divana, (Fred Carpenter's mother), slept in the deckhouse. There were lots of dogs on deck, tied all the way up on the bow. As kids we would get to sleep on the sacks of oats and tea and then as he traded it away, we would end up coming back sleeping on beds of fur like polar bear and arctic fox and seal!"

Some of the fifty dogs that North Star regularly carried on deck, plus one wolf.

This was the common way that the Inuit travelled. The Arctic Ocean could freeze up at any time and with bad weather, the ship might be stuck in port for the whole winter. The roles in the family were very traditional with the men bringing back the kill and the women cleaning and cooking it. If the ship and the men were to disappear for a winter, the women and children would have a harder time of making it until spring.

Fred Carpenter and Peter Esau with bearded seal.

Albert Elias recalls his father's routine with the schooner Fox. "My father trapped at Banks Island as well. Based at Sachs Harbour most of the time. Sometimes when the weather was fair they would see the mainland and instead of stopping, just swing west to mainland, but lots of times we had to stop at Baillie Island."

If the Sachs Harbour convoy met up with ice along the way they would make the ships fast to the ice and collect water. If possible, they would try to get the ships into shore on another island where they would again wait for the ice to recede and maybe replenish their fresh meat and do some trapping. "Soon the snow on the land melted. We put our boat back in the water, loaded it up, and weaving our way from our way among the ice floes; we moved our winter camp to a beautiful little inlet. We set the tents up on the gravel shore, with gentle rolling hills as a background. Here we waited for the polar ice to leave the sea before we set out for Aklavik. The days were warm and we made the most of them by cooking and eating our meals outside."[16]

**North Star moored to an ice floe in Beaufort Sea to
await clear water. Photo credit Dr Hohn.**

"The voyage to Banks Island in a small boat requires navigational skill and
good seamanship. On a clear day Nelson Head is visible from the main land,
yet one dare not attempt the crossing without knowledge of compass travel
and dead reckoning. Fog and storms can strike suddenly, and ice frequently
presents an additional hazard. These dangers were traditionally faced with no
other navigational aids than a compass, a watch, and a leaded line. Auxiliary
power was generally used on the crossing, particularly as calm conditions
were preferred, so the schooner owners also required knowledge of their
engines and ingenuity to repair them if necessary."[17]

**Many Bankslanders helping to haul walrus ashore
with North Star in the background.**

This ingenuity was played out countless times as once the Inuvialuit were in their remote camps or out at sea, they only had themselves and limited resources to draw upon. An example of this occurred aboard North Star in the late 1930's. "Once on Banks Island, one of the most God forsaken remote places in the world, Fred and Jim Wilkie (Wolki and probably Fred Carpenter) bent the rudder shaft of their large boat. They had no facilities to pull its many tons out of the water where they could get at it. Also they had few tools to work with. Before the ocean froze, they figured out their problem. They pulled the boat in the shallowest water that would float it, then it froze in solidly at the stern. After this they chipped the ice away and got down to the balky rudder.

Inland several miles, they found a vein of poor quality coal. They obtained a bit of this with their dog teams. With packing box boards they made the frame work of a bellows and their women made a sealskin cover for it, sewing the seams and making them airtight. With this outfit they made them a forge, and removing the crooked rudder shaft, heated it and beat the heavy iron out straight again. I do not think one white man in ten million could have done this job."[18]

The traditional route that Carpenter took with North Star to the mainland was to head east to Baillie Island, using dead-reckoning. With Baillie Island in sight and the weather clear, North Star would then be turned towards the Delta. If ice or weather conditions were poor, then the ships would put into Baillie where they would often meet up with the Baillie Islanders and with other small traders making the same trip.)

During Dr Hohn's voyage aboard North Star they found themselves weaving through small ice bergs for the first day. At sunset two small whales passed close to them and he saw a lot of eiderducks tending to their eggs on the ice pans. The next morning he awoke to find that Carpenter had moored North Star to an ice floe, as had Reindeer, since their way south was blocked by ice. The worry was that the ice would not break up enough to allow them safe passage and at a certain time they might have to weave their way back to Banksland or to the trading post of Holman Island off of Victoria Island or just to Baillie Island for safe harbour. Hohn and the others spent the day walking around on the ice. "It was a beautiful scene - a clear blue sky over the darker blue water and the shimmering expanses of ice, while to the north we could see the cliffs of Nelson Head, the most southerly point of Banks Island."[19] In the middle of the night a polar bear came walking along the ice floe, stopping to follow the scent of the ships and the dogs. The men quickly pulled out their rifles and dispatched him. They were all soon on the ice, carefully skinning and quartering the large male.

The ice made the choice for them and so North Star and Reindeer went in to Holman Island where they met up with the local tribe and the Oblate father. The Father was very concerned about a report of some very sick people further up the coast. A side trip in a small scow to rescue two sick women from a smaller settlement resulted in a longer delay for the ships. The decision for the women to go aboard North Star to Aklavik was not taken lightly even though they were in need of medical attention, for it meant that the patients would most likely not be able to arrange transport home for at least one year.

The ice being blown into the harbour is a regular danger for Arctic sailors. Sven Johansson advises that, "When you are sailing in the ice pack it is more important to watch behind you than it is to watch ahead. If the ice closes in behind you, it is all over."[20]

North Star and Reindeer were well and truly iced in and it seemed as though this voyage might have come to an end for that year. By luck, the Hudson's Bay ship Nechilik was in the area and spotted the iced in ships. With her flat, steel hull she broke through the ice and towed the ships as far as Baillie Island where they put in and were once again caught in the ice. Hohn was down below in the focs'le where the meals were cooked and where the stove gave everyone some break from the cold. He looked around at the situation and recorded it for posterity.

"The space is triangular following the lines of the ship's bow, about ten feet long with a table running down its length and a narrow sitting shelf on either side with a stove at the base in one corner of the triangle and a ladder leading up to the deck in the other. Beside the ladder is an opening leading into the front of the hold where the Pokiak family sleep. Sitting in this opening two little Pokiaks are arguing at the tops of their voices in Eskimo. Beside them, Susie, Peter's wife, is crouched on the floor. She is fortyish and has wisps of black hair hanging over her face. She has rather a long nose, which her daughter Navaluk has also inherited. An intense discussion is going on between mother and daughter. Beside Susie again is Andy Carpenter rolling a cigarette. He is a young man of about twenty showing almost no sign of Eskimo blood and looking like any farmer's son outside. Near Navaluk is Frankie, the youngest Pokiak. He is generally seen wearing nothing but a little shirt and his cherubic behind is much in evidence. Angun, his 11-year old brother is just climbing the ladder to get some water for Frankie while at the same time the husky Pat is trying to come down bellowing at the top of his voice that the wind has shifted and 'we'll jolly be stuck here for a week.'

Andy Carpenter.

I'm sitting on the floor which is littered with odd bones from the last meal and scraps of paper which the children have made into toy sleds, almost certainly humming some cowboy tune, as that is all we've heard on the gramophone for weeks. Opposite is the oldest Pokiak girl, about seventeen. Her long black hair frames an attractive oval, rather full-lipped face and she has exceptionally large black eyes. Nearby is her youngest sister Iliguk with a more Mongolian type of face, flat with high cheekbones, nice eyes, full lips and very white teeth. At my right is Andy's sister, Agnes, about eighteen. She also has much of her black hair hanging over her face as she reads an old schoolbook with great concentration. Visible in the hold is mama Pokiak looking rather shapeless in her ankle-length 'Mother Hubbard' parka, trying to restrain the argument between her two younger children. A bit further in the hold father Pokiak is sleeping peacefully through it all. Outside the wind rages, slapping waves against the hull and every now and then the dogs on deck drag their chains and let off a dismal howl."[21]

Hohn and North Star made it safely to Tuktoyaktuk the next day. Upon arrival the wolf was so eager to get ashore "that she jumped over the side three times and hung there dangling on her chain. Luckily for her she was pulled back each time."[22]

In the Arctic Ocean there are no navigational markers or buoys as these would be shifted or torn out by the ice. Instead, the Bankslanders would measure depths with a lead line and pay attention to things like the direction that the kelp was streaming to determine the ocean currents. "When you are in the open sea and there is no means of getting your bearings you can use the floating seaweed (qiqquaq - kelp) for this purpose. The root of the kelp is floating on the surface and its frond is submerged, positioned by the tidal current. From this you will be able to tell what course to take (the frond of the kelp points downstream). This is a good method of finding your way especially when you cannot see the sun."[23] The difficulty of navigating the MacKenzie Delta was clearly explained by Kroetsch in the Northern Review, "There are many channels, many currents, the occasional whirlpool and much shoal water, willow-covered islands and muskrat ponds and oxbows and sandbars and walls of black spruce and unseen deadheads, there in the Mackenzie Delta. The water itself carries enough silt so that it is difficult to see beneath the surface. When on a riverboat pushing loaded barges into the Mackenzie Delta, toward the diverging and joining channels, it is neces-sary to take soundings. ... To enter into the Mackenzie Delta on a riverboat or in a canoe or a fishing craft or a flat-bottomed boat is to enter into the oral tradition."[24]

The difficulty of navigating in the Beaufort Sea was recorded when a survey crew were waiting for Angus Elias to bring Fox to Sachs Harbour in order to get them to Aklavik before freeze-up. Angus had left the Delta and thought that he was heading for Sachs but missed seeing the coast and ended up travelling in circles out on the ocean before finding his way back for the charter. That's when the real trouble began. It appeared that Angus had left Tuktoyaktuk about September 3, but had first gone to Stanton to take some supplies to the Roman Catholic Mission. After leaving Baillie Island he apparently became afraid he might miss Banks Island and get out into the Beaufort Sea. To avoid this he turned more and more east, and after travel-ling for over 50 hours without sighting land, he arrived at the head of Prince Albert Sound. He was then sure that he really had gone west of Banks Island and got to Melville Island, so he headed south, reached the mainland which he thought was Banks Island, and went west until he reached Pearce Point, where he met people who told him where he was. He then crossed from Cape Parry to Nelson Head, and so along the coast to Sachs Harbour.

"As it was a fine night and we wanted to make the mainland during daylight, we left at O200 hours, but ran aground going out of the harbour and lost an hour or two. We met a little ice at about 1000 hours, and had to go 10 miles or so to the west to get around it. Soon after this, a strong easterly wind got up. Owing to the delays it was dark before we sighted land. The obvious thing to do in these circumstances would have been to sail west, being sure to keep well off land, but Angus preferred to heave to with all sail up since there was no means of reefing it. Soon after midnight we struck bottom and the breakers threw us onto a beach which we later found was the northwest point of Baillie Island. Had we been another 100 yards west we should have drifted harmlessly into Liverpool Bay or run into the lee of Baillie Island. Fortunately the bottom was soft, and the worst of the sea was breaking before it reached the boat. At the first glimmer of light Angus was anxious to get his valuables ashore and up the little cliff partially sheltered beach for a while. As the wind showed no sign of slackening off we turned back and camped at a more sheltered beach until the following evening. This time our rounding of Nelson Head was less eventful and we ran along the coast to Sachs Harbour arriving on the morning of the 29th; on the way we saw a large number of bears. The breakers over the harbour bar were quite high, and we nearly came to grief when a wave swamped our engine, but fortunately we dried it in time to cope with the breakers. We had to unload in the surf on the beach, and were afterwards glad of Carpenter's house. The Eskimo were all at Tuk, but Carpenter had offered us the use of his house, and had left us a welcoming letter. We had a short sleep there, and then devoted our time to unpacking and repacking specimens, repairing and strengthening our damaged tent, and sorting out food and equipment, which took us until midnight on July 31. We left immediately in order to round Cape Kellett before the wind changed or rose. There was a fairly heavy sea off the cape, and the Defence Research Board's ship Cancolim II was drifting a mile or so offshore. We twice swamped our engine and had to make for shore to dry it and rig up a baffle to keep the waves out before we rounded the cape, after which we had a wet run in to the western coast.

As we travelled south from Storkerson Bay the weather became milder and the lakes were safe to cross. On the 14th we reached the Kellett River valley, where there was no snow, and finished our journey with rucksacks. Living at Sachs Harbour until around noon the following day. Fred Carpenter and others had just arrived, but Angus Elias, the native sent to pick us up, had not yet come in, although he had left first. A rendezvous date was September 18 and we remained at the settlement until then, but after that we felt free to walk over to Cape Kellett. We returned in the evening of September 21 to find Angus in harbour. He had been wandering all over Amundsen Gulf with a poor compass', a worse idea of navigation, and an impossible map. On the way back we ran ashore under the cliffs of Baillie Island on the stormy night of the 22nd. Angus was convinced the boat was lost, but Manning rallied the crew, and on the 27th we were again on our way. On the 29th we arrived at Tuk, but the post manager was unable to contact Aklavik on the radio sched, the aircraft at Aklavik were anxious to leave, and the harbour froze next day, so we were forced to remain until November 15 in Tuk, where we spent most of our time trapping small mammals. We then stayed at Aklavik until the 24th, arriving at Norman Wells for the weekly C.P.A. flight on November 26 to Edmonton."[25]

North Star with some Carpenter children aboard, Aklavik, 1955.

As they made harbour, their years of experience coupled with the knowledge that had been passed down to them the Bankslanders showed a lot of confidence in their ship-handling. "..he swung the boat around and headed full speed for the rocks. ..Like many old-time Inuit, he had an astounding geographical memory and knew every rock and ridge along hundreds of miles of coast."[27] "By the 1930's, schooners were in such widespread use that most men had become familiar with the operation of such vessels. Yet only a few had learned the rudiments of navigation, usually through summer employment on Hudson's Bay or CanAlaska vessels. Such men were essential for crossing to Banksland, and this was an important reason for travelling in convoy."[28]

There are a handful of old 8 and 16mm movies as well as some slides showing North Star weaving through the ice along with the other schooners. Albert Elias recalls, "You could expect to see ice when we're heading south in early summer because ice would still be floating around. It never really caused much problems, we would go around though we were never really caught in heavy ice."

David Jones ran the Imperial Oil Station in Aklavik and remembers North Star's annual trip in to his docks to get the winter oil drums for heating. "Fred would come in with the North Star about once a year. Always in the middle of the summer to the Imperial Oil at Aklavik. Fred - he was a friendly sort of a guy. He was very friendly, very plain. He wouldn't talk too much. He'd have his family with him and some others. Maybe ten people. I don't remember any dogs. Fred would bring North Star in every year. He'd have ten or fifteen empty fuel barrels that he would drop off and then pick up the same number of full ones. North Star was a nice looking ship. I was aboard her quite a few times." "It wouldn't be just us that would go. The Pokiaks would go and everyone who was related to us, "remembers Joey Carpenter.

Part of the thrill of travelling aboard North Star, Omingmuk, Reindeer, Only Way or Fox was the drama that surrounded the Atlas engine. North Star's

157

was the last one built by the Atlas company and as noted earlier, they had to cobble it together with spare parts as Carpenter demanded that this be the motor for his ship. Aboard Fox, Elias also had a hand crank Atlas, though of a smaller size and the distinctive thump-thump-thump of the motors was part of the back drop of any trip. The engines were used hard, run for days on end at times and repaired on the fly with whatever materials could be found. There are numerous stories of North Star towing in boats whose engines had died at sea and it was not uncommon for Elias to take North Star in tow when her engine was down. This was part of the safety net that the Bankslanders used, knowing that they could rely upon one another should trouble arise. Albert Elias has fond memories of hearing Fox's engine going. "That engine. I don't know if you read up on it on the Internet. It was a re-build Atlas. They were not building new ones any more for a long time. They always had a lot of problems. Our boat, our schooner, we towed North Star several times, you know, engine troubles. On the Fox, we had Atlas - 2 cylinders - big hand crank. I can hear that engine sound when my Dad got her going. I used to like to hear that when I was a kid. It meant we were going to leave, eh? It's kind of boring sometimes when you're a kid."

Sometimes Albert's Uncle Noah would ship aboard North Star as the engineer and Albert would be invited aboard by his Dadak, Fred Carpenter. "He (Fred) used to sit up in that chair. You know the pilothouse has a hole uh? When it was real calm weather like the McKenzie River we'd be on top of the pilothouse and he'd have his legs through the hole and steer with his feet. Bernard (Pokiak) was engineer most of the time and my Uncle Noah, Noah Elias. They'd take apart the engine when it was being towed and that and try and fix it." The hole that Elias refers to is a hatch that was designed into the ship for this purpose. Oftentimes there was so much cargo, gear, dogs and people on deck that the helmsman could not see what was ahead, including sheets of black ice, growlers or bergy bits. Carpenter often steered this way, with his legs hanging through the hatch, or sat on a chair atop the pilothouse and called down to the 'pilot' if he saw anything to steer clear of.

"The summer voyage back to the mainland was not normally a difficult one since daylight is continuous at that time, Ice is then only a barrier and a cause of delay, but not a hazard, and indeed its presence can serve to reduce waves in stormy weather. The outward voyage in September, however, could be dangerous, since one might have to contend with both darkness and ice, and strong northwest gales appear with suddenness and severity at this season. Waves can be so high that boats are lost from sight when in their troughs. Most Bankslanders have memories of the tension and anxiety of waiting out the darkness while pounding and tossing in a heavy sea, with their family possessions below, hoping that dawn would bring the light of a safe harbour. There were many rough crossings, and some near disasters, but it is a tribute to the resourcefulness and skill of the Bankslanders that in 30 years and well over 100 return voyages, never was a person or a boat lost at sea."[29] Their skill is duly noted but as you will read in the chapter on storms and sinkings, there were many adventures, some tragic, on the Beaufort Sea crossing.

Besides trading their fur and buying the coming year's provisions Fred Carpenter and the other Captains could act as 'gate-keepers' for those who wanted to try the isolation of Banks Island for a winter and perhaps even grubstake them if they wanted to trap. Usher adds, "the schooner owners normally took another family or two with them, and perhaps a young, single trapper. Almost anyone who showed interest could arrange to go. If one did not own a schooner, one's father-in-law or brother might, for the schooner owners generally chose close kin to accompany them. The transport of another family assured the owner of sufficient labour to man the vessel, to load and unload, to beach it in the fall, and paint, repair and launch it the next summer. Such labour, in exchange for passage, was generally considered a fair bargain."[30] The schooner had also become an instrument of immigration control. The informal passage arrangements of the early years gave way in the 1940's when more and more people sought to go to Banks Island, while the number of available schooners declined. The schooner owners were in a strong position to dictate not only who made the crossing but at what price they would pay to do so. In some cases, passengers were required to purchase shares in the voyage, in others to pay a designated fare in cash or fox pelts. Passage charges were designed to cover gas, oil and paint and to return a goodly return to the owner, in fact the usual sum was about $500.[31]

On the return trip to Banksland, with their holds and decks full of the supplies needed for the following winter a stop was often made in order to mine coal for heating and cooking. To do this, North Star was made fast to the shore at the bottom of a coal seam. The families then climbed to the top of the cliff and hammered and chiselled away blocks of coal which then fell down to the ship, sometimes right onto her deck, where it was bagged in gunny sacks and stowed dry below. Kathleen Hansen relates the procedure, "the people that goes to Banks Island used to get coal from here. There was lots of them that came here. Over there on the shore of the lake they worked there and went way in. They make stairs up on it. Then before they go in too much, from up the steps, they make the coal fall down. It's very far when you go in there. And when you go way in, a person gets very tiny when he is standing at the end of the mine."[32]

The story of North Star of Herschel Island and trapping fur is one of extreme highs and lows. There were banner years of fur but then it would take several years for the fox to replenish themselves. As well, some years the western Arctic was choked with ice and other times it was clear sailing to the mainland. In North Star's first year in the Arctic of 1936/37, there was too much ice to make it to Banks Island and so Carpenter and Wolki had to draw the ship close to shore and freeze her in by Cape Parry on the mainland. Their new investment was left to the elements and was forced almost out of the ice and onto her side in the bay behind Cape Parry that is now called North Star Harbour. There is also a North Star harbour on the NorthWest coast of Banks Island where the first North Star was frozen in for three years.

After spending so much on North Star and then being stuck on the mainland, Carpenter and Wolki also found that the trapping was very poor and they ended up not being able to pay back their creditors in the Delta - the shops that outfitted them with ammunition, groceries and traps. Captain C.T. Pedersen had left the Arctic but was still Carpenter and Wolki's biggest supporter. He worked with investors in New York who were appalled to learn that the combined debt of all of the Bankslanders was around $20,000 to them. The partners were ready to call in the debts and take back whatever capital the Bankslanders had which would have included their schooners. Pedersen recognised that the reason the Bankslanders were in the red was due to ice conditions that he was more than familiar with, coupled with the natural cycle of the fur bearing animals that they were trapping. He not only did not call in the debts but convinced the New York suits to advance an additional $25,000 so that the Bankslanders would have enough supplies to go back onto the land and trap all winter.

North Star, Fox, Reindeer and the other schooners made it to Banks Island and the Inuvialuit set off on the trap lines, laying hundreds and hundreds of traps and staying out for weeks on the land, sleeping in ice houses and working long days. By the time that spring came around only 1,700 foxes had been taken, less than half of what would have been needed to satisfy the debt.

At this point, with the Bankslanders in deeper debt, Pedersen completed the sale of all of his business to the Hudson's Bay Company. The HBC did not have the same optimistic view of the trapping forecast that Pedersen had had and refused any more credit. This was the end of the trapping life for many but the more successful trappers like Carpenter, Wolki, Elias and Pokiak were able to struggle through with what they had managed to save.

The season of 1939/40 was one for the record books with over 6,500 foxes trapped. Usher recorded that "the leading trapper and his wife together obtained 1,300, a record number which has never been equalled in Canada, and probably not in the world. This bumper harvest however, coincided with a nadir in the market price. For example, the 1,300 foxes which brought about $15k in 1939 would have fetched 100k ten years previously. Still, earnings were sufficient for most families to clear long standing debts and even have some credit left."[33] Usher doesn't name who the leading trapper and his wife was but it was most likely Carpenter or Wolki. In the years since those boom days I have spoken with a half dozen retired trappers and read the accounts of dozens more. Over time, it seems that their memories are of having regularly completed much higher takes.

The next season of 1940/41 produced another great run with 5,500 foxes taken with the added bonus that the market was improving and so profits were enormous. These were the years that established the reputations of the Bankslanders and when the crowds at Aklavik saw the thousands and thousands of snowy white fox pelts being offloaded from North Star. It was as exciting as watching gold being unloaded from the Yukon. Pelts were used like cash in many places. In December of 1941, Jasper Andreasen - who described himself as a 'full-blooded Eskimo', wrote away for a periodical subscription: ' I am sending one white fox, if you will please get me started in getting The Beaver magazine."

With all of their new-found riches and the opportunity to spend it the Bankslanders were in no great hurry to make the schooner crossing back home at the end of the summer. Mother Nature was again against them and winter came early and with a vengeance, freezing the ships into harbour at Aklavik. There was no way to get back to Banks Island now. Those who had decided to stay on the island that summer would have to fend for themselves and live off of the land while the Bankslanders like Fred Carpenter had to make a living trapping in an unfamiliar area.

Generally though, with a lot of money in their pockets, the wintering over in Aklavik was enjoyed, perhaps even over-enjoyed, by Carpenter and his fellow Bankslanders. There was very little trapping done but a lot of money changed hands at the gambling tables, either in Peffer's Hotel or around the deckhouse table aboard North Star. In the spring the entire Delta turned out for ratting or muskrat hunting. Trapping muskrats produced a better quality pelt but many were taken by shooting them which harms the pelt. At the end of the spring the locals had done better than the Bankslanders but even the top ratters pulled in less than five thousand dollars. "Accounts of Delta Life that winter indicate the Bankslanders were spending money rather faster than they were making it. Gambling increased in the Delta during the early 1940's.[...] Some of the Bankslanders had credit in the tens of thousands of dollars, and they were not only in a position to gamble for high stakes but also to purchase large outfits, luxury items and gifts, to stay in the Aklavik Hotel, and generally to flourish their wealth."[34]

The Second World War pumped the economy and creditors increased their stake with the trappers. Between 1942-48 "wartime prosperity was accompanied by greatly enlarged credit extensions and heavy spending. $20,000 outfits were purchased and some men contracted debts of over $10,000. Such well being proved short lived. In 1944, freeze-up occurred while the Bankslanders were en route home, and they had to winter at the Boothe Islands. Most men got 10 or 12 foxes, with even the high man only taking 30. They were thus unable to take advantage of the high fox prices in 1945.[35]

After a long stay at Aklavik the schooners headed back to Banks Island in the fall of 1944. The weather deteriorated quickly and the little ships were out in mountainous waves, the seas so large that they lost sight of one another when they were down in the troughs of the waves. With their rounded hulls for ice survival and negligible keels, the boats rolled their guts out. The shrieking of the wind and the howling of the dogs chained on the foredeck being covered in wave after wave of freezing Arctic waters presented a very grim situation. The Inuvialuit held on for dear life. The children were kept down below, many of them vomiting and miserable. Water sloshed around the bilges, mixing oil and sea water with spilled food and vomit creating a living hell. At the crest of the waves, Fred could see the entrance to calm water in the bay at Booth Island. The convoy followed him in and the rocking of the ship died down as the storm anchor was let go. Everyone needed a break and the Captains knew that they would have to wait for the storm to play out before they made their final leg back to Sachs Harbour. The wind continued all night and drove the scattered ice of the Beaufort Sea right into the harbour, trapping the ships. They were stuck for the winter.

Tensions were running high throughout the fleet. The Inuit do not seek out conflict. They are masters of diplomacy and look for a peaceful way to sort out problems so that there is no loss of face and peace can be restored. One problem that had been brewing was between Fred's second wife, Ada Gruben, and Jim Wolki's wife. While they liked and respected one another, they found it difficult to live together aboard North Star.

One solution was for Jim Wolki to trade off his half-share in North Star. He was interested in one of the smaller schooners, Nanuk II, that Fred's sister, Susie, had inherited when Jim's brother Fred had died. The deal was struck and in 1944 Susie took on half ownership of North Star with her brother.

The forties were tough years for the Bankslanders. Fashion trends were changing and the prices for white fox were not great. During the next few years, prices fell by 75 percent, and the trappers went further and further in debt. Severe ice conditions continued to plague the Bankslanders in most years throughout the 1940's. In the summer of 1946 three of the boats at Sea Otter failed to reach the mainland. The winter of 1946/47 produced the only outstanding fox harvest of the 1942-48 period, but prices were already down to about $13.00. In 1947 the boats had only just returned to Sachs when freeze-up occurred and 25 trappers were forced to winter at that site", rather than working their way around to other harbours on the east and west coast of Banks Island.[36]

The next big year was the winter of 1951/52 when large numbers of fox were taken and after a decade of being indebted to their backers, every Bankslander was able to repay their loans. The next few years remained fairly consistent until a new problem entered life for Bankslanders when large packs of wolves began to decimate the fox population. The wolves not only went after the live fox but destroyed traps and shredded trapped animals rendering the fox fur useless on the trading market. Usher reports that fully 25% of trapped foxes were destroyed by the wolves. The Bankslanders made a pitch to the government who sponsored a wolf poisoning program in 1954/55 that had mixed results. "In the 1940's and 1950's, Banks Island Eskimos all but wiped out the wolf population at the southern end of the island in an effort to protect their arctic fox trap lines from scavenging."[37]

By the mid-fifties Sachs Harbour was seen as being the most reliable place to live and the community that seemed to be doing the best in terms of living conditions and trapping success. By the fall of 1960 the families who had traditionally wintered at De Salis Bay, Sea Otter and Lennie Harbour upped stakes and moved to Sachs Harbour. Cargo planes and barges were now making regular stops at Sachs Harbour and in the summer of 1960 the Fox made her last trading voyage to the Delta. In the fall of 1960 Albert Elias hauled his schooner Fox ashore and she has sat there ever since. In 1978 he and Ted Pedersen's son toured the boat and after only a few minutes of tinkering were able to fire up the old Atlas gasoline engine. Albert continued to maintain the boat until his death. His son, Angus, is now her owner and caretaker.

Ashore at Sachs the villagers began to build permanent wooden homes and sketched out ownership of different trap lines to the satisfaction of all of the trappers.

North Star made her last fur trading voyage in 1961. Clara Gully, Susie Sidney's daughter remembers her mother as being Captain of North Star. "I was born right on that boat, May 23, 1944. Right on North Star. I'm the only child of hers. She recalls that they "have loaded aboard one hundred cases of little mandarin oranges" at Aklavik before heading back out to sea. "That's what everyone lived on when it got rough. My mother never slept. We tied up the Primus stove with rope - even the coffee pot!"

When North Star and the other schooners returned to Sachs each fall there was a rush on to get them hauled out before they froze in. North Star was frozen in at least three times in her career at various harbours, including Sachs. The risk of the ship being crushed or pierced by jagged ice and then sunk was very real and so the whole village would turn to and help haul her out. "Upon arrival in September, the schooners, containing the complete winter's outfits, were unloaded, and winched up on the beach. For their winter dwelling, each family erected a frame tent of lumber and canvas which they had brought with them. These were small, usually 10' x 12' or 12' x 14' and were insulated by a complete covering of moss, then surrounded by ice blocks. Small coal ranges served both cooking and heating requirements. Such a dwelling required about five tons of coal, or perhaps six if used in conjunction with seal blubber. As a ton of coal cost upwards of $200.00 the families naturally tried to conserve their supply as much as possible."[38]

Lena and Susie Tiktalik and Florence Carpenter in front of Susie's tent, Easter Sunday 1959. Note that the tent is insulated with blocks of ice. Photo credit Bob Knight.

Later in this book it is documented how the Canadian government asked Fred Carpenter to return to Banks Island to show Canadian Arctic sovereignty. When the government's representative, LACO Hunt, subsequently visited Sachs Harbour to inspect the community he reported on its development. "Fred filled me in on his adventures. The voyage across to the island in the schooners had been uneventful, except that they had seen several pods of bowhead whales, the species that had almost become extinct until an international treaty strictly forbade killing them.

The little community had plenty of fresh meat - caribou, Arctic hare, seal and bear. Their dogs had never looked better, and there had been no sickness. I brought the mail, including letters from Fred's two sons, Noah and Frank, both going to school in Aklavik. These boys went their separate ways in later life, Noah to become the first Canadian Inuit medical doctor, and Frank to become a pilot.

North Star's rigging was often used for drying pelts.

Half of the families had gone to Storkerson, a hundred miles farther north; on the following day we would visit them. With Fred Carpenter in the co-pilot's seat to point the way, we flew to Storkerson, where we found a level area of hard-packed snow on which to land. There were several igloos, and I followed Mrs Wolkie, (Fred's sister, Susie) into hers, where from under a pile of caribou hides, she fetched out two Wedgewood cups and offered me tea.

This group, which had gone its own way to hunt and trap, was as successful with its fur harvest as was Fred Carpenter's party. Around the cluster of snow houses, there was a bicycle, a sewing machine and assorted toys for the children, looking incongruous at Storkerson Point on Banks Island, latitude 73 degrees North. A huge polar bear pelt was drying on a frame, and there were seals waiting to be stripped of their coats...more here if needed.

Back in Sach's Harbour, Fred Carpenter and I discussed the possibility of turning the camp into a permanent settlement. There were quite a few things Fred wanted, especially better access to Canadian radio, so he could pick up something other than Moscow or Fairbanks on shortwave, or sporadic reception from CHAK. But basically he agreed with me; the experiment had been a success...

I did not return again to Sachs Harbour until the winter of 1969. There was indeed a permanent settlement, an airstrip, a weather station, a community hall and a school - all the amenities that Fred Carpenter and I had spoken about. On that trip I accompanied Ernest Cote, deputy minister of the Department of Indian and Northern Affairs and he was amazed at the way I was greeted by Fred and his family. By then the community received regular broadcasts from the CBC and Sachs Harbour was no longer totally isolated. There was also a regular weekly flight from Inuvik, and Northern Transportation sent over a supply ship each summer from Tuktoyaktuk."[39]

Chapter 13
Fred Carpenter's Leadership

The Inuvialuit have never held formal elections to choose their leaders, though in recent years political positions have been held through standard voting methods. It goes against their philosophy of each member of society working to do their best for all without harming anyone else. "So foreign was the idea of an authority or 'man in charge' in Eskimo communities that there was no word for it in Inuit or Yupik languages. The closest term, in one Canadian Eskimo dialect, means 'a very bossy one' and was used as an insult."[1] As a close knit society with members often related by marriage or birth, they have always tended to watch out for one another. "Nobody ever tells an Eskimo what to do. But some people are smarter than others and can give good advice. They are the leaders. We always try to help each other, that is the best way. Everybody works together, but if you don't do the right things, then people won't help you."[2] Even when Fred Carpenter and Jim Wolki decided to have North Star built they thought that it would be good for all of the Bankslanders to have a large ship capable of helping all of their neighbours transport their winter's catch of furs to market. Certainly North Star was far larger than the other 'schooners' and more than enough boat for one or two families. In later years, as the other 'Arctic schooners' fell into disrepair, it was North Star that continued hauling the Banksland furs.

Without a formal election, certain leaders have always been recognised. Nugalik, Billy Banksland, Thrasher, Pokiak, Gruben and others have been looked to for their level heads, experience and knowledge in different communities over the years. On Banksland this honour and responsibility was placed on Fred Carpenter. "In order to survive in our climate, the people had to have very special and superior hunting skills. The best of our hunters became our leaders. A hunter became a leader only by proving himself over a long period of time."[3] Eskimos were very different from other people, in that they had no chiefs, or leaders, in their bands. There was no government, no council, no voting on what the group should do, or where they should hunt. No one was elected to tell others what they must or must not do. There were unofficial leaders, however. The bravest and most successful hunter in the band was entitled to respect, and was often consulted on matters that related to the group as a whole."[4]

Fred Carpenter profile.

Fred Carpenter once explained where some of his confidence came from. "North Star. A really good boat and I trusted her, but you had to have a good head as Captain. Lots of people, they ask me, ' Fred, you're even better than white people. You got good head, never changing.'

Eddie Gruben is one of the last of a quickly dying breed of fur trappers who like his brother, Charlie, spent decades out on the land, trapping and hunting in order to support his family. He is a no-nonsense man who does not offer false praise for anyone and has little time for those whom he doesn't respect.

He has seen foreigners arrive with their fancy equipment and bravado only to be humbled by the Arctic weather and the rugged lifestyle that life on the land demands. One man whom he called a friend and whom he has undying respect for is Fred Carpenter. Squinting his eyes at a black and white photograph his face lit up."That's Fred. You recognize that guy from anywhere - every time. You see him from the front, from the side, from the back. That's the really smartest Eskimo I ever run into in my life. That guy, he never went to school, not even grade one. But he's smarter than a lot of university educated people. That's the only Eskimo that had money in the bank. That's how he bought the North Star. He bought it for only twenty-five thousand but that was like a million bucks in those days. He never went to school. No education of any kind. He learned from his friends. Everything you learn in life, it comes from your brain. He told me that with effort, nothing is impossible. Use your brain." The Canadian Government's Sub. District Administrator of the Western Arctic, LACO Hunt, described Fred Carpenter in a report to his superior in Ottawa, G.E. B. Sinclair, dated November 16th, 1951. "Fred Carpenter is a Sergeant in the Ranger Corps, an extremely capable mechanic and one of the most intelligent Eskimo in the country."[5]

Fred didn't fit the image of the strong, silent type. He was renowned for his healthy sense of humour and in many interviews over half of his answers to interviewers' questions ended with a long, hearty laugh. He had a great interest in how people were making out, how they were coping with the winter and with their supplies. He recognized that many of his neighbours found it difficult to make it through the nine months of the Banksland winter without their food or trapping supplies running out and so in 1958 he and Agnes started up a small store.

As earlier stated, the business was run mainly on credit. A person could pick up some canned food, traps or fur-stretchers and then pay him in fur or put it on account until they had traded on the mainland during the summer. This service was very much appreciated by his neighbours and they grew to rely upon his store being stocked so that if they started the winter without enough 'white-man's food' to get through until spring, they knew that they would be all right.

Fred was certainly a man with his own mind. He did a lot for a lot of people, setting them up, establishing them. Sometimes, when people had nothing, he would buy them boats, dogs, traps. He had a certain responsible idea about the way that things should be done and as a result had quite a few run-ins with the government, so that they didn't establish themselves in the community. "They (the Government) tried to invite the people of Sachs into Social Assistance. Fred didn't want none of that. If you were from Banksland you had to work", says one of his grandchildren. Fred Carpenter had long been a leader of the Bankslander community. The cabin he built at Sachs Harbour in the 1930s is the oldest building still standing on the island and, as late as

1953, very nearly the only building. In 1958 Carpenter opened the island's first trading post, again at Sach's Harbour, and life was changed forever. Outpost camps at Sea Otter, Lennie Harbour and DeSalis Bay were abandoned and by 1961 everyone lived at Sachs Harbour. Frame houses were built, and Catholic and Anglican missions were opened in 1962. No longer tied to the mainland for trading, people began to live at Sachs Harbour all year round, and schooner traffic came to a rapid end. The Fox made her last voyage in 1960 and the venerable North Star in 1961."[6]

Throughout his life Fred always had time for anyone he met, from child through to senior citizen. Because of his recognized stature, many people recall the thrill that they got from Fred taking an interest in them and encouraging them to be the best that they could be. These inter-generational relationships perhaps explained how Sachs Harbour managed to produce so many people with a strong work ethic, a desire for knowledge and a friendly attitude towards all. Martin Goodliffe was Fred Carpenter's son-in-law and remembers Fred's positive attitude towards everyone. "One thing Fred used to say, no matter what the person was he'd say, 'there's some good in everybody'. No matter what the person was, he could find good in everybody, no matter how screwed up they were - there's always good".

Young people were drawn towards Fred by his friendliness and by the respect that they had for him, since stories of his time out on the trap-line were legendary even to them as they grew up. Old timers recall that you didn't mess with him, but he was friendly. He always wanted to know what was going on. Of course, whenever anyone in the community came back from hunting Fred would be right over wanting to know how he did. Albert Elias grew up on Banksland and remembers how well Fred treated him. "I was 10, 12 years old. Yeah, we used to sit up on top, on top of North Star's pilothouse. Fred Carpenter was my grandfather, not really biological; his sister was my real grandmother, Ivy Raddy. They had the same mother. They were brother and sister. Fred always told me 'never call me Fred, call me Dadak', which means grandfather. Fred Carpenter - he liked to be with the people. He was a great leader. Spoke Inuvialutuk mainly. Just a natural leader, just a go-getter. His motto, he had broken English, he'd say 'ahead of time', he always said 'ahead of time', be prepared. You'd sit up top of the pilothouse, that was like an honour though". Many people recall that when they were children he would let them sit on top of the pilothouse and just be looking out over the ocean. It was a big deal when you got to sit up there with him.

In regard to the Banksland children, Fred once said, "I'm so glad I worked for them for a long time. They say I work for me. I work for them, the kids. I like that kind of life, my life. I'm glad that the kids' lives are good. I'm so glad they will help me and I help them, too. Hee-hee."

Fred Carpenter and son.

The motto 'ahead of time' was something that many interviewers remembered about Fred. While showing no modesty about his abilities or achievements he was always aware of what was going on around him, how he could help someone else and how he needed to be ready for any emergency from keeping his store well stocked, his dogs healthy and well-fed or North Star painted and ready for the season and the hand-crank Atlas engine ready to turn over at a moment's notice. In his book about St. Roch, <u>Plowing the Arctic</u>, G.J. Tranter describes North Star's skipper. "In Fred Carpenter the mixture of the breeds showed itself at its best. The Eskimo-half showing itself in his easy good nature, and his natural skill with machinery; while the other half showed in his foresight and ability to anticipate trouble."[7]

Eddie Gruben remembers sailing aboard North Star with Fred Carpenter and is highly respectful of the manner in which the ship was kept. "I know Fred Carpenter. I know I go on his boat. Holy smokes! When you go to Herschel Island. From here (Tuktoyaktuk), you go to about...depending one week, maybe two weeks maybe to go to Herschel Island. After staying at Herschel Island, come back here to Tuk. Heading for Sachs Harbour now, after. Aye, it's a good ship. I know Fred Carpenter. He's a man that never went to school. Really! But he could speak English. He learned that from the white people in Herschel Island. He learned to speak English. He had a full bredded Eskimo Mom, but a white man dad, I don't know who."

One of Fred's hobbies was photography and film-making and he took great delight in filming life around Sachs, perhaps partly for posterity but mostly for the joy that it brought to those who watched the films. In the pre-tv and internet era he also filmed scenes from life outside whenever he had a chance to travel south. As a wealthy trapper, this was a luxury that not all on the island could enjoy and no doubt the first time many of them had seen a skyscraper, a train or a construction site were when Fred shared his films. Captain Henry Larsen of the R.C.M.P. vessel St. Roch was another of Fred's friends and he spent an Easter weekend with Fred and his family, the highlight of which was watching Fred's home movies.

Nowhere was Fred's leadership shown more than when he was commanding North Star on her annual round-trip to Herschel Island and the mainland. This was where Fred's skills as a sailor and a navigator came into play. His natural skill at reading the weather and navigating are legendary. Using what now are considered the very basic navigational tools of compass, barometer and depth-sounding, Fred was able to safely complete around thirty seasons of travel in the Beaufort Sea. The Arctic Ocean is particularly difficult to navigate because of the amount of variation in the compass readings due to the high magnetic fields. "Scotty Gall, who spent forty-three years in the Hudson's Bay Company's northern service, had learned his navigation in the MacKenzie Delta. 'I knew where all the reefs were; I'd hit every one,' he remembered. 'Some of the Scotsmen who came over were linguists, others studied the Inuit. I was much more interested in finding out how the aboriginals can travel without any navigation aids. I came to believe they have an inherent sense of direction, reading the sun, wind, snowdrifts or the lichen on rocks.'[8] The number of ships that have been wrecked in the Arctic are often attributed to being crushed by the ice, a not uncommon event. Just as many have been taken by vessels driven onto the numerous reefs and shoals that surround the entrances to ports. These hazards coupled with the extreme weather make for a huge navigational challenge. A compass alone cannot be relied upon and the Captain's sense of direction coupled with the effects of tide, current and wind must be razor sharp in order to make safe passage. "Fred Carpenter had developed skills at using the magnetic compass in spite of the magnetic anomalies and wild variations. He seemed to be able to interpret the results and could remember the compass behaviour from previous voyages. He would only go as far as Baillie Island before heading north into the open Arctic Ocean and cross the 100 nautical miles towards Sachs Harbour," recalls Sven Johansson.

He always did this voyage at the end of the navigation season, so that he could take advantage of the Northern dusk. Timing his departure from Baillie Island he could use the glow from the windows in the houses at Sachs Harbour to take a bearing for the final stages of the voyage. He was also capable of taking bearings on the sun and the polar star to make intuitive decisions about the course he should follow. "Eskimos seldom used sea charts. Traditionally, they would never leave sight of land in their travels. To do so was generally considered too risky and the possibility of becoming disoriented and unable to make a landfall too great. "They are good sailors, cautious ones. Before embarking on a cruise the barometer is carefully consulted, hours in advance; and the sky is scanned for the faintest sign of stormy weather. The result is that though their schooners are habitually over-loaded with supplies, dogs and Eskimo acquaintances to whom they are lending a helping hand, one seldom hears of a case where an Eskimo boat has been lost at sea."[9]

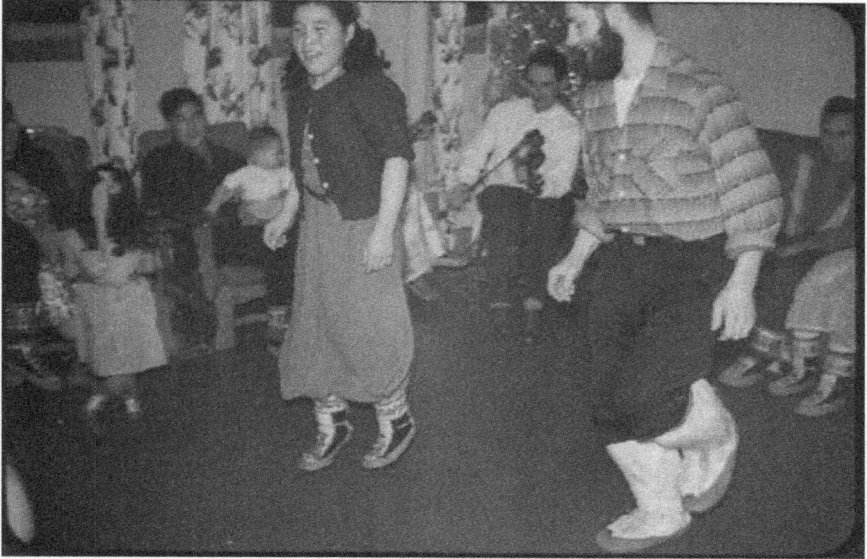

Sachs Christmas 1957. Barbara Carpenter, Geddes Wolki, Leslie Carpenter, Lena Tiktalik, Fred Carpenter on violin, Bill Benedek, RCMP Peter Esau dancing at the D.O.T. Photo credit Bob Knight.

To make a major voyage the Eskimos used the local knowledge gained by individuals in each community who may have visited locales in their region. They would have to take one of these local guides to show them the way to the next destination. These guides knew the configuration of the coast-line and the sailing directions to the other nearby destinations. They also knew about ice behaviour and the local weather signs. Fred Carpenter once proudly said that people had told him that he was "better than the white man. Lots of people tell me, 'you've got a head like a rock.' You got to have a good head to be a Captain. Lots of people tell you, 'Where's the Banksland? Where's the mainland? You can't tell me?(I ask). I know what we're doing. I watch wind, storm, cloud, everything. I know the North Star. I see it at night time. I read all that all my life. You tell me (ask me) something, I tell you. When I start to see the water change colour, and the fog and the wind, the land and the island. I see the water change colour. Blue water - deep water. Things like that I keep in my head."

In the Dictionary of Maritime Heritage Fred's skills are documented. "One exception was Fred Carpenter. Fred, a Bankslander, who was arguably the best Arctic navigator of his day, who had accumulated exceptional knowledge which enabled him to 'eyeball' the passages to islands over the horizon."

Occasionally they were caught in the ice. One time Carpenter was leading a flotilla of seven other schooners when they were caught in an ice-pack. Fred recalls the narrow escape. "I was at Baillie Island, too much ice. I wait and wait. Big ice year. I wait for the right wind, the big wind. After that I could cut out. I go out in the ice. I go about half-way, about eight hours driving through the ice. I get stuck in the ice. I can't go ahead. I can't go back. I can't go other places. Seven schooners follow me." The ice-master Captain Pedersen had taught him that in a case like that he should find a very large piece of ice and shelter the vessel behind it so that the pack ice could not bear directly on it. They were there two weeks eating seal and bear but unable to find a route through the ice. When Fred later recounted the story he said that, "it's a good place for hiding your boat, look for the big heavy ice knolls. I told my Dadak that if I find that, I go there," using the Inuvialuit word for grandfather, Dadak, as a sign of respect for Pedersen.

A natural leader, the others deferred to Carpenter to make the decision on what to do. They would tell him, "Fred, you have a good head ... just like a rock.' But after two weeks the crews of the other boats were anxious to get home. Fred scanned the clouds on the horizon looking for the dark reflection of open water. When he saw some to the east he gave the decision for the other schooners to follow his boat, 'just like mother' back to Sachs Harbour. ""Follow me," I said. "Follow the North Star trail." After seventeen hours of travel they finally saw Cape Kellett and knew they were saved. "Most people start to applause then," said Fred but after the return one woman told him, 'Fred good thing you returned. One more day and I put a bullet in your head!' Fred said, "Go ahead. I'm not scared of a bullet in my head. I think you're quite pleased," (to be safe). Then everyone start to laugh.... but I'm happy no one put a bullet in my head," he added.

Diane Carpenter remembers her father telling her of the same event, "my dad said one time they got stuck, cause it froze up too fast before they got to Sachs. They were stuck in the ice for two weeks. He said everybody was just nervous. The guys on board were afraid not to survive and everyone just wanted to get back to the island. There was the North Star and the Fox. People were getting really anxious by the second week and my Dad said, 'No, we're going to make it, something's going to open.' He was kind of nervous too but you couldn't show that in front of the people, otherwise they would get scared too."

Being able to read the on-coming weather in order to survive storms at sea or to have enough time to make a snowhouse while on the trap-line was a necessary quality of all those Inuvialuit who ran their vessels to the mainland after their trials ashore during the winter. They did not seek out bad weather in order to prove themselves and they would find nothing entertaining about present-day 'adrenalin junkies' risking their lives and sometimes others lives when they are called upon to rescue them, only to have the thrill of being out in bad weather and surviving. It would seem utterly foolish to them. "We (as Canadians) have little talent for excesses of any kind and little patience for anyone who believes that heroism is worth achieving - except by inadvertence. There exists a vague link between heroes and weather, which remains Canada's most essential reality. Our frigid climate reflects the selectivity of how we pick our heroes: many are cold, but few are frozen."[11] "Among Native people there is a very high value placed upon individual self-reliance. Ability to cope with harsh or unexpected circumstances through one's own ingenuity and resourcefulness is a much admired quality. It is particularly apparent in the esteem extended to 'tough travellers' who are able to hunt and trap successfully under unpleasant conditions."[12]

A lonely North Star waits by the shore of the frozen Beaufort Sea for the brief summer.

These Inuvialuit were not only skilled at what they did but were hardened after a life in the outdoors to men and women who faced adversity with humour and togetherness, always looking out for one another. The incongruous marriage of the qualities of caring and ruggedness seems almost a cliché, but their history indicates otherwise. "Whenever an Eskimo hunter killed an animal, the first thing he did was share with others. Anyone who needed food got a share of the meat - women without husbands, other hunters who had not been successful that day. Before the hunter and his family enjoyed a meal, the choicest portions were given away. To be able to share was considered an honour, rather than a duty. The hunter who shared was obviously skilled, and was worthy of the respect of his community."[13] "To cheat nature they had to be tough". E.J. Scotty Gall, a veteran HBC trader, recalled that while building a boat in Tuktoyaktuk, he once saw his Inuk assistant pull nails out of the hardwood planking with his teeth. That story may or may not be true, but Father Frans Van der Velde, the veteran Arctic missionary, reported that an Inuk used his teeth like a third hand."[14] There are numerous accounts of Fred working through his injuries, carrying on as though nothing had happened. Bill Pringle was stationed at Sachs Harbour in the '50's and he shared a photograph of himself with Moses Raddi and Fred Carpenter all sharing a laugh. Fred's arm is bandaged up and Pringle recalls that Fred had dropped by to have a dressing change due to a "freak accident where he got burned. I was doing daily dressing changes and I.M. antibiotics for him."

Bill Pringle, Moses Raddi and Fred Carpenter at the RCMP Station when Fred was having his injury checked.

In 1941 reports were being sent back and forth as to what to do about the Bankslanders and their request for a liquor license. These offer a unique character assessment of Fred Carpenter, Jim Wolki and Susie Sidney. In those days liquor was only sold to First Nations people in restricted quantities. Up until 1940 Eskimos were allowed a liquor permit and could then buy perhaps a year's supply at one time which would have suited the Bankslanders' way of life. Records show that Fred and his first wife, Lucy, as well as Fred and James Wolki all did this on an annual basis. After 1940, Eskimos and 'half-breeds' were switched to the same provision as Indians and became ineligible for permits. Some people switched to making home brew, an art that had been practised for many years - a Northern version of moonshine. If a person was caught making home-brew then their future liquor licences could be cancelled.

A rumour had been picked up that the Bankslanders were making home-brew and Sgt. Henry Larsen responded to this. "From my various conversations with these natives and half-breeds, especially Jim Wolki and Fred Carpenter, who are the acknowledged leaders of the Banks Island community I came to the conclusion that these rumours were started by various people who are envious of the prosperity of the Bankslanders who possess excellent equipment and in good years make exceptionally large catches. This is itself proof that they are industrious and hard working and would have little or no time for brewing or drinking. Quoting both Jim Wolki and Fred Carpenter whom I have personally known for many years - 'We like to have nice things and equipment and lots of good grub for our families and we are not at all interested in drinking, and there will never be any brewing in our houses.' Larsen's memo was replied to by Sgt. Covell in Aklavik in regard to the rumours that he obviously believed. "Although no evidence of brewing was found on the occasion of Sgt Larsen's patrol to Banks Island I would not put too much faith in their protestations that they never make it. Fred Carpenter, Angus Elias and other Banks Islanders have had liquor permits in the past and are always agitating for them now that they are classed as ineligible for them. Therefore there is no doubt that at certain times they get together and have an occasional brew. However they are a good class of native and there is no reason to believe that they make a practice of this or indulge in drunken orgies which might be followed by acts of immorality."[15]

"Life in the Arctic, even now, is hard. In the old days it meant a constant battle and struggle against nature and the elements, fights against animals and sometimes even against human beings. It included a perpetual movement and mobility according to the cycle of nature. Often they encountered tragedies, some remembered and told and others still unknown, buried deep in the ice or below under the sea. Everything in life was met with patience, humility and serenity in defeat, as well as in victory,"[16] wrote Father Lemeur.

In 1966 one of Canada's most widely read authors took one of his many trips to the Canadian Arctic. While in Aklavik he met with one of Fred and Ada Carpenter's daughters, Mary. In his book, High Latitudes, Farley Mowat shares the recording that he made of Mary describing her father. "My dad, Fred Carpenter, was born at Sachs. His father was a white man working for Stefansson who married an Eskimo woman. Dad had three wives - two died on him - and thirteen kids, and he looked after all of us kids real good.

He trapped enough foxes so he could buy a schooner, the North Star, and summertimes the whole family lived aboard her. Dad would freeze her in someplace where he and the older boys could trap white foxes. Sometimes at Baillie Islands near the mainland east of Tuk, sometimes around Banks or Victoria Island.

He set up as a trader at Sachs because there was no trader there. He's kind of a man who works 'til he drops. He's a good man though - a good thinker, too, who hates welfare. He tries to keep the people from Sachs from going on welfare. There's one widow there now taking welfare and she's the only person who is. Dad tries to get people to help each other the way they used to in the old times. He says once they get you on welfare you can say goodbye to your freedom.

I was actually born in the summer of 1946 when the North Star was in there getting supplies to take home to Sachs for the winter. For the next five years I lived free as the wind, just travelling around to wherever Dad thought there's be good trapping. In wintertimes we kids used to ride on the dogsleds, right up on top of the loads, where we could keep a lookout for foxes and polar bears. If we spotted one we got a lot of praise. Summers was mainly at Sachs with a bit of travelling in the schooner to hunt white whales; do a bit of trading; or go hunting caribou, musk ox, whatever you needed."[17]

A responsibility and leadership position that Fred took on that was perhaps different than that faced by others is that when North Star left Sachs Harbour she was often carrying four or five families plus all of their possessions, dogs, sleds and all of the fur that they had taken over the last nine months. If the ship were to be wrecked all, literally, would be lost. Added to that was that North Star was the lead vessel in a flotilla often measuring up to seven boats, each filled as North Star was with families and their possessions. The Bankslanders, as most Inuvialuit did, carried everything with them, as a return trip was not guaranteed and they might find themselves stranded on the mainland or another island for the next season or even for years to come. If a person chose to stay behind on Banksland, he or she might stand ashore and wave good-bye to the fleet not knowing when or if he or she would ever see them again. "North Star. When you sailed it, it wasn't a boat. It was like a community sailing away, you know, because we had everything, you know, we had the dogs on there and everything; we had the people and their food. We had our trade and we had the families and the kids", recalls one of the grandchildren, Les Carpenter.

**Note the amount of gear that North Star is laden
down with for a summer voyage.**

North Star fully laden.

Jumble of gear and docks on North Star's deck as she crosses the Beaufort Sea.

One of Canada's most esteemed historians and writers was Pierre Berton, who met Fred Carpenter and his sister, Susie Sidney, in Aklavik. "I met only one native on the Delta who lived like a white man. His name was Fred Carpenter, and it was a paradox that this Eskimo with the English name should be the wealthiest man in Aklavik at a time when most of his fellows were facing privation. I walked down to the waterfront one afternoon to visit him, and an odd experience it was. Carpenter is another Canadian Eskimo who wears the Queen's Coronation Medal. There his resemblance to Idlouk (another medal recipient) of Baffin Island ends. He greeted me from the deck of his twenty-eight thousand dollar schooner, which is more like a yacht. His sister, in a bright print dress, was doing the family washing in a new gasoline-powered machine. (His wife was in the hospital suffering from TB).

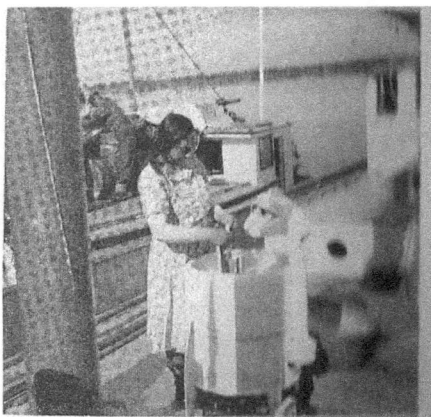

Susie Sidney using washing machine on North Star's deck.

His children ran about, dressed in neat little suits. Carpenter, a long-nosed, freckled-faced man in a new plaid shirt and pressed slacks, looked about as much as the traditional grinning, parka-clad Eskimo as Anthony Eden. We sat on the antiseptic deck and discussed basic economics. Carpenter's father was a white whaler, but he himself was brought up without schooling in a snow house and a skin tent. Now besides his other assets, which were impressive, he had fifteen thousand dollars in the bank and was perhaps the world's richest Eskimo. He lives on Banks Island, a storied rectangle of tundra rising out of the ocean to the northeast of the Delta and prominent in the journals of the early explorers. Here he is the nearest thing to a king, in the old-fashioned sense that remains. 'I got another washing machine just like this one up there, and a sewing machine too, of course, and I got three radios altogether, one here in the cabin, one on Banks, and another at my place on Tuk,' he said in a flat, matter-of-fact, almost sheepish voice. On his Arctic desert island the king had erected a palace, lit by electricity, laid with linoleum, and furnished with chesterfield suites bought by mail order. His children do not eat raw seal meat; they have cornflakes for breakfast. His two eldest sons are each worth ten thousand dollars. The king wanted to buy an airplane for one of them and make a pilot of him, but discovered to his chagrin that the boy did not have the necessary qualifications.

Schooners at Aklavik, 1941.

The collapse of the fur market hit Fred Carpenter, the provident Eskimo, as it hit everybody. But he is a man who saves his money or reinvests it into equipment. He earns an income from his boat and sells his furs for top prices at outside auctions. When white foxes sold at forty dollars a pelt, Carpenter brought in nine hundred of them in a single year."[18]

Fred's ingenuity and wealth allowed he and his family to move into modern times faster than others around him. He was way ahead of his time in many ways. He harnessed the wind through a small windmill that he built which charged batteries so that he and his family always had a ready supply of electricity. Carpenter was always trying to improve the quality of life for himself and for his children. He made sure that everyone lived in strong wood frame houses and that they had electricity. The RCMP detachment at Sachs Harbour was still using candles and kerosene lanterns while next door Agnes and Fred had electricity and many modern conveniences like an electric stove. In the 1950's he recognized the value of green power and built a windmill to charge six volt batteries that provided some luxury for them. Agnes Carpenter smiles when she recalls, "even where we were living we had a windmill of our own with wet batteries. We always had electricity - even before the RCMP had it. They didn't like it, that we had it and they didn't."

When North Star returned from her summer voyage it was a big occasion at Sachs Harbour. All worries were cast aside and those who had stayed ashore turned out to get news from the mainland, collect mail and to see what the furs had been traded for. Some of the trappers who had sent their fur with North Star only found out upon her return whether they had turned a profit and whether their orders for a winter outfit had been able to be filled. "Yeah, and when she rolled back in there was a big cheer from the community. Sachs Harbour, Banks Island, Fred Carpenter and the North Star were all synonymous, you know, one and the same. The Carpenter family - it's just one big identity. When you travel, if people hear you are from Sachs Harbour, Banks Island, they'll ask you about the Carpenters or some people will know about the North Star. It's something that those of us, some of us now, mainly my family, we've always been proud of that. Try to do good and be the best that we can be in whatever because that's the way it was. First and foremost, you were taught that you were a Carpenter. There's no coming in second", proudly states Les Carpenter, one of Fred's grandchildren.

Families, including the Pokiaks waiting aboard North Star for voyage to Delta. Note the flowers on the window sill.

Leadership might be something that a person is born with, but in many cases it is something that is learned by watching others. This is the Inuvialuit way. "Fred – he was a stately man. You know – somebody special. When he walked into a room he had an aura about him. He commanded respect. "He was a wise man. A hard man. He was a real worker. If he got cold he would just keep going." People who ask questions rather than observing are considered rude. In this culture it is better to watch an elder and learn their ways by doing than just asking for a quick answer. "Because the world around them could not be changed and had always been the same, old customs were followed and old people's wisdom was not challenged. It was bad manners to ask many questions, to try to change people. People learned by doing things and by observing, for there were no books. They knew a great deal about wild creatures, the weather, and all the things which today we call geography, zoology, and other names."[19]

Captain Fred Carpenter aboard North Star.

One of Fred's daughters, Margaret Hawkins, recalls a story about her quiet, observant father. "Tom Butters used to edit The Drum, the Northern newspaper, out of Inuvik. He knew Fred well. Fred used to go to all of the town meetings and sit in the back, never saying anything. One time the editor asked Fred why he didn't step in when they were having these debates with all of these young people arguing and Fred answered "because nobody asked my opinion". He also said that,"yes he did know the answers", but he wanted the young people to grow up and take responsibility and learn leadership."

Chapter 14
Storms/Sinkings/Ice/Tows

And through the drifts the snowy clifts
Dis send a dismal sheen
Nor shapes of men nor beasts we ken-
The ice was all between

The ice was here, the ice was there,
The ice was all around:
It crack'd and growl'd, and roared and howl'd,
Like noises in a swound!

by Coleridge

The Inuit and Inuvialuit certainly faced their fair share of storms, ice and bad weather, sometimes even ending in shipwreck. Their vessels were small, though, compared with some of the large trading and exploration ships that came from far away. When one of these ended up sinking, the Inuit saw this as a windfall for themselves. If they arrived in time they would help with safeguarding the cargo and making sure that all aboard got off safely but after that the broken ship became a gold mine of material; wood for building ashore or for sleds, metal fastenings, copper from the ship's bottom for ulus, cordage for dogs harnesses etc. A shipwreck that washed ashore would be visited again and again until there was nothing left of her. "To the Inuit, of course, a wrecked ship or one abandoned in the ice floes was a gift from the gods. Here was wood for their sledges, tools and handles, here were nails to be used in making harpoons, knives and needles. The most trifling bit of material is a treasure in this forsaken country where no tree grows. And in addition to this booty when a ship was wrecked, the Inuit had a good laugh at the white man, those clumsy Big Eyebrows who imagined they could fight the sea and the ice, and "for what, I ask you?"[1]

When Investigator was abandoned off of Banks Island after becoming trapped in the ice, Inuit travelled hundreds of miles to strip her of her riches before the ice finished its deadly business by crushing and sinking her. Anthropologists studying the people and their reliance on musk-ox discovered at the North end of Banks Island almost 600 muskox skulls, dozens of food caches and the evidence of tent rings. This was peculiar to them since musk-oxen and people had all disappeared from Banks Island by 1850 and muskox were not seen again there until 1952. Struzik, in his 2009 book, The Big Thaw, writes, "An alternative theory suggests the presence of an abandoned ship, Investigator, which had been used to search for the lost Franklin expedition (1850-53), attracted so many Inuit to the north end of Banks Island that they eventually depleted the muskoxen population." [2] (There are now over 64,000 muskox on the island and the local joke amongst hunting guides is that a rare trip is one where no muskox are seen. In the sixties, Fred Carpenter was encouraging a new market for musk-ox wool. "Combing the fine fur inside the hair. Some people want to buy it. One pound get two or three hundred dollars). Getting back to scavenging, roughly one hundred years later, in 1949, the Royal Canadian Air Force lost a plane near Bellot Strait whose metal was stripped off by the local Inuit who used it primarily for sheathing the hulls of their boats for use as ice protection, including Kavavouk's little schooner, Seal.

The Arctic Ocean and in particular the Beaufort Sea where North Star was operating is notorious for its severe and rapidly changing weather. Storms spring up fast and the strong winds, coupled with the relatively shallow water produces large, standing waves very quickly. Added to this mix are the icebergs, floes and the small refrigerator sized ice pieces called 'bergy bits'. The Beaufort Sea shoals quickly and there are many outlying reefs. The challenge becomes even greater with the pea-soup fog that is often part of the mix.

Fred Carpenter was known for his great seamanship and navigation skills. A contemporary of his was Billy Thrasher who was Captain of another Kneass-built ship, Our Lady of Lourdes. As an experienced Captain, Thrasher had a healthy respect for the Beaufort Sea and was not against calling upon a Higher Power to help him through the worst of the weather. "I used to hear him, my dad Billy Thrasher, on ship when he says his prayers. When it get really rough on ships he would say his prayer because sometimes its big waves; it's got too rough even to land. We just stayed in one place. He just closed his eyes, still praying. And I remember his Hail Mary, he would say it real loud. Sometimes my grandfather would say Lord's Prayer in Inuit and Hail Mary. This one here (rosary) is very old and this one beside is new. It's broken. You know why? It's because I carry it in my pocket."[3]

Families waiting to sail aboard North Star.

Billy Thrasher.

"Another experience awaited the Lady of Lourdes in the summer of 1947. Pedersen had told the Bishop that she wouldn't ever be crushed by the icepack, but if anything, the ice would lift her up. She didn't share the fate of so many ships travelling in the Arctic being crushed by the ice as the Fort James and the Lady Richardson, which were wrecked and pushed to the bottom by the violence of the ice pack. 1947 was a very bad year for navigation. Too much ice: old ice, glacier ice, moved all over the ocean. From Paulatuk, on August 8th, she proceeded east, looking for leads on her way to Holman Island. But wind, turning to a gale, and snow flurries etc... limited the visibility, and the only thing that could be seen was ice and more ice, travelling fast. There wasn't any more question about maintaining a course. The only thing then was to remain afloat and avoid the impact of the huge pans of ice. Suddenly, the look-out sighted a lake on the ice floe, and full speed we entered in, and there as a duck we turned and turned until the ice pack closed in and lifted the schooner out of the water and piled up underneath and all around the hull. Fortunately and miraculously nothing seemed to have been broken. The only inconvenience was that they were prisoners of the ice and travelled at its caprice and whims..now easterly, then westerly.. and they couldn't do anything about it."[4] Aboard the "mission schooner, the thirty-five ton Our Lady of Lourdes, had often been caught in the ice, and even on occasion given up for lost". Roger Buliard was aboard Our Lady of Lourdes during that voyage.

Our Lady of Lourdes meeting up with Margaret A in ice clogged waters.

He wrote in his diary that," we were scarcely underway when a tornado of wind and snow burst upon us, a fifty-mile-an-hour gale, with which we are obliged to travel. For ten hours we give up trying to maintain our course and merely try to remain afloat, while the sea treats us like a bit of straw. 'Our Lady' leaps from the crest of one wave to the next, and rises to a frightening height before smashing down into the next swell. Then the real worries begin. Huge pans of ice dance madly in the waves, threatening our hull. Striking one, at our speed, would smash the hull to splinters. Then, as we safely pass the ice pans, the lookout cries from the crow's-nest: 'Ice! Solid ice ahead!' There is no open water, no 'lead'. We bear down upon the long white line, approaching the ice barrier at terrific speed, and it seems certain that we will be smashed to bits. Just then, beyond the barrier, we see a sort of a lake, closed off at the entrance by a narrow bar of ice. We prepare for the impact. But a great wave lifts the ship, and her keel grates on the ice as she clears the mouth of the lake. We are safe again for the moment. .....Before the engines can be stopped, a tremendous shock rocks the vessel, cracking her planks and raising her above the water. Jagged shards of ice appear, higher than the deck, then we fall back with a noise like a giant bridge collapsing. The ice closes in on the ship, embracing her.....we wonder how long the ship can endure the pounding."[5] In 1944, from the RC Schooner "Our Lady of Lourdes", Buliard continues, "we saw the Olga go down off Tuktuk, in a raging storm. We stood by, but there was nothing we could do, for the waves were already sweeping the ship's deck and tearing her apart." "In 1945 a little trading schooner sank with her captain and nine Eskimos. A few days later, on a crossing to Bank's Island, the "Beluga" foundered." "In 1947 three schooners bound for King's Bay met with bad luck. One, the Lady Richardson, went down in a storm. Another, the Krochik, was tossed ashore like a log and smashed. The third, the Blue Fox, made it, but her smashed bow and waterlogged cargo told the story of her trip."[6]

Joey Carpenter remembers his father telling him of the sinking of Beluga. "North Star was making the crossing with Beluga. Beluga began to take on water and the caulking was not holding. Dad circled around and went up next to Beluga. All the people came over and all the fur and all of the dogs and everything. Dad started to tow Beluga but she was taking on more water and sinking. He tried to get her into shallow water but the (tow)line kept getting tighter. The line broke and she went down."

Other accidents at sea were caused by simple human error. Fred Inglangasuk recalls "my granddad (Isaac Alunik) bought a boat from Qiqtaqruk - from Ole Andreasen, I guess. They bought one and they used it. Alunik had an accident with the boat called Kaligraq. "He started to fix the tank on the boat. He heated first the gas tank, then it explode on his head. That is how he had an accident with it. They never touch again since that time. He was working on his gas boat tank and tried to heat it up with a blow torch or something like that. A gas tank and then it got hot. Anyway, it blew up. The whole tank went to his head and split his head in half. He was alive for a short time and then he died."[7]

Johny 'One-Arm' Togluk earned his unfortunate nick-name while travelling by schooner in the early thirties. While lowering the anchor his arm became entangled in the rode and he went by the board. The weight of the anchor pulled him down to the seabed. His shipmates immediately hauled on the rode and dragged him up the ship's side to the capping rail (or a'cock'a'bill for the sailors) with the anchor but in doing so his arm was crushed and later had to be amputated.

George Burnham was in the employ of the Hudson's Bay Company in the early thirties. One of his team's jobs was to build the first HBC post at Tuktoyaktuk in 1935. He often sailed aboard the HBC schooner, Sea Otter, up to Banks Island and then to Coronation Gulf. On one of these trips, with Sea Otter as laden with trade goods as any Banksland schooner they met some typical Beaufort seas. Not a storm but a very uncomfortable ride during which they lost overboard some large timbers to have been used in constructing trading posts, an iron stove and a case of oil. These things would have been lashed down but their loss was considered business as usual for travelling by sea in this part of the world.

Margaret Hawkins was out on North Star with her family when a storm brewed up. "I remember one time we were out in a big storm. It was terrible, with the ice all around and the waves crashing on deck. It went on for days. My mother was very angry and upset and she and my father got into a big argument. "I want off this boat right now", she was yelling. "It's either me or this boat!" With that, she pulled off her wedding ring and threw it into the engine bilge. All of us kids were watching this and wondering what would happen. The next morning it was calm and my parent's were laughing again. They were just like that. My parents spent hours looking for that ring but never did find it."

When Margaret first related this story to me, I began a copious search of North Star's large bilge. For years I would spend a little extra time sifting through it after doing the regular engine maintenance. My hope was that I could find and return the ring to Margaret in memory of her mother, Ada. When I was speaking with Margaret and her husband Lyle Hawkins about this book, I mentioned the ring. Margaret looked surprised and then said that she thought that actually the next morning her parents had found the ring where it had landed, hanging on a bolt on top of the engine. Out of habit and hope I keep watching for that ring, but I am sure that Fred and Ada are watching down on North Star and having a good chuckle over my futile search!

Fred Carpenter recalls that, "I was never scared in bad weather. You slant the boat - you controlling everything. My engine, sailing, same thing. Sometime when steering the boat through rough weather, make it through. Take the sail down. I learned from Fred Wolki at the beginning."

Sarah Meyook, who was born in 1925, recounts her memory of travelling in the icy Beaufort Sea. "As we travelled with a boat named Nibiluktarak, there was lots of us when we left from here. I had told them, 'How are we going to travel in icy ocean?' My aunt and Meyook said if we reached where there is no ice then we could make it to Delta then. We had trouble with our engine on our boat then. They were working on it. There was lots of us. Also we were short of water and we had anchored too. And there was young ice on ocean water now."[8] "I was afraid of the wind and the huge waves. I was afraid for Margaret and the children. We had the nine of them with us, as well as Agnes, our granddaughter. That made ten children in all. David Andreasen and his wife were on board also."[9]

One of the Oblate priests, Father Dehurtevent, recalls how the Mason River was named. "Mason River, they used to call it Kuugiaksuk. They call it from Stanley Mason: he was foreman on reindeer herd at...they had a herd of reindeer around Stanton and then Stanley Mason was the foreman. Charlie Rufus was the owner of the herd but Stanley Mason was the foreman. Then all of them drowned. They went to...they had a boat...a schooner and they used to go every summer to Aklavik to get a new supply for winter. And so they went there and coming back, they had been caught by a storm and not far from Cape Dalhousie, not far from there and they drowned. They knew they couldn't go farther so they tried to go ashore and at least, to save their lives but they could not make it. The boat was touching bottom and then the waves, it was shallow so the boat broke anyways, broke to pieces and then everybody drowned not far from Baillie Island and then Cape Dalhousie, little bit west. In between Cape Dalhousie and Baillie Island there is Husky Lake there and then they go deep inland those Husky Lake close to Tuk. So they drowned not far..not too far from Stanton. Kuugiaksak; kuug means river but I think when Stanley Mason died, they called that name, that river, by his name."[10] "Inuvialuit people tell a similar story where Charlie Rufus and his family (except Peter) drowned in a storm while crossing to Baillie Island."[11]

Because the crossing between Banks Island, Herschel Island and the mainland was so dangerous, the boats almost always travelled in convoy. If one of the boats got into trouble the others would try and get close enough to lend a hand. Nuligak aboard Bonnie Belle recalls one time when he and his crew were able to rescue the legendary Captain Pedersen. "Long before we got there, we could see the Belvedere from far off. She was held on all sides by icebergs, about a mile and a half from the coast, far from any natural shelter. The ship was crowded with people - there were members of two crews aboard, for Captain Pederson had abandoned his two-masted schooner the Elvira, cast ashore by the ice. Unloading their provisions, he and his men had taken refuge aboard the other ship."[12] Fred Carpenter adds that as North Star was the largest schooner that he would often end up towing the other boats. "Them boats, sometimes I towed behind for twenty-two, twenty-three hours. We go eight miles an hour steady. That boat good for sea, big wind, good for everything."

As the largest of the Banksland fleet and with Fred Carpenter or occasionally in the first few years, Jim Wolki as Captain, North Star would always lead the other 'schooners' between ports. Eddie Gruben recalls, "There were four or five other schooners. They would follow Fred. One time they left Baillie Island early in the morning and when they got halfway across to Banks Island, maybe another hundred miles, maybe more, Fred Carpenter was in the lead and it was nice calm and we had another hundred miles or so to go to Sachs Harbour from where they were. Baillie Island was the last stop. It's about 150 miles maybe, from Banks Island. One morning when we got up there, we was about halfways, another boat leaking. We pull up the boat beside him. Hollering at Fred, "Okay, the islands right here go crossing from Baillie Island." Big black clouds coming on the west side! So Fred Carpenter he head this way on the right side of Banks Island. Just when we got there - Holy Man! a big storm! Fred turned around to the right side of Banks Island. He seen the black cloud coming from the western side. If he didn't turn and go on the east side of Banks Island they would have got into big storm. Would have run into it, but Fred, he read the clouds, you know. Shoot. But that's why he went to east side to a harbour there. Storm came, man. From the west there. If he went on the side to Sachs Harbour we would be hit. If we went that way we would have been caught in the gale, in the big west wind storm right there. But he went over to ...Desallis Bay, they call it. So he went there and waited and then went to Sachs Harbour." Eddie Gruben continues his praise for North Star and Fred Carpenter's seamanship, "That's a solid boat, that one. All the Eskimos, they follow that boat when they go from Banks Island to come to the mainland here and from her to Aklavik and from Aklavik they go to Herschel Island and back to Tuk and from Tuk back to Baillie Island back across to Sachs Harbour. He's really smart that Fred Carpenter. Everybody listen to him. Everybody look up to him."

An early government guide to preparing for making a passage by schooner in the Beaufort Sea makes the strong suggestion that "a schooner not less than forty feet in length, heavily timbered and, preferably sheeted with metal or iron bark, should be used. Anchors of a greater weight than would normally be used for the tonnage of the boat, together with ample lengths of anchor chains, should be provided, as much of the coast is but poor holding ground with little or no shelter. Spare anchors should be carried as experience has taught that during a season's operation, when ice conditions are even normal, one or more anchors will have to be sacrificed. During almost any season a trip along the length of the northern coastline will necessitate the riding out of at least one blow. As the harbours are few and far between it is unsafe to count on running to shelter when the blow comes up." The missive then describes the necessity for gear aboard including at least 1,000 feet of warping cordage as well as copper nails, lead patches and engine spares.

Reindeer underway. Note hunter with rifle atop pilothouse.
Photo taken from aboard North Star by Fred Carpenter.

A true sailor could be defined as one who is totally self-sufficient while at sea and this is also a trait of the Inuit who many explorers noted were able to fix things on the go, to rely upon their own natural mechanical skills to get themselves out of tight situations. Persis Gruben recalls being in that type of situation one year on DeSalis Bay with the schooner, Reindeer. They had spent a wonderful summer hunting, fishing and collecting berries and were anticipating leaving with the thaw towards the middle of July to head over to the mainland to sell their winter's cache of fur. Their mechanic had decided to overhaul the engine and had dismantled it entirely before leaving to go hunting. With no sign of him returning anytime soon, Persis and Charlie were effectively stranded and knew that they would have to rely upon their own resources in order to leave DeSalis before freeze-up. "We found ourselves in a precarious and dire situation. We came to DeSalis Bay aboard the Reindeer, the Lennie's schooner, but now in summer the snow all thawed and the ice pack began to move away. It looked as if we would be stranded there at DeSalis Bay. To our dismay and disappointment, we realized that although the schooner was in good condition and in need of only common, usual repairs, it was not so for the motor. It was all in pieces there in the engine room, and the cargo room, all scattered. Sam was our engineer and mechanic. He wanted to overhaul the engine and had left without finishing the job, thinking maybe to be back in time before sailing time. However, there we were with a boat and no engine to propel it. Sure the schooner was rigged with a sail, but only one jib. For us to cross from Banks Island to Tuktoyaktuk and the mainland, that was not safe enough. To picture, describe or even write down our dismay and dejection, words wouldn't be recommended, and to state that we didn't know much about the engine would be understating our ignorance. Oh sure, Charlie knew enough to start it, run it and do minor repairs, but to practically rebuild it was another matter, and at first seemed to be out of the question and surpassing our power and resourcefulness. The least we could say then was to express our resentment and discomfort in words not to be printed or broadcasted."[13] They moved the ship to a small cove and set up camp. "Our work detail was set and our days occupied in cleaning the schooner, refitting ropes, and getting everything ship shape for the crossing. However, work would be abandoned whenever our meat supplies ran low. Then Charlie and John left camp for hunting."[14] "In those days time was not wasted."[15] Persis got set up in the engine room with the manual and schematic diagrams. Persis would read each section and then translate it into Inuvialutuk for Charlie and then the two of them would work as a team to try and re-build the motor. "From the engine manual and from the schematic, we struggled to identify the parts, and many there were. Once identified, he put them together, a slow job indeed, as I first read the manual trying to understand the mechanical jargon and translated it to Charlie. How many hours and days we spent at that job. Whenever I felt tired and thought that I had had enough, Helen would replace me. So back at the manual, reading, decoding, studying words and schematic and unravelling the mysteries behind the words to Charlie in the Inuit language."[16]

The job proved to be too difficult and they were very aware that with each passing day they were running the risk of the ocean freezing over, leaving them without their ability to secure their much needed supplies for the coming winter. On top of that, their own food supply was continually running low and so they had to take breaks of days at a time in order to go hunting. They finally gave up and headed out on an eighty mile trip by land to get help. When they finally arrived back at Sachs Harbour they met up with the crew of the RCMP schooner Jennings who were dealing with their own crisis. Their winter supplies had been off-loaded to shore, the previous day just as a storm had hit. All of their food, fuel and supplies for the coming winter were scattered all over the beach and they were hurriedly trying to save as much as they could.

Persis and Charlie lent a hand and the Jenning later delivered them back to DeSallis Bay where the RCMP helped in getting the motor back together. "After several unsuccessful trials, finally our efforts were rewarded, and how sweet to our ears sounded the humming of the engine. It sounded good enough, although perhaps running slower than usual, but this would have to do, even though we were not too fussy about it."[17]Using their self-sufficiency and ingenuity Helen and Persis made a new suit of sails for the Reindeer using the canvas from their tent for the sail. For lines, ropes and standing rigging they used uhhiuk or walrus intestines, braiding the innards into strong cordage. The engine was not running very healthily and they knew that once at sea they might need to rely upon their sails.

By this time the foursome and their children were again almost out of food. They sailed out of the harbour, bound for Nelson Head and Sachs Harbour. Charlie wanted to make up for lost time and head straight for the mainland as originally planned in order to trade their fur, but Persis insisted that they return to the safety of Sachs Harbour. Persis recalls, "My husband said 'I'm going to set sails and we'll go straight across or we won't have enough fuel.'"[18] As mentioned, it was unusual for the schooners to travel alone and now that the season was well underway they both knew that the other vessels were already over at Aklavik trading their fur. Their argument continued as they motored slowly out into the icy sea. The Reindeer began to rock violently as the rollers beat down upon them and Persis went down below to stay with their children and try and get some rest after all of their work in getting underway. "I was glad to lay down if only for a moment and forget anxieties, as long as the rolling and pitching of the schooner, the creaking and groaning of the timber, amid roaring swirl of wind and waves would permit."[19] "It was anxious work with the schooner tearing and plunging over the waves, before a cold wind. He (Charlie) was entirely soaked with water, seal oil and fuel. The waves didn't give time for rest or shelter as they dashed over the deck and chilled him. This deluge of water emptied the seal oil barrels and the mixture soaked him anew. In the galley, although protected from the wind and water, "we didn't fare too well either. The children and I laid heavily and listlessly on the bunk, feeling all the impact of the bow against the waves. My only vision consisted of water rushing, dark water and foam. The only sound covering the motor, the whirling wind in the rigging, the pounding of the treacherous waves loud and angry. Then something happened to break the monotony and dispel the fear that gripped us. Charlie saw something among the waves and whitecaps, something even more white, swimming beautifully and not at all hindered by wind and waves - three polar bears swimming in their element for land. He asked Willie to take his place and spell him for a little while. Charlie took aim and killed the three bears. "My husband shot three polar bears, he said to me to hold the stern wheel of the schooner while he skinned part of the hind quarter of a bear to slice meat from the ham. He said to cook it but there was a strong wind and waves. He lit the Primus stove and I was holding pot all the time while the meat was cooking. He had sliced very thin pieces and after they were cooked, I fed my children who hadn't eaten for quite some time.

We were still travelling very slow. It was like if we were drifting. By now it got so rough you could see waves by the porthole windows. The dogs were tied on the deck, scared and howling. When the schooner would roll, the water would come in by the side that was open on cockpit that we used as bedrooms and kitchen. The water was mixed with oil from engine splashing and the fox skins that are hanging. But there were waves, wind and snow! The drift made it worse as it was dark."[20]

Soon after the hunt, Charlie resumed steering and swung the schooner a little bit and it was at this precise time that the rudder didn't answer or respond to any command. They were at the mercy of the wind and waves, rolling and rocking heavily. "The rollers heaved the schooner, she slid down the incline and then leaped and bounced with the waves from one to another, while Charlie worked fast to fix cables and pulleys. At each new wave, from the crest I could survey the bluffs, cliffs looming ahead of us, menacing and threatening, coming closer and closer. Charlie slowly turned once more the schooner into the wind and put more distance between us and the shore. We began to breathe freely again, it had been a close call indeed."[21] "Water seemed unreal, splashing all over the deck and dripping through all the holes and cracks, spoiling everything in the schooner, including our fur catch. Our winter catch of white foxes looked like coloured foxes, smeared with fuel and seal oil. What a sight and what a waste of time last spring."[22] After many more hours grinding their way through the waves, past the rocks along the shore they were finally able to turn and enter Sachs Harbour. Then the engine died. After many tense minutes and with shipwreck still a possibility after all that they had been through they got the motor running and made it to shore.

At this point Reindeer had delivered them safely but the boat and her crew were a mess, completely covered in thick oil and dirt. Charlie: "Myself, I was soaked from head to toe from ugyuk (bearded seal) oil that had been stored in 45 gallons of oil. There wasn't anymore oil, it was mixed with water. The engine quitted on us after we came in. Somehow, we finally started the engine once again. We arrived about four in the morning. I had about 1,000 fox skins and 17 polar bear skins. They are good for nothing when you have nothing to eat. We had lots of money on boat but you can't spend it. It's no good for nothing."[23]

With no money and all of their trapped fur seemingly ruined the Reindeer crew's spirits were at a low ebb. A mechanic from the Department of Transport visited the boat and was able to fix the engine. As a bonus he agreed to buy the three polar bear skins that they had taken on their wild ride to Sachs Harbour. Then Timothy Lennie agreed to join up with them to help get them to the mainland. Their problems seemed to be coming to an end until they tried to start the engine. The battery was completely run down and there was no spare or way of re-charging it. Using Inuit ingenuity again, Persis suggested using the 12 volt motor from her electric sewing machine to jury-rig the starter. Initially her suggestion was laughed down by the others. The thought of a small sewing machine motor being able to turn over a schooner's heavy engine seemed ridiculous. With nothing to lose they rigged it up and the Reindeer was back to life.

"Somewhere near Atkinson Point we sighted two schooners and as they came closer we identified them as the North Star and the Fox, belonging to Fred Carpenter and Angus Elias. As they were on their way to Banksland and Sachs Harbour, Timothy left us and joined them, he wished to spend another winter at Sachs Harbour. After saying goodbye, we proceeded again to Tuktoyaktuk."[24]

The spring's adventures and the recent storm had made a big decision for Charlie and Persis. Their days of living on the edge and of living an isolated existence had come to an end. Once in the harbour and ashore on the mainland, the welcome of the land to the men of the sea was warm and generous. We had decided to call it the end and resolved not to return to Banks Island, nor the surroundings."[25] "We arrived to Tuk and never left again. We had enough harsh life and never again we travelled to Banksland. Every trip we made with the Reindeer something always happened. Sometimes the North Star was there for a helping hand when the engine would break down. Since then we never went back. This was the fall of 1954-55" says Charlie."[26]

Hope Gordon remembers a storm that they battled in their schooner until they were finally able to get an anchor down to ride it out. "About in front of the Blow River, we reached the frozen ice. It was really lots of frozen once that we reached. Around there we anchored with a big north wind like that. Then when got slushed in, but we were glad to be anchored. Then the anchor busted! The anchor rope busted and it was made out of iron. And they hard to buy all right, eh? It just busted and let us have an accident." Hope recalls "it got dark on us then and it got north wind storm too. Right then we stayed there for awhile and then the ice broke the anchor line. It was good it did happen because the boat will be gone then because of the ice rubbing on it. Then we finally made it to Running River. All of us went ashore. After everything was out of the boat, the boat sank. All this time the bottom of it was almost breaking because of the ice in the ocean. We were all sick then."[27]

On one voyage, perhaps the '61 trip, North Star got lost in the fog and huge winds. Clara Gully was sixteen years old and remembers that rough passage. "It was everybody's last trip. I know that Fred Carpenter, (Clara's Uncle), was piloting. Andy and Frank Carpenter were on board. We had left Baillie Island, maybe three hours. Big strong wind came up. Big waves. We couldn't go back to Baillie because it was too rough and too dark. Fred Carpenter and Timothy Lennie said that 'we might as well stay close to shore. Maybe the weather will get better.' That night the storm got bigger. We were in sixty foot waves. The dogs were all chained on deck and howling. Some were washed overboard, hanging there. Frozen solid. The front of the boat started to crack. It was splitting from the weather. The boat started splitting! They were looking at it trying to figure out how to fix it. They started spilling fuel oil or gasoline to make the water smoother. Five or six guys got on the front to keep the boat from sinking. They had chains and things to hold it together. We were in that sea for five days. They said 'North Star is a goner." The winds and the currents took the ship far west and when land came into sight they were off the Russian coast. Clara Gully continues, "We just turned and followed the coast all the way back to Sach's Harbour. Everyone was so hungry. We hadn't eaten for days. We put the lifeboat ashore and got forty or fifty ptarmigan and my mom (Susie Sidney) made a big pot of ptarmigan soup. She was cook in the North Star and the pilot, then. She sailed that boat. She knew the way. Almost all of our dogs were lost that trip - just washed away. It's awful when you have to travel under the water! There were pointed waves. The waves were piling up and hitting the whitecaps on the next wave but my mom could manage that boat anywhere. That time when we were sailing, the boat kept filling up from the bottom. Everyone was seasick. We were pumping and pumping and pumping." When we made it back to Sachs Harbour my mom said she was going to sell the boat. She didn't want it no more." It was during this storm that the huge gyro-compass that had been firmly bolted to the top of the deckhouse was ripped off by a wave and lost into the Beaufort Sea. The compass was mounted ten feet off of the waterline which lends some perspective to the size of the seas that they were in.

John Bockstoce is an Arctic historian and adventurer based in the United States. In 1973 he was attempting a NorthWest Passage with an Inuit crew in a traditional umiak - a large open boat made from walrus skin - when they were hit by a storm. While running for shelter in the face of a gale past Warren Point, Bockstoce was worried for the safety of his umiak and his crew. After dragging their vessel ashore and making camp behind it they turned their attention to the inlet. "We had noticed a fifty-seven foot schooner at anchor in the little cove - the first vessel we had seen all summer. She was now bucking hard, with two anchors out on heavy chain. The next day, the wind had died somewhat. The barrier bar was visible again, and inside her the schooner was now riding peacefully. Jim and Mark and I launched the umiak and went out to her. On her stern in handsome letters was NORTH STAR OF HERSCHEL ISLAND. It was a sturdy and seaworthy wooden boat. From her lines we judged that she had been made quite a few years before, for she had a handsome bow that is seldom seen today. She carried a pilot house aft and had the look of a small North Sea trawler. We pulled alongside and one of the crew asked us to come into the pilot house for coffee.

North Star was immensely strong and well cared for. As we sat sipping coffee (and shedding our halo of caribou hairs, picked up from our sleeping skins), we learned that she had been built in San Francisco in 1935 and been brought north on the deck of a fur trade vessel to Herschel Island, where she was sold to Eskimo trappers who lived on Banks Island. The new owner and captain, a Swede named Sven Johansson, who was asleep below decks, had bought her in the mid-1960's on Banks Island after she had been ashore for nearly a decade. He used her in the summers, primarily on charter to the Geological Survey of Canada, and spent winters in the Arctic mountains west of the MacKenzie, trapping and guiding."[28]

The storm that North Star had been riding out had measured winds in excess of seventy-five knots. The anemometer - the device for measuring wind - had blown off of North Star's masthead at that strength. This was Bockstoce's first encounter with Sven. He would later hire Sven to skipper his ship, the Belvedere, in what became the first ever successful sailboat transit of the NorthWest Passage from west to east.

Sven recalls this storm from his perspective. "It was the biggest storm I had ever been in. We went into the bay to seek shelter and dropped anchor. We began to drag towards the shore. I put out our second anchor and the strain on the anchor and the chain was almost too much. I ended up running the engine and holding the gear in forward all night, just to take the strain off of the rode. By the morning I had been up all night and so never met John that trip because I was too tired. The ship had no room to drag because there was a shoal just twenty feet astern of us."

One thing that Fred Carpenter, Susie Sidney, Angus Elias, Jim Wolki and many other Bankslander Captains were very well known for was their ability to forecast the weather. The fleet almost always headed to Baillie Island from Sachs Harbour or upon their return from the mainland in order to take advantage of the harbour there should a storm arise. The instruments aboard were invariably only a compass, thermometer, barometer and a lead-line for taking depth soundings. A lead-line is a line marked by the fathom with a heavy lead weight at the end. By throwing or 'heaving' the lead forward and into the ocean the navigator can not only find the depth but also, if the end of the lead is 'armed' or coated in a sticky substance such as beef tallow or peanut butter a sampling of the seabed can be taken so that an estimated position can be determined if, for instance, the ship is crossing from an area known for a mud bottom to one of sand or shell. Albert Elias whose family owns the Fox adds about navigation, "About returning, Yeah that could happen (not returning). Ice and whatever. You know those years, no radio. No nothing. Just barometer and a compass." The skills the people have. When I could remember, they had thermometers - they had them on the wall.[29] Lucy Inglangasuk adds "and by the sun. You know when there is a rainbow around it, they say it's going to be stormy. After two days it gets very stormy. My grandfather used to look at the sun and the clouds around it. I could tell little of it sometimes, when it's bad weather.[30] "But they could tell when they are going to get wind bound. It depends on the weather. They could tell better than the weatherman." adds her husband, Fred.[31]

The Beaufort Sea is one of the most dangerous and unpredictable of waters to navigate on. The weather changes quickly and with the relatively shallow bottom, seas build up in no time. Added to this is the danger of ice as well as the few places for a vessel to seek harbour.

Fred Carpenter was well known for his navigational abilities as well as his skills in meteorology. As a leader, he gladly passed on his knowledge to the younger generation. Albert Elias remembers to this day how Fred taught him some of the tricks of the trade. "My mom would take me out hunting and teach me about hunting. Once in the fall time my father got hurt and got torn up. He couldn't do much after that. When I first got to Sachs Harbour I didn't know nothing about the coast, about trapping, about the ocean. Fred Carpenter told me, 'if the wind is offshore, it is very dangerous". You could tell which way the current was going, because he would take a little piece of white paper (and drop it in the water) and you could tell then because it is clear water. Things like that, you know, is very good to know how to do. Sometimes, there is strong wind in one direction, the current will buck the wind and it is very strong in there. Things like that are taught about by the elders for safety."

Fred Carpenter was also an expert in forecasting the weather. He shared some of his tips aboard ship. "You know, there's no one way that you recognise the weather, travelling like that. In the first quarter of the moon is the bad weather, last quarter it's going to be good. One way I get a long life. People follow me. They think, ' what a man!' Ha, ha, ha, ha. If you got sun dogs - stay behind. Don't go if there's sun dogs in day light. When the stars ringle, the wind come pretty soon. If the moon got a ring around it, bad weather pretty soon. Moon get yellow - bad weather. Moon clear, ocean dark, stars got ringles - good weather. We know then good weather twenty-four hours. Predict twenty-four hours with no ice."

The wind direction also determines what type of weather to expect in the Beaufort Sea. North wind - Ungalaq, West wind - Kanaknaq, East wind - Nigiqpak, South wind - Kiluaknaq. Lily Lipscombe recalls that sea-birds could also be used for weather forecasting. "Qaqrauq (loons) were sacred in a way that they didn't really hunt them. Because ...they used to go by, how they make the noise for weather. Like right now, the way it's making sounds, it's suppose to rain or be wet out. You know, cloudy and wet, foggy or whatever. The way they make that 'qaqa' sound. and then if they make that real sharp high sound, that's when it's really gonna be sunny and beautiful, or so the story goes anyhow."[32]

Peter Thrasher continues, "They would know right away about it, long ago those Inuit. Just by looking at the sun and the moon, and the clouds too. In the summer and in the fall and at night they would know about the weather, how it's going to be. You know, the moon. Every month there's a (when it's a full) moon, they know there's going to be bad weather. They knew when the weather is good them days, our parents. They would know when to stay away from the ocean if it's too big wind. They know when it's going to be shallow water. They know all that."[33]

Raddi Kowichuk remembers being aboard their schooner and what an expert his father was at reading the weather. "My Dad however didn't show his feelings nor express them; he kept looking not at the schooners, but at the skies and the clouds. He seemed a bit worried as the wind began increasing slightly and the boat to rock a bit more now. Coming out of his silent observations, finally Dad told us that he didn't like the weather outlook very much and for safety sake and before darkness, he wanted to go to the shore and there wait for the next day and for good weather. He gave the orders and we tackled the sails, altering course for land, the coast being near. This was certainly a wise move and decision, though I would have liked to continue and be with the others and reach Baillie Island as soon as possible. But Dad was the old man, and his words were laws, be it on land or at sea. His good judgement was rarely in fault and that day it confirmed again his knowledge of the sea and weather. Before we had reached the bottom of the bay, the harbour winds became tornadoes and gales. The sea and waves tossed our schooner roughly. Rain began to pour down heavily upon us. Our stovepipes were knocked away also.

Akrale! What a storm. Believe me; securing the boat ashore didn't take us long. Then in semi-darkness, Orsoatsiak and myself went inland searching for fresh water. We were completely out of drinking water. We found a small lake and the water was drinkable and fresh enough. On our return, in complete darkness, of course then no flashlights, we had to walk slowly and carefully, making sure not to stumble, fighting the wind and the rain battering our faces. Even before we arrived home to the schooner, we were all soaked and looked like wet rats."[34]

Every year there are storms in the Beaufort Sea, some more memorable than others. "Fred Wolkie, at seventy-two, the Inuvialuit elder had been around long enough to remember most of the big storms that had hit the Beaufort coast over the decades. He and his father, the son of a German/Swiss whaler who jumped ship in Alaska and made a life for himself in the western Arctic, had several close calls over the years. The storm that made the biggest impression was the one in 1944 that washed away several buildings. 'Charlie Rufus's boat went down with him and his family aboard in that storm' he recalled. 'I was just a kid back then, and really only remember what we were told. But that same storm washed away most of the buildings on Baillie Island, where the Hudson's Bay Company had a post in the 1930's and 1940's. In the end, the Baillie Islanders all moved to Tuk because everyone realized that it was too dangerous to stay there. Many here are descendants of those people. They forget that."[35]

The main danger though in travelling in the Arctic Ocean is hitting or being caught in the ice. Sailors are a superstitious lot and Inuit sailors are no different in this regard. While aboard their boat hunting walrus, some Western Inuit were overtaken by a storm of hurricane force " I noticed a small clump of little finger-length, ivory knives tied together with a twisted piece of sinew which rattled against the heaving bulkhead. They had been put there, Kumalik said, to help cut the weather."[36]

Even ashore in a storm there are hold-backs to ways of bringing good luck to those caught out in a storm. For the old residents of Tuktoyaktuk, Mangilaluk is the real founder of the village. As for Kaopkruna, Mangilaluk's mother, she thought a lot about her son and prayed for him in her own ways, humming and chanting some errant tunes. According to the old custom, inside their little dwelling, she hung her son's caribou boots on the ceiling, after filling them with shaving chips of wood. At night her thoughts went to her son and sometimes she could hear the boots fastened to the ceiling just above her, dangling and swinging, moving to and fro, as a man walking. Then she felt relieved, 'my son is alive and safe on the treacherous ice, walking and on his way home.' A quick inspection of the interior of the boots confirmed her feelings. From inside the boots, the shavings had moved upwards. Cheerful and lighthearted, she told the Baillie Island people not to worry anymore."[37]

Seal wrecked in the ice.

In 1951 the schooner Seal owned by Kavavouk was attempting passage accompanied by another Inuit in a whaleboat with all of their families, furs and supplies. They were caught in the ice but could see leads further out and so began the back breaking process of sawing and chiselling through the ice to try and get to safety. Too soon the ice pack shifted and the wind drove a massive wall of ice towards them. "The poor old Seal was first caught and pushed by the big floes - coming at us from the south west and rubbing along the edge of the shore pack - part way up the sloping sides of the high part of our iceberg, only to be brushed off again, with her sides crushed and keel torn out on the floes' return and change of direction, and to fill with water and slob. She was sinking when a huge tongue of ice was thrust under her to hold her until the next squeeze hoisted her high on top of a confused mass of pressed up. broken ice, where she remains at this moment, stern down and bowsprit pointing high in the air, as weird a looking wreck as could well be imagined; a very monument to the futility of our effort when the blind, giant forces of nature which encompass us move in the wrong direction."[38]

One famous trader who often dealt with the North Star was Slim Semmler. Anna Olga was his boat, another vessel built by Kneass shipyards in San Francisco. Slim Semmler was born in Oregon and came north as a trapper in the late 1920s. His reputation of 'superhuman strength and endurance' preceded him no matter where he went. Bern Will Brown remembers the story that first most impressed him. "Perhaps the first was the story of how he had saved the Mission schooner at Coppermine (Kugluktuk). It seems that the Mission boat was stranded on a reef near the harbour. The crew had laboured in vain to free it when Slim happened by and plunged into the water. By brute strength he single-handedly lifted the bow enough for the boat to float free. Everyone was astonished."[39] Slim ended up opening a trading post in Inuvik after losing two schooners loaded with trade goods in the Arctic Ocean.

Slim Semmler.

One time Slim was sailing with a full ship of goods to trade for fur at Tuktoyaktuk. Rounding the entrance to the unmarked harbour, Semmler cut in too close and drove the Anna Olga onto a reef. The waves began to pick the ship up and drop her onto the rock shelf just below the water. The mast was jumping in its step and the rigging began to give way. With each blow Semmler could feel the force of the sea driving through the planks and into his body. The planks began to split and water quickly began to fill the hull. Semmler was too far from shore to swim and in any case the icy waters would have caused immediate hypothermia and death. With all hope lost Semmler cast his eyes around the horizon. There, making her way towards him was North Star. Fred Carpenter manoeuvred North Star round by the deep water at the Anna Olga's stern and got Semmler aboard. They managed to rescue some of the cargo but very quickly after Semmler was safe aboard

North Star the sea completed smashed Semmler's boat and the rest of the cargo was lost. Slim Semmler lived to see his one hundredth birthday.

There are many examples of the ingenuity of the Innu in being able to get themselves out of tight situations but the same qualities of character have also been well documented in many other Northern adventurers. Certainly for every level-headed southerner who has survived their own Arctic trials there are a dozen examples of others who failed to recognize the importance of following the locals' example and froze or starved to death. A happy example of the former is that of the Ledyards who saw the need for their own Peterhead in order to do their missionary work in the North. "Our first experience in pulling the 100 pound mud hooks with the entire length of chain was fearfully disappointing. Before we got them very far, a huge berg with its dark green, fantastic-looking bottom had moved in on us. To pull the anchors now with the bottom of the ice fastened on our anchor chains was impossible. We were drifting back at the speed of the ice, and to take up the slack of the chains before we were crushed in the ice behind us (was impossible). I started the engine while Komak and Chris worked on the chains. It turned over the first crank, but something was wrong. Water was spurting out the side of the block. Power was sadly lacking; it was firing on only three cylinders. With a prayer for strength for the men up front pulling up the anchors, I opened the throttle fully; and steering right for the ice, we gained enough speed over the approaching pan to get the chains loose from the ice. Once the anchors were free from the bottom of the bay, we let them hang in the water until we were out from behind the ice and in the clear again. When we were in open water, I took out all the spark plugs. One cylinder had salt water in it! Our engine had rusted out during the years and was leaking salt water in the inside. An examination showed that water was being sucked in through a crack in the intake manifold. We plugged both this crack and a hole in the block with pieces of walrus hide. Since the sides swell up when wet, this made a perfect temporary repair."[40] In the 200 mile trip Sojourner - named for Abraham who sojourned in a strange land and to whom God had promised to be with - went through eighteen quarts of oil!

Anchoring one night to ride out a storm, the Sojourner's crew did not get much rest: "By three o'clock in the morning the wind was whistling through the ropes and cables. The boat was sweeping a wide area each time we went over a wave. Finally at about six in the morning the tempest really started to rage. Three times in quick succession the bow of the boat took a quick lunge upward and with a violent crash staggered back down, with water pouring in through the engine room hatch and windows by tubfuls. Not only were we getting soaked, but the engine was drenched and so were our sleeping bags on the bunks...I went up on deck to watch for awhile, and besides, the bilge was filling up at an alarming rate. Bracing myself inside the tiny wheelhouse, I could see what was happening. The boat soon tried to leap another of those monstrous waves. Just as the boat was ready to go up over the crest, an angry wave broke, spilling tons of water over the deck, washing it clear of everything that was not tied securely. We could not take much more of this pounding. Desperately holding on in the wheelhouse, I prayed fervently, then worked my way to the hatch cover and down to the engine room just before another wave washed over the deck. Komak was gravely concerned about the center section of the boat, so I crawled through a hole in the bulkhead into the hold. Water was coming in between the planking where it was beginning to separate.

Then I went back up on deck to the wheelhouse. There was not much hope of saving the boat. The urgent question was - how could we save ourselves? A reef ran between us and the shore. Our anchors were dragging. If it were not for the rocky reef, we could let the boat drift back until it grounded, where we could possibly get to shore safely. Of course, the boat would be pounded to bits. But the reef blocked all possible chances of our drifting close enough to land."[41]

They saw another vessel weave their way through the reef and decide to follow suit. The plan to just let the anchor rode run out was not possible since the ends are bolted to the bottom of the chain bin and so their only hope was to weigh anchor in the gale and then get through the reef. "On a calm sea the job is not pleasant or easy, but with the added strength of a 60 to 70 mph wind it was next to impossible, especially while hanging on to something with one hand. ..the Sojourner was seesawing back and forth. Each time it was at the limit of the chains, we could feel the anchors drag considerably. After we had one chain in about halfway, the boat started to drift at a terrific rate. The only thing to do was to start the engine and try to help Komak by keeping the slack up on the chains while he pulled them up. His back had troubled him for years. I suggested he run the engine while I pulled the anchors, but because of his limited knowledge and dislike for the mechanical part of the boat, he yelled to me to go back.

The engine never started as quickly as then, but all hope of keeping the boat straight was shattered when I got hold of the wheel. It was nearly uncontrollable. The small hand winch on the deck was a big help, but, oh so slow! A huge wave was forming out in front of the boat. As we worked around, I could see that it would hit the boat right at the crest. To yell loud enough for Komak to hear would be impossible. With his head down, he would never see the wave when it hit. Without holding on he would surely be washed overboard. From my view the wave appeared to be like a volcano ready to belch foaming lava over a helpless person. I prayed that God would save Komak. At the instant the wave was about to swamp us, the bow rode exceptionally high taking Komak above the water and dropping him with the same momentum as a roller coaster. He turned around and looked at me as though to ask what in the world had happened? Not a drop of water had touched him, but our boat crashed violently into the other side of the wave. Komak was spared, Praise the Lord, but how long could the boat stay together under such pounding?

Finally Komak signalled...the anchor was up!..Because the wind caught the small wheelhouse it was impossible to get the boat turned away from the wind. We were drifting sideways uncontrollable over the end of the reef. Each time a wave lifted us high in the air and let us down to the very bottom of the trough, we expected to feel the crash on the rocks any moment. Air was picked up from the foam of the waves, and the engine speeded up as though our propeller had been knocked off. Somehow - some way, we passed the reef. The engine idled until the boat headed into the wind...as soon as we had control of the boat we were able to ram it in ashore. For five stormy, windy days we clung tight to our sandy beach with every piece of rope and chain, burying our anchors in the earth and piling rocks on top. We heard later that the wind had varied from 60 to 75 miles an hour."[42]

Raddi Kowichuk recalls another close call when the legendary Billy Thrasher stepped in to save the day. "We had time to enter into the harbour and to secure our schooner, when we sighted the two motorized schooners coming our way also. If Old Bennett Ningarsek aboard his Shamrock progressed steadily, though rather slowly, it was not so for Angik, the Ugiyuk being in tow hindered his march and its headway seemed very laborious and trouble-some, the two boats not riding the waves at the same time. We were now in safety, hopeless spectators, watching their progress and battle against the raging sea, praying that everything would be okay. To our dismay and awe, suddenly we saw and realised that the Ugiyuk, Akayak's boat was on its own, the line couldn't and didn't sustain all the strain, tugs and pulls. It snapped, and now free, on its own and out of control, it was at the mercy of the winds, waves and current. The elements in fury pushed the Ugiyuk towards the shore which at that place was only high banks right to the water's edge. We were completely powerless and expected to witness a sudden and violent ending for all, for the boat and its passengers on the first impact with the cliff, when to our amazement and also great relief we saw the Ugiyuk as if propelled and swallowed by a hand in the swift current alter course and travel parallel to the coast and the sand bar where it then headed towards the harbour. They were in trouble yet and in dire difficulties. Billy Thrasher, a master in sailing and always very helpful as well as daring and fearless, wishing to help them he set out in a small dinghy to meet them. Needless to say, he was certainly welcome aboard. He took command, set up the sail and brought them safely into the harbour, boat and passengers. All was well that ends well, but it had been a very close call indeed."[43]

As previously noted, when North Star made her annual passage there would be four or five Inuvialuit families living aboard with all or most of their possessions, hundreds and hundreds of fur pelts, food and supplies for two or three months and, of course, their most valuable asset, their dogs. It was not uncommon for North Star of Herschel Island to be carrying fifty or sixty dogs, all chained on the foredeck with one wolf. When storms came up ashore the practice was to stake the dogs so that each had its own area and would not fight with the others. The dogs would curl up with their tail wrapped around their nose and the snow would blanket them.

Dogs were a very important part of life in those days and were well cared for but often were put in positions of misery, being chained ashore or on deck in storms as waves broke over them, causing some of them to die from exposure or being flung overboard by waves to hang by their necks. Aboard St. Roch, under the command of Henry Larsen, a crew member complained of the constant howling of the terrified animals. "'Can't something be done for the dogs?' Hunt moaned as the dogs howled their protest against being chained, being seasick, and the motion of St. Roch. Even Larsen's temper began to fray under the constant onslaught of howls, wind, fog, and other annoyances."[44]

Aboard North Star and the other schooners there was no such luxury as space. When the storms rose up the dogs would be left chained up. "At times when there was a gale even our dogs were not able to stay on their feet."[45] With the ship rolling, bucking and heaving through the Beaufort Sea it wasn't uncommon for dogs to be washed off the foredeck where they would hang by their necks until dead. Their frozen bodies would bang against the hull with each movement of the ship. When the storm died down they would be cut away.

In 1936, when the HBC ship Fort James became caught in the ice her crew hung on for three days listening to the giant bergs squeezing and crunching the planks. Finally the order was given to abandon ship and they were able to walk across the ice to the St Roch. "She listed heavily to starboard, her keel wedged beneath her, and soon, with a great cracking noise, her keel snapped off. The crew jumped onto the ice and walked to the R.C.M.P. "St Roch", fortunately close by, while somebody took a revolver and shot the frightened dogs on the St James' deck. In an hour's time, the ship had disappeared, and over the wreck the heedless ice slid on."[46]

Arctic storms come up suddenly, particularly on the Beaufort Sea at the end of summer towards the end of August and early September. Joey Carpenter adds that "it was windy in the fall time. Sometimes the third week of August. Sometimes there was a delay coming across and we had to stay in Tuk for the winter." Bessie Andreasen agrees, "soon now, at the end of September, the sea would begin to freeze and young ice would form preventing us then to reach Kent Peninsula. Our schooner, although well built and heavy, was not yet an ice breaker and young ice is treacherous and dangerous, it cuts through timber like a saw. Everybody told them to wait, Alex more emphatically than the others."[47] On a clear day some Innu were out walrus hunting when the wind was suddenly upon them. "Anowavingaluk! A huge wind!

Avudalungivosi, we're going!' I looked at the last bull walrus lying dead before us and thought, We can't just go and leave behind that last great animal we've killed. But the anchor was being hauled up fast and in no time the hurricane hit us with a rising force that frightens me even to remember. The first great smashing wave that engulfed the Peterhead broke and carried away two halves of the canoe. I wished to God then that we had seen no walrus and had instead run for safety. I wished that we'd never come on this perilous hunt.

It was all I could do to hang on, then slide down the ladder in a torrent of water along with Kumalik and Kopikolik. We were soaked to the skin. My sleeping bag was floating but I was too scared to feel the cold.... ... ... the engine had cut or they had stopped it. Fortunately, Kalingo and Irving, at the last moment, had been able to storm-tie the helm and set the sail, though it was torn by morning."[48]

**Storm at Sachs Harbour, Banks Island. Photo
taken from ashore by Earl Esau, 2012.**

More recently, Steve Solomon and his colleague Gavin Manson were on Banks Island when a storm blew up "in 2000, when 95 kilometre per hour (59 mph) winds were lashing the coast" said Solomon. "It was blowing so hard that this old boat, a derelict that was abandoned some time ago, got washed away in a surge that night. It was quite the sight watching it get spun around by the waves. That was the last time that boat went out to sea. All they found the next day were parts of an engine."[49]

Canada's RCMP vessel St. Roch under the command of Henry Larsen is one of our Canada's most revered ships. St Roch was built for the RCMP at Vancouver's Burrard Dry Dock Company in 1928 and named for a 14th century native of Montpellier, France who nurtured plague victims in Northern Italy. The ships, St Roch and North Star of Herschel Island, are very similar in construction and as they were both purpose built for the icy waters of the Canadian Arctic, a parallel can be drawn between them. As the Inuit employ an oral tradition and those of European descent use writing as a means to memory, it is I believe acceptable and necessary to use some of the latter's accounts of life at sea in a purpose built wooden Arctic boat in order for the reader to better appreciate what conditions were like aboard. Bear in mind, though, that the North Star is forty feet shorter than the St Roch yet carried more people, a similar if not greater cargo and a similar if not greater amount of dogs aboard. Perhaps the biggest difference is the amount that each ship draws, that is the measurement from the waterline to the bottom of the keel. St Roch enjoys a 121/2 foot draft while the North Star measured in at 41/2 feet during her Arctic service, the better to be able to manoeuvre in close to take on or discharge crew or cargo. The deeper the draft, generally the more stable the ship in rough weather. North Star's short keel allowed her to enter shallow ports like Sachs Harbour.

Patrick White served aboard St. Roch and recalls what it was like to be aboard her in thick weather. "As soon as we got to the tip of (Vancouver) island, Henry made a beeline for the Bering Strait, right across the North Pacific. I remember looking out and seeing what looked like green mountains, except they were moving. The Roch stood on her head and stood on her tail and rolled both rails under. The seas broke right over the cargo load out on the bow. We used to have to tie ourselves into bed. We'd tie a rope to the rails on either side of the bunk. You'd just fly out of bed sometimes without that rope. If it was really rough we'd put a rope from the back aft up to the wheelhouse. You'd wait for a wave to crash over and then you'd grab this rope and run to beat hell up to the wheelhouse before the next one crashed over. You could barely keep the boat on course in that weather. The wheel didn't have any power assist or anything, so sometimes it took two of us just to hold her in a straight line.

The Roch was designed for Arctic service, you see. She had a rounded hull, so that she could rise up on top of the ice when it pressed in. When you have a straight-sided hull, the ice just wedges up against it and it can crush the hull. With her bathtub shape, the Roch might have been proof against the ice, but the way she handled on the way there it felt like you were going to capsize long before making it far enough north to the ice. Yes, Roch was what she was called and rock was what she did."[50]

The round hull was deliberately designed to allow the ship to be pressed up out of the ice rather than be crushed. The round hull also meant that the ships designed for the Arctic did have a tendency to roll in heavy seas. Albert Elias, in comparing his ship to North Star said, "North Star was good for the rough water 'cause it's got a good keel. Our Fox is more rounded. It's got a keel but still rolls."

Bill White recalls that St. Roch was so cold and clammy below that the mate, Fred Farrar, lit the coal heater and soon conditions down below were more like a sauna with all of the wet gear giving off moisture. It was so uncomfortable that Farrar opened up the hatch's door to let some fresh air in. "A column of water came driving down, the full size of the open door. With every pitch it sluiced from one bulkhead to the other taking with it a collection of paint cans stowed under the steps. With a few pitches the water was all colours of the rainbow. There was paint over everything - woodwork, bedding, stove, gear - and the smell of turpentine was so strong it was worse than being sick. There was nowhere else to lie down on that bloody boat and we were too tired to get up."[51]

Sometimes a schooner would have to take more than one try in order to make it to their winter trapping grounds. Randi Kowichuk recalls seeing one of his friend's schooners arriving after battling a Beaufort Sea storm."One day we sighted a boat coming in our direction from the east coming slowly at half speed. When it drew nearer we recognized it, Tadjok's schooner, a two mast. It entered into the harbour and anchored there. The passengers came ashore in a small boat. Levy and Tadjok then told us their story. After leaving us at Tutkrayak they had travelled for a few hours without any incident, but suddenly a strong gale had come up and they were caught in the storm. So violent was the wind that it almost tore down all the sails, the waves heaving the boat as if it were a cork. They had no other option than to sail before the wind and hope for the best. Luck directed them and they swayed their dismantled schooner into a small creek. After such misadventure and setback they rested first and made some rough repairs to the canvas and decided to come back to Tutkrayak to do a thorough overhaul of all masts and sailcoths before setting out to sea again. The job done, they left for Baillie Island and once more we were on our own."[52]

Perhaps the worst storm that North Star was ever in occurred on Agnes Carpenter's honeymoon voyage. The year was 1956 and Fred and Susie were a little late in getting away from the Delta. The trip to Baillie Island was a nightmare with huge wind and waves but after a short lay-over the brother and sister decided to push on for Sachs despite the unsettled weather rather than risk being iced in for the winter short of their goal. Agnes recalls the night when as a teenaged bride, leaving her family behind for the first time she found herself alone in the pilothouse watching the waves with her husband and sister-in-law lashed to the top of the deckhouse. "There was a big west wind. We were out in the open of the Beaufort Sea. We were cross-ing the middle of the ocean. One or two schooners went down that night. Everybody was out all night. I was scared. There was a big black wall of water, it was like the parting of the seas and there was black ice all around too. There was just myself aboard and Susie Sidney and Fred. They were brother and sister and they were piloting the boat. They were steering from atop the pilothouse. There was a gyro-compass there - a huge one - on top of the deckhouse. We would take soundings. The most important thing was the current. Fred would navigate by the stars. During the storm Fred and Susie were lashed to the top of the deckhouse for 36 hours, that's how long it took us that time from Baillie Island to Banks Island. The storm started at night, right after we left Tuk. I was in the pilothouse and was just seeing big black water. The waves were as high as, higher than the mast was - 75 feet, 60 feet. The waves were all around us."

Agnes knew of the ship's past and the storms that she had been in. She knew that she should trust her, North Star, known as the Queen of the Banksland fleet - a ship known throughout the Arctic for her adventures, strength and beauty. Still, the ship rolled, dipping forty degrees from side to side as waves hit the bow and then broke over the two helmsman sitting twenty feet off of the water. With silent prayers, Agnes held on through the night and 36 hours after giving her wedding vows, she heard the engine wind down, felt the waves lessen and saw land around her as the two tired navigators wove the ship through the sand bars outside her new home of Sachs Harbour.

Recently, Cameron Dueck and his crew met up with North Star of Herschel Island in Victoria, B.C. before they made their successful transit of the NorthWest Passage aboard Silent Sound. Dueck recorded the voyage in his book, Voyage Through the NorthWest Passage. They made a stop at Sachs Harbour and before long were enjoying the hospitality of Joey and Margaret Carpenter. Joey recounted to them that, "My father's schooner..she was a beautiful boat." Dueck surprised Carpenter then, "I know the North Star because she was docked near Silent Sound in Victoria's Inner Harbour, perhaps the only schooner of her type and generation to remain afloat. She was originally rigged as a schooner, (author's note - actually a cutter). It was clear most schooners did not fare as well as the North Star. When hauling freight was no longer profitable, schooners were left on the beach to rot." "When the government created the NTCL (Northern Transportation Company Limited), they started hauling freight from Hay River to Tuk and all along the coast," Joey said. "They could haul freight cheaper than it cost to operate these boats, so there was no need for these boats. So they put them up on the beach and that's where they have stayed since the early '60's."

"As we travelled east we came across more wrecks from the Arctic's rich sailing history. Just down the beach from BayMaud lies the Eagle, a long liner fishing boat. She was purchased in Tuktoyaktuk in 1954 by Father

Steinman, a German Catholic priest. He towed the boat to Cambridge Bay and it leaked badly the entire way. Later that year, before he had a chance to refurbish the Eagle, he was transferred by the Church. He was forced to leave his boat behind. The Eagle sits on the shore just south of the stone church the priest built."[53]

Chapter 15
The DEATH OF FRED WOLKI

Fred Wolki was married to one of Fred Carpenter's sisters, Susie and Fred Wolki's brother, James (Jim), with Fred Carpenter was one of the original partners in North Star. Fred Wolki died in 1939 and as one of the most successful trappers in the Canadian Arctic he died a rich man and with a large estate. Normally a judge would have looked out for his estate's interests and decided upon a fair way of distributing it, however weather precluded this and so the Canadian government's most senior person in the area was dispatched to do the job. This man was Henry Larsen, skipper of the R.C.M.P. vessel St. Roch. The ship had already been hauled ashore and winterised at Baillie Island and so Larsen put together a crew, hitched up the dog teams and they made their way west to Banks Island. By coincidence, Larsen had been considering putting in at Sachs Harbour for the winter but learned that the harbour would be too shallow for his ship.

Henry Larsen was a well known and well respected Arctic man who was one of only a few 'outsiders' that the locals accepted as having skills similar to their own. Not everyone was that impressed with him, though. A young Anthony Aparkrak recalls, "There was a big surprise in August. The RCMP schooner, St. Roch, called in at Tuk. It had come all the way from the other side of Canada. A man called Larsen was in the pilothouse. I was told he had set some kind of record for sailing the northern seas. But I knew better. My dad was the champ when it came to sailing the Arctic. He had put more waves and ice under him than any man."[1]

Larsen's reports back to the RCMP as related in the book, Plowing the Arctic, explain how the situation was passed along to him. "A couple of days later Larsen told Peters to help him get ready for a trip to Banks Island for, among other things, there was the Wolki estate to go over and settle, Wolki having died leaving a considerable estate consisting of schooners, houses, and other valuable property. This must be settled according to the laws of the land, and in the absence of attorneys, the responsibility for proper disposition of the estate must rest with the Mounted Police."[2]

Henry Larsen and RCMP patrol leaving St. Roch, 1941, for Sachs Harbour. Note St. Roch buried in ice for insulation.

On March 17th, 1941 Captain Henry Larsen left his command, RCM St. Roch for an overland trip to Banks Island. He took with him two men, Constable G.W. Peters and the employed civilian G.W. Porter. They took two large komitik sleds with a team of seven and a team of eight dogs. "The purpose of this patrol was to investigate various complaints and rumours in regards to infractions of the NWT Game Act... ..., and to interview Mrs Wolki in regard to her estate, and to register native firearms."[3] What made the division of the estate most difficult was the regular practice of co-ownership of large items and the necessity of determining a fair market value for partners to buy his estate out or to trade their shares away. Sven Johansson recalls the event, "Fred Wolki - he must have been a great operator to get a "large" estate in trapping, trading and boating."

The men left Walker Bay and made 25 miles that day, which was to be their best day's run on the whole trip to Sachs Harbour. They camped with a native family on the first night. After that it was hard slogging. The komitik sleds were very heavy and unwieldy. They practiced the Inuit way of coating the sled's runners with mud and then smoothing it with ice until it formed a slick surface. As they got further out into the ice they encountered very rough sand cliffs with protrusions of coal and rock which knocked the mud from the runners slowing them down. At one point they resorted to caking their sled runners with oatmeal when they couldn't find any mud and another day they tried making a mixture of flour and a little mud and then freezing it to the runners. From the rough terrain they made their way into deep, soft snow which tired the dogs out and slowed them down. The men walked ahead of the dogs doing the heavy work of breaking trail, while encouraging the tired animals along.

"The men were pulling hard on the heavy sleds now and were almost on the verge of collapse when ' Look!' Larsen cried. 'Look!' He pointed to a group of well-painted frame houses that looked down with friendly eyes upon the harbour. 'That one,' he pointed to one of the snuggest, 'is Fred Carpenter's'.[4] "On March 31st they made Sachs Harbour and "found the three native schooners pulled out here, also the five families had their main camp here..... 'Glad to see you! Glad to see you!' Fred Carpenter was coming to meet them with outstretched hands, ready to help them unload, and before long they were gathered around the coal stove yarning about this and that.[5] Where's Susie?' Larsen asked, referring to Fred's sister, Susie Wolki, the main beneficiary in the estate they were about to settle. 'Oh, she'll be along shortly,' Fred said casually. 'She's out on the trapline with a dogteam. Got her niece with her.' Larsen nodded and Fred went on: 'Two of us always travel together on the same trapline, setting the traps alternately, for there's plenty of foxes for the two and it isn't very safe going alone. Never know what might happen.' He settled himself down to smoke in a large comfortable chair. 'Jim Cockney and I trap the same line.' He paused then and Larsen primed him with an enquiry as to how trapping had been this year.

'There's lots of foxes around here. Got good fox country,' Fred boasted, 'mostly rolling sand and gravel hills with moss; plenty of moss and lots of long stretches of tundra with lots of low willows and roots for the lemmings, rabbits and ptarmigan, and that's the kind of prey the foxes go for.' He puffed on for a while. 'Only trouble about it is,' he frowned, 'when there's too much food the foxes don't have to travel very far to get enough to eat, and they get awful fat; and rubbed and dirty from the clay and mud in their dens...and when they can get lemmings and rabbits in plenty, they don't come after our bait. "He, (Fred Carpenter), got up then and started preparations for a meal, while Peters inspected the house with eyes that missed nothing; the high-powered radio, the sewing machine, the lamp that gave a light comfortably bright, and the stove that threw heat to every corner of the room, burning coal that had been brought in at high cost from 'outside'.

'I wish Susie were here', Fred said as he set the table, placing the knives and forks neatly in front of each place. 'Susie's a pretty good cook,' he commented, 'in addition to being able to trap as well as any man around here.'[6] In an interview with Usher, Carpenter recalled the event. "Larsen. He always asked people what they trapped like. He stayed here quite awhile."[7]

Larsen and his crew settled down in Fred Carpenter's house to rest up after their long trip to Sachs Harbour. Larsen must have recognized how comfortable life had become for Fred Carpenter, a man who had grown up living in snow houses and tents on the ice, often going hungry and struggling to survive in the frigid climate. "Next day Susie arrived, her face radiant above her caribou parka which was luxuriously edged with wolverine, a fur expensive and hard to come by, providing as it does the perfect frame for a face, not only because of its becoming softness, but because of its resistance to frost; while her supple body gave to the skin garments the subtle beauty the trunk and branches of an elm lends to its plain green leaves."[8]

'I'm glad to see you're making yourself at home,' she (Susie Sidney) said heartily, eyeing the clothes they had spread out to dry and the pots of dog feed they had on cooking.

It did not take her long to change from the Arctic clothing into a neat cotton housedress and mix up a batch of sourdough biscuits, which she baked on top of the stove from a recipe passed on to her by her grandfather, and before long they were on the table and being washed down with piping hot coffee.

'I never saw anyone that could make biscuits like you, Susie' Larsen complimented her, 'so light and fluffy.' He took another bite; then reaching for another biscuit, slathered it with butter, before settling down to discuss the pros and cons of settlement of the Wolki Estate. At last Larsen, his head reeling from the facts, figures and 'whereases', got up and suggested that Peters look after the Wolki estate while he took a team and went up to Storkerson Bay to see what was what. Susie Wolki chuckled her delight. 'The things we must discuss are too tiresome for you.' She was smiling at him understandingly. 'Then you may go; but,' she urged, 'you will be back for Easter?' Larsen grunted his surprise.

'Next Friday is Good Friday,' she reminded him. 'The people will be gathering for services and festivities: Saturday night we're to have a square dance, on Sunday there will be services, and then in the afternoon we will have moving pictures.' She was breathless with anticipation.

'I'll be back, ' Larsen promised, 'long before then,' and he went out to look the dogs over and set himself to the task of culling the two teams so as to leave himself with the best of the lot for the trip up to Storkerson Bay."[9] "Larsen assigned Constable Peters to remain behind at Sachs Harbour "To finish up work in connection with the Wolki estate, also to interview Mike Amos and to look after the remaining dogs."[10]

The next leg of the journey was to head up to Sea Otter Harbour (European name Storkerson Bay) in order to complete their inspection and the local gun registry and to enquire further in regard to the Wolki estate and to interview the people there. Larsen would have to make up an inventory of all that was to be divided up and to ensure that all of the goods belonged to the estate. He also had to look into any debts owed to Wolki at the time of his death. This is one aspect of the job that the RCMP in remote communities are called upon to do, relying upon their honesty and good judgement to get the job done.

Carpenter kindly loaned them his toboggan for the trip, no doubt surprised that Larsen had made the rough trip to Sachs with the cumbersome komitik sleds. "' Fred Carpenter came up behind him (Larsen).' I don't like to butt in,' he said in his quiet way, but those sleds of yours are not going to be any help to you in getting back for Easter; they're too heavy,' He struck a match and lit a cigarette. 'Now if you want to borrow a sled, you've only got to say the word, and I'll let you have one of mine.'

Larsen accepted with alacrity, and went through the two teams picking out the dogs to be hitched to Carpenter's basket sled, then set out to follow the trap-line northward, the dogs trotting out in fine style ahead of the light sled, while Larsen's eyes took note of everything. Word had been coming through that the natives had not been lifting their traps in accordance with the laws imposed by the Government which insists that all traps be lifted at the end of March, and Larsen had strict instructions to watch for any traps still laid.

It was something of relief he found everything in order and, inwardly cursing people who were forever stirring up the police with false leads, he turned back to Sach's Harbour, arriving there in time to go sealing with the natives."[11]

Before heading back, Larsen stayed at Sea Otter with Jim Wolki at Wolki's camp and learned that Bertram Pokiak and Angus Elias were in the area, on their way to Sea Otter Bay. After a few days of waiting out the weather in camp, Larsen and Porter returned to Sachs for one night and then went on to Blue Fox Harbour to continue the survey of Wolki's estate. At Blue Fox harbour was Wolki's fish boat and a building that was left vacant during the winter. The two then returned to Sachs and interviewed Bertram Pokiak (Larsen spells Pokeak), Angus Elias and Moses Raddi. The RCMP team then spent a few days hunting seal for dog food and preparing for the return trip. "The men were busy hitching the dogs to the sleds, and loading on the canoes which they would need for retrieving their quarry (of seal). Soon whips were cracking and they were off to find open water for the hunt, while Fred Carpenter issued last minute warnings to Larsen to be careful with his team which was new to this kind of work.

Larsen well knew the danger of crossing the ice in this part of the country where an open water lead has a way of closing in suddenly if there is the slightest wind, and in calm weather acquiring a frangible covering of young ice which might provide sufficient support for the weight of a dog, but which would 'give' under the sled-runners.

They let Fred Carpenter and the others lead the way, but more than once their dogs dashed across a patch of young ice in their eagerness to catch up with the others, only to find the runners cutting through the thin ice and the rear dogs getting their paws wet so that they strove frantically to get away from the spot, while the sled seemed suddenly immovable and nothing was gained by the short cut. The dogs did not take too long to learn their lesson and soon they were content to follow the older dogs, zig zagging around to avoid patches of young ice until they came to a wide lead, where they were anchored.

They had not long to wait until a seal poked his head up through the dark water and looked around curiously. Another joined him; but they were still out of range. They disappeared for a moment and came up again closer in, only to have Carpenter lift his rifle to his shoulder.

A moment later a canoe was being pushed into the water. Two of them climbed into it and paddled off after the dead seal, which they picked up and brought back to be loaded on one of the sleds and hauled back to camp."[12] 'It's all so easy here,' Larsen deplored, 'with open water and the equipment they have. The time when you enjoy seal hunting,' he told Peters, 'is when you go out with a native that has little more than his wits to work with. All this,' he waved a hand that took in the frame houses, the canoes, the telescopic sights on the rifles and the cartridge box - 'it's all too civilized.'

'But,' Peters offered, 'if you're going to own a schooner like Fred Carpenter's, you've got to have money; and if you're going to have money you've got to work with the best equipment money can buy."[13]

Larsen and his men took their time to look around Carpenter's camp before Easter dinner. Lying on the beach near his house was Fred's pride and joy, North Star. As a fellow Arctic sailor Larsen had an eye for a good ship. 'The North Star's a sweet little vessel, Larsen admitted, 'and she set Fred Carpenter back a pretty penny.' His voice had a touch of envy in it, for the North Star was a thing to make a man envious."[14]

On Easter Sunday, April 13th 1941 Larsen reports: "Everyone gathered at Fred Carpenter's house for big feed and Easter celebrations. Moving-picture show given by Fred Carpenter. Projector run by six-volt battery." "Easter Sunday came, following hard on the Saturday night dance, and after the services everybody gathered at Fred Carpenter's house, Susie Wolki greeting them in a smart, trim, navy tailored suit that she had bought and worn in Vancouver the year before. The men were profuse in their compliments.

Susie Sidney and Fred's daughter, Agnes.

'She had her hair permanented while she was there, too, ' Fred told them.

'But it's grown out now,' Susie said regretfully, smoothing her dark, straight hair with an anxious hand, and patting it into place with her fingers.

Larsen admitted the clothes were becoming to her, praising every feature, then finished with, 'But up here, skin clothing looks best.'

Susie tossed her good-looking head. 'I put these clothes on,' - she broke off, and nodded to her niece who was entering the room in a lacquer-red dress, made in New York, that might have been designed to set off her olive skin and dark hair and eyes. 'My niece too; just to please you.' Susie could not hide her disappointment. 'I thought it would be nice for a celebration for you to see women dressed like they are 'outside,' she sighed. Susie's niece, whom she had raised, was Fred Carpenter's daughter, Agnes.

Larsen hastened to assure her all over again that she looked lovely; her niece looked lovely; that he had never seen either of them look lovelier; and then finished with an obstinate, 'But up here skin clothing looks best.'

Susie gave up the argument then with, 'Maybe after you've had something to eat, you'll be better humoured.' Already she was setting the table, bringing out the best china and silver, and opening pickles and preserves as luxuries for the Easter feast, in the same way women in North Dakota and British Columbia would be doing, giving a polish here and a rub there, and seeing that the salt and pepper were on the table, and worrying about whether there would be enough for everyone to eat, and whether the gravy was thick enough, before she called to them to bring their chairs up to the table and get started while everything was hot.

'Roast caribou.....m-m-m-m-m.' Larsen ate it, wondering aloud why women seemed to put more flavour into the things they cook than a man can. He blushed then at his unfaithfulness to Dad Parry (the cook aboard St. Roch) and added quickly, 'Dad Parry's an awful fine fellow; and some things he does wonders with; but this caribou is far and away the best I have ever eaten.'

'More?' Susie enquired, holding her hand out for his plate, which she refilled, piling it high with meat and vegetables.

When that was finished, 'No more caribou for you,' she told him. 'I want you to have room for something else.'

She brought on cakes, pies and doughnuts and set them on the table, urging her guests to help themselves while she and her niece brought in the coffee.

Larsen ate as if he would never get enough. 'It sure takes a woman to cook,' he said, when he had finished and was bringing out his pipe. 'My wife is a wonderful cook,' he bragged. 'Fancy cakes, pies...all these things she cooks better than anyone I have ever seen.' Catching the look on Susie's face, he hurried on with, 'of course nothing better than what you cook, Susie,' he assured her. 'I don't know how you do it.' He looked around the gathering. Forty-three people, he counted them, cooked for and served in a room that would seem small to the average city woman."[16]

"The dishes were cleared away in the same efficient manner in which the food had been served, and then Susie suggested that her brother get his projector out and show his pictures.

Fred got up and went easily about his arrangements for the movies while Larsen lent a hand. 'The projector is run by a six-volt battery,' Fred told him with some pride as he settled himself down behind the machine to run the film while he gave a running commentary that was remarkable in its lucidity and brevity."[17] One reel after another was run off, pictures of 'outside' that Fred had taken coming first, and the natives watched with intense interest; but it was the objective interest any audience gives to a place and people foreign to them. Fred brought out another film, adjusted it into place, and new scenes flickered on the screen. The North Star, Fred's schooner, came into sight and the interest of the audience took on a warmth and delight that had been absent before.

One film showing local natives on a seal hunt brought almost hysterical delight; another showing Bertram Pokeak, Angus Elias and Moses Raddi coming in from their traplines at Storkerson Bay brought a cry of a re-run of the film, while friendly joshing of the three men went on among the rest. And soon it was no longer Easter Sunday, but well into the day after Easter, and everybody went to bed."[18]

Next morning Larsen and Peters made all of the last-minute preparations for their return journey, Fred Carpenter helping them and offering suggestions, and when the noontime meal had been eaten, Larsen pulled himself to his feet."[19] The team left Sachs Harbour the next day and had a rough trip back to St. Roch negotiating the snow and the ice.

Chapter 16

Fred & Agnes marry - /food/pastimes/young marriages/traditional medicine/superstitions/tattooing

Up until the early 1900s the practice of people getting married at a young age in the Western Canadian Arctic was still accepted and encouraged. This was the norm in Arctic society. 'My father married my mom when she was 12 years old. Even not too long ago, after I came back from school [...] they were still getting married at 12 years old. Fourteen years old, that was old if you're marrying at 14 years old! Now, there, they go to court when a woman is 17 or 16 because it's too young. Those days, they're all getting married at 12 years old,"[1] says Jimmy Jacobson. "In the Eskimo tradition, love at the age of fourteen is natural and clean. We die early. We go by nature, not by the books. Girls have perfectly natural children at fourteen, some at twelve..."[2]

When Fred Carpenter and James Wolki were growing up marriage was perhaps less about finding true love than in matching up partners who might produce children to help with all of the work on the trap line. Young girls might be paired up with boys slightly older than themselves or in many instances with men who were twice or more their age. Part of this had to do with the established roles that each gender played. The man would hunt and provide the meat for the woman to cook. He would trap the fur but it was the woman's job to flense them and to sew any tears. From a young age a girl was taught these skills by her mother and grandmothers while the boys would be following their father and grandfathers out onto the trapline.

According to the Inuit Way - a guide to Inuit Culture, "Marriages took place when the girl was approximately 14 years of age and when the man was entering early adulthood, around twenty. Marriages were usually arranged by parents based on economic reasons or as a means of strengthening bonds between families. It was common for people to arrange marriages for their babies, sometimes before they were born."[3] This was perhaps due to the 'transient' way of life where a family might not know when they might see each other again but with a recognition that having children was important to the continuation of the culture as well as for the parents to have help in old age. With a high infant mortality rate the parents tried for many children, a concept that is foreign to our culture today but was also common across Canada at the time.

Marriages were performed at Herschel Island when a minister was in residence or when ministers visited the island. Traditionally, marriages were arranged by the parents. Dora Malegana explains that this was still the case in the 1920's when she got married. "My husband found me when we used to go for Christmas somewhere. He was from Alaska. He was a reindeer herder. [...] We used to go to Alaska for Christmas, that's when we meet and got married. They all wanted me to do so! In them days, it was not your choice to marry who you wanted. So, I just had to marry anyone, even if I didn't want him, I had to marry him."[4]

Eddie Gruben recalls those days. "Yeah, hard working people. Old timers. They depended upon themselves. Never depend on government like they do today. Very independent people in those days. Those days, young man fifteen years old - you have to be a man when you are 15 years old. You're on your own already. In those days, when you're a little kid, you learn from the elders by the time you are 15,16 years old then, more or less, you earn your supper or you suffer. You're really smart. No schooling. Those days. People don't go to school in 1927. Epidemic flu in Aklavik and all over this area. Lots of people die, eh? Lots of kids that had no more parents. Mostly elders in their 30s and 40s died, but the young boys in their 20s and 15."

"Yeah, you got to learn how to build a snowhouse when you're a boy. About fifteen years old, cause whenever you're travelling out in a blizzard - no trees, no nothing - you never go out without a good snow knife or a small saw - something - kind of a thing that you could use for a wood saw. You pack that, it's good for cutting snow too. It takes you about an hour, maybe less to build a snowhouse, depends what size you build. Ohhhhh, they're comfortable man! But when you build a snowhouse, when you set your door, you have to have a hole in the bottom, a hole in the roof so to let the air circulate - you don't do that you can suffocate or die."

Fred Carpenter adds, "Mostly we used snowhouses. A single tent, that's all we know in springtime in fishing time. A double tent is good for winter time so long as you've got thick blankets. Now we find out that nobody uses snowhouses anymore. That was a good life. I like snowhouses. Hard work to build one snowhouse. Have to fix it up after one or two nights. No drips, nothing. Never get cold at night. Shut the stove down, warm a little bit, not get too shaky. Inside, nice and warm. I like the snowhouse at night time. Can I still make a snowhouse? Sure, I'm number one! Nowadays, young fellows say, 'what do you mean snowhouses? That's old timer life.' No one goes to that kind of work anymore. I know, too much work. Once they're made they're good for the year - a whole year. It's nothing. Go there and make a cup of tea inside, leave door closed. We used to do that trapping."

The authors of <u>The Inuit Way</u> sum up the marital relationship in the north with, "the relationship between a husband and wife was one of equal partnership and cooperation. The amount of effort and knowledge required to survive and raise a family in their environment made mutual dependence between a man and wife essential."[5]

It was the same case with Fred Carpenter and each of his three wives. His second two marriages were to younger women. A trapper, especially one who has grown accustomed to societal gender roles in a small community, would find it hard to change the way that he did business. The division of labour, with the husband and wife each knowing their roles worked for him and his peers. By the time that Fred and Agnes were married, Fred had eight children and he was not able to raise them and work on the trapline, so a wife was needed. Agnes was younger than some of Fred's older children but the young ones, still needed rearing. In addition, hauling home dozens and dozens of fox and leaving them to be cleaned, flensed and dried was the only way that a trapper could get back out on the trapline and make a living.

"Traditional Eskimo families were very self-sufficient. A husband and wife, working together, could build their home, hunt for food, make clothing, and raise a family, but such an existence would have been very tenuous. If the husband died, his isolated survivors would soon perish for lack of food. If the woman were to die, the man would have no one to butcher the meat, make clothing, and keep the house warm."[6] Other than love this was perhaps a major reason why Fred continued to get married. As one of the top trappers he needed the traditional partnership with a woman who could assist him in keeping the family business going. He also had many children with each of his wives and needed the support of a mother figure for them.

"Traditional women's work among the Inuit is associated with making clothes and other skin items such as tent covers and dog packs. The ulu is the traditional half moon knife, sharpened on one side that the women use for everything from preparing food to flensing fur. In some cases it was reported that it could also make a deadly weapon and in one case a woman was able to throw it Frisbee style and hit a target with great accuracy. "Ulu. Really good machine, that ulu. the men do all the skinning. The womens only know how to use ulu. The women clean all the fat." Women had to follow certain taboos on how to sew properly so that the hunter wearing the clothes would have good luck while hunting. Sarah Meyook remembers' when we sewed for men, we always watched our hair. We tried not to put hair on our sewing - the person hunting might get cramps. They always tried to keep their hair away from their sewing. Long ago, they always had long hair. They told us 'watch your hair when sewing because the hunters get cramps when they have hair on their clothes. Gee! those elders knew a lot about living!"[7] Fred may have also thought that a younger bride might be more likely to produce heirs who would then be able to aid him in his retirement. "Mom got married to Dad in 1956. My Mom was sixteen years old. My Dad was forty-eight. My Dad worked with Stan Peffer and Jacob Peffer. They would buy foxes and they worked together a lot because they would travel back and forth to Sachs. He, my Dad, liked my Mom."

Fred and Agnes wedding photo.

"Fred's first wife (actually first two) had died and like all Inuit, he needed a wife. A wife was a necessary part of a household. She was needed to raise the children, sew the clothes, prepare pelts, cook, and keep house. Agnes was younger than one of Fred's children. While I was in Aklavik in 1956, Fred Carpenter married Agnes Pfeffer. Rev. Gibson performed the ceremony at All Saints Anglican Church. The bride wore a white wedding gown and the groom a well-tailored suit. However, the church was one hundred meters away. It had rained the previous day so the streets were very muddy. Most of the distance was along streets that had been lightly gravelled. Unfortunately the gravel, which had cost sixteen dollars per cubic meter, had sunk deep into the mud. The only vehicle in town was a pickup truck, in which, I suppose, the front seat was muddy. The only way for Agnes to get to church without muddying her gown, was to ride standing up on the back of the pickup, with Fred holding her steady."[8]

Agnes and Fred's wedding in muddy Aklavik. Agnes' mom, Ethel, behind Fred.

One thing that differentiated Agnes from many of the other women in the western Arctic was her interest in being out on the land, rather than waiting for Fred to come home from the trap-line. "I was the only lady in the western Arctic that was travelling. There was one on the eastern side, but I was the only one on the western side. So, we're sort of a different race altogether. Even then, I was the only woman from the west that was travelling. And I birthed here. And being a trapper. Well, I was no trapper. I mean, sure I trapped but I did not get one fox, but all the rabbits I wanted - by the bushel. Everybody laughed and said that I was a rabbit trapper. Arctic Hare trapper. I had my own team of dogs. Seven dogs. My history goes from very remote to modern and then back to remote and back to modern again. I've done everything that a man does or a woman does." Inuvialuit women were equal partners with men in ensuring survival. In all hunting endeavours success depended as much upon the skilful women as the skilful hunter."[9] It is hard to say who had the tougher job, the man setting and recovering traps while being alone with his dogs for weeks on end or the woman, at home raising the children while also dealing with the dozens, if not hundreds of furs to be flensed and cleaned. "There was the sewing which had to be perfect in order for the Inuvialuit to keep warm during the coldest months. There was the constant travel which required much hard work from both men and women. And, after every successful hunt, the women spent hours efficiently preparing the meat to prevent spoilage. So important was the woman to survival, that a hunter without a wife was considered incomplete."[10]

Perhaps due to the necessity of sharing a small space and the lack of privacy that resulted, Innu children learned about sex from a young age. It was nothing to be ashamed of and nudity was seen as a natural part of living. "In communities of Inuit, sexual mores vary considerably from those of North American society at large. Everyone learns about sex at a very early age. Sex acts are regarded with a relaxed, natural attitude, as just a part of normal life and growing up."[11]"Family life was characterized by security, intimacy, warmth and less restrained displays of affection. ..Perhaps the most obvious indication of the closeness of the family was that the family slept together on a common sleeping platform with the youngest children closest to the parents."[12] When the Roman Catholic priest, Bern Will Brown, visited North Star while doing his rounds by dog team, he had noted that the whole family slept together under caribou skins. "When survival was constantly at stake, there was little time to evolve elaborate rites of passage for the young. Add to this the lack of privacy in the days of the nomadic snow-house life, and you have no room for any sort of sexual mystique. Relationships between adults were straightforward, and youngsters grew up fast."[13]While visiting North Star of Herschel Island in recent years, Margaret Carpenter Hawkings confessed to peaking down the skylight to watch one of her siblings being born.

The trading of the fur towards the end of August was a make or break time for all of the trappers. At Herschel Island, Carpenter and the other trappers could choose between Pedersen's CanAlaska Company and the Hudson's Bay Company. Later, when the trading center moved to Aklavik and later still, Inuvik, the choice was between Simmler's, Peffer's and the HBC. Peffer and Carpenter entered into an agreement where the fur would be sent to auction and then Peffer would share in a percentage of the sales for doing the service. Fred had all of the fur that he had trapped himself on his own lines, often a record number. In addition to that, Fred brought to the table all of the fur that he and Agnes had traded for at their post at Sachs Harbour. By bringing in these record amounts of fur, Carpenter had a bigger bargaining chip. Diane Carpenter recalls a happy day for the family. "One time my Dad would buy foxes from the people at Sachs for nine dollars each and they would send it to Winnipeg for auction. At auction they gave them $12.00 each so they made a profit. Then the price went way up. One time my Dad said he didn't know what was happening. He heard this noise and it was Stan Peffer and he was dancing! No music. Stan said, 'we made $250,000!! At that time, in the '30's - it was a lot of money. He was dancing too. No music."

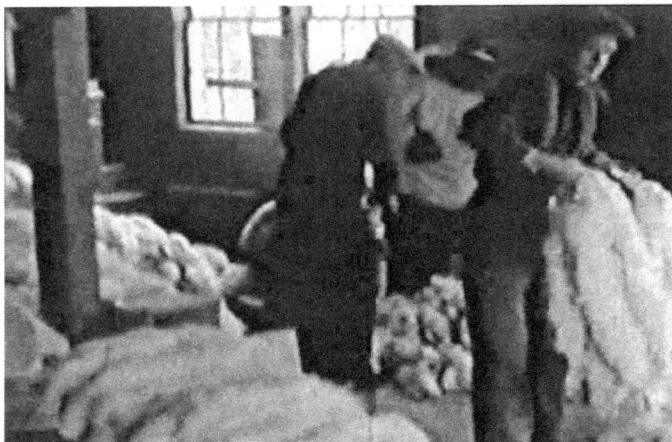

Sorting furs taken off of North Star and other schooners, Aklavik, 1940's.

With the Inuvialuit of Banks Island and the Delta moving from the nomad life of following different game in each season into a trapping life where they had more contact with southerners, many of their past times and rituals went by the board. Part of this was due to the church now playing a large part in their lives and part of this was just becoming aware of how other cultures lived.

One custom that ended quickly after hundreds of years was that of facial and hand tattooing. This custom was done to young women as a way to beautify them. Different designs on the face reflected different beliefs or were copied from an ancestor for whom the young woman was named.

Susie Titsalik was a very famous woman on Banks Island who was respected by all for her wisdom, kindness and the fact that she could out-shoot and out-trap just about anyone in the Western Arctic. When her husband died she chose to remain single and raised her two daughters by herself, taking them off on long hunting journeys by foot with just a couple of dogs packing some of their gear. "Susie - I remember her for my birthday one time, she gave me Arctic Char and it was cut up really nice. First time I went to her place, we didn't speak too much because she only spoke Inuvialutuk but I'd go there and she'd cook bear meat for me and it was good! She was real tough, tough - a widow. She brought her children up by herself - every man in the community respected her 'cause she would go - she only had a couple dogs with packs on them - she'd go walking- didn't even have a sled- they didn't have skidoos then - she just used her dogs, walked inland, found food and came back. One time there was this thing that happened to her. She said she was inland, just by herself - didn't even have her rifle. She's inland - there was three polar bears surrounding her. She was so scared and didn't know what to do. She had this seal hook and she just started swinging it, twirling it. Then she started to sing. Bears were coming closer and she was singing in her native language. They must have thought she was crazy and went on their way", recalls Diane Carpenter.

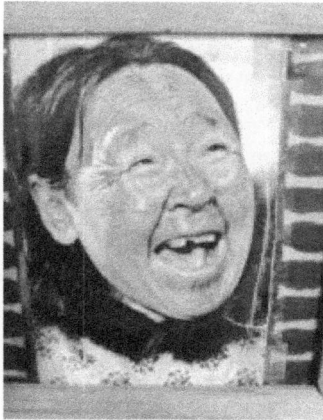

Susie Titsalik.

Susie bore the tattoos that were once commonplace. Margaret Carpenter Hawkins was sitting on North Star and looking at a picture of Susie's beautiful face, the lines and wrinkles of ages and wisdom now entwined with the faded tattoos that she had acquired in her youth. "They put a lot of pressure on me when I was a young girl to have my face tattooed, but my mom stepped in and said, 'Absolutely no way is she going to do that!'. It was brutal the way they did that', Margaret commented, with a shudder. Diane Carpenter adds, "Susie Titalik's teeth were real worn down from chewing the Ukie bottoms - bearded seal - so that you have waterproof mukluks".

Inuit couple with Fort Garry tea. Note woman's facial tattoos.

To make boots, the women would use bearded seal skin or sometimes whale skin. The soles would be made from beluga whale. "First, we chewed the skin for sole and then we soaked it in water. When it was well soaked, we stretched it out and cut it out. When we finished cutting it out, we would (put) pleats on heels and toes. We would chew pleats maybe for fifteen minutes, I guess. When you use your own teeth it doesn't take long. They are not like these pliers we use now. With teeth, when you chewed pleats, when you did them right away and with a scrubber you shape it to your size. That's how we had shoes,"[13] said Sarah Meyook.

The method of facial tattooing used is much different than the modern tattoo gun or the traditional pricking of skin with a sharp bone and then adding ink. The Inuvialuit way was to take a needle, either steel or bone, and then thread it with fine sinew from the back of a caribou leg or if it was available with cotton thread and then coat the needle with soot from a fire-pit. "To tattoo, a woman first marks out the pattern with charcoal on the patient's skin. This consists of one to four single or double lines ordinarily copied from the patient's mother, but possibly from another woman. The woman doing the tattooing lifts a bit of her patient's skin between her own thumb and first finger and then pushes the point of an awl through its so that the skin is punctured in two places. She then immediately pushes through the holes a one-foot strand of sinew previously prepared by wetting with water (except for the initial end left stiff so it can be pushed through the holes in the skin) and a coating of char. The process is then repeated using the second hole of the first puncture as the first hole for the second puncture. The stiff end of the sinew is put back into the second hole and pushed out of the second hole of the second puncture. When pulled tight by pulling on both ends of the strand, no part remains to pass through the second hole of the first puncture. The procedure continues in accordance with the length of the tattoo line desired."[15]

Many of these tattoos would run from the chin to the lips and then carry on right up to the forehead. Line after intricate line. The soot would be left below the skin and would remain embedded to form the tattoo. "When tattooing is done on the chin the ends of the strand of charcoal-coated sinew are finally cut off close to the holes from which they emerge. The chin swells up and the girl eats only cold soup (if a girl ate hot food at this time her chin would rot). In a few days the swelling goes down and the strand is pulled out. After about two days the end of the strand is pulled a little to test it. When right to come out, it will pull easily. The taboo on eating is then ended."[16] It was a long, bloody, painful procedure. "And the ladies by here, because they want to be pretty, that is why they put them on. They all have meaning when they are to put them on themselves. Even when someone doesn't want them, they could put them on."[17] "Them women. They got no tattoos in their face. I like it that way. Women with tattoos, when they were big girls they put them on. When they want to attract men they put those on, and on their hands.

But these here - it was when they were good doctors and when they were chiefs or good storytellers,"[18] remembers Peter Thrasher. The face was the main area tattooed but it was common to also tattoo fingers, hands, wrists, arms and breasts. The women almost exclusively received geometric designs. Men were less commonly tattooed but when they were the symbols were realistic such as a whale's flukes to signify that the man was a good whale hunter. Not every girl was tattooed either by choice or if she couldn't stand the pain. The penalty for not being tattooed might mean that prospective suitors might find her less attractive or as Osgoode writes, other girls might say to her, "You look like a boy." Fred and Susie's mother, Divana, had facial tattoos. In one of the only surviving photographs left of her that was taken aboard North Star, the intricate lines cover her face from her forehead to her chin.

Another tradition was of facial piercing for labrets. A slit was made in the skin below either end of the lower lip and pieces of walrus tusk or decorated whale bone were inserted. This was one way of showing their wealth and success. "Men who killed a bear wore tutut, ornaments of stone or ivory fastened between their cheeks. When girls and boys reached the age of twelve or thirteen, their teeth would be filed down with sandstone, and the boys would have their cheeks and ears pierced ready to receive men's ornaments. The MacKenzie Inuit was the only tribe to mark the growing up of boys and girls in this way."[19]

Avumnuk and his wife at Herschel Island in the 1890's. Note that he is wearing labrets of bone and large, blue glass beads indicating his high status. Photo credit A.C. Stringer.

Living in the north requires a lot of self-sufficiency, even when it comes to medicine. With no western trained medical doctors around for hundreds of miles, miles that cannot be traversed in many seasons, people had to learn how to heal each other. The Inuvialuit had a centuries long tradition of using Shaman or medicine men to help with their ailments. Once the missionaries arrived these practices were for the most part, put out of sight, however folk medicine carried on. Here are some examples. "You know, my grandfather used to be a good doctor. You know, when they cut people. You remember that time they used to cut people? Old Bennett, he used to cut people to take the sickness out of them. To heal it back. Just let it heal by itself, heal by having a rest, even headaches, bad eyes. He cut on the side if you had bad eyes or if you had bad headache. They know right away 'cause they feel it like this. And if it's got too thick with blood, they know where to cut it."[20]

"They did that to me one time, Mary Archie, my auntie. I used to have really bad migraines and my head used to be just thick with that stuff. She just feel my head and she said, 'I have a really bad head'. So, she just feel it and then she just cut it and water just pour. Then after that, it was just like blood and then it just turned into just like jelly. After that it's just like you have no more headaches, your eyes get much more better...That's where they cut old blood pouring out, when it pour out, it starts getting good."[21]

"A little bit later my younger sister Winnie got very sick and had to stay in bed with a high fever. We were all very concerned about her, especially my parents. Finally Dad decided to make an incision in her head and from then on her health improved."[22]

"My grandfather nearly died that time. He said he had a little mouse for medicine. They would skin them, have them raw and stick them in his back. He said the pain always go away when he do that."[23]

For frostbite there were many remedies including for Sir Hubert Wilkins, who in the Steffanson party to cache food and goods for a trek across sea-ice from Martin Point to the north of Banks Island in 1913-14 felt superior to the Inuit who were guiding him. He consistently dismissed their suggestions and found himself again and again shown up, often with near fatal outcomes. After disregarding their example of wearing snow glasses, an eye mask made of wood or bone with a slim, horizontal slit), to protect his eyes he found that his eyes 'felt as though full of dust particles, making the lids grate over the eyeballs. Soon the dust began to feel red-hot, accompanied by a splitting headache, with a stiffening of limbs almost like frostbite....The correct treatment would have been to have dropped adrenaline solution into the eyes, but Wilkins had none, even had he known. In despair, he tried putting granulated sugar into his eyes, and when that failed, had a go with tea leaves, both wet and dry."[24]

**Snowglasses or goggles were made from bone, antler, or
wood and protected the wearer from snowblindness.**

For snow blindness, Buliard writes in <u>INUK</u>, "we have a local remedy, short-lasting but effective. I have used it many times and respect it as much as I dread having to use it - a few drops of kerosene in the eyes. The first searing pain passes quickly and the immediate impression is one of relief. At least we think so. And anyone who has experienced the anguish of snow blindness knows that any diversion, even just a change of pain, is worth a try."[25]

Fred Carpenter used to run traplines a hundred miles long and he would be gone with his dog team for about two weeks at a time. Agnes would go with him until their children were born. Fred had taken many of his sons out on the trapline with him and when Frank and Andy were ready, they ran their own lines. Frank built himself a cabin at the end of his line, so that after a week of tending to the traps he would have a dry, warm place to sleep in for a night or two, before heading back to Sachs. While on the trapline Fred and other Bankslanders would sleep in snowhouses or in the spring, double walled tents. The snowhouses could be used again and again until the warmer weather came and they started to melt. "Oh, it's really warm, a little bit of drop, you don't even notice it. The heat on your body is good enough to keep the snow house warm. Ah, sleep in a deer skin. To put down in the snow. You just pull it up and then your eiderdown parka on top. Really comfortable and you have pillow and everything. Shit, really comfortable. In a tent you f*&%ing freeze to death," advises retired trapper Eddie Gruben.

Banksland was a natural breeding ground for the white fox and justifiably had the reputation as the 'white fox capital of the world'. "All winter the foxes came around the house and even on top of the roof. They were all over and around the camp."[26] Before the white man came, the Eskimos had little use for fox. "They made trim out of it, children's clothes, ornamental parkas or underwear. The skins tear easily, and for day to day hard wear caribou and seal clothing were preferred."[27]

The arctic fox is a dimorphic animal, that is, it occurs in two colour phases blue and white. It is only white in winter and in summer is more of a yellow colour. The blue fox is a sort of grey-blue in winter, and during the summer its coat becomes a little darker. "The white fox will frequently watch from an ice hummock while the hunter sets his traps and, before he is out of sight, will poke around only to be caught in the cruel iron jaws and slowly freeze to death or to be later dispatched with a blow to the head. At one time the Eskimos considered the white fox worthless and used it as a towel to wipe their greasy hands upon. At the time of my visit, however, they were getting as much as forty and fifty dollars apiece for these pelts. It had been a 'good white fox year' along the coast and quite a number of Eskimos and their families had trapped as many as two and three hundred of these little animals and sold them to the traders for an average price of about thirty-five dollars apiece, enabling them to purchase motor schooners, high powered rifles, gramophones and even cameras."[28]

Fred Carpenter, Geddes Wolki and others motoring alongside a polar bear.

When Laco Hunt made a visit to Banks Island, after asking Fred Carpenter to take North Star there years before to hold it for Canada's ownership and sovereignty he was unsure whether he would be greeted by starving, impoverished families or if the rumours of abundant white fox were true, in which case the Carpenters and other Bankslanders would be doing fine. "We pointed the nose of the plane north, and since compasses do not function properly so close to the Magnetic Pole, we could only hope we were flying in the right direction.....Then we saw what appeared to be masts sticking up from the huge snowdrifts: we had spotted the schooners North Star and Reindeer.

Our welcome was spontaneous and warm. I had always believed that Inuit are by nature undemonstrative, but this was an emotional scene, and a happy one. We unloaded the fuel, fruit and candies that we were carrying as gifts. We made for Fred Carpenter's house, small but cosy, where we would have to sleep on the floor. After we had eaten heartily, Fred took me to a small unheated back room, where hundreds of white fox pelts were hanging. There were other pelts too, including polar bear and seal. Without asking any questions, I knew the winter had been a very successful one for the Bankslanders.

I told Fred the price of white fox was rising, but he had already heard that news, broadcast in English and Inuktitut from Fairbanks, Alaska."[29]

Life at Sachs had a rhythm to it, with each season designated for hunting specific species. Fox hunting was the real reason to be there but in the winter when the schooners returned from the mainland, the Bankslanders would go sealing out on the ice. The seals would be cut up and put in the icehouse, primarily for dog food. Caribou hunting was during the winter and a trip to Egg Lake was made in the spring to collect the snow goose eggs. Banks Island is part of the migratory path of snow geese and it was an exciting time for the village to travel the day and a half to Egg Lake in order to collect their stock of eggs. After egg season was goose season. All of these animals and birds, once dispatched, would be stocked below ground in ice houses for future use. "One thing about living in the North, though, or living at Sachs was that each season had a different thing you had to do to survive like hunt geese. Each season had something you had to gather or collect or store. You can't get bored. I thought that living in an isolated community you'll go bonkers, but there was always something to do, so you never, ever, ever got bored. You can always find something to do," remembers Fred Carpenter's son-in-law, Martin Goodliffe.

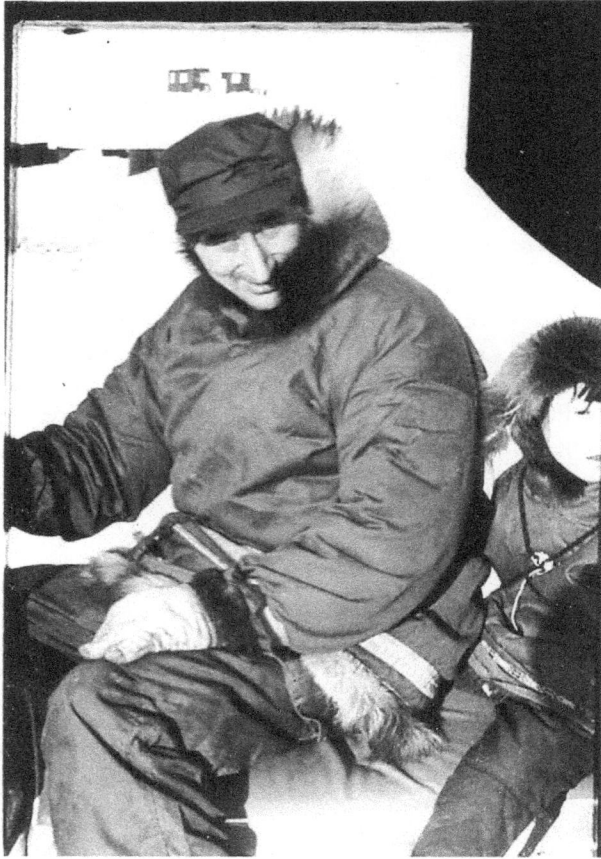

Fred Carpenter and child aboard his new snow machine.

Other chores included collecting ice for drinking water. Carpenter would travel by dog team to nearby frozen lakes and then saw out blocks of ice to take back to Sachs for fresh water. Martin Goodliffe, joined him one year. "He wasn't trapping then, he was getting on in age and after his accident he really wasn't doing too much of that kind of stuff. He bought a brand new skidoo and had a skid, so we went to get ice together. So, we went out to this lake to cut some. Sachs has a river but there's a lake he wanted to go to. He gets out and he's got his axe and his snowknife. He's checking the cracks. He tells me to shovel here and so on and he gets down and he sort of looks at the ice. Really slowly he starts chiselling out a little V. I'm thinking, he must be getting so old 'cause he's not hitting very hard. He cleans it out and he's going real slow and then he turns and starts hitting it on a certain angle and the next thing there's a crack about six feet long and all these big chunks of ice that we had to cut up to take to the sled. Here I am trying to cut up like crazy and with one hit he's got all this busted ice!" Gontran de Poncins in his book, Kabloona, describes his own similar experience in collecting ice. "With an eight foot crocodile-toothed saw, a breaking back, and aching muscles, we cut long strips of ice, about eighteen inches wide. The strip was then chopped into squares with an axe, after which we strove with hooks to raise the plunging, circling blocks out of the water. That done, the block was trimmed and the load dragged up to the Post. Eventually, we raised a high wall of pale green, translucent ice that glittered like crystal when the sun shone through it. But it was killing work. We cut thirty blocks the first day - less than a third of the winter's need. Next day the freeze was harder, the ice was twenty inches thick on the lake instead of the ten inches possible to work, and we had to put off the rest of the job until the clear water froze and we could cut again in the same channel before."[30] The ice would be stacked on skids beside the tents or homes and it was a good insulator for their homes. It had to be covered so that it wasn't fowled by the dogs marking their territory.

Joey Carpenter.

It wasn't always just work at Sachs Harbour. In between hunting seasons when most of the villagers were home there would be dances, feasts and games. One of these was a dogsled race, something that Fred Carpenter looked forward to every year. At Christmas and New Year the Sachs Harbour community would get together and visit. One of the events was a six mile dog sled race. Fred Carpenter was usually across the line first until his son Frank began to look into how to breed a faster and stronger dog. With the 1/4 strain bred into Frank's dogs, Frank became the number one racer leaving his father behind. "I thought I had the fastest dogs," Fred once said, "but Frank's dogs with the wolf were much faster."

Life was tough and the men and women put up with great hardships to make a living, but they also recognised that while the rest of the country had been suffering through the Great Depression, they had escaped it by maintaining their lifestyle. Complaining was not done, for it showed a lack of backbone. "One of the most important and respected attributes of a person in Inuit society is their degree of Independence and ability to meet life's challenges with innovation, resourcefulness and perseverance. Traditionally, these were traits that would greatly increase the chance of survival for the individual and the group."[31]"Inuit place a high regard on the right of individuals to lead their lives free from interference of others. This belief strongly affects the way people interact with each other."[32]Inuit are uncomfortable responding to direct questions concerning other people and their motives. It is considered a violation of that person's privacy to speak for them in their absence."[33]

An example of this occurred when three of the Carpenter boys, Frank, Andy and Joey went out with their treasured dog teams to hunt polar bear. "One time, me and Frank and Andy went out to Nelson Head, three dog teams on the ice. When we got to the Nelson Head area, lots of rough ice. We just made one dog team and we stayed in camp. Frank and Andy went out on the ice to look for bear. When they came back - real, real quiet, both of them. Frank had a real good dog, a real leader. Good bear dog and in rough ice they let the dogs loose to chase the bear down and prevent it from running away. I think they let three of them loose. Two of them came back. His leader never came back. Both of them were quiet. Next day we just stayed there a long time and finally decided to go back to Sachs. Quiet all the ways. Even when we got home - quiet. Boy, about four days later, in walks his dog. He gave me one of his older dogs. Even the hair on his belly was getting thin. He made a caribou skin and tied it up to the back to keep his belly warm," recalls Joey Carpenter.

Dogs had great significance to the Inuvialuit of Sachs Harbour since without them there would have been no trapping, hunting or ability to travel any distance during the nine months of winter. On the trapline at the end of the day, the trapper would first cook the dog's meal in the dogpot before feeding himself. If anyone was going to eat a good, hot meal at the end of the day, it would be the dogs.

Patrick White was a Mountie based at Herschel Island and remembers that "we were set to bring twenty or twenty-five dogs on board at Herschel Island, so we needed all the cheap seal and dried fish we could get our hands on. We did have some kind of powdered dog food on board, but you had to boil it up and it smelled horrible. That's one son of a bitch of a job, cooking up food for so many dogs. It was a hell of a lot easier just tossing them a piece of raw seal. Seals are the best dog food you can get. Only drawback to feeding them seal and fish is the bastards start to fart and stink, holy Christ. Sometimes when we were going into the wind it would just about turn your gut."[34] Bradley 'Dino' Carpenter remembers his father, Franklin, telling him that "it's either Prime or Akita that's buried right on Main Street at Sachs where the roads cross. My Dad said they built the road right over him. So one of his leaders is right there. That just shows the significance dogs had at that time."

The dogs of Sachs Harbour became famous over the years for being fast and strong. Fred taught his sons about the best way to match up bitches and studs and introduced the idea of having a wolf as part of the mix. He continues, "Frank caught a wolf in a trap. We had her a few years. Couldn't touch her, couldn't get close to her - make lips funny when we get too close. Frankie grab it first in the trap, we put the canvas on the head. We want to tame it, put muffler over the head. Frank put the muffler on we made out of rope and canvas, tied up the nose - can't come out. We put it on the sled, take her home. From there, Frank got pups. No other dog can keep up. We got like half-dog, half-wolf, you know, really fast. When the dog race come, even me, I stay behind. I'm the closest one all right. Closest one, me all the time. Even my dogs start to holler, they get left behind. Frank says, 'You feel the wind when you sit in the sled. Have to put the head down - big lumps (of snow) go right over your head. Dogs running like that is like caribou - they throw the snow behind their heads. Those snow lumps, they hit your head you get a black eye. Everyone go to Frank. They want one for the fast race."

Bradley Carpenter adds, "My Dad's team was quarter-breed. They actually caught the wolf in a trap, eh? Fred told a story about a wolf that caught in a trap and my Dad put a muffler on it. He used the word muffler instead of muzzle! What he meant was a muzzle, wrap canvas around it. The wolf was so weak by the time they got to it that they were able to put it in a sled and tie it in and take it home. I think my Dad said it was a female wolf and he tied it up. He said she would walk around in circles and she'd put her jaw on the ground on the ice when walking. Wild, eh? He said you couldn't get close to her either. She had the first pups in the wild too. Couldn't get close to those. The quarter breed was what he used for the dog team. Big, big dogs." Joey Carpenter adds, "His Dad, Frank, was always proud of his dogs and bred them well. So, it was important to have a good dog team. If you didn't have a good dog team you struggled. "Nearly every person has his own ideas about feeding and caring for dogs. In times when fish and dog feed were scarce nearly every person had his own way of coping. As 'filler' in dog feed one used strips of old cloth rags and caribou sleeping skins, another utilized used tea leaves and coffee grounds, others used various lichens and grasses, and one used sawdust from the Aklavik sawmill....The test of effectiveness is a pragmatic one: if the dogs do not howl with hunger, then the strategy was effective."[35] For the most part though, the dogs ate as well or better than the trappers. Cornmeal was added to fish or seal meat and cooked up.

Eddie Gruben has made up hundreds, if not thousands, of 'dog-pots' to feed his teams over the years. He recalls that he would, "stay on trapline about a week, two weeks sometimes. I used to go two weeks. For the dogs, I always pack food, right from here. Cornmeal, seal meat, char, blubber. Boil in the water. After it starts boiling, cornmeal. Cook that up really thick and when it's cooled off - really good food. Oh man! Seal oil. Seal blubber. Month of April dogwood, you mix it up with chicken. Real healthy nice dogs. Strong." Fred Carpenter used to bring in one thousand pounds of cornmeal in one season, just for the dog pots. "Winter time, spring time, you need enough seal for the good (dog) feed, cornmeal too. The only way to cook it is with seal meat. No use killing caribou for dog food."

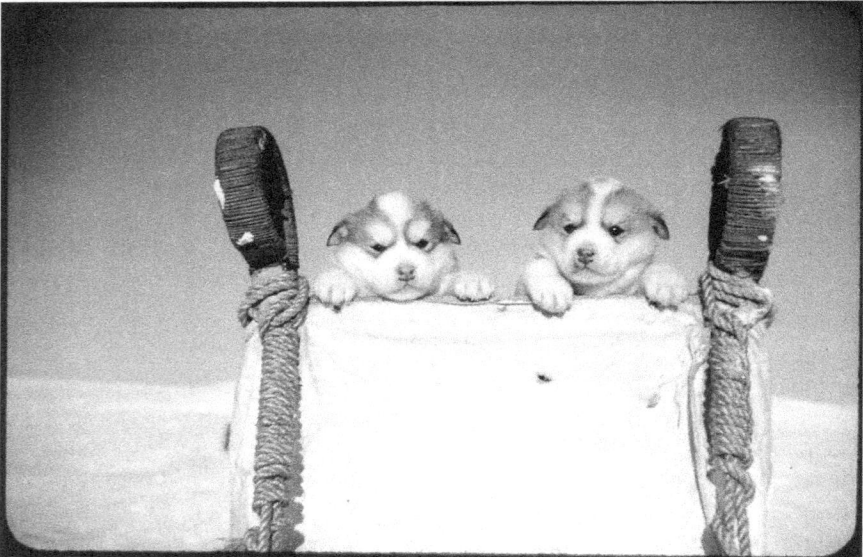

Two Sachs Harbour sled dog pups. Photo credit Bob Knight.

In order to have a good, responsive dog team the Inuvialuit would start working with the dogs when they were just pups. Eddie Gruben continues, "When they were little pups, just like this, just learn to walk, I used to talk to them just like I'm talking to you. Spoke to them like a human being. When they're a year old, not even a year old they understand every word what I say. But they can't talk back to me. When I'm travelling some place coming home, I say 'go home' to the dogs. I get out and I can keep up with them. As a young man I can really run like a dog. I can keep up with them a little ways but not for long. They don't gallop, they pace. Boy, they can travel. One time I was going to jump on. I was running out (beside sled). The dog coming home too, huh? They want to go home. I tripped in the snow and I missed my sled. My dogs are really good. They must have been a couple hundred yards away. When I got up, my leader's name is Nasty, I yell, 'NASTY!!', He turned around and go and pick me up."

In Sachs Harbour "each family has dogs, nine being the usual number. The Mounties are raising Siberian dogs. The Eskimo dogs appear to be cross-breeds. They are longer legged than the Siberians and as big as German police dogs. They are clannish and attack a strange dog. Each dog has a name; when an Eskimo father or mother or other loved one dies, it is customary to give a dog the deceased's name. "It makes us all seem closer to the deceased", Angus Elias told me. "The dogs are chained at discreet intervals; and no matter the weather they stay outside at all times. Occasionally in bitter 50 degree below zero weather a dog is frozen although Fred has never lost one. The dogs are fed once a day; a nine dog team will eat at least one seal a week."[36]

"When they were hunting caribou with their dog teams Fred explained that the dogs would all start to "holler." "They have a lot of power, seven or nine dogs, so you come up next to caribou and then throw out anchor. The dogs so excited sometime you lose (break) your tow-line and lose your dogs sometime - one or two dogs. (You get) close enough to shoot sometime. I put down anchor and start to shoot. I shoot one or two. Let the dogs go to caribou. I sit down, shoot some more. (Laughs) We use Nome harness. Two dogs side by side two by two. When chasing caribou the pups no good for straight harness, not good for what they call crazy harness. They get all tangled up. So, I use Nome harness."

Eddie Gruben, 2011.

Challenges on Banks Island would come up that had to be dealt with and these were done in a studious, methodical way. There was no use in getting angry since that would just slow down the solving of the problem. "Along with the emphasis on self-reliance on pragmatism and experimentation there is a high value placed on patience. I recall only too well being stranded near the Arctic Coast by a broken outboard motor. The owner of the motor spent two days patiently taking the motor apart and putting it back together in different ways, and yet another two days in patiently cutting and fitting a series of gaskets from old rubber boots, shoe soles, tin cans, aluminum cooking pots, rubber groundsheets, tar paper, and cardboard boxes. I finally became angry and frustrated, and my companions were startled by my outburst. My closest friend took me aside and chided me for 'acting like a white man,' and explained that there was nothing to do about the situation but try with the best means available to remedy the predicament, and that only babies acted with such obvious frustration. This emphasis on patience extends to difficult physical tasks, endurance on the trail in bad weather, necessary tasks which one dislikes and social situations in which the outcome is not clear."[37]

One is struck by the peaceful, orderly progress of camp life. Tasks are done with a minimum of fuss and noise. 'Barking,' noisy behaviour (even in fun), and overt conflict are much disliked. Children who want to play noisy games are encouraged to move out of earshot from the campsite. Quarrels and fights between adults are rare, both in camp and in the settlement unless intoxication is involved. Noisy and quarallous behaviour is believed to infringe the rights of others to peace and quiet; pushy behaviour threatens the autonomy of others. The gentle, somewhat effacing manner and quiet speech characteristic of Native people in their own surroundings has complex meaning as a cultural lifestyle. ..There is little opportunity for physical privacy in crowded tents or one-room cabins. Quiet unobstructive behaviour in this context is a means of tension management."[38] The quiet, peaceful nature of life at Sachs Harbour and in similar Inuvialuit villages and hamlets of the Western Canadian Arctic did not mean that the children never had fun. Agnes Carpenter pointed out that "back then, everyone had large families," and so the children always had lots of playmates.

There were snow forts to be built and tunnels to crawl through. Diane Carpenter adds that "when I was little I would play outside in the snowbanks, make little tunnels all through the hills - igloos and stuff. There was a lake below my parents place and we would run across it - loved it - just before the ice would break. We would have a skid and go on it when it had just melted. We had a lot of fun outside." One game that all of the children at Sachs Harbour used to play, was to sneak aboard North Star and Fox for hide and seek and other games. One time the boys were playing on deck a war game that involved taking prisoners. One of the Carpenter boys ended up being tied to the foremast while the others scrambled up on top of the pilothouse and then decided to pretend to shoot him with the harpoon gun mounted there that normally would have been dismantled and moved ashore. "When we were kids we used to play on North Star all of the time. We would explore around in her and hide and stuff. I remember one time we had tied someone up to the mast as part of the game. Grandpa had left this big whaling harpoon gun on top of the deckhouse and we were swivelling it around and pretending to shoot this guy tied to the mast. Afterwards we found out that the gun was still loaded! We laughed so hard at that!", recalls Larry Carpenter. Diane Carpenter adds, "I lived in Sachs for quite a few years after school. I remember walking in the moonlight - just walk around town and then go up and go visit people. My parents brought in a polar bear and they had a big cage, about the size of this room, like a wooden cage. They have a slide with me standing beside the cage with a polar bear behind, just small. Once it gets used to your scent, you can feed it." Polar bears are very common on Banks Island and the children get used to looking out for them. Being a hunting community, sometimes a sow was taken by mistake and then her cubs had to be dealt with. Fred wasn't against bringing them home for his children to have as temporary pets, until the bears were old enough to fend for themselves. He built a large pen one year for a cub that Diane Carpenter quickly claimed was her own. "My Dad and Frank and Andy used to have a lot of polar bears - some of them were pets."

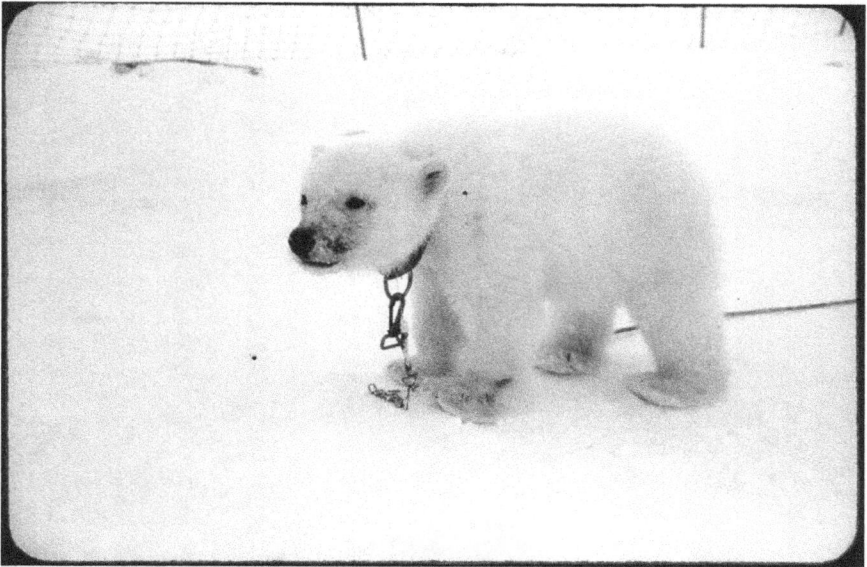

Pet polar bear cub at Sachs Harbour.

"Sometimes they would kill the mother and then have the babies. What happened after they got to maturity when they could mate they would tell them to get away because they would get more violent - so at a certain age they had to make sure they went away," says Diane. Agnes Carpenter adds that "one thing I'm known for is never being afraid of animals. Polar bears. Especially with the polar bears. They always come up to my yard every year. They go right up to where I pump my fuel. Every evening when I go out the door. Even to go out and shake the carpet. The only thing I fear from those is for my children. I fear for my children going to school but they're right in the area, between ourselves and the RCMP. There's always bears all over. Polar bears, they sort of stay away. You don't bother them, they don't bother you. I've always been good with animals. I've always loved animals."

On Banksland the only thing higher on the food chain than polar bears are humans. Martin Goodliffe remembers his father-in-law, Fred Carpenter, telling a story of how he learned of another animal taking a polar bear. "He said that when they used to trap, when he was going along the coast up by Norway Island near Sea Otter Cove on Banks Island and he came across a polar bear that had been killed by a wolverine. What had happened was that the wolverine must have got on the ice by Paulatuuq, 'cause there's wolverines over there and I guess it was hungry and it seen this bear and I mean, they're a pretty vicious animal and it ran up in front of it , chewed its neck to open the vein and then ran off 'til it was dead. Ate what it wanted of the polar bear."

Polar Bear cub secured for transport.

On several occasions Fred was able to sell the cubs to various Canadian zoos. Dave Jones was the Imperial Oil Agent at Aklavik and he recalls seeing

North Star come in to his fuel dock at Aklavik with a polar bear cub in a cage on deck. "The little cub was in a cage right on North Star's deck and after getting his fuel he was sending it down to a zoo, in Edmonton, I think". Another time at Sachs Harbour Fred built a pen beside his house and kept a polar bear cub in it over one winter. Some of the dogs got loose and entered the pen and killed the cub overnight. Before the introduction of hunting laws the Inuit upon finding that they had killed a mother bear would have killed the cubs since otherwise they would have probably starved to death. The game wardens specified that bears must be of a certain size before they were killed which caused a rift between the hunters and themselves. The demand for bear pelts also meant that they were hunted in the spring since this is when their fur brings the best price, rather than in the fall when the meat tastes better after a summer diet.

Food was kept fresh year round at Sachs Harbour by keeping it in an ice house. Digging through the frozen ground is a difficult undertaking. When Father Dehurtevent moved into his Arctic community he had the challenge of doing this and of learning the local language. His main purpose was to keep the seal and fish fresh that he would be using for dog food. "So you have nice fish for all winter, for the dog feed anyway. He dug it himself .... study Inuvialuktun and now, after dinner, dig the icehouse So I used to work three hours everyday. So after a few months, I have a little pit deep enough... it was not much room, maybe 6 feet wide, square, not even maybe 5-6 feet down."[39] I cleaned out Fred Carpenter's ice-house many time times for him," recalls Martin Goodliffe. "It probably goes down 13 or 14 feet, then it sort of follows around and then there is another community icehouse out at the point." Families would share ice houses and put their own food in different tunnels, though the Inuvialuit have a tradition of always sharing their food. "Inuit continue to share the meat of animals with everyone in the village, just as they believe that the animals are sharing their energy with the hunters. It is a system of high and treasured reciprocity. If a hunter betrays this system of sharing, this country food, then the community shuns the hunter. In turn the animals supposedly withhold themselves from being hunted."[40] The sharing of food amongst the community was commonplace, though the unwritten rule was that one always took care of their family first. "There remains a very strong family orientation among Inuit. People feel that they can always depend on their families for assistance and support if it is needed. Family loyalties generally outweigh any other obligations a person may have, including those to the community at large."[41]

As the money rolled in from the sale of fur, Fred soon was living in a wood frame house year round, rather than in a double walled tent. His decision had been made to live out his life at Sachs Harbour. The house was a far cry from what he had grown up with and with what some of his friends still had, living out of tents, ice houses or mud huts with windows made from dried walrus intestines. "My grandfather used to get seals from Herschel Island;

they just used them to make windows. They made it real good too. No wind come in through it, they don't tear."[42] Diane Carpenter remembers the house as being comfortable but cold. "We would hang blankets up in the doorways in order to keep the heat trapped in," she recalls. She also remembers that "we had outside what they call the honey hole. Inside the house, we had chamber pots, but we called them honey pots!"

Fred and Agnes would order furniture from the Eaton's catalogue and the goods would arrive about a year later on the Northern Transportation barge. By the time that National Geographic wrote a story about Banksland in their May 1964 issue, Fred and Agnes and their children were living quite comfortably in their sturdy home. "We had William O. Douglas, a sitting Supreme Court judge, a guy named Parker from Scotland and an Anglican Bishop from England all staying with us at the same time when they made that article for National Geographic. Everyone just slept on the floor. It wasn't that cold," remembers Agnes. Martin Goodliffe recalls that at one time "there was about fourteen of us living in this four bedroom house - Fred, Agnes, Diane, David Peffer, Helen Peffer, Georgie, Linda, Marilyn, Fred Jr, Tina, Visto...a lot of people!"

The small house was a great meeting place for the whole Hamlet of Sachs Harbour and people were always stopping in for a chat and a cup of coffee. Meals were a time for family and friends to get caught up on news and any visitors to the island were almost invariably invited to come for dinner, spend the night or even stay at another of Agnes and Fred's businesses, the North Star Inn. The locals were used to the country food being served and looked forward to it while southerners sometimes had a harder time with it. The popular Canadian travel writer, Lynn Hancock remembers, "Take okshuk for instance. Agnes and Fred Carpenter of Sachs Harbour introduced me to okshuk, which is bearded seal oil gone rancid. It is a popular condiment in Inuvialuit communities. I was strolling past the Carpenter's house with Miluse, one of my southern friends on her visit to the North, when Agnes called out through the window, "Lynn, I've just got some fresh apples in on the plane. Come and have some apple crisp."

As soon as she heard that Miluse hadn't tasted country food before, Agnes discarded her offer of apple crisp and whipped up several sumptuous dishes of swan, goose and caribou. And when Fred heard that I hadn't tried okshuk, he encouraged me to try to it. "If you eat it long enough, you'll get to have an Eskimo stomach. You'll be able to do anything, even grab snow in winter without gloves. Every hunter eats some okshuk with his dry meat or fish."

Agnes added that her kids never had colds when they ate okshuk because it was chock full of vitamin C. She explained its preparation. "We cut the blubber of the bearded seal into strips, put it in a large can, let it melt and marinate for a couple of weeks. Then we keep it in the deep freeze but it doesn't freeze. It's an amazing oil. Try some."

I will always try something new in the North, but this is one time I wish I hadn't. With Miluse, Agnes, Fred, and a roomful of Carpenter kids watching, I dipped a chunk of dry caribou into the pot of okshuk and in agony of shudders and grimaces, managed to force some down despite my shrieking tastebuds. My audience shrieked too - but with hilarity. Grab snow in winter without gloves? I didn't think I'd ever be doing anything again.

To my consternation, Miluse tried some okshuk without being asked and even went back for more. Surely she was just being polite. Surely she didn't enjoy it. I begged for apple crisp. I don't think I'll ever okshuk again, not even if I'm starving." Frozen caribou eaten raw is best" Agnes said.

She also explained how to cook a Banksland staple. "In regard to the best way to cook seal meat: "The blubber she said is cut off and used for dog food or for baiting polar bear traps. The seal meat is on the back. It should be boiled with onions and a lot of salt."[43]"Fred spoke up to say that his favourite seal dish was Agnes's recipe with the seal meat cut into small bits so that the dish could be eaten as soup."[44] In regard to eating the seal liver. "The best of all," he (Fred) said. It is rich in vitamins and keeps us all healthy."[45]

Another staple food on Banks Island is fish. Several times a year a Capelin run would happen, when large schools of the sardine-like fish would come close enough to shore to be dip-netted. If they were further out then the Bankslanders would go out in canoes and dip-net them, dropping the catch right into the sole of the canoe. These could be eaten raw, cooked or dried or smoked. "There are many lakes on Banks Island that offer lake trout. In the rivers are arctic char, the fish Fred Carpenter calls 'salmon'. The Eskimos use nets in the rivers and bait or spears in the lake. Much of the lake fishing is done through the ice that holds all the waters of the island in its grip for 10 months of each year. The low dwarf willow is sometimes used in the summer months to smoke the fish. More commonly, they are dressed, split and frozen....Raw, frozen fish is excellent" Agnes said. "Very seldom (do we cook fish). The older people here like the fish raw, provided it is frozen. Fred spoke up to say that frozen fish and frozen caribou eaten raw seem to provide more 'strength' than cooked food. But today, caribou meat is usually cooked."[46]

Fred Carpenter loved to fish. He described his favourite fishing spot at Husky Lake, near Tuktoyaktuk, "big river, too many fish. The fish going up the river get fat. You use a hook, never a net. Catch the fish, split them, hang them up. Enough for winter. In spring, lots more fish coming." Fred used to 'jiggle' for fish, as well. This is where a lure is jigged and when the fish approaches it is speared. "You have to know when they want to eat," he confides. "Seven in the morning before it gets too high is good." On Banks Island he and his neighbours would string nets before freeze-up. "We catch lake trout for the dogs. Sometimes you get Arctic Char all right. Sometime when you play with a hook you hit the hook in the right place. One time I pulled in the fish backwards with the hook in its tail. Arctic Char has the small mouth, won't bite the hook, not like the Lake Trout - he bite."

Another food besides seal, fish and caribou is Polar Bear. "Fred said it (polar bear) was good, especially younger bear. The older bear tastes strong and takes a lot of boiling."[47]

While being known as the white fox capital of the world and in taking hundreds and hundreds of the animals each year, most Inuit do not seem to like to eat the animal. Fred adds, "A fat female fox freshly caught is very good. But if it has been in a trap a day or so, we feed it to the dogs."[48] The Island is also rich in birds to eat. "Two species of ptarmigan, the willow and the rock, frequent Banks Island and supplement the Eskimo's diet."[49] It seems incongruous that the Bankslanders and there fellow Innu have always remained so healthy when their diet seems to lack the wide range of foods that southerners find are necessary."No milk, no cheese, no butter, no fresh vegetables, no fresh fruit, no sugar in the Eskimo's diet? I asked."[49]

"There wasn't until recent years" Fred said, "And we were always healthy. Look at our old people's teeth, and you will see they are strong."

'He (Fred) became serious'. "A great change is going on. Our children are in school at Inuvik. They have candy and the white man's diet, and their teeth are decaying."

'How about the people of Sachs Harbour?'

"Their diet is changing too." Charter planes bring in food from Hudson's Bay stores. Our people. if they have the money, can eat what people in Edmonton or Vancouver eat."

'Are there many Eskimos at Sachs Harbour who are still on a traditional meat diet?'

"Only a few. Come, I will show you."

'Fred took me to the general store he runs, stocked with canned meats, soups, stewed fruits, powdered milk, a powder that makes soft drinks, jack knives, snow glasses, and many other goods.'

'Do your people take to the white man's diet?'

"Yes" Fred said. Then with a chuckle he added, "except for macaroni and cheese."

'Why that exception?

"I don't know. Agnes and I like it very much. But none of the other Eskimos do."[51]

Life at Sachs Harbour seems to have been one of harsh extremes but one that elders now look back on as being the best part of their lives. Hard work, close families and neighbours and a reward for your labours at year's end. No one went hungry and people cared for one another. "Sometimes they (the leaders) would tell stories. The stories would always help the young people to learn ways about doing things and ways of behaving. Their words were full of information and wisdom and our people respected the elders. When individuals behaved in ways which hurt the camp, the leaders and elders would try to counsel them. If they refused to change, despite repeated warnings, they would be shunned by the others in camp. It was as though the person did not exist."[52]

Martin Goodliffe remembers when he first met Fred and Agnes and lived in their home at Sachs Harbour. He has fond memories of the two of them sitting and talking in the morning and it wasn't until later in life that many of Fred's lessons showed their true value to him. "I remember first meeting Fred Carpenter, well yeah, I was going with his daughter for awhile and ended up I had a little place that I was renting and that ended and I didn't know where to stay and so they invited me to stay at their house and that's when I first met Fred. In the morning we used to see who could beat each other to get up first - get up first to make the coffee, 'cause he made real strong coffee. I used to go 1/2 and 1/2 with his coffee, 1/2 water and 1/2 coffee. We used to sit in the mornings and in the aboriginal communities people would stay up late and get up late cause there was not much to do. He spoke great English and we used to have coffee. Then he would tell me stories, things like which way the drifts go when you're trapping and what do you look for when you wake up in the morning, when you look out on the land. He would actually look at the flag and see which way it was blowing and then look around from there 'cause that will tell you lots about what's going to happen. If there's a small ring around the moon at night, or a large ring around it. It's like sailors or whatever. What kinds of clothes mean and stuff. He used to tell me stories of being stuck in the ice, everyone was all upset and he said' 'you gotta wait it out' He was a very patient man."He taught me how to pack ice properly and stuff like that and I went hunting with him a few times. When you see caribou, you just drive along beside them. It looks like you're leaving them when you're just passing them and then you just angle your way in on the skidoo. We used to have caribou all over the place. When we first got to Sachs, they's be pretty plentiful. We'd shoot them and he'd show me how to butcher them. It was fun. I only had a year or so with him. Most of his stories didn't mean much to me 'cause I was pretty green. Later, the stories come a long way to guide you in life. He believed that no matter how bad a person is, there's some good somewhere and he basically believed in God, the Bible and stuff. He was always working, always doing something. It's a rough environment to live in the Arctic. You have to, you just can't go to the corner store to get something, you know?"

Chapter 17

Florence Carpenter – the Language Keeper

There have been countless interesting, strong and independent people who have been involved with North Star of Herschel Island through the years. In the majority of cases it is the men's' stories that have been recorded and survived. One woman who ended up joining the Carpenter clan did so when she fell in love with Fred Carpenter's eldest son, Frank, when North Star came into the port of Aklavik to trade their winter catch of fur. This is her story.

Florence Turrel was born October 17th 1930 to Gwich'in parents near Aklavik. She had a brother, Stan, and two sisters Rosie and Dolly. Her parents could not afford another child and so she was given to another Aboriginal family to be raised. This was not an uncommon practice in Northern Aboriginal communities. It was Sarah and Albert Ross who took her in as their own and at some point she attended school in Aklavik for a few years where she first met some of Fred Carpenter's children. Her formal schooling was at most a few years as she was needed at home to help her father with hunting so that the family would have food and in taking care of the home. "By her late teens she was the main breadwinner for the family."[1]

Her son Les recalls that "Aklavik was the Mecha at that time for hunting and trapping. As such, Fred Carpenter and his sons Andy and Frank were well known for the huge bounty of white fox skins that they would haul in every year. The whole town would come out to see the huge ship (North Star) and what would come off. I guess during that time, at a dance or something, they met and fell in love."[2]

Her son, Bradley was told a slightly different story by his mother. "She said she was about twenty year's old, maybe a bit younger than that. She asked her Dad if he had some money because she wanted to go to Peffer's Store to buy some candy. She liked the toffee he had. So, Ross pulled a quarter out of his pocket and said, 'See my girl, that's all I got!' He gave her the quarter, she was thankful for it and she said she was clutching that quarter as she walked up to Peffer's Store. Peffer's was described in the book Canadian North. The "store is typical of such places in the north. In it are stocks of every conceivable Indian or Eskimo requirement. Tinned foods, tea, kettles, tobacco, pipes, moccasins, mitts, parkas, dog-harnesses, knives and all the rest of the paraphernalia of Arctic living and hunting are arranged in neat rows on its shelves. In another room I saw some of the things that customers bring in return. Polar-bear skins, the skin of a Barren Lands grizzly bear, and pelts of silver foxes, crossed foxes and white foxes hung on the walls. The scene would not have been very different in a fur-trading post any time in the last two hundred years."[3]

Bradley continues, "She went in and she could see these plywood boxes, 8x4 feet, two or three of them in the middle of the floor. She said there were a bunch of Eskimo women walking around the store. They don't shop by the yard - they shop by the bundle! She said they were walking and taking what they want from the shelf and put it inside this box. They go over and get it and put it inside the box. Go over and get something else and put it in the box. That's how they shopped. When they were all done they'd leave and Peffer would go and write everything down. She said she was standing there watching this happen and that was her first encounter with the North Star, the people from Sachs Harbour. She said that all of a sudden she just got embarrassed and thought, 'what the hell am I doing her at twenty years old with a quarter in my hand watching these people shop like that?' So instead of buying her candy, she turned around and walked out embarrassed. Started walking home and she could hear, 'Hey, what's your name?' She looked back - Frank Carpenter was chasing her. He caught up to her, asked her who she was. You were forbidden to have any type of relationship back then, especially if you were Indian and Eskimo. Just couldn't do it. So she said they spent four years courting one another, four consecutive years. The reason for the rift between the Indian and Inuit peoples was as a result of a long running feud. "The forest dwelling Indians and the Eskimos of the treeless tundra were traditional enemies. This was particularly true in the MacKenzie Delta, where both the Gwich'in, originating in Alaska's interior, and coastal Alaskan Eskimos, moving slowly into areas formerly occupied by another Eskimo culture, were competing for the food and fur-rich territory."[4] Aklavik had been a traditional place where the Gwich'in Indian and the MacKenzie Inuit would come to trade in peace. In 1912 the NorthWest Mounted Police and the Hudson's Bay Company both opened shop here, somewhat formalising the town of Aklavik, named for the barren ground grizzly.

Even though the intense feuds and fights to the death between the two groups had cooled by the mid 1900s, "Atavistic fears die hard: when the Arctic Games were held in Coppermine (Kugluktuk) in the late 1960's, one of the competitors was a Chipewyan woman from Fort Resolution on the south shore of Great Slave Lake. She was terrified of being killed and eaten by the Inuit, though she actually was treated with great hospitality."[5]

On the fourth year of their courting when "the North Star came back, she asked my Dad if she could go to Banks Island with him. He said, 'Geez, Florence. We can't. We'd be living in sin' and my great-grandmother was very strict, very religious lady. My Dad was scared of her, didn't want that sort of thing to happen. So he told Florence, 'Can't do it'.

So, she packed her bags when she went home that night and next morning she knew North Star was leaving. She got down to the shore and she was going to jump on the ship whether he liked it or not. She had had a rough go in Aklavik you know. She said when she got to the shore, North Star was pulling out and she had missed the ship and so she had to wait an entire year for him to come back." It would have been a haunting and heart-breaking sight to have seen the young lady standing desolately with suitcase in hand on the banks of the McKenzie River as North Star faded into the distance.

Bradley continues, "my Dad tells the story that he had a picture of my Mom and on that same trip he was going back to Banks Island, he had it in his Bible. When everything had settled down and no one was around and they were just sailing, he would open his bible and just stare at Mom's picture. The two of them were definitely in love and on the next year when North Star came back, my Mom was scheduled to go the nursing school in Fort Smith. So she told Frank, 'Frank, you marry me now or never.' She went home and told her parents. Her Mom forbid the wedding cause he was an Eskimo. 'You can't marry an Eskimo.' All her Dad said was, 'Geez, my girl. What am I going to wear?' They got married in Aklavik that year, 1954."

"In an excerpt from a CBC documentary produced in 2002, Florence told a slightly different story of her and Frank: "We did go to school together for about a year or a year and a half and then I met him again in 1950 in Aklavik and then I never seen him again until the next August. I was working at the hospital in Aklavik and then the boats came in from Banks Island so that night Frank's Dad asked me to come down to the North Star, that was their boat. So I went down there and he talked to us and he said his son needs a wife because they have no one to sew for them, no one to look after them. So, that's how I got picked to marry Frank."[6]

"My older sister, Rosie Larock, she just said, 'why are you going to marry an Eskimo?' and I told her that because I'm sure that he's going to treat me good and he's going to be kind to me because I was raised poor, eh? But she was married to an Eskimo too so it was really funny. I don't think they were happy that I was going to marry an Eskimo but what could they do? My mind is just like a rock that you can't move."[7]

Florence and Frank Carpenter's wedding.

In any case, on August 23rd, 1954 Florence and Frank married. Frank's brother Joey recalls, "I remember that day pretty good. I was on North Star and with Uncle Tom on the day of the wedding, Tom Moss had really fancy clothes on. He had slippers and mukluk on. Gee, I thought. What's going on? 'He's the best man', they told me. There's no significance (of best man) to me except best is really, really good. I had no idea what he meant - best man, when I went to church with him and the fellers. Dino continues, "My Mom said my Dad had to get a bit of liquid courage to go through with the ceremony. He was a quiet man, very quiet, so before the wedding some of his best friends plied him with some rum. She said as they were walking out of the church he stepped on her veil and pulls it off her head."

After all of the years of watching North Star coming into port and her aborted attempt to jump aboard with her suitcase, Frances finally made it aboard and Fred steered the ship towards Banksland and her new home. As the ship rolled along, Frances became very seasick. On that voyage, the ship ran into some typical early fall storms. Working though her own queasiness she worried about the young children aboard and tied them all to the mast below. "I've never seen the North Star, but she says the mast goes right down through the boat and she'd tie the kids to the mast because the boat was rolling and she didn't want them to get hurt, so the kids would get tied to that thing. (Laughs) I don't think they were her kids, 'cause they were just married, but I think there were subsequent trips made where she would have had Les and Barb. Barb might even remember getting tied to that pole!"

"Fewer than one hundred people lived year round in Sachs Harbour. Frank built a house behind his father's house. It was insulated with sod. It was their home, when they weren't living on the land. She trapped with my father and it was a whole new life for her, a whole new language, a whole new culture. And it was hard and during that time they always wanted a huge, huge family. I think she had six, if not more, miscarriages. Others joined our family which was an opportunity for us as well as for them and that's how we ended up with the family that we did. That opportunity was adoption. And for Florence, for whom language was important, the word adoption had lost its true meaning and thus, its use."

"She would never say that. It was a dirty word in the house. If you mentioned adoption in the house she would throw you out. In some instances, I think she actually believed that she gave birth to me. That's how strongly she believed in her children, and so they were all her own. As each one came along we were spoiled but you never stayed spoiled. The next one would come along and everybody would spoil that child and then another child would come along and we'd all spoil that one. So, we all had that taste of being a special child for a while and then we ended up being a very special and in my opinion, a unique family. You know at the same time that she had our chips in and first of all being accepted into Inuvialuit society, as children we had to deal with some of that too because half of our relatives were Inuvialuit and half of our relatives were Gwich'in and so, depending upon where you spent the summer or winter, you always got teased - either teased about being Eskimo or teased about being Indian. Sometimes it wasn't so kind but being the parents they were, they taught us to deal with it and get over it. Don't let it bother you. What you had to do was learn to love your family first and so we became really closer knit as one family within two different cultures,"[8] remembers Les Carpenter.

For a wedding present for Florence and Frank, Fred Carpenter took a saw and cut Agnes's and his house in half. Then he hooked a dog team up to Frank and Florence's half, towed it a few meters away and then boarded up the backs of both houses. The fuse box remained in the original house and Fred was able to monitor their use. "He proceeded to spend the next four or five years controlling their heating bill. Couldn't turn that heater up unless you were cooking!" adds Dino.

Even with the Carpenters' status in the one hundred person strong Hamlet of Sachs Harbour there was still racism. The Carpenter children were used to being called 'half-breeds' and worse. Diane Carpenter and Martin Goodliffe's children were called 'white niggers', an insult that Diane and her siblings had also received as children of a 'half-breed' marriage. In the hierarchy of racism though, nothing was worse than the union of an Eskimo, half breed or not, with an Indian. "In the fifties, marriage between Gwich'in and Inuvialuit was not common. Historic animosity lingered from before the days from contact with Europeans because of blood feuds and battles between the two peoples and later there was competition for trade. Florence and Franks' marriage carried the weight of history, social stigma and personal pressures."[9]

"Florence was immersed in her husband's culture but she remained devoted to her G'wichin heritage, in particular, the language.'In a way I think that even though she pretended to be hard nosed about how things fell into place, I think her language was what always kept her, in her heart, G'wichin, and that was always the one thing that she could probably do better than just about anybody else and she used that to reflect, to remember, to plan, to speak and used it as a tool as well. Something that she held very, very close to her heart.'"[10]

Frank followed in his father Fred's footsteps and was known as one of the best trappers in the Canadian Arctic. Florence worked the lines with him, some of them so long that they would be camping out in snowhouses and double walled tents for weeks at a time as they went from one end to the other. Rising early to check the weather in forty degree below temperatures, then cooking up dog pots, harnessing the dogs and travelling from trap to trap was not for the weak. My Mom often talked about writing a book. She never did. She was going to call it 'The Good Old Days - Bullshit!'", recalls their son, Dino.

**Florence and Frank Carpenter and Joe Apiana outside their
Sachs Harbour home. Photo credit Bob Knight.**

Frank and Florence ended up raising eight children. Another addition to their family was Joe Apiana. In the fifties, the Inuit of Holman Island fell on hard times. Hunting dried up and food and fur was so hard to come by that some Inuit starved to death. In desperation many of the community moved to Sachs Harbour and were taken in temporarily until they could get back on their feet. Frank and Florence were so generous to Apiana that he felt he was a true part of their family. Even though he was only two years younger than them, he called them mom and dad and stayed with them until their move to Inuvik years later.

The move came as a result of their two eldest children, Barb and Les attending Stringer Hall residential school, about 500 km south. The tightly knit family felt like it was coming undone. They were faced with the same dilemma that so many Inuvialuit before them had felt. Their work was on the trap-line and there was no local school. If they followed their children to Inuvik they would have no way of supporting themselves. "I think it was my mother who talked him into becoming an RCMP because that way there was a stepping stone for them to get to Inuvik because my mother was having a hard time with dealing with my sister and I being away in Stringer Hall for so long. And so, he joined the RCMP, gave up trapping and then in 1966 got transferred to Inuvik and worked as a special constable for a number of years until they adjusted the program even then as somebody who was not a young recruit, he became a full fledged constable,"[11] recalls Les.

As the children grew older and began to fledge, four of them followed in their father's footsteps and joined the RCMP. Frances started looking beyond her home, not only for a job, but for work that would recognise her roots. She pitched an idea to the CBC and was hired in 1984, when she was 54 years old, to host her own radio show in her first tongue, Gwich'in. The show was called Nuntai, which simply means 'People Speak' and it immediately became very popular. Formerly, the local radio waves played mainly country and western music. Frances not only played G'wichin songs but interviewed elders, spoke about current events and weather and on occasion even took on the role of counsellor while on air, and all in the Gwich'in tongue. Her popularity as a radio host extended to her work in the community. She was well known for cooking up extra food and then taking it around to the homeless shelter or taking warm clothing and blankets out to people in need. Florence stayed with the show, tackling any new technology thrown her way until her retirement in the early 1990's.

Frank retired from the RCMP and soon after was diagnosed with prostate cancer and soon after Frances was struck with breast cancer. Frances continued to take care of Frank right up until his death on December 2nd, 2004. For his funeral RCMP from across the country were flown out to Inuvik where they joined the whole town in honouring his life. Shortly after Frank's death Frances discontinued her treatment for breast cancer, telling her friend that she missed her husband too much and she couldn't stay very much longer. Florence passed away on December 6th, 2005 roughly one year after her husband.

Gordon Pinsent called her a 'language keeper' and recognised that through her show that she 'kept her language alive and thus her culture.' "<u>When God Comes and Gathers His Jewels</u> was the song that she played to mark a listener's death. Florence Carpenter was a jewel, to her family, to her people, to the mosaic of our country."[12]

Chapter 18
Sailing and Trading to Herschel Island & the Delta

Agnes and Fred Carpenter in front of their home, Sachs Harbour, 1959. Photo by Bob Knight.

In 1936, when Captain Pedersen sold North Star to Jim Wolki and Fred Carpenter he spent the summer trading as usual and then sold out to the Hudson's Bay Company. The year after, the HBC closed its trading post at Herschel Island and the majority of trading was transferred down to Aklavik in the Delta. Aklavik was more accessible to more people, since the mainlanders needed neither a schooner nor a plane to get to it, the center became very busy and a party atmosphere was created as people from all over the Western Arctic convened on the town. "Aklavik then attracted all trappers, the Capital of the Delta, where stood the stores, the Administration, the boarding schools and hospital. For us coming from Banks Island after a winter of isolation everything and everybody interested us of course."[1]

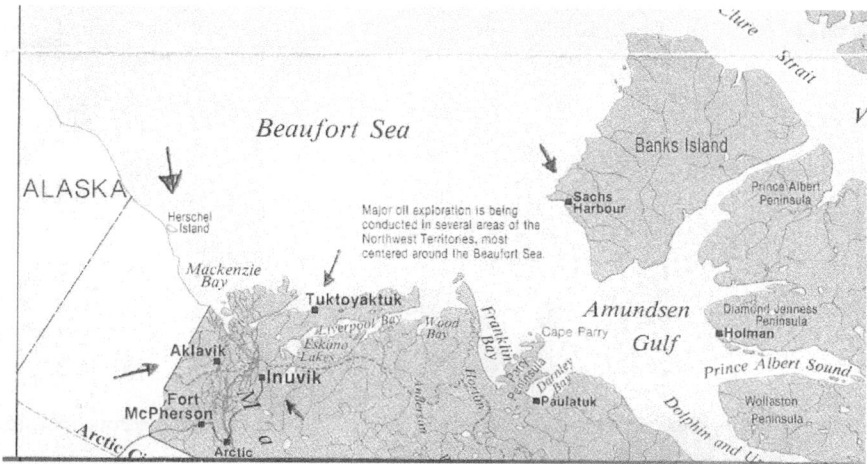

Chart of North Star's stomping grounds.

While trading was the primary reason for the trip to Aklavik, it was just as important as a meeting place. The highlight of the get together was always the dance held at Peffer's Hotel. Sometimes the dances would go on for days at a time. Alice French recalls the atmosphere, "There was a dance at Peffer's Hall that night and my dad promised to take me to it. When we there he taught me the waltz and the two-step. I felt proud to be dancing with him. At eleven-thirty my grandmother Susie said that there was an Eskimo dance that they would like to go to, so we went back across the river to our camp where these dances were being held. It was not as exciting as the dance at Peffer's Hall."[2]

Peffers was probably the most popular meeting place in town and with their myriad of services from restaurant to store and trading post they covered the gamut of services that locals and visitors needed. They employed locals giving many of them their first paying job. Peter Thrasher was one of them. "I stay working for two dollars a day at Peffers and I got a raise after that of three dollars a day. That was lots, lots of money. With one dollar you could buy when you go in a restaurant a cup of coffee was ten cents and one piece of pie was twenty-five cents. That was one dollar for four lunches for one day."[3] During their yearly visit the downy, white furs are turned first to cash, and then into sewing machines, guns, gasoline, canned goods and yard goods. Candy and fresh oranges are especially sought after - all to the tune of much good natured visiting and joking. Their favourite Aklavik trading post is Peffers."[4] "The trappers made trips to these centres and others, such as Aklavik, to trade their furs for goods and perhaps to visit the mission. The trading post became a kind of meeting place for Inuvialuit men. They visited briefly with one another, exchanging stories and information."[5] The facilities at the Aklavik Hotel in the early 1950's were not glamorous but were better than life out on the trapline. There were six hotel rooms that shared one washroom containing a basin, a tub, and a honeybucket.

The schooner fleet at Aklavik, North Star second in. Omingmuk in foreground.

When Thrasher was a young boy he remembered how exciting it was to see the Banksland Fleet arrive. "I remembered as a small boy in that first year at mission school seeing trappers in the spring coming into Aklavik with big smiles on their faces, their sleds heaped high with furs. You could hear them celebrating around their brew pots in the huts out behind the Anglican Church. They were making a good living from trapping then. The prices were good, the furs plentiful.[6] But as the years passed, I saw their smiles turn to frowns. Fur prices were falling. By 1957, it was no longer possible to live by trapping alone. Half of the population of Aklavik was relying on government handouts. It was either that, or join the white construction gangs, or starve."[7] When the American scientist Charles Gillham visited Aklavik in the late thirties he was struck by the sight of all of the schooners festooned with the drying furs of muskrats. "After the trapping season, which ends about the first of May, the schooners pull up stakes and come into Aklavik. The schooners are a primitive sight, sliding up the river. Festooned, often from bow to stern along the sides, are hung strings of blackened dried muskrat carcasses. Chained to the top of the deck are sled dogs, in such profusion one can hardly walk among them. Swung from lines on the masts are babies' diapers drying, or perhaps other apparel, or maybe a polar bear skin. It is a festive occasion. The schooners tie up to the banks, the dogs are taken ashore and staked to the beach, and visiting commences. The length of the stay in Aklavik by the Huskies (a common derogatory name for Inuit at the time) depends upon when the Distributor, the old steam boat arrives. If there is a lot of ice in Great Slave Lake, it may be delayed a bit. However, there is little hurry, for much dancing and visiting needs to be done, and anyway, the boat eventually arrives. When it does, there is another delay while it is unloaded and the goods put out for trade. After a while the deals are all consummated, and not long thereafter the schooners pull out. This time of year is about identical with the arrival of the first mosquitoes, and the natives have little love for them. They head for the cold windy coasts where the pests are not too numerous. Here they put up fish and hunt white whales."[8] He continues in his description of Aklavik. "Along the shore schooners were thickly anchored. Some were so close one could step from deck to deck. Around the sides of the crafts bunches of muskrat carcasses were draped, dried almost black and, denuded of their skin, they were anything but appetizing to gaze upon. The teeth of the rodents protruded in grinning derision, and the long, hairless scaly tails did not add to their appearance."[9]

"The Banks Islanders usually timed their annual visit to coincide with the arrival of one of the Hudson's Bay Company's paddle-wheeled steamers. In normal time this happened three times a season, and then 'shiptime' might well be a synonym for holiday time."[10] The brief visit to the mainland was hectic and exciting, for summer was far more than a time of trade and resupply. It was also the occasion for reunion with families, relatives and friends; for the exchange of news, stories and experiences, and for enjoying the summer flowering of activity that characterized Herschel Island and Aklavik in those days. Boats were everywhere. Schooners came in from all parts of the Arctic coast, sternwheelers came down the MacKenzie and steamers came round from the Pacific. On these boats were people from all races, nationalities and occupations, bringing the latest inventions and merchandise from San Francisco, Vancouver and Edmonton, as well as news and mail from around the world. There were new things to see, like cows and airplanes, and other places to visit like Shingle Point and Tuktoyaktuk. Little work was necessary, as the Bankslanders lived on their boats and the dogs were put ashore and fed on fish and scraps. There was plenty of time for such popular pastimes as dances and games of chance. The Bankslanders soon earned a reputation as top trappers, shrewd traders and big spenders. This richness of life contrasted strongly with the long winter's isolation and hardship on Banks Island, where feelings of loneliness and monotony sometimes descended on the camps and hung there for days and weeks."[11]

Despite the holiday atmosphere for years there was no drinking allowed and when this ban was eased it was only done so for white people. Years later non-whites were allowed to drink, but only at a bar and they were not allowed to buy bottles to take outside. There was a lot of moonshine or homebrew concocted that was left out in the bush but the emphasis was on the trading, gambling and the dances. Agnes Carpenter who had grown up in Aklavik and at her father and uncle's knees behind the till at Peffers recalls those days. "In that time no drinking was allowed. No liquor. The parties and the dancing would go on for days at the hotel. People had their own brewpots at home but they wouldn't bring that."

Mable Stefansson, Alice Simon and Ida Aleeluk perform a traditional dance.

A local journalist described the scene. "In December, a large crowd gathered at Peffer's Aklavik Hotel to welcome in 1956. On Monday January 2nd 1956, a drum dance was held at the Aklavik Hotel, sponsored by the native women of Aklavik with help from Agnes Carpenter. With all the celebration going on, Louis Paul, clerk for Stan Peffer's company trader, pleaded guilty to a charge of selling shaving lotion by the half-dozen bottles and then being picked up drunk with the same customers. Again both Peffer's Hotel Aklavik and the North Star Inn have been closed on liquor nights to avoid fights, broken equipment, etc."[12]

A citizenry meeting was held to discuss among other things, the new alcohol problem in Aklavik. The government had recently opened a liquor store with strict rules about serving only to white people. As a result, the non-whites had begun to abuse other products, much to the naive amazement of the council. ..." a temporary system of liquor rationing was put into effect immediately. Under the new system, persons in Aklavik entitled to buy liquor will be rationed to two 26 ounce bottles a week. ..people around Aklavik are actually drinking hair lotion, cologne and other mixtures containing alcohol and their sales has (sic) (or hic) reached scandalous proportions, and it was being used to make home brew. The government tried to build a case that the liquor problem and drunk problem lies with the traders selling the hair tonic, cologne and other mixtures containing alcohol."[13]

"The holiday atmosphere produced by the arrival of the season's first river steamer called for a dance in Aklavik and other river settlements. A lady tourist who arrived in the Delta on the steamer in 1926 describes how crowded Aklavik was with Eskimo camped in tents near their dogs and with Eskimo schooners anchored offshore. At night Eskimo dancing accompanied by a ' flat one-sided drum held by a handle' took place in the village hall. Non-native persons with permits drew the first liquor they had seen in nine months, and some got 'dead drunk'.[14] An informant confirmed the association of alcohol with celebrations in native Aklavik. Homebrew drinking on such occasions, he claimed, increased in the '30's when muskrat fur was growing in value. The reason lay in the switch from raisin and sugar wine to malt beer. The malt enabled the brew to be more quickly completed, and this, in his opinion, contributed to heavier consumption. Jigs, square dancing, and other old-time dances accompanied by a fiddle, provided standard means of celebrating weddings and holidays."[15]

Canadian author and Northerner, Pierre Berton, once watched an old-timer seem to come to life with the Aklavik festivities. "He was a wiry, wizened, brown little man, the last time he needed a doctor he walked thirty miles through the snow to find one. A few nights later I watched him nimbly dancing the rabbit dance at exhaustive length, on and on through the night until four a.m.,capering to the sing-song music of a fiddle, never missing a beat, never changing expression or uttering a word, with no apparent fatigue though he was seventy-three."[16]

"The dances, like the music, they were probably learned in the 19th century from Hudson's Bay Company employees who hailed from Scotland or, as an informant claimed for the fiddle music, from Red River Métis whom the lower MacKenzie boat crews met at Portage La Loche."[17] Also the gramophone became a popular source of music; Robert Service (1945) heard an Eskimo at Fort McPherson in 1910 playing recorded hymns. The description of a Red River Jig performed by the chief and his wife at Old Crow, Y.T., corresponds closely to the style of dancing we observed one night in Inuvik. In this dance the man never moves from one spot. His steps may occasionally take him on little excursions of a few inches to the right or left, forwards or backwards. But that is all. His body stays erect, his arms hang at his sides and his face looks down to the floor. He would be motionless were it not for the rapid agitation of his feet. They perform continuous series of small, light, jerky steps which take their rhythm from the rollicking jig tune played by the fiddler. Little waves of motion pass from the dancer's feet upwards over his body.

She faces him at about an arm's length away. Her body too is erect, her hands are at her sides, and her downcast eyes watch intently his pattering feet. Her own steps are more subdued and yet more expansive than his. She does not lift her feet from the ground as he does, an inch or two with every step. Her footwork cannot be called more than a dignified shuffle. But she makes this shuffling movement in little circles about six inches in diameter. She follows slavishly every slight position made by her partner. If he shifts to the right, she follows. If he tends in the opposite position, she does likewise. But whereas he moves in short straight lines, she never swerves from those circular progressions. And whereas his whole attitude is lively and gay, hers is quiet and coy.

Periodically a man amongst the onlookers walks into the middle of the room to relieve the male dancer. The latter promptly retires, the newcomer swings into the jig, and the squaw continues the jog with him. Then another squaw will step forward from the audience and similarly take the place of the female dancer. So the jig continues with partners constantly changing until the fiddler tires and the tune dies."[18]

The visit to town also allowed the trappers to visit church. Many of the Inuvialuit population had converted to the Anglican faith and visiting the Aklavik All-Saints Cathedral was an important part of each year's visit. The church was a beautiful building. The stained glass windows in the Baptistery were donated by Fred Carpenter, his sister Susie and Charlie Smith and melded the fur trade, the Inuvialuit culture and the Anglican Church in an uncommon portrayal of the story of the three Wise Men. "The left one, with a seal in its lower portion, was given by Susie Wolkie in memory of her husband, Fred. The middle window, given by Fred Carpenter in memory of his wife, Lucy, shows a polar bear, and the one on the right, donated by Charlie Smith in memory of his wife, Lily Sarniak, pictures the three wise men, one dressed as an Inuit, with a sled dog below."

When the All Saints Cathedral was being constructed in Aklavik Fred Carpenter, his sister Susie and Charlie Smith commissioned a large three panel stained glass window for it. Smith chose an image related to the three wise men from the nativity scene but in this window they are Inuit accompanied by a sled dog. Susie's panel was of a seal and donated in memory of her husband Fred Wolki while Fred Carpenter's was made to honour his first wife, Lucy Wolki and is of a polar bear. The church has something of the air of an early average English parish church in the days when heathens were still being converted. Its alter-piece is a painting of 'Epiphany in the Snows'. A fur-clad Madonna and Child are receiving gifts of white fox pelts, walrus tusks, and a young beaver from a white trader, an Eskimo trapper, and an Indian hunter respectively; while a Royal Canadian Mounted Policeman and sleigh dogs and reindeers look on. The altar cloth is made of moose hide and caribou skin decorated with porcupine quill work. In summer the pews are crowded with Eskimo and Indian worshippers."[19]

The stained glass windows commissioned by Susie Sidney, Fred Carpenter and Charlie Smith.

The church also recognised the common currency of Aklavik and promoted a unique way for parishioners to fill the collection plates in an annual event known as Rat Sunday. "Even the Missions had to go along with the muskrat currency. The Anglicans had instituted a unique and combined 'Harvest-Home-Thanksgiving-Day event, commonly referred to in Aklavik as 'Rat Sunday', when the collection plates were heaped with skins donated by the regular church-going families."[20]

Rat Sunday. Muskrat skins were put on collection plate.

One of the more influential members of Aklavik society at the time was Dr Leslie Livingstone. Dr Livingstone had spent the first half of his medical career in Canada's Eastern Arctic. He moved to Aklavik in 1938 and combined his theological career with very successful forays into farming. His hard work and open nature made him a friend of many, including Fred Carpenter. An article appeared in LIFE magazine about his successful ventures into raising cattle and growing vegetables in the 24 hour sunlight, making him famous worldwide and helped to dispel the myth that the Western Canadian Arctic is always in a deep-freeze. He was so well thought of that people wrote to him asking advice on everything from medical problems to letters from local young men who had gone off to war. One letter that he wrote back to a home-sick soldier reads: "There are not a great many changes in Aklavik since you left, except probably a larger number of planes than in previous years. The season for muskrat was very favourable and with the high price there is plenty of money in the country. They are paying up to $2.50 for rats this spring and now returns coming in show a price as high as $4.50 - so that you can imagine the amount of money flowing around.....the Bankslanders all came in with large white fox catches and received around $40.00 per skin. Fred Carpenter had four hundred."[21]

Dr Livingstone, Aklavik, 1939.

Evelyn Steffanson pays homage to North Star in her book, <u>Within the Circle</u>, though she makes the common error of combining Carpenter and Wolki's ship with her namesake. "Eleven months of the year they spend more than three hundred miles north of the Circle, hunting and trapping, but late each summer they arrive at Aklavik to trade their winter's catch of white fox and polar bear. They come in excellent ships loaded to the gunwhales with dogs, children and skins. One of their ships is the famous North Star, which played a dramatic role in Steffanson's Canadian Arctic expedition of 1913-18. Three families together own the boat which they purchased for $25,000. It takes a great many white fox skins to make up that amount, but Banks Island, so rich in animal life, is able to supply them. Other families have equally good ships, the Nanook, the Omingmuk, tidy schooners with shining engines and scrupulously clean interiors. One of them even has a red and white colour scheme carefully carried out on the galley. The men smoke cigars. These families pay income taxes up to $10,000, which are collected by the RCMP Inspector."[22]

The two individuals, Dr Leslie Livingstone and trapper Fred Carpenter must have been cut from the same cloth. In his retirement Canon Trevor Jones said of Leslie Livingstone, "Les Livingstone always found something good in a person, however down-and-out that individual may have become." These words mirror that of Fred Carpenter's son-in-law Martin Goodliffe who said of him, "He always said there was good in every one."

**Fred, Agnes, Andy, and John Carpenter aboard
North Star. Photo credit Dr. Otto Hohn.**

The scene in Aklavik when the Bankslanders arrived in their schooners must have mirrored the Herschel Island days. Rows and rows of traditionally rigged sailing ships moored bow into the shore with an anchor out astern to hold them into place. Many would raft together, so that a person might cross from one vessel to another to visit with friends and family that they might not have seen for a year. "The Eskimo-owned schooners from the coast, and the smaller and quite different river boats of the Loucheux Indians, were moored side-by-side with bows to the river bank. The masts, riggings and family clothes-lines were hung with meat and fish; wind-dried, shrivelled and preserved for winter use. Good sanitary conditions did not exist along the waterfront. It was no wonder that occasional cases of typhoid broke out."[23]

Of all of the schooners that visited Aklavik, North Star was the one that was most closely watched for. When the Queen of the Banksland fleet was rounding the corner crowds would gather to watch as she nosed up to the muddy shore. "Word would be radioed from Tuk when they were on their way. The adults would always be sending the children down to the beach 'go look for the North Star. Tell us when you see the North Star!" When the ship did come over the horizon, the whole town would come out to watch her dock and then it was a big party," remembers Margaret Carpenter Hawkins. Part of the excitement over North Star's arrival was a collective sigh of relief that the ship had made another successful crossing of the dangerous Beaufort Sea but it was also the anticipation of seeing old friends and relatives and finding out how their winter had been and what the fox trapping had been like. The emotions were mirrored by those aboard the big white ship for they were no doubt starved for the latest news and the chance to interact with a larger group. There were also many who were more than ready for a change in their diet after a winter of eating supplies that may have been stored on the island a year or two ago.

"It was the annual custom of the North Star that Captain Fred Carpenter sounded her whistle within sight of the settlement of Aklavik. It was a glorious sound. The residents of Aklavik understood this and it was a yearly event that both parties looked forward to and when the noble whistle sounded everyone headed for the banks of the Peel River. It was delightful to see the diverse groups of people: Inuvialuit, Dane, Métis and whites with their smiling faces and new clothing waiting at the Peel River to greet the Bankslanders and to help tie up the North Star.

The Bankslanders usually arrived at Aklavik about the same time as the Hudson's Bay Company's paddle-wheeled steamers. One of the contributory causes of boat-time excitement was the Bankslanders Festival which was kind of a Field Day featuring a tug-of-war between Inuvialuit and Dene/Métis women, with races and contest for all. There were balloons, hot dogs and ice cream, and the proceeds were usually donated to the Red Cross.

The inhabitants of Aklavik all made new parka covers and re-trimmed their parkas with wolverine, wolf, and beaver and had new mukluks and moccasins made especially for this occasion and for the few days the North Star was moored. Aklavik held a grand festival to welcome the Bankslanders. All the residents held open house and every night there was a dance at Stan Peffer's Aklavik Hotel and the local talent would play their fiddles, violins, and guitars; instruments and music inherited from the Scottish traders and whalers. The dances would start about ten o'clock and last until eight the next morning and were held at Peffer's hotel because it was the biggest building in Aklavik at that time," writes Mary Carpenter Frost.

"The presence of so many boats at one time was an indication that the spring muskrat hunt had come to an end. This was a time of affluence. Even the children wandered from store to store 'spending' their muskrat skins which they carried in bundles on lengths of cord reeved through eye holes. Although there was some cash in circulation, people had little need of it. Muskrat skins had become the currency and barter medium. But on rare occasions, even small, one-ounce pokes of gold were traded-in having been panned by white trappers from the creeks that flowed down from the nearby Rocky Mountains."[24]

"Anything up to 200,000 rat skins may be brought into Aklavik during those few weeks. The Eskimos bring other furs as well. Commonest and loveliest among them is the coat of the little white fox. Thousands of these come into Aklavik every year. Other fox furs come too: silver, blue, red, and crossed of various shades. They fetch quite good money, and some Eskimos are well off."[25]

Fred Carpenter was a very good businessman. Despite having no formal schooling he knew how to drive a hard bargain and learned early on how to secure the best prices for his furs. Sven Johansson believes to this day that Fred Carpenter was the sharpest business person that he has ever met. In regard to dealing with brokers of auction houses, Fred would play them against each other, telling each house what the other was offering. His daughter, Margaret, remembers, "He communicated by telephone and by Morse code. He dealt mainly with Joe Lavine at the Edmonton Fur Auction. He would go to the Army signal Corps in Aklavik to use their radio to do business." Because of the large amount of fur that North Star would bring in, Joe Lavine, a fur broker that Fred had met through his RCMP friends Alexander and Lambert, could usually secure a good price and this would be paid through Peffer so that they both made a profit. Peffer would then take charge of shipping the furs off to market. In 1954 and '55 Cal Alexander of the RCMP in Sachs Harbour organised a way for Fred and two of his sons, Andy and Frank, to sell their furs directly and by-pass the middle man. "In 1954/55 we organized Fred and Andy and Frank to send their furs to the Edmonton fur market. They netted $18 a pelt!" Other years, when the money was needed right away and extended credit was rare; it made more sense to send the fur to the Hudson's Bay Company. This way, the funds became available right away and could be used in the Hudson's Bay trading post. Once the credit was posted the Carpenters would start shopping for the coming winter's supplies.

HBC plane crammed full with white fox pelts.

"The stores were never busier than at this time of year. The traders' warehouses were piled waist-high with thousands of skins, all to be packed for shipment before the close of river navigation. Even the hotels cashed-in on the wealth from the spring hunt. Harry Peffer, an enterprising American who was getting on in years, ran his store and hotel mostly for the benefit of Eskimos and Indians. The proprietor spent the morning hours frying bacon and eggs, which were served to customers on enamel plates in the communal-style dining room, in exchange for muskrat skins."[26] The local slang for eggs was kackelberries.

The author Malcolm Macdonald spent some time with Jim Wolki one summer in Aklavik when Wolki was still half-owner of North Star. "Jim Wilkie (sp) is an outstanding example. By the time that we reached Aklavik most of the Eskimos had sold all their furs, spent all their money, enjoyed as good a time as they could conceive, and started again on their return journeys north. But a few still lingered, and amongst them was Jim Wilkie. He could afford to stay after others, for the schooner that he owned made the voyage more quickly than did their smaller craft. He need not allow as much time for getting through the MacKenzie River's mouth before ice stopped navigation. He paid $25,000 for his schooner, the famous North Star. In her youth she played a part in the history of Arctic exploration on one of Steffansson's expeditions. We saw her lying at her mooring. Aboard were two or three families who make the annual voyage to Aklavik under Wilkie's command. Their tents were pitched on the river bank alongside."[27] The author attributes North Star's ownership to Wilki and confuses North Star with her namesake but gets the spirit of North Star's participation right in Aklavik during schooner days.

Raddi Kowichuk shipped aboard North Star with his wife one year in the late thirties for a season of trapping at Banksland. "The next year, we were back to Banks Island when Jim had the North Star. I went with him and trapped. I did have lots of traps and didn't really trap. My wife was ill but somehow I managed to get 500 foxes. For Jim Wolki, his catch was 700. Some trappers got over 700 to 800. Foxes at that time maybe 30 to 35 dollars. Well, when we got back to the mainland, I sold all the good foxes, about 200 of them for 5,000 dollars. I had no debits (debts) at that time. I just put 5,000 in the bank to the Hudson's Bay book. The foxes that I had left, I sold them to Peffer's Trading Post."[28]

Malcolm Macdonald continues with his assessment of Jim Wolki's comparative affluence to the other Inuit he had met. "Wilkie (sic) is not completely cut off from the rest of the world when he goes trapping on Banks Island in the dead of winter. Thousands of miles of ice and snow may separate the solitudes where he and a few companions live from even the outer edges of populous civilization. But he has an excellent portable wireless set, and listens-in most days to music and talk in the great American cities. He always tries to hear the news of victories and defeats on the distant war fronts. He is also the proud owner of a cine-camera, and has taken good films of the home life of white foxes and polar bears.

His is not a typical example of modern Eskimo life. In most parts of the Arctic conditions are still primitive. The Eskimos who trade at Aklavik are probably more sophisticated than any others. Even amongst them small capitalists like Jim Wilkie are the exception rather than the rule. He is the wealthiest of them. But some others do not lag far behind. An Eskimo woman who owned a small schooner which we saw anchored beside the North Star had recently spent $5,000 fitting it with a new diesel engine. A better sailor than myself might have felt tempted to make a proposal of marriage."[29]I wouldn't be surprised if that 'Eskimo woman' was Susie Sidney who was well known as an excellent schooner captain and through the years kept all of her vessels in fine truck.

Aklavik became almost a fantasy land for the Inuvialuit and the mainlanders as old friends and relatives converged on the town. It was a once in a year time to catch up on all of the news. Mail delivery only happened twice a year and there were no telephones, so there was always a lot of news to share."Children shouted at their games and played happily on the river bank, or raced back and forth along the unsteady planks leading to the boats. Tethered dogs barked and tugged on chains moored to lines stretched out along the bank. People came and went to and from the boats wearing a variety of costumes. Most of the men were in shirt-sleeves, but many preferred lightweight cotton parkas. The women all wore store dresses of one sort or another. The Eskimo women showed a preference for Mother Hubbards with fur-trimmed hoods, loose fitting garments that hung straight from the shoulders to the ankles."[30]

The hardest decision for the families to make was when to load up the schooners and leave for Banksland. The return trip was often rough and at the end the families were faced with isolation and the back breaking work of life in the remote Arctic. One year the fleet tarried too long at Aklavik and the first winter storms came early. The whole Banksland fleet was iced in at Aklavik along with the LaCheux Indian boats and the independent white trappers. Being iced in was no excuse not to work and so the trappers carried on with their business, only this time the target was muskrat or 'rat' fur. "By July that year, my dad and my two brothers and I had close to twenty-five hundred muskrats and lots of ducks and geese. The meat we didn't eat we put in our ice house for later use."[31] Immediately there was some resentment from the Delta mainlanders who felt that the Bankslanders and the mainlanders from Tuktoyaktuk were encroaching on their territory. "I can remember 1940's that's when they started dividing the land among themselves without noticing Tuk people. They put a borderline to Tuk people and they just divided the land among themselves. Trapping areas. That's why the Delta people say it's their area. They divided up so Tuk people couldn't go in there anymore, where Tuk people used to go in there every spring and trap muskrats,"[32] remembers Persis Gruben.

Charlie Gruben recalls with some pride: "the last time I was in Delta hunting rats, I got over four thousand rats in the springtime. Then I went to Banks Island. When I came back they've been putting border line so we can't go in there anymore. Because I triple all them Delta people. I think I kind of spoiled it. I got too many rats."[33] The resentment towards the outsiders resulted in a division of the land with only the locals being given licenses for 'ratting' in the area.

Another reason to visit Aklavik would be see to Dr Livingstone and get medical treatment. For nine or ten months each year the Bankslanders had to attend to their own medical problems as did other Inuit living in remote areas. These were tough times and the Inuvialuit were tough people. After living out on the land, building snowhouses to sleep in or bunking down in tents when the temperature regularly hit forty below; going days without food when there was no game to be had and dealing with their own medical concerns as they arose since there was no doctor for hundreds of miles to see to them. Thrasher recalls an example of typical Inuit 'never say die' attitude of the time. "From Cambridge Bay, we sailed to Cash Haven and left the same day for Perry River. There I met a man who had gone through the ice on his trap line out in open water. He had frozen both feet. When the skin on his ankles and his feet went bad, he cut off his legs below the knees. When I saw him he was walking on his knees and still trapping."[34]

Mary Carpenter Frost recalls a life-changing incident when she was aboard North Star on one of the Beaufort Sea crossings. "It was the summer of 1947 and the North Star was anchored off Baillie Island in the Western Arctic. Shortly after everyone had gotten off the schooner for a picnic, a violent storm developed and Ada Gruben found herself alone to cope with her two younger children, Noah and myself. The schooner jostled and Ada trembled as she attempted to comfort her two wailing offspring who were both clinging to her delicate body. Since I was older than Noah, I hollered more loudly hoping that the clan would hear us and return to reassure us that our world was secure.

Fred Carpenter appeared and he communicated rapidly in the Siglit dialect with his concerned and beautiful wife. Our mother gently removed us from her as our father encircled Noah and I into his arms, making Inuit love sounds reassuring us that we were safe. I remember snuggling into his fur parka and gaining comfort from the scents that I at age four associated with my family and familial security. These scents were the blend of all the wild animals of the tundra and the Beaufort Sea which my father and adult relatives killed for our food and shelter and in which the women made into warm and comfortable clothing for all of us to wear.

The air suddenly exploded with human sounds and laughter! Everyone was relieved to be back on board the North Star with the clan. They all seemed to be talking and laughing at once while the women prepared the tea as it is the Inuit custom to drink endless cups of tea as each person tells his version of the story.

Apparently when all the women and young girls went into a bear cave to relieve themselves, they woke up a hibernating bear which created confusion for all the parties involved. The men had deemed the cave safe for use and then walked a short distance, politely looking in the opposite direction from the cave. Since there are no trees higher than one's ankles in the tundra, this was one way of giving the women and young girls privacy.

When the men heard the screams of the women and saw them running along the beach with their pants down, they looked and started to laugh. This laughter ceased as they realized that their women and daughters were in danger from a brown bear. The hunters shot the bear dead and the women collapsed with relief and then went onto the beach to finish their toiletry and laugh. I remember examining these brown faces as I listened to their embellishments and feeling an inward joy that all the humanity that I cherished at age four were back and that my world was intact again.

As my father rubbed his unshaven beard playfully onto my plump cheeks, while my beautiful mother, adoring grandmother and aunt looked on, making their Inuit love sounds assuring me of their love affection and adoration, I was happy. I appreciated my Inuit world. I was loved.

Polar bear hunt. Inuvialuit use every part of the animals that they kill. Photo credit Bob Knight.

As Fred Carpenter took his place as Captain of the North Star on top of the pilot house, the clan women moved to the top deck and left me to play the universal game of hide-and-seek with my freckle-faced sibling, Noah, and our Gruben cousins on the lower deck between empty fuel barrels.

The North Star is a 55 foot schooner and she was loaded down with about 25 people, 30 vicious Arctic husky dogs, bales of fur and empty fuel barrels. One can imagine with all this cargo how close the ocean water was to the gunwales.

The Inuit are anthropologically renowned as keen observers. What happened next may be attributed to the excitement of the brown bear incident at Baillie Island or to the expectation of visiting with relatives and friends at Tuktoyaktuk and Aklavik whom we had not seen since the previous summer.

"Lie down - NOW!", my loving mother shrieked. "Lie down Tungoyuq, my baby daughter!" I responded immediately to this desperate plea from my caring mother. I seized Noah and we laid face down on the deck among the empty fuel barrels in our polar-bear jumpsuits, my young arm over his tiny shoulders, poor bodies pressed close together. Noah started to scream and as

275

I turned my fur-clad head to peek up I saw the deadly paw of a rabid polar bear frantically trying to scoop us into the Beaufort Sea. I started to holler too. The sounds of human anguish and barking dogs that ensued are etched into my memory. That primal cry from parents about to see their children annihilated penetrated all psychic barriers. I lost my childhood that day on the North Star sailing over the Beaufort Sea and my trust in dogs and adults.

What came next was a barrage of rifle shots and blood, lots of blood, and as the blood of the polar bear drenched our young bodies, I knew our world had changed forever. A vicious husky dog got loose and as it sank its teeth into my arm I had around my younger brother I lost consciousness.

When I woke up I was lying between my parents and I gleaned no comfort from their Inuvialuit murmuring love sounds. It is a favourite memory of mine that my parents and my extended family of numerous relatives showered me with loving attention during every waking moment of my first four years of childhood and this memory of being loved was enough to sustain me for the traumatic changes that were to occur a few days later in Aklavik. ...As Ada held me and sang her Inuvialuktun song for me which consisted of two verses repeated over and over, I remember my mother's gentle voice and caresses as she tried to calm my terror. As my mother held me and sang my special verses I remember her Inuit woman's wolf ruff delicately brushing my face as she turned from me to cough repeatedly and took up the enamel container which she kept beside her to spit up her blood."[35]

The arrival on the mainland allowed the Bankslanders to loosen their purse strings a bit and purchase not only the necessities for the coming year but also some luxuries. "Consumer goods abounded among the Eskimo in the '20's: iron bedsteads, linoleum, canned foods, yeast bread, sewing machines, cameras, hair clippers, thermos bottles, and even typewriters. One Eskimo home in Aklavik had electric power. The average winter outfit purchased in 1930 at Aklavik by an Eskimo family going off to trap white fox on Banks Island cost between $5,000 and $6,000." Once they left the mainland, though, they became fastidious in never throwing anything away that might have some possible value or possible use in the future. While ashore they were also very aware of the value of a dollar, despite their predilection for gambling. With no store to run to when something broke, they would use and re-use items rather than just throw them away. Persis Gruben adds, "Long ago people knew how to make living - they don't throw away their fish nets. I used to see Auktalit's dad's old folks wash their nets, hang them, dry them, mend them, weave them. They didn't throw out nets unless they were really worned right out. They were making their own nets."[36] The nets Persis was referring to were made of braided caribou sinew that loses its strength and becomes waterlogged when soaked for too long. Lines or ropes were made from bearded seal skins. This was a time when no part of an animal's carcass was wasted. "From earliest days explorers have told of the remarkable skill with which an Eskimo could invent, build, repair all sorts of mechanical devices. One has been known to fix the first outboard motor he had ever seen. Another had a dollar watch which stopped after a year or two of service. Although he had never seen the inside of a watch before, he took it apart, cleaned, oiled and put it together again - and it ran."[37]

The arrival in 1947 at Aklavik was a sad one for the Bankslanders as Fred's second wife, Ada, had to be admitted to hospital for tuberculosis, the disease that would take her life as it had so many other Inuit before her. She had put off being hospitalized for at least one year, choosing instead to be with her husband and children. "The 1947 Bankslanders Festival (in Aklavik) was overshadowed by Ada's obvious illness. While their young children were still asleep, Fred and Ada Carpenter hiked up to the Anglican Mission Hospital to get the missionary medical staff's assessment of Ada's predicament. It was not good. Ada had to be admitted immediately to a hospital or face death within a year. Our stout-hearted mother was diagnosed with tuberculosis. This diagnosis was devastating to my parents. They loved their children and stepchildren, their extended families and their Inuit nomadic culture. With Ada's illness confirmed, my parents had to make a decision.

I watched them return from atop North Star's pilot house where I was pretending to be a captain and I hollered to my devoted parents the first English word I had recently learned. "Candy!?" My mother smiled weakly and held up a brown paper bag brimming with sweets. My father had his arm around Ada and he murmured my Inuvialuit song of endearment as they ambled up the gangplank." What Mary's parents had decided on their walk ashore was that Ada would be admitted to hospital and that the children would be placed in the mission school. It was a huge change for the family and a decision that would have life-long repercussions for the children. "Fred and Ada Carpenter had on their beautiful Inuit parkas trimmed with the Delta braid design which is unique to the MacKenzie Delta area and specifically to Aklavik. Their Sunday clothes. I had no idea that Ada was never to return to the North Star or to Banks Island ever again. She was destined to languish in the Anglican Mission School Hospital and to die eight years later. Ada was to see her husband for about a week every year thereafter when he came from Banks Island to trade his annual catch of furs at the Hudson's Bay Company in Aklavik. As I watched my parents disappear behind the Imperial Oil tanks, I remember them holding hands as they walked together. I also remember that as they whispered their private thoughts to each other, Ada never looked back."[38]

"Nearly all Inuit then lived in camps. In late June, they came to the ancient coastal camps to hunt whales and net fish, vital winter provisions for themselves and their sled dogs. In September, the people scattered across the vastness of the Delta, and to 'bush camps' to the east and west. We trapped all winter Alex recalled, 'and then, in spring, we went by dog team to Aklavik to sell our furs. We bought grub and ammunition and went again to the whaling camps. Some years that beach below was covered with tents and we took twenty or thirty whales a day.'"[39]

Fred Carpenter, Jim Wolki and Susie Sidney would join the rest of the fleet at the whaling camps, using rifles and then harpoons to take the beluga. The shot from the rifle would kill the animal while the harpoon would have a float attached to it so that the whale did not sink and go to waste. For years Fred Carpenter researched purchasing a large harpoon gun, cannon style, for North Star. The paper work went back and forth to various ministries and shows how much red tape a person had to go through even back then. Carpenter shows great patience in these letters, he being a hunting expert knowing what he needed and trying to explain this need to someone on the other side of the country who most likely has never been hunting, much less whaling in the Beaufort Sea. In the end, Carpenter acquired a large whale gun harpoon for North Star which was generally mounted atop of the pilothouse.

Gambling was a big part of the Bankslanders visit to the mainland and Fred Carpenter loved to play poker, perhaps something that he had inherited from his mother, Divana. Joey Carpenter recalls a lesson he learned one crossing aboard the family ship. "First time I poke around North Star in the mid-fifties, Joe Burk, big guy eh?, He wanted a ride Tuk to Aklavik. These Indians used to go work in Aklavik in summer or something. So, he's haggling with my Dad and we start playing poker. I owed a couple hundred bucks, five and ten cent games. Then, he won all the clothes from my bag. I remember, 'Oh Geez. I got nothing. Before we reached Aklavik he came over and gave me my money back and my clothes back. I've been playing poker for over 45 years now, 50 years." Susie and Fred's mother, Divana, was a gambler. "They would dock in Aklavik and she'd walk into the poker game. Divana is the woman in the picture standing on deck, looks like Susie Titalik. Many years ago, nobody had two names. Just one name and Fred's mother was Divana, nothing else," recalls Joey Carpenter.

The family histories of the Peffers and the Carpenters are as linked as those of the Carpenters with those of the Wolkis and Grubens. In all three cases the connection is through marriage with Fred having married Lucy Wolki and upon her demise Ada Gruben and then upon her demise, Agnes Peffer. As well, Susie Carpenter married Fred Wolki as well as traded the schooner Omingmuk to James Wolki in return for half shares in North Star of Herschel Island.

The Peffers, aside from becoming Fred Carpenters in-laws were also indebted to him and Jim Wolki for agreeing to trade with them for a substantial amount of fur that allowed them to get out of serious debt. In 1929 the brothers Peffer, Jake and Stan, had been stock-piling furs that they had traded for or trapped themselves for many years. They had been waiting for the prices to rise so that they could have a big payday. They had over six thousand skins including beaver, marten and lynx. After studying the market, they plotted where they would get the best prices for each of the types of fur. To get the fur from Aklavik to market required loading the fur bales onto a horse drawn cart which would be driven to Fort St. John where they were then sent to Fort Vermilion. From there they were taken on another horse drawn cart to the rail line and then shipped by train to Grand Prairie. The furs were then shipped to Calgary, Edmonton, New York and London England. The brothers calculated that the expense of shipping the fur would be recovered quickly as their latest information was that individual pelts were selling for about forty dollars each.

The news of the stock market crash reached them by telegram shortly thereafter. "The furs were worthless. A very few sold for fifty cents a skin. Some were burned. ....The Peffers owed over $17,000 in Grande Prairie to the different wholesalers plus some wholesalers in Edmonton which left them without credit."[40] The two brothers went back to work running their hotel in Aklavik with its restaurant and their other business of operating a sawmill. Their horses died and economically, things looked grim for them. Time passed and they continued to look for a way to acquire large numbers of furs so that they could make enough money to pay off their debts to their wholesalers and to move forward with other business plans. In the mean time, they continued to work hard, running the restaurant and Jake started his own trapline.

"Then one day, via the grapevine, some Eskimo friends of Stans said some Eskimos from Banksland and Melleville Island were on the way to Tuktoyaktuk. They had over one thousand white fox skins and that Mr. Pedersen was coming round the Arctic Ocean with his boat to buy the skins at Tuk. Somehow, Stan's friends contacted a Fred Carpenter and Fred Wolki who were the trail bosses for the Eskimos. They talked them into bringing the white fox furs to Aklavik because of better conditions for them. The restaurant, the movie shows, the dances, ice cream and Indian girls. A change from Eskimo girls. Stan got all the furs. This was the first bit of luck since the 'crash'. Peffer didn't have enough supplies to fill all the Eskimo orders. He went to the RCMP, RC Mission, Semmlers and Knut Lang and got enough supplies to help fill the orders."[41]

"Peffer was now back in the fur trading business and in a big way. The spin-off helped the whole town of Aklavik. For many years after, the same group of Eskimos did business with Peffer and the rest of the town. This also sparked a proposed sale to Holt-RenfreFurriers."[42]"In Canada between 1950 and 1960, nearly 400,000 arctic foxes were trapped and traded, with a total value of $5,065,937. The top year was 1954/55 when 81,783 arctic foxes were taken. During these same ten years the price for arctic fox pelts fluctuated from a low of $8 to more than $24 per pelt."[43]

One year there was a very special event at Aklavik when Agnes Peffer married Fred Carpenter. This union of one of the top trappers and the patriarch of Banksland to the daughter of one of the most influential men in Aklavik was a significant event that all of Aklavik turned out for. "Fred Carpenter wed Agnes Peffer - Jake's daughter - in an impressive ceremony witnessed by Reverend A Holam August 31st and left the following day on their honeymoon in Fred's schooner to winter on Banks Island."[44] In the same month that Fred and Agnes were married the "rations were lifted - the two bottles per person liquor rationing rule which had been in effect in Aklavik since the council meeting of Jan. 18 was lifted. Aklavik liquor sales were $5200 in Oct, $4,600 in November and $9,100 in December."[45] In 1957 the liquor laws were changed so that "everybody including Indians and Eskimos in the Territories be allowed to drink beer in licensed tap rooms."[46] The law prohibiting the sale to Indians and Eskimos of liquor or beer in a bottle remained in effect.

With the change in liquor laws, many entrepreneurs recognized an opportunity and "at least three residents of Aklavik have asked to open a beer hall at the new town (of Inuvik). They were not aware that Stan Peffer had already all liquor outlets tied up."[47] Stan Peffer passed away March 19, 1999 at age 87 in Edmonton.

"As September approached, the Bankslanders regrouped for the outward voyage. Some were absent, because they did not wish to return....(but) ...as always there were the real Bankslanders, that core of about a dozen families who returned year after year. Together they gathered behind the sandspit at Baillie Island, sometimes stopping at the post to pick up a last sack of flour or box of ammunition, or some other article remembered at the last, and waited for fair weather so they might set out for the great headland which beckoned them from across the gulf."[48]

Chapter 19
Residential School & the Banksland Children

"During the 1930's and 1940s, many and most probably all children attended the mission schools for at least a few years. Later on the children spent the greater portion of their youth in school, especially at Aklavik. Children attending the residential schools were away from ten months of the year, and if they lived any distance away, did not go home at all. Many of the Banksland children never saw their homes for years at a time and saw their parents only briefly in the summers when they came to Aklavik. There was little opportunity, therefore, for these children to learn the way of the life of a trapper and in any case, having grown up in a completely different physical and social environment, Banks Island was not really their home and it offered little if any attraction to them when they left school. Those born in the 1940s and leaving school in the last 50s or early 60s quite naturally took wage employment for their livelihood rather than trapping."[1]

In the 1940's the Canadian Government put into law that all Canadian children must attend school. This was a mixed blessing for the Inuvialuit of Sachs Harbour and surrounding areas. On the positive side, this meant that their children would be given the opportunity to learn how to speak and write English, do arithmetic and perhaps have more choices with what to do with their lives than live in a fur trapping society. On the negative side, it meant that their children would be exposed to others' ways and to take on their values and rules. It meant that a parent would not be able to pass on their own knowledge to their own children and everyone recognised that this would sound the death knell for their way of life. A trapper could live his life out doing his job but would have no one to pass on his skills or his trap-line to once he wanted to retire. The most difficult part would be that their children would live away from them for about nine months each year and in the case of the Sachs Harbour children, it was later determined, that they would not be transported home at all - ever - as Sachs was seen as being too far away. "I had to stay in the school all summer, for there was nowhere else to go. It was pathetic to have only a few of us rattling around inside a big building that was made to house hundreds of children."[2] Fred Carpenter's eldest children would not return to Banks Island until, in most cases, their education was complete at Grade Eight. The excuse given was that Banksland was too far away from Aklavik and that the flight across the Beaufort Sea was too dangerous. "The Carpenter kids never went home. The other kids did. They had a policy. They said it was too far and too dangerous to take kids in a one engine plane. They had students from James Bay, Holman, Cambridge Bay. They had the Anglican Church ship the Beacon and the Roman Catholic Messenger. They went to Tuk and Paulatuk, but wouldn't go to Banksland," remembers Mary Carpenter Frost, the unfairness of the decision still weighing heavily upon her decades later.

Mrs Holman, another student and Mary Carpenter kneeling at All Saints Hostel Residential School.

Mary Carpenter Frost started at the mission school in Aklavik when she was only five years old. She was not allowed home for the next twelve years and witnessed many disturbing methods of discipline by the staff there. One that sticks with her was the method that staff used to teach one of the girls who was encopretic not to wet her bed. The other girls were told to urinate in the poor girl's bed in some misguided attempt to correct the situation. Years later Mary told her story of life at the school to Farley Mowat. "I was five when I was put into the mission hostel at Aklavik. I never got back to Sachs Harbour 'till I was seventeen. All those years I didn't get home in summertime. Instead, they kept me at the Anglican hostel in the summer. My mother was there in Aklavik in hospital for a while before she died with TB, and my father would sail in for two or three weeks during the summer, so I sometimes saw them but, you know, the hostel was so strict they would not let me spend the night with my father or my mother. I had to be back in the dormitory every night.

I used to hide behind my father's legs and cry not to let them take me back. But I had to go.

There was both Indians and Eskimos in the hostel, but more Indians, so they were always the bosses and, you know, from old, old times Indians and Eskimos didn't get along too good.

There were four dormitories: A, B, C, and D. We were divided up according to ages, the youngest in A dorm. After 8:30 at night it was like Lord of the Flies in any of them. .....It was the monotony that was the worst. The food was mainly fish and tapioca. You couldn't talk your own language. If you did, and you were caught, you got a beating. Everything was in English. In the end, most of us lost our Native language.

You know what I got out of my twelve years' schooling? I lost my Eskimo language. I lost contact with my parents, with most of my brothers and sisters, with the old people who were my relatives. When I left Aklavik mission school they sent me to Yellowknife. That was even farther from home. After Grade 12 they finally let me go home to Sachs at last. That was the first time since I was five. I didn't know the place. I didn't know what to say or what to do. I didn't know my parents. I couldn't talk Eskimo no better than one of the hostel missionaries!

But you know what was the worst thing of all? I didn't know who I was anymore...." she rightfully laments."[3]

Mary Carpenter Frost continues with some of her memories from residential school. "All our teachers came from Europe. I did not have a Canadian teacher until I entered Grade 8. I did not know I lived in a country called Canada. Since our teachers were from the British Isles, we thought we were British. We were socialized to become Boy Scouts and Girl Guides and strangely enough, we learned to knit and crochet for church rummage sales to send money to missions in Africa and China.

Our family and Inuit disintegration has its roots in the missionary schools. What the missionaries did was wrong. They should have followed what Jesus said in the Mathew Gospel - "I tell you the truth, whatever you did not do for one of the least of these, you did not do for me."[4]

Fred Carpenter sired seventeen children and the ones who made it to school age were sent to residential school at the All-Saints School in Aklavik. Fred had never spent a day in school in his life but probably recognised that the world was changing and that an education, at least learning basic arithmetic and English would stand them well. "It was hard for the Inuvialuit parents to decide whether they would send their children to school. The mission was offering to teach their children to speak, read and write English, and to do arithmetic. The Inuvialuit saw that these skills were very important in their dealings with the Tan'ngit. On the other hand, parents would have to be separated from their children. Most parents were hunting and trapping to survive. They could not stay in one place to enable their children to go to school. Their children would have to be left in the hands of the mission from fall to summer."[5]

Fred and his wives' wishes were a moot point, in any case, as the Federal Government passed a law in the 1940's that all minors must be educated. Mary Frost Carpenter recalls she and her siblings being sent off with the RCMP when the ship was in Aklavik. It was 1947 and Fred's second wife, Ada was very ill and needed to be admitted to hospital. She was put into quarantine and the only time that the children could see her was when they walked over and stood below her second floor window. She died in hospital years later.

sidebar?

Ada Gruben-Carpenter, A Cherished Mother (by Mary Carpenter Frost)

Each day I would go see you
Standing in the cold
to your second-floor window
I missed you at first
You were still warm to me
I knew you loved me
but I did not understand
Why you were behind that clouded pane
And all I could see was your waving hand

For days, weeks, months, years
I met you like that -
From the chilly outside, looking up
to that blurring window
In that immured hospital

What pain you must have felt!
What were your thoughts (dear Mother)
watching me grow away from you
Hell is separation but you were strong

Forgive me for scorning you - Ada...
I understand now...
I missed your love and care, Mother
I missed your sunny smile

I missed the haven of your arms!
I missed ....

....I still miss you - MY MOTHER!

"You were supposed to be six, but I was four," Mary said. Once at the school the Carpenters and the rest of the Aboriginal children were thrust into a world so different and at times so harsh, as to be unimaginable. "How could there be so many people living in one building? I was so scared that I hung onto my father's hand. I did not like it there and I did not want my father to leave us."[6]

"We quickly learned not to speak our own language in the classroom," remembers Inuit Ann Meekitjuk Hanson. "When we did, our hands were slapped with a wooden ruler. I remember being very silent. We could not speak English because we had not learned it, we could not speak Inuktitut because it was forbidden..We stayed silent. Only our eyes communicated."[7] This way of speaking to one another is part of the Inuktuk language. "Affirmation was indicated by wrinkling the nose and admiration was expressed by putting out the tongue."[8] When the staff caught the children doing this, they were punished.

The girls and boys were divided up and from that point on were not allowed to socialize or speak with one another. They soon learned to communicate silently or face the humiliating consequence of being whipped or insulted. For all of the children, it was their first time in a 'white man's world' with more rules, different food and separation from their family. Many of them were quite young and away from home for the first time ever. "We were not allowed to associate with each other, us siblings. It became like the Stockholm Syndrome. We were taught to mimic white people," says Mary.

Margaret Pokiak Fenton of Sachs Harbour recorded her experiences in residential school in two books, fatty legs and a stranger at home. In the former she describes walking into the school for the first time. "All around me was glass and wood. An enormous photograph hung on one of the clean, painted walls. In it, an outsider wore a fancy sash. Medallions like coins hung from his chest - I would learn later that he was king of all of the outsiders. They told me he was also my king, but I knew that my family listened to no one but Mr. Carpenter and Mr. Wolki, who owned the North Star."

One boy's experience was probably fairly similar to a lot of the children who were shipped via the mission ship, Our Lady of Lourdes, from above the tree line, down into Aklavik. Tom Thrasher grew up on the Barrenland where there are only scrub plants. He remembers being aboard the mission schooner Our Lady of Lourdes as they approached Aklavik and the residential school. "I remembered when we left Tuk, eh, when we got to Tunniq eh, like you know the trees start there. I was with my dad in the pilothouse and we seen these trees eh? We was in the Lady of Lourdes heading down the river, going to, looking out our window. 'Daddy lots of people up there,' I told him. (chuckle) It was trees, eh? (chuckle), I just seen that funny face ah, he was laughing at me. Here it was trees. I'd never seen them before. And then when we landed in Aklavik, hundreds of people on that shore, eh. Holy Smokes! I never seen that many people in my life at once. I was scared to go up that gangplank. And my dad was holding my hand, I was walking behind him, he took me up that bank, I guess eh. Us we weren't important, people were there to meet the Bishop and Fathers. ..I just let my dad's hands go and took off through the bushes. Chuckle. He had hard time to bring me back, eh. I'm scared I never seen so many people in my life."[9]

The missionaries felt that if they could make English the children's first language and then teach them how to read and write it, that the children would then assimilate into the white man's culture and more readily accept the Christian religion. Sometimes they had to be creative. "According to Eskimo historian Sam Hall, the missionary was asked about the meaning of 'daily bread' in the Lord's Prayer. 'What is this daily bread that is so important that you must ask the (white man's) God for it every day? The missionary responded with the amended translation 'Give us this day that which tastes good,' but the Inuit were still not satisfied. 'Are there no seals in your heaven?' they asked. Eventually, (the missionary) capitulated, changing the translation to 'Give us this day the seal meat we need.'"[10]

When the schooner fleet started to arrive each summer to trade their furs and in some cases, pick up their children, the vessels' horns would be sounded. All of the children and teachers would rush down to the shore to see which boat was coming in and whom else they had aboard.

One time, Joey's older sister played a practical joke on him. Margaret said, 'North Star's coming!' and so we all go down and we walk past RCMP. "'Where you going, Joey?' 'Anxious to see my parents. We're missing them. North Star's coming, going to wait for it.' He stopped me. You know they have the radio from detachment in Aklavik for the communication in the fifties, so he knew if any boat was coming. Margaret was just pulling a joke on us. I had to turn around and walk back to that hell-hole".

Another time, Joey's luck was with him. He and another boy had been getting into trouble and had taken off to hide in their dorm. "I was upstairs and I kept running upstairs - that fucking bitch is after me. Oh she is... was older - '50's. Anyway, in one dorm there's a window that opened and a wooden slide fire escape. My friend went down there and took off and then she came upstairs and I just repeated what Wilber had said,..'fuckin' bitch' or something to that effect. She just stopped in her tracks and she just started crying. She didn't expect to hear that from me. My brother Noah and two other guys were always saying, 'Quit hanging around with these people - bad influence'. "I know but they're my friends.' So that's been the story of my life, eh? Anyway, she went down and I could hear Mister Holman coming up the stairs. I know

I'm really going to get it. Next thing - BRRRRRRRRRRRRRRRRRR - I hear North Star's horn. He never touched me. Even he knew the sound of North Star's horn!"

Mary Carpenter Frost remembers "we saw him (Fred Carpenter) every summer for about two days. When we heard the whistle - he would stop and blow the whistle right outside the classroom. One time there was an open window and I jumped out and slid down the fire escape. I had a nightgown on. I would hold onto his leg and never let go and he would drag me around."

While North Star was in Aklavik the Carpenter children spent as much time as they could aboard the ship with their father and in some cases, their mother. Other family and Bankslanders would be aboard and the children soaked up the attention and ate as much as they could. "It was a big thing when North Star came. Stay there all the days. My Dad used to buy apples and oranges, case by case. Things we don't eat in school. We would sit there all day and finish a whole case of apples and oranges. Night time I have to go back to the school. When North Star and other boats came, it was a really nice break."

The food at the school is not remembered with any joy and is described by Joey Carpenter as being 'just enough to let you survive.' He and some of the other boys used to sneak into the cellar at night to try and find anything to eat. "Oh Yeah! We used to go in there and munch away on raw potatoes." Bradley Carpenter was told by his parents, Frank and Florence, that "they had a whole bunch of dry meat, lot of dry fish and peanut butter. The boys used to sneak down at night and fill their pockets with peanut butter. You didn't get enough to eat then. Boys walking around with those flannel pants - grease stains - you could form the peanut butter into a ball. My mom said she couldn't understand why they could have all kinds of dry fish and dry meat and different things in the cellar, but the kids never, ever saw it on the table. Kids never got it."

Many of the Carpenter children ended up graduating at Grade Eight from the Mission School, formally called the All-Saints Anglican Mission. Because of the great range of ages, siblings would see one another go without knowing when they would see them again. Margaret Carpenter Hawkins was desperately homesick during her time at All-Saints and longed for the day when she would return aboard North Star to Sachs Harbour. "Dad had promised me that when I finished grade 9 that I could go home to Sachs Harbour. When I did finish I was so happy that I was going home. One night, all of the students were kept inside to watch a movie. Suddenly I hear the motor on North Star start. I took off out the door and went running along the shore right beside North Star, calling out to him. I was hysterical. Next thing I knew it was morning and I had been put to bed in one of the teacher's places. That morning I was told that my dad and the head instructor had decided that I would be doing more school and they flew me all the way to Sault Ste

Marie, Ontario. When I finished there I worked in a hospital with children who have cleft palettes. It was so expensive to get back home. I saved my money but still didn't have enough and so I paid for tuition to secretarial school. I didn't go back until the birth of my first child, Terry."

Margaret's sudden departure had a sobering effect on her younger sister, Mary. "Margaret left when I was in grade three. I never saw her go. I thought, you had to keep quiet or you'll disappear too. I could not see Joey or Noah. I was scared when I went there." Mary was so angry with her father that for years she would only refer to him as 'Mr Carpenter', when she was speaking to him. "I always called him Mr Carpenter, when I came to the age when I could leave that is what I started to call him. It was the only way that I could cope with why he couldn't/wouldn't take me home. I don't know if you are aware of the intensity of the feelings of being left there."

Their brother Andy was encouraged to continue his education. He was born aboard the schooner Blue Fox "to Fred and Lucy Carpenter, at Sea Otter Harbour, about fifty-five miles from Sachs Harbour. Andy's mother, Lucy, passed away when he was very young. His father sent him to the Anglican residential school in Aklavik for five years. Andy remembered being a bit of a brawler then. He was taller and stronger than most youth. "I was wild, always getting into trouble. Never big trouble, but I got into a lot of fights,' he laughed. "My Dad wanted to take me to school in Edmonton, but I wanted to come back here to hunt and to trap. I was fifteen, didn't want to go down south."[11] Andy ended up becoming the head of the Inuvialuit Hunters and Trapper's Association and followed as his brother Frank did in their father's footsteps to be considered leaders of the community in their own right.

One Carpenter child whose education was very successful was Noah Carpenter. Noah ended up studying medicine and now is a highly regarded surgeon at the Edmonton Hospital. When National Geographic wrote an article about Sachs Harbour in 1964 they interviewed him. "Red headed, freckle-faced Noah Carpenter entered the University of British Columbia in 1963, and plans to go on to medical school. Noah looks forward to his career and hopes that education will lead other Eskimos into similar paths. He, too, has a sense of mission, a desire to see his people in the forefront in all the professions.

"But how about the Eskimo language," I asked him. "There is no instruction in the schools in Eskimo," Noah replied. "Only English. So I have forgotten most of the Eskimo I ever knew. I would probably pick the language up again if I were in an Eskimo community." After a pause he added, "But I do not expect to be."[12] Diane remembers one time when Noah returned to Banksland. "He left when he was really, really young for residential school. He didn't have much experience with hunting and trapping. After he became a surgeon he came home and one time, in Sachs, my dad was cutting up a seal and my Dad says to Noah ' Do you want to try?" and Noah said, 'Dad, you know I can do it to a human being, but I can't do it to a seal". Noah ended up donating copies of his medical degrees to the mission school in hope of inspiring other students to further their education.

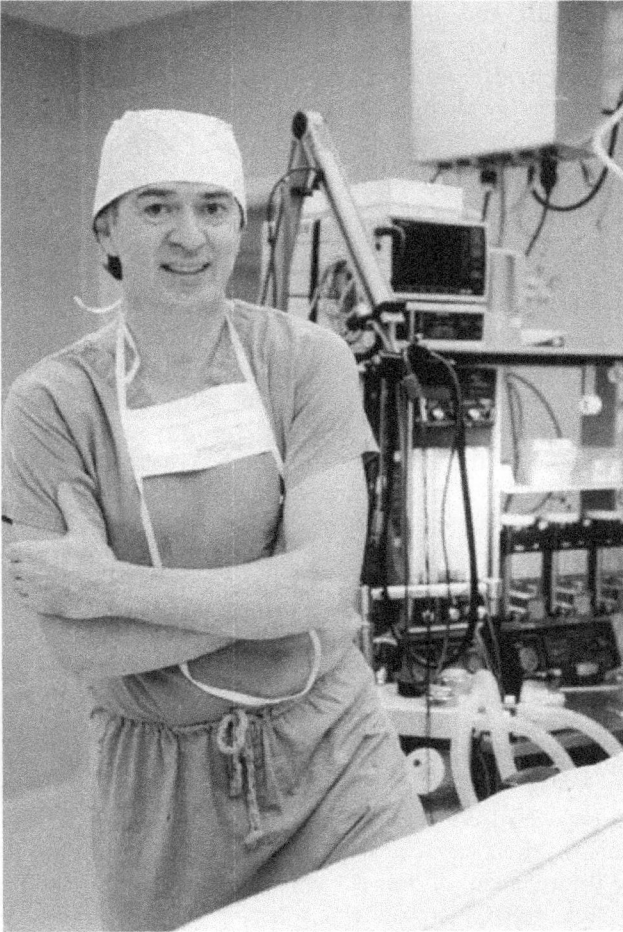

Dr Noah Carpenter.

Not all outdoors skills were lost at the Mission School, though what they did was a poor comparison to what life would have been like for them had they stayed on the land. For instance, each winter the children were issued traps for the muskrat or 'ratting' season. "Even in school we were given two traps and taught how to use them. So, in the spring our walks included lakes and channels which had muskrat houses. The pelts we sold to the Hudson's Bay store and the meat was roasted for us to eat at school."[13] The trapping seems to have been less about retaining or learning traditional hunting skills than about finding an avenue for the students to earn some money towards their keep. "Trapping at school? That was to raise money. Muskrats. Sometimes they'd buy a radio or a stage - something that benefits all the kids, eh?" remembers Joey. Boarding schools in Aklavik insisted on chores, including mending, sweeping and laundering, and to promote continuity with the Delta's economic mainstay, muskrat trapping. Aklavik pupils practiced trapping on specially registered land and in the kitchen of the Anglican school could have the meat cooked for their own meals."[14]

"The result was a lost generation, neither white nor Inuit, alienated from their parents and their past, their culture, and their land. Many sought solace in alcohol, and thus the North's 'terrible liquor problem,' as former NorthWest territories commissioner Stuart Hodgson called it, was born."[15] Fred Carpenter was very aware that once his children were exposed to modern life at Residential School, they would not be eager to step back in time to the traditional trapping life. "What child who finishes school at Inuvik will return to Sachs Harbour? Fred Carpenter thinks fewer and fewer will return home to trap the white fox and hunt caribou, polar bear, and seals; to flesh hides and clean furs; to live without modern comforts. They have running water in the hostels at Inuvik", Fred said. "Will they come back to cut ice from the lakes, and to haul it miles for drinking and cooking? He paused and after a moment continued. "In Inuvik there are flush toilets. Here there is only the 'honey bucket' to empty. In Inuvik there are electric lights and movies; here only lanterns. Will the Eskimo children after high school come back to Sachs Harbour? I don't think so."[16]

Perhaps the missionaries plans ended with an ironic twist. By educating the Inuvialuit in the white mans' way, the written and oral English culture, the politics and societal rules, they did not foresee that this education thrust upon them would come full circle when the graduates became able to research and debate their rights. Ultimately, this resulted in the Inuvialuit Land Claims Agreement that awarded self government to the Inuvialuit as well as the land and oil rights on their land as well as the exclusive hunting rights on their traditional hunting grounds. Many, many Inuvialuit were involved in this but particular thanks were given to Fred's sons, Andy, Frank, and Joey.

Chapter 20

Our Lady of Lourdes – the Anglican Church's Schooner

The other Kneass built ship that was the closest in size to North Star was Our Lady of Lourdes, a vessel commissioned for the Roman Catholic Church Missions. Her main purpose was to transport cargo such as food to each of the Western Arctic Missions of Oblates. She was also used to move Brothers and Priests as they made their rounds between missions and in the fall and spring she would pick up and drop off school children between the Residential School and their villages. She was built in 1928 and sold by Pedersen to Bishop Breynat. She was a very familiar sight along the coasts of the Beaufort Sea. "On one of his visits overseas to Rome, Bishop Breynay mentioned his project to the late Pope Pius X11. The Pope listened with great attention and interest and encouraged the project. Even more so, he pledged financial support and donated a substantial sum of money (for the purchase of the ship)."[1]

Our Lady of Lourdes was almost a proto-type for North Star. She was slightly beamier and a little shorter but drew two feet more which restricted her ability to enter many of the Arctic harbours, including Sachs. Her iron-bark cladding and the short keel with the rounded hull allowed her to be pressed out of the ice much like North Star. Father LeMeur recalls the planning of Our Lady's design. "The ship was to be just over 55 feet in length, 16.2 feet in breadth and 5.4 feet in depth. Equipped with a 75 horsepower diesel engine, she would average eight knots. Moreover, Captain Pedersen added that with a rounded keel or hull and drawing only some five feet, she would sail in shallow waters more easily and avoid being crushed in the ice. How thoughtful and how wise and true. This was to be proven later on many voyages."[2]

When Pedersen loaded Our Lady of Lourdes aboard Patterson she was still far from complete and the crew worked to fit her out as the Patterson travelled north in the Pacific. This was a common practice and spoke to the myriad of skills that Pedersen's crew had. "Our Lady of Lourdes was finished construction in San Francisco on May 24th, 1930. She was then ready to be shipped on the whaling ship of Captain Pedersen. She wasn't entirely completed yet and during the voyage sailors worked on her until she finally landed at Herschel Island. There they lowered her down into the sea."[3]

Once in Arctic waters, the ship was crewed by Inuit who knew the coast and the weather. The rest of the crew was made up of Brothers from the Church. Thomas Edouget remembers with pride his father's role aboard ship. "My dad captained all those 'cause he was born in that coast, so the Roman Catholics hired him ah. He was an Anglican before that, so he got a better deal so he got baptized (Chuckle). He was gonna be an Anglican priest, minister, he already had the uniform from the Anglican mission, but he got a better job offer so he moved over (chuckle). Then he became Catholic."[4]

In The Incredible Eskimo a more detailed description of the crew is given. "Father Griffin's motley crew on Our Lady of Lourdes comprised the pilot, Billy Thrasher (half-Eskimo, half-Black), a whaler from San Francisco; Brother Kraut, the engineer, from Germany; Bishop P. Fallaize, who had made the first overland contact with Coppermine Eskimos; Father Biname from Belgium, and, of course, Father Dehurtevent and me."[5] The crew were taken care of but not usually paid any money for their work. Instead, the church would just see to their needs. "He would be paid just with food. Well, they never had money that time. When the big ships used to come we get one big slab of bacon. It was about four feet by four feet long sometimes. They would give that to my Dad. And a big sack of beans, about five or six sacks of flour, those one hundred pounds. Also tea, maybe the tea would be 30 to 40 pounds, and shell and one whole case of tobacco, 48 in one case. They give it to him for whole year worth. Sometimes we get kargi - calico cloth. They make dresses and their own clothes. At times they even make their own socks." He, my father, was always a Captain on boats. He would just sit sleepy sometimes. He would just set his compass and fall asleep sometimes. He's got his rosary right there and sleep. Sometimes I hear him say, 'Hail Mary full of grace..' and he get up."[6]

Our Lady of Lourdes was often a family affair. For years Qimiqsana otherwise known as Billy Thrasher was her Captain and often his wife was the cook aboard as was Kuvlualuk, with Peter Thrasher helping out with deck work as he got older.

In 1935 Our Lady of Lourdes was involved in a rescue of the Hudson's Bay ship Fort James, near Tuktoyaktuk Harbour. The Fort James was hard aground on a reef and the Lady was used for towing her off before the HBC ship was wrecked.

Father Dehurtevent hated travelling aboard the ship as he was very prone to motion sickness. The rounded hull and short keels of the Arctic ships make for a very uncomfortable ride and he avoided travel aboard her as much as he could, preferring to travel in much smaller vessels that have less motion or to wait for freeze-up and go by dogteam. "Not much except when I was moving...when I came from Aklavik, when I went down and once I went to Tuk..I went with the Lady of Lourdes and I can't....Oh sure, but I don't like to travel by Our Lady of Lourdes. I was seasick very easy. Oh boy, bad. (laughter) No. We had just one storm, I think. But I went to bed. It was the only way to feel less sick. No, I am no good for the sea. But in the small boat, you don't care."[7]

Albert Elias recalls one summer when he was travelling with his father aboard their schooner, Fox. "I remember one time we waited at Port Dalhousie, not too far from Baillie and the next year, spring I guess, we were still there. Lots of ice. We seen this ship, Lady of Lourdes and she was out there. Looked like it was stranded. We ended up towing it to Tuk. It had a broken shaft or something. My dad's schooner is not that big, but so dependable."

In the fall, the ship was hauled ashore and then launched in the spring in a very similar way to how North Star was put to bed. "In those days tractors were unknown of, at least on the coast, and brutal strength and a bit of ingenuity was a must. After laying the skids, beef fat was generously applied to them. Two cables were lashed around the hull and fastened to the capstans, then inch by inch men turned the capstans. The ship progressed very slowly, but safely out of the water. She was then securely tied up. The engineer would disconnect pipes, etc and cover the engine with a piece of heavy canvas."[8]

In the spring the crew would arrive and begin their annual inspection, checking the keel bolts, propeller, shaft, engine, rudder, the rigging and sails. Then the hull was sanded, a job that could take weeks before a fresh coat of paint was added.

To launch "was a very simple operation. The cables were replaced with ropes and tightened as a violin string. At the command, two men armed with an axe would cut the ropes and after just a few seconds of hesitation, she slid into the water again. For a few days she was wet and soaked by the water infiltrating through the cracks and small holes in the timber. The pump was kept busy for a few days and soon the timber, well soaked, sealed itself."[9]

Once the ship stopped taking on water the year's supplies for the missions would be put aboard. "For cargo - beans to jam, rice and lumber, coal, dog food, calicots, fish nets and ammunitions. It would be a very difficult and hard year for the missionaries if some items were forgotten. It would mean rough trips, sufferings, shortages and a struggle for life. There was a very special item, especially looked after and very important for the Mission - the mail! There was lots of noise on deck and the schooner was always loaded to capacity, if not overloaded and all corners were filled as well as all parts of the deck. Very often dogs were lashed on deck and near by some sleighs and dried fish and even sometimes barrels of seal or whale oil. What a bizarre cargo indeed!"[10]

In 1942 Our Lady of Lourdes left for a re-provisioning voyage but immediately ran into thick ice. The ship was locked into the ice and drifted, helpless to break free from the pack. A 'strong easterly gale' sprung up and they drifted between four and twenty miles a day. Their only hope was to try and get to the lee side of the ice and so the decision was made to drive her up and over a floe, where she lay protected, but imprisoned. "On September 14th, we thought that we were on our way for Tuk and that our trials were ended, open water all over. However, around 9 a.m., when Billy Thrasher went up to the crow's nest to have a better view, he signalled ice, ice again ahead of us. The nightmare wasn't finished yet. Ice extending right to the shoreline prevented us from continuing, so back on over the ice floe, at anchor to wait.

Underway again the next day, even after killing a polar bear, food was still running low. "Now a decision was hastily taken. Weather wasn't improving, temperature was already below zero, fuel supply was very low, and a wintering location should be found as soon as possible. Near the Smoking Mountains, among the old ice and behind them, we found a natural harbour - an improvised harbour. There we drove the 'Our Lady' ashore. Water was deep enough, and the grounded old ice would provide shelter for the schooner."[11]

Our Lady of Lourdes worked the Arctic Coast travelling between Missions from 1931 until 1957. She began her last voyage` on April 22, 1967. For the same reason that North Star's service had become redundant, Our Lady of Lourdes now found herself hauled ashore. After a few years she was given to the trapper Eddie Gruben who in turn handed her use over to another trapper but neither man got as far as launching her. The upkeep of the old wooden boat was too much. With a grant from the Northern Transportation Company she was lifted from the Beaufort Sea for the last time and installed on a concrete slab overlooking the harbour at Tuktoyaktuk, a proud sentinel and reminder of when wooden ships provided the only link between the islands of the Western Arctic Archipelago and the Canadian mainland.

Chapter 21

Arctic Sovereignty, Fred receives Commonwealth Award & Her Majesty Queen Elizabeth II visits

In his report, The Bankslanders, Peter Usher wrote: "With the current talk over how Canadian Arctic sovereignty would be enhanced with more oil and gas production on Banks Island and in the Beaufort Sea, it should be noted that the Bankslanders have proven that their fur trapping is viable proof that Canadians have been making their living as well as habitating this area of the far North. Indeed, not only were Bankslanders such as the Carpenters, Wolkis, Pokiaks, Elias' and many more the Canadian pioneers in this area, their flagship and continuous proof of this is of course what was once known as the Queen of the North, North Star of Herschel Island."[1]

In recent years, spurred on by climate change, the opening of the NorthWest Passage and the discovery of vast reserves of oil and minerals in the Canadian Arctic, there has been a lot of pressure for Canada to assert its authority over its Northern waters. While these recent events have accelerated the discussion, it has been going on for over a century and North Star and Fred Carpenter have played a large part in maintaining Canada's sovereignty in these waters. "On the 31st of July 1880 an Order-in-Council was passed by which all the 'territories, islands, inland seas and waters lying north and west of Robeson Channel, Kennedy Channel, Smith Sound, Baffin Bay and Davis Strait as far as the 141st meridian of West Longitude were included in the Dominion of Canada.'"[2]

The discussion continued into the next century. "In 1907 the Honourable Pascal Poirier made the motion, 'That it be resolved that the Senate is of the opinion that the time has come for Canada to make a formal declaration of possession of the lands and islands situated in the north of the Dominion and extending to the North Pole. He contended: 'It is somewhat - I do not know if I may call it jarring to read occasionally in the United States papers such paragraphs as this - 'the Captain of the whaler so and so has hoisted the United States flag on a certain island, or that some United States navigator in the Arctic waters has planted the United States flag on another island and taken possession of it, when by referring to our atlas we find that these islands and lands are situated in Canadian waters."[3]

When Prime Minister John F. Diefenbaker visited the Arctic in 1950 he was disgusted to learn that some Canadians, specifically from Old Crow had to use American stamps on their letters and then send them with Alaskan airlines in order to be processed. He also noted that there was a lack of health services including primitive methods of handling sewage and of obtaining fresh water and electricity.

In the early 1940's Fred Carpenter and many of the trappers from Banks Island had been trapping in the Delta for several years. Banks Island sat uninhabited at the entrance to Canada's NorthWest Passage. A more strategic island for enforcing sovereignty could never be imagined. Both Russia and the United States were showing an interest in extending their footprint in our North. "Apart from the purchase of Alaska, the Americans showed little interest in the north until the 1950's."[4] The Government of Canada sent its representative, Laco Hunt, to ask Carpenter to take North Star and transport as many people as he chose to move to Banks Island in order to assert Canada's ownership of the island. There was a secondary reason for this as the Bankslanders were showing their trapping prowess and this was affecting the Delta trappers' income.

Fred was initially reluctant to move all the way back to Banks Island. He was doing well trapping fur in the Delta and one of his sons had been hired aboard a ship making runs out to Herschel Island. Life in the Delta was easier than being hundreds of miles away on an isolated island. Fred negotiated that he move, in concert with the schooner Reindeer, provided that the government build a school at Sachs Harbour so that the Banksland children would never have to be sent away from their families again. He also asked for an airstrip and perhaps in a selfish mood, better radio reception so that he could receive the CBC signal rather than only stations from the USA.

Hunt was the government official tasked with convincing the Bankslanders to return to their island home. The Canadian government wanted to see Banks Island populated by Canadians and the logical first choice was to ask the first residents to return there. He writes: "..as the Government's man in Aklavik, I had work to do. I had been asked to make a contact with a group of Inuit known as the Bankslanders who had been living on the mainland for 12 years, and to help them return to Banks Island. Their leader was Fred Carpenter. Because of the war and resulting low prices for white fox, he and the others had decided to leave the island and settle at Tuktoyaktuk.

There was a problem with this, because the coastal Inuit, had insufficient resources for their own needs. The Bankslanders, better hunters and trappers than the coastal Inuit, picked up the lion's share of the game and fur harvest. Since there had been no fur or game taken on Banks Island for 12 years, it was generally agreed that it could now support sustained harvesting.

There were also compelling reasons for moving the Inuit back to their original territory on the island. Occupation is the logical first step in establishing sovereignty over a region."[5]

In this postwar period, there were difficulties with the United States government over the Arctic weather stations. The United States wanted these weather stations to supply meteorological information that would be vital if long-range bombers ever had to be sent over the Arctic. The shortest distance between Moscow and Washington was over the North Pole, in Canadian airspace. Canada insisted that the weather stations be jointly manned and that the senior person in each station be a Canadian.

For Canada, it was politically expedient to have the Bankslanders return to their island, which is as big as the province of New Brunswick, where they would be Canadian citizens in residence on Canadian soil. Sinclair of the Hudson's Bay Company explains the process in a memorandum from March of 1951. "I began to negotiate with them, knowing there was no time to lose. Summers are short on the Arctic coast, and it took time to mount the kind of expedition I had in mind.

Fred Carpenter owned a 57 foot schooner, North Star, the pride of the Banksland fleet. Fred Wolkie owned a smaller vessel, Reindeer, and both were very seaworthy. Both could handle cargo plus a number of families with all their supplies. It seemed to me these boats could accomplish the big move. The initial talks with the Bankslanders were encouraging. I insisted that the decision must be theirs; they alone would select those to accompany them. It seemed to please the people that the government was taking an interest in their affairs."[6] G.E.B. Sinclair was Director of the Northern Administration and Lands Branch based in Ottawa, also adds that two other vessels, Omingmuk and Fox were also capable of making the trip back to Sachs Harbour, but in the end they didn't cast off for another year.

At this point it should be noted that the Bankslanders had been making out a good living trapping in the Delta but were not pulling in the huge harvests of fur that they had enjoyed at the height of the schooner days. Over the 1950/51 winter Fred and his three sons "filled their marten quotas on the Anderson River, a total of 100 marten, besides a lucrative summer, his boat, the North Star, made two trips to Herschel Island, and one of his sons was employed by the M.V. Fort Hearne."[7] Many were still paying down huge debts to the traders who had grubstaked or jawboned them. The government agreed to pay off some of these debts for them if they returned to Banks

Island to hold it for Canada. In addition to this the government set up a program called the Eskimo Loan fund which allowed the Bankslanders to borrow against future trapping earnings.

"Fred Carpenter was a skilled seaman, and had learned the rudiments of whaling in his younger days. As it turned out, he wanted desperately to return to Banks Island. I told him that the government would guarantee his group's debts with various traders, and promised to fly to the island the following spring with the medical officer. I wanted him to know that the government was indeed concerned about the Bankslanders' welfare. Fred agreed to do all he could to persuade a selected number of Inuit to travel with him and Wolkie back to the island.

In late September, having been assured that all was well and that 27 Bankslanders would return home, I flew to Tuktoyaktuk to watch their departure. The two schooners were loaded to capacity with lumber, drums of fuel, crates of everything imaginable and at least 50 husky dogs hitched around the deck.

Some of the Inuit were apprehensive about embarking, especially the younger ones, who had never been to Banks Island. They were sailing into the unknown. The whole population of Tuktoyaktuk turned out to bid them goodbye. I was confident the expedition would be successful, barring accidents. Storms are frequent in the Beaufort Sea, but Carpenter's skills and seamanship would surely get them safely home."[8] Some old-timers remember watching the ships leave 'Tuktuk' and that the ships were so heavily loaded with all of the supplies that they would need for the coming year and for starting the community, that the ships' railings were very close to the water. One story that I heard was that some of the children were hanging their arms through the forward portholes and touching the water. Normally these portholes are about six feet off of the sea.

"The Northern Administration and Lands Branch became anxious to see the Bankslanders return to the island, and indeed would have preferred a trading post established there to encourage more permanent settlement and less dependence on the mainland. The Cold War also made strategic considerations important. Canada had both to ensure the loyalty of its northern peoples in the event of outright warfare in the Polar Basin, and to assert its sovereignty over the Arctic Islands in the face of an increased American strategic interest in them. The resettlement of Banksland on a more permanent basis could usefully serve both ends."[9]

"In late September of 1951 the ships cast off.... and what many believe the 'official' founding of Sachs Harbour began. Even though many families had made Sachs their winter quarters for many years, it was at this time that Fred Carpenter built a wood frame house and put down roots. This would be his permanent residence until his death. When the Minister visited Sachs

Harbour he told the villagers that he saw housing as their most immediate need, and would ensure that it was provided. Many took this as both an insult to their own houses and a bribe to deflect their concern over the exploration programme" (for oil and minerals)."[10]

Fred Carpenter heading out on the trap-line.

For the next few years Fred and his sons Andy and Frank ran their traplines and solidified their reputations as three of the best, if not the best, trappers in the Canadian Arctic. The Government came through with their end of the bargain and many of the local Inuvialuit were hired to construct the school and runway. The radio signals were strengthened and the Canadian Broadcasting Corporation as well as the local station from Inuvik were able to be picked up by the Bankslanders.

Fred Carpenter paddling a walrus skin boat at Sachs Harbour.

With the community now established the RCMP moved in and set up across from the Carpenters. Fred Carpenter recalled that "when the police got here in 1954 they said to me, "Thanks, Fred for holding this island for the Canadian Government for all these years. I laugh. Good fox country, that's why I'm here." "He used to joke that the people of Sachs Harbour were responsible for keeping the land "for the Queen. He knew this island was important to Canada," his son Joey Carpenter remembers.

During World War Two, Canada, Russia, and the USA were all allies, fighting on the same side. At the end of the war new hostilities grew between the United States and Russia and the growing distrust of each other resulted in each building up their own military strengths and scoping out territories that would be to their own advantages should the Cold War erupt into actual fighting. The biggest scare was that of atomic weapons. Should either country decide to fly bombs to drop on one another, their air routes would be right over the Canadian Arctic and so in 1955 the Distant Early Warning Line (DEW Line) was set up. The sites were meant to warn of any enemy missiles or planes being sent from Russia. There were primary sites with large radar and antennas and secondary sites used primarily for relaying the warnings or information. In order to keep the DEW Line personnel entertained on their off-watch the sites often contained bowling alleys, bars and community centers. As relations improved between the two countries, the staff were relocated back south and the sites were abandoned.

Fred Carpenter and Simon Bennett hauling Blue Fox ashore with a winch.

Banks Island's strategic position made it a logical site for a DEW line radar station at the beginning of the Cold War. Canada and the United States were worried that Russia might try and invade from the North and so a series of Distant Early Warning radar sites were set up across the Arctic. "The Inuvialuit were hired in great numbers to help construct the Dew Line "Probably for the first time they saw Canadians making a real effort to protect the North from a perceived invader."[11] As a side note, it is interesting that the wires connecting the DEW line to the smaller repeater stations were laid along the ground. As time passed the wires proved irresistible to the arctic fox who chewed through them to get at the insulation. Miles of this one inch thick wire was bucked off and replaced. The damaged wire was left aside and at some point Fred and later Sven scavenged this very high quality wire, cut out the damaged parts and wired North Star with it. To this day, the DEW Line wire is still being used aboard, just another part of her amazing Arctic construction.

The Dew Line was constructed since there was a perceived threat that Russian military aircraft could fly in to Canada from the North at low-levels undetected and drop atomic bombs on cities in Canada and the United States. The Joint Defense Board of these two countries invented the Distance Early Warning system to be a net of radar stations that eventually extended from the Aleutian Islands to Greenland and Iceland. There were main stations, auxiliary radar stations and linking all of these were unmanned intermediate stations. By the late 1960's communication technology had increased to the point that the intermediate stations were abandoned by the Federal electric Company. The construction of the site also had provided work for some of the Bankslanders and for many it was their first wage job. The contrast of working a 9-5 day for money as opposed to spending weeks on a cold trapline and then still having to wait to trade their catch for goods was a huge one. Many still preferred the latter and returned to their traplines and the freedom of working for themselves out in the fresh air.

Her Majesty Queen Elizabeth II returned to the North in 1959 and Mary Carpenter was one of a handful of Inuit children chosen to be part of the celebration of her visit. "I met the Queen in 1959 at Acadia Hall in Yellowknife. They selected four students. We sat across from the Queen and we were instructed not to talk to her. Not to talk at all. I don't think the Queen would have talked to us anyway. Two of the boys had just arrived the day before from a camp and they just ate everything with their hands. It was disgusting!" Fred and Agnes Carpenter were presented to Her Majesty Queen Elizabeth II and Prince Philip, Duke of Edinburgh again on this occasion. The official pamphlet for the visit on Monday, July 20th, 1959 reads that "at 2:50 the Mayor introduces ....a small group of Eskimos and their wives."[13]

Fred Carpenter's contribution with his ship North Star to Canada's Arctic Sovereignty did not go unnoticed in political and monarchal circles. "In 1970, the Queen, Prince Philip, Prince Charles and Princess Anne toured the Northwest Territories in celebration of its Centennial. When they arrived in Inuvik the townspeople were surprised but delighted that the family was not surrounded by throngs of press recording the event. Inclement Arctic weather had delayed the press plane indefinitely in Tuktoyaktuk."[14]"The Queen and Prince Philip came to Inuvik and mom and dad were presented to them. Prince Philip was very taken with dad's lifestyle and he told him that he often wished that he could just trade jobs with Fred," remembers Diane Carpenter.

On another visit from the Royals, Fred and Agnes were invited down for a gala in Yellowknife. Diane recalls the event. "My parents saw the Queen and Prince Phillip at a ball here in Yellowknife. My mother gave The Queen and Prince Phillip an emblem of the Northwest Territories. My mother had hand sewn it. It was on a red velvet background, with the emblem being sewn in sealskin. My mother was shy when she handed it to the Queen, so she didn't hold it up until she got to the Queen. The Queen held it up for all to see. It was a beautiful emblem-my mother is an excellent seamstress! My parents were told they were welcome to stay at Buckingham Palace anytime they went to London! My father said that he and Prince Phillip talked for a bit. Prince Phillip told my dad that he would gladly be in my father's shoes for a day - just to see how it would be to not be under the watchful eye of the public. Don't get me wrong though - Prince Phillip loves everything he is doing - just a passing thought he gave to my father."

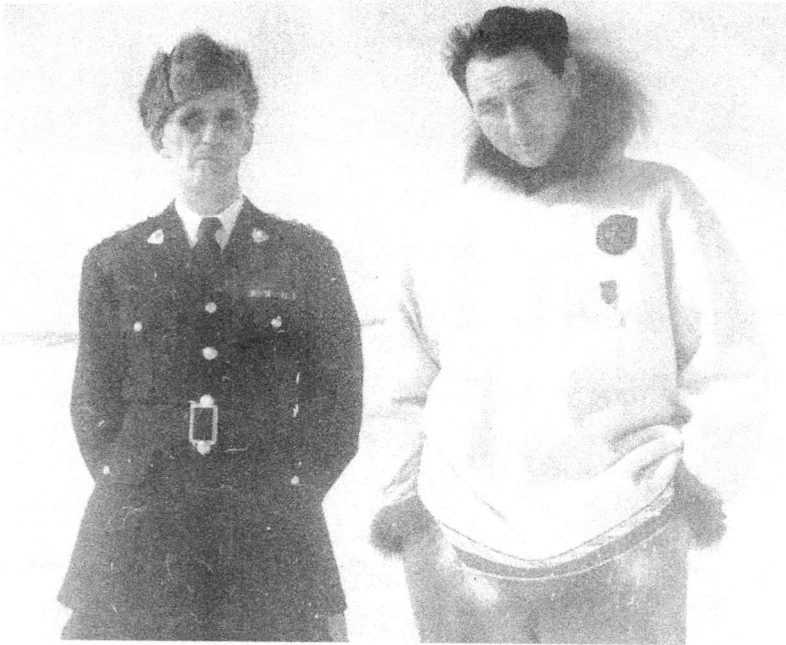

Government official and Fred Carpenter, who is proudly sporting his Commonwealth Medal on his anorak.

Fred Carpenter was invited to be at the assembly because of his work in settling Sachs Harbour and for all of the donations that he had made in purchasing Victory Bonds during World War Two and in encouraging other Inuvialuit to do the same. He was awarded the highest honour that the Queen could bestow on a Canadian subject, the Commonwealth Medal. From the moment that it was pinned onto his tuxedo, it never left his wardrobe and in every picture taken of him from then on the medal can be seen, including pinned to his caribou skin anorak when he was outside trapping. "Dad was given the Queen's award for all the work that he had done with raising money during the war and for taking all of the people to Banks Island for Arctic sovereignty. That's why he got his medal, because he helped build the community in Sachs Harbour. He helped with the war effort. He collected money and put the money towards the 2nd World War effort. He made sure that the island was inhabited. He got a medal from the Queen in 1953. Larry (Fred's son) has it. Andy took it home and now he has it. Plus there was a plaque that the Queen gave him in 1953," adds Diane. "There is a record that the energetic half-breed Fred Carpenter, through Leslie Livingstone, invested some of his money in Victory Bonds."[15] It should be noted that the Canadian Inuit were very generous in buying Victory Bonds as were their neighbours, the American Eskimo. Charles Gillham discusses this in his book, Raw North. "Most interesting was the attitude of the natives towards purchasing war bonds. They gave everything they had. Their income was inadequate to buy the bare necessities for their families, yet they gave what little cash they had. In addition they offered to throw in their dog teams, food supplies and squaws."[16] "My Dad was presented to the Queen and Prince Philip when they came to Yellowknife. Philip took Dad aside and said "what do you think of my wife?" Dad said "well she's the Queen of Canada" Philip kept pushing him - "Come on, man to man - what do you think of her?" "I can't. I respect her too much." Finally Philip said within earshot of the Queen "Tell me!" Dad looked at him and said "Okay - she's not bad - for a white woman." The Queen overheard and started to laugh," remembers Mary Carpenter Frost.

The high recognition for Fred's and other's work had been announced on "December 1st, 1953 - Presentation of Coronation Medals to Eskimo. The Honourable Jean Lesage, Minister of Resources and Development, announced that twenty Eskimo have been awarded the Coronation Medal. The medals will be flown to the Arctic and presented by officers of the R.C.M. Police."[17]"Fred Carpenter, Disc No. W3-240, Banks Island - A hunter and leader of the Eskimo group at Banks Island."[18]

Fred and Agnes were also feted years later in Yellowknife. "Each year the Commissioner (of the Territories) would host a Legislative Ball, and representatives from all the settlements would arrive to participate in one glorious spree. In 1973, my wife and I accompanied the Governor General and Mrs Michener to Yellowknife for that year's ball, which honoured the 100th anniversary of the Royal Canadian Mounted Police. We met many old friends and acquaintances, including Fred Carpenter from Sachs Harbour, resplendent in a tuxedo."[19]

**Agnes and Fred Carpenter and Commissioner Hodgson
at Legislative Ball. Fred resplendent in tuxedo.**

Canada's waxing and waning interest in the North has always been a puzzle to its most Northern citizens. Even back in 1952, Prime Minister Louis St. Laurent made a speech in the House of Commons regarding Canada's neglect of the Arctic. Twenty years later Prime Minister Pierre Elliott Trudeau expressed his dreams for the Arctic. "I hope that the Northwest Territories Centennial will encourage Canadians in all parts of the country to increase their knowledge and their understanding of our northland and its people."[20] Prime Minister Jean Chretien, who was probably more familiar with the North than any of his predecessors having served as the Minister for Indian and Northern Affairs for two terms was often encouraging more support for the role that the Canadian Arctic plays in Canada. In 2011 Prime Minister Chretien telephoned me aboard North Star of Herschel Island and we discussed her history. He was very enthusiastic about North Star of Herschel

Island's story and impressed that she is a living symbol of our Canadian history (and that my wife and I have raised four children aboard!).

In the end it is the Inuvialuit who shake their heads and wonder why there is even any need for a discussion of Canada's Arctic Sovereignty. "I hear on the radio that the United States and Canada are squabbling over who has sovereignty in Arctic waters. What they are talking about is my people's hunting grounds. We were hunting in the Arctic Ocean before the white man came to discover America. I hope they leave us a little salt water."[21] Fred Carpenter's son, Joey, points out that "We did use the ocean summer and winter. We have always had land use and occupancy between here and the mainland." That is perhaps the hard part for southern Canadians to understand. Canada's Arctic Archipelago looks like a series of islands on a map. To the Innu, however, it is one solid piece of territory. Often the water is frozen, but that does not stop them from using it. When the ice melts, they have continued to use it in their canoes, kayaks, umiaks and of course, schooners such as North Star of Herschel Island. Gontran de Poncins explained it this way in his book, Kabloona. "For the sea here is the great winter highway that joins camp to camp, family to family. It is the hunting-ground that yields not only sustenance for a season but reserves of provisions against the lean months to come. It is the habitat of the Eskimos, the 'land' on which his igloo is built, and he lives on the sea and not on the land through many months of the year."[22]

On the 25th anniversary of the IRC, Inuvialuit Robert Kuptana said "I used to live there, I step on it, I hunt on it, I get my food from it and it's my 'store'. And if the government said, 'We need to preserve this land for Canada', we had to say, 'Are you saying we are not Canadians? We were the first Canadians!'"[23]The Eskimo has no such background of attachment to the soil. He lives by the sea. From it he obtains his food, the seals, the walrus, the polar bears. From the sea mammals he obtains materials for much of his clothing, fuel to heat his house and cook his food. The ice cover of the sea is his winter highway and his hunting ground. He often builds his house of snow on this ice cover. He spends the greater portion of his life on or close by the sea. When we draw a map we outline the peninsulas of the land; when the Eskimo draws a map he outlines the bays and inlets of the sea."[24]

The decision that Fred Carpenter made, when he chose to leave the relative easy life of living on the Delta to move his friends and family aboard North Star and Reindeer to the uninhabited Banks Island in order to preserve Canada's Sovereignty over it and the surrounding waters, including the entrance to the NorthWest Passage must never be forgotten. If anything, North Star of Herschel Island is a living symbol of Canada's Arctic Sovereignty and should be respected as such.

Chapter 22
Fred retirement – North Star on the beach

North Star made her last voyage from Sachs Harbour to the mainland and back again in 1961. By then she was the last of the Western Arctic schooners plying her trade, her raison d'être, and it was still lucrative due to her size. Besides that, it was tradition and something that many Bankslanders still wanted to do, not only for the adventure but for the connection to the ship and their ancestry. Many families could make the trip in order to sell their winter's catch and to pick up their food and kit for the following winter, but with the price of fur falling and fewer and fewer people choosing the lifestyle of being out on the trapline for weeks and months on end, North Star's fate was obvious. Planes now made regular stops at Sachs Harbour and could also be chartered almost anytime to take Bankslanders to the mainland. Max Ward, one of Canada's most enterprising pilots had formed Polaris Air Charter Company based in Yellowknife in 1946 and it was so popular that in 1957 he bought a Bristol Air Freighter capable of carrying heavy equipment into the high Arctic. Some of this equipment was used for building landing strips near remote villages. Recognizing the role that the schooners had played, he purchased a DC-6A freighter plane that could manage fourteen ton loads to these villages. A ninety minute airplane ride is much easier to face than days or weeks being tossed about in the Arctic Ocean with the danger of ice ever present. In addition, a Northern Transportation Barge was coming in to different villages, sometimes as often as every two weeks, delivering purchases ordered through catalogues by telegraph.

**Fred and Frank Carpenter getting ready for the tra-
pline. Photo credit Bob Knight.**

Upon her return to Sachs Harbour, North Star was hauled ashore over greased skids one last time. Laying ashore abeam her sister Fox, North Star took on the look of an abandoned, decaying building. There was no life to her at all, except when the Sachs Harbour children would risk the wrath of Fred Carpenter and sneak aboard to play. Diane Carpenter remembers playing aboard North Star with some of her childhood friends. "For sleep, they had bunk beds underneath, more forward. We used to play on it when it was docked - go inside and play around inside it. Just jump around, tear on the bunks - we didn't dare touch nothing - we were scared to touch the engines or anything. We'd go around on the beds - as many of us that could fit in." Each winter North Star's boom and rigging would be pressed into service as drying racks for polar bear, white fox and other pelts. One man who had visited Sachs Harbour in that era recalled that there were polar bear skins hanging everywhere and there were stacks of polar bear and fox pelts piled all over the deck.

North Star lying weathered on the beach at Sachs Harbour.

LACO Hunt sums up the situation. "With the increasing use of aircraft came the means to transport, within reason, almost anything to any destination in the North. It opened up a whole new vista of possibilities. A few years before, all merchandise had to be shipped by boat through the Mackenzie River system during the ice-free months. Now, you could order and receive goods any time during the year - except during the "in-between" weeks of fall and spring, when ice was forming or breaking up on the river."[1]

Fred and Agnes recognised that it was more financially viable to ship their furs by plane to the mainland and so there was no need to risk the crossing with North Star and the expenses involved with maintaining her. Fred took North Star's Atlas engine apart for wintering and for maintenance. The electrical system attached to the engine had been causing some problems but there were no spare parts available and so it was left dismantled for another day. With no parts to be had he would have known that his beloved Atlas would have to be replaced. Fred still wanted to keep the old Atlas going but the trend now was to purchase fibreglass speedboats that could make the crossing in very little time as well as being able to speed around to hunting or fishing grounds.

Fox and North Star on the beach.

North Star and Fox sat on the beach, being beaten by the weather as reminders of the schooner age but no one showed any interest in resurrecting them. So many schooners around the Western Arctic were lying in a similar state. Some of them were broken up for firewood, others burned to the keel when children got aboard and played with matches. In the words of Canadian folk singer Stan Rogers ."the boats are so few, Too many are pulled up and rotten."[2]

Chapter 23
Sven Johansson pre North Star

Sven Borje Johansson was born in a city known for making marine engines, Säffle, Värmland, Sweden on the 29th of August in 1924 and grew up at Torskog, Bohus län, near Göteborg on Sweden's Atlantic coast. His father, Anton, was a cabinetmaker and wood sculptor and owned a factory. His mother, Ester, was a patron of the arts, but Sven remembers that it was his father in the 'dirty thirties', who was the more artistic one, often grabbing a couple of blankets to act as back-drops and then putting on plays in the park for the town to enjoy. Sven was the middle of three brothers. The family home was filled with books and music and he has many fond memories of lively debates and discussions about arts and politics around the supper table. He never saw his parents show anger and they had a mutual respect for one another. Sven stayed in the Swedish school system until grade six when the Second World War put his formal education on the back burners. For the next couple of years he went through an intensely religious period, questioning all and seeking out faith in what he now saw as a cruel world. He read the Bible and every other Swedish translated religious book that he could lay his hands on. Sven found that for himself, "religion doesn't measure up. It's a construction of answers formed by belief, not proof."

From 1941-44, starting at age 16, he gave three years of his life as a non-commissioned officer in the army. In his teenaged years he, like many others, was affected by World War 2 and man's cruelty to man. Sailing and being out in nature seemed to lift his spirits. "When I was 20, I'd sailed a friend's small sailboat whenever I could," he remembers. "It gave me a good sense of the wind and helped me become a serious boating professional." In his late twenties he worked aboard a thirty foot craft on a chain of lakes in Northern Sweden where he learned his boat handling. "Our boat carried whole trucks hanging over the bow - there wasn't much regulation in that remote part. Sometimes I'd be so sleep deprived I'd see things that weren't there - great training for transiting the Northwest Passage. But I never had an accident and I had great fun."[1]

Having fun in life is a goal that Sven set at a young age and one that he has kept. He also decided that he would never have a formal, life-long career. "I wanted to live, not make a living." He also did not see the need for formal education and quit school at age twelve.

By his early twenties he had become a deep thinker and found that he was better suited to living a life in nature, as he had become disillusioned with people in general. He set off with his rucksack to live off of the land in Sweden's LappLand to 'contemplate life's mysteries'. This period of his life was marked by a dark depression with the black dogs of sadness constantly in his thoughts. He once described in a draft of his life story that he entered into "a period of depression and lived the life of a hermit for two years." By living out in nature, he saw that it was not just man that could be evil. As he began to see, nature could be much crueler than people but still retain its beauty, and this seemed to pull himself out of his depression. "After World War Two I had to go right into the wilderness. I was kind of an idealist, wondering what human beings were doing to each other. Nature is so balanced and beautiful and harmonious and, my gosh, I realised it is also so many more times evil than Hitler could ever be. I went to live in nature to find that balance. Look at the white fox. If there is lots of lemmings then the white fox has a big litter. In the third year, when there are no lemmings, the white fox has sixteen pups and eats them all. The starvation is the thing that keeps the numbers down. By living out in nature I found out how nature works. The universe doesn't give a damn about you as an individual and in nature, evolution of all forms of life is not well served by harmony." From then on, it was an idyllic life for him and he learned many skills first-hand that would help him in his future careers in Canada's Arctic. He explains his time as a 'recluse - gaining understanding of existence in nature, human existence in nature and existence in the cosmos. "What affected me most was the contrast between life at home and the cruelty and greed that happened outside my home."[2] "I learned from those experiences that if you can't change something you have to accept it."

He learned to herd reindeer by the Sami Laplanders in Northern Sweden. This is where he learned reindeer husbandry and it also allowed him to spend a lot of time out on the land. "I was working with Laplanders and reindeer, and also hunting and trapping."[3] The work only involved helping them twice a year with corralling; otherwise he was just living directly from the wilderness hunting moose, rabbit, birds and fishing.

In 1951, on one of his hunting excursions with his closest neighbour, Mikkelerik Koljok, they decided to go north and hunt ptarmigan which was considered to be a fantastic delicacy in the local restaurants. "We agreed to go up to the Norwegian border where we figured that there would be a lot of ptarmigan. We hired an airplane and flew over Sorva and into a tourist cabin at the Akka Mountains." They spent their days hunting, leaving the game outside to freeze overnight. After bagging enough of the little birds to make it profitable, they set them out on a runway for the plane to pick them up later and decided to ski the forty km back to Sorva the next morning.

Ptarmigan in their winter camoflouge. Photo credit Trait d'Union.

Sven Johansson in his trapping days.

That night as they were standing outside their cabin before retiring, they saw across the frozen lake a big fire coming from one of the cabins. This was distressing enough in itself but was compounded by their having not seen anyone for the whole time they had been up there. "There was nobody there. We thought it must be an accident or something. We also thought that we could have been accused of setting the fire since we were the only ones there," remembers Sven.

The next morning they set out on their skis to investigate and because they were hunters their rifles were loaded and ready to go. The smoke was still coming off of the burned cabin but strangely there was also smoke coming out of the chimney of an adjoining cabin. Sven kicked off his skis and banged on the door, asking if whoever was in there was all right. "A guy came out and screamed something. I didn't understand him but Mick heard him saying, 'GET OFF, GET OFF! You go or I will shoot'. I just called back, 'We came to see if you need help'.

We started skiing away over the lake. There is no shelter and it is all ice. Suddenly, the man from the cabin fired at us. We were maybe 250 yards away. He shot high above us. On a shooting range you hold up a spade and wave it when a person misses and I held up my ski pole and waved it like that (as a joke and a criticism of the marksmanship). His second shot missed as well. The third shot went right by Mick's ear and he yelled, 'He's trying to kill us!' We now realised the seriousness of it. We took off away from each other. Another shot rang out and on the fifth shot he hit me. I was bent over and the bullet ricocheted up off of the ice and ploughed right through my hindquarter and out again. The impact of a bullet is so enormous that I fell flat on my back. I lost my skis. I rolled around and aimed to fire back. What stopped me was that I saw myself in a courtroom defending myself. I lay there. I had no skis, only my rifle and a ski pole. I limped over to some willow patches and lay down. Six shots came just ahead.

Meanwhile Mikk had seen me get shot and fall down. He was thinking, 'Sven is killed' and so he took off skiing to Sorva to get the police. We later found out that the man firing at us was named Thor Bjorn Hanson but the police and press had given him the moniker, 'The Desperado.'

I got up and started limping towards shore. It was 35 below. I found a ring of rocks and sat down in them for some shelter. I got out my binos (binoculars) and stayed watching for any movement. I was watching as the second cabin goes on fire. There were two eagles soaring up in the warm air above the fire. Dusk came and I felt around the wound. Blood was still coming out. I passed out with my head in the snow.

When I woke up I made it back to a Kota, a round structure for people to holiday in. The man had been there before and he had thrown all of the food and everything outside, so there was nothing there. I made a fire and sat there watching the door with my finger on the trigger.

The next morning at six o-clock I managed to make it back to where Mikk and I had stayed. There was food there and I made a fire and stayed watching the door with my rifle pointing right at it. I was there two nights and on the third morning a plane came. Men were getting out with their guns. They thought that I was the 'Desperado'. Mick had told them that I had been killed and so they assumed that it was the 'Desperado' in the cabin. I called out to them and eventually I was put into hospital.

One of the men borrowed my rifle and after a manhunt where he killed two police, the Desperado was wounded and arrested. We ended up in the same hospital. Reporters were everywhere and they offered me five thousand dollars to stand above the criminal and point at him. No way. Two men had died and they just wanted this photo." It is one of Sven's deepest life regrets that he didn't end it right then (killing the man who had shot at him), sparing the two officers' lives. "People think I'm a gruff, muscular, unfeeling person," he said, "It's exactly the opposite; I'm over-sensitive, just about to a fault."

In 1958, Sven married Margit and the following year acted as the midwife in the birth of his first daughter, Asa, while they were camped out in the wilderness. The young family enjoyed the exciting, rugged life out on the land and were quite content to stay there until the Swedish Government decided to build a massive Hydro-Electric Dam that would flood the Upper Lulea Basin where he was living. "They published a plan of hydro power development in the last remaining wilderness area of any size in Europe,"[4] he said with a sigh of sadness."

Sven knew at this point in his life that he wanted to remain working in an Arctic environment and when, in 1962, he heard that the Canadian Government needed help with their own reindeer herds he applied for and was accepted for that position. "It's easy to become an expert in such a narrow field. I wanted to immigrate to a land with wilderness. Canadian Immigration seemed interested in my knowledge of boats and reindeer. In 1962, I ended up in Inuvik with the task of turning around the reindeer industry."[5] He was hired to reorganise the industry from intensive herding to modern, extensive herding methods.

Until his arrival, the reindeer were being held in small spaces and were dying from malnutrition so Johansson introduced free-range herding which successfully turned the project around. He and his workers would herd the reindeer using sled dogs and sleds. In order to transport the reindeer carcasses for processing he acquired the arctic schooner, Nanuk II, a heavy government schooner that was missing planks and a motor. In a bit of foreshadowing over his future acquisition of North Star, Sven and the local Inuit installed a motor and re-planked the ship. Prior to re-fitting Nanuk II, Johansson and his Inuit crew had to transport the reindeer meat with canoes, tugs and barges. He referred to the job in a recent interview as the Canadian Reindeer Project, adding somewhat sadly, that it's a project the federal government gets 'hot and cold' about".

Three years into the five year contract he and Margit divorced and she returned to Sweden with their daughter. Sven threw himself into his work and made a success of the industry which worked him out of a job. However, while on a business trip to Inuvik he met Norma Buchanan who was working as a secretary there. They married in 1967 and two years later Silva Esta was born.

When the contract came to an end he decided to stay on in the North and built a log cabin in the remote wilderness, accessible only by a small plane on pontoons or skis, depending upon the season. The lodge was one hundred air miles from their nearest neighbours. He called the cabin Rocky Mountain House and opened a business for guided hunts of large game animals. In order to get back and forth for supplies and to pick up customers he took flying lessons and became a pilot after only two weeks of instruction and after that purchased a plane, a Piper two-seater Cub and put floats on it. In order to take his customers out into the bush he had kept his large sled dog team from the Reindeer Project and purchased six horses as well for that purpose.

He also hired on guides to help take customers out shooting. One of these hands was Albert Elias, a young Innu who met Sven one day in Inuvik. Elias was barely out of his teens and had no experience with horses, in fact had never seen a horse before, having been born and raised on Banksland, but the money was good and it sounded like a good adventure. Albert's father owned the Arctic schooner, Fox, a ship that often travelled with North Star. It might have been their discussions on the trail or around the campfire that spurred on Sven's idea of one day owning North Star.

One day Albert was wandering around Inuvik and wondering how he was going to find summer work when he bumped into Sven. "The last time I saw Sven was the summer I was wrangling horses for him. That summer Sven Johansson was looking for hands, $15 a day including Sunday. That's pretty good money in them days. The horses were huge. He had a hunting lodge in the mountains. I was just looking for a job in town here. He said he was looking for guys to hunt with him. This was on horseback. I never saw a live horse in my life! But I needed the job, right? Fifteen dollars a day, food included. Better than bumming around down here. Month and a half of riding horses everyday. I really enjoyed it, I'm telling you! I fell in love with those horses the first time I saw them. Not everybody's like that. Lots of people want nothing to do with them - with a horse. Me, I thought they were beautiful and the horses knew that I could trust them. At the end of the six weeks, Sven Johansson flew us back to Inuvik in his SuperCub. We got to keep one 30:30 carbine as a bonus."

Throughout his long and adventurous life Sven Johansson has never worried about money. "I've always disregarded money. That's why I can do so many things. I don't let the lack of it stop me. I jump in headlong and the money comes. Money is a resource you must use immediately to make life better."

In 1977 Sven was hired to narrate a TV program called The Northerners for the Canadian Broadcasting Corporation (CBC). He and the host, Bob Switzer, travelled around to communities in the MacKenzie Delta and Banksland interviewing people who had made significant contributions to Canada's Arctic. In 1979 Sven was elected a Fellow of the Royal Geographical Society and in 1994 he was invested as a Member of the Order of Canada.

Sven Johansson receiving the Order of Canada.

There is some great footage of a tuxedo clad Sven awaiting his prestigious Member of the Order of Canada award on the floor of the House of Commons in Ottawa. He had never asked and always assumed that it would be in recognition for his work with North Star of Herschel Island. It was not until he was on the red carpet that he was told it was for his work with reindeer husbandry and the look on his face is a mixture of pride and confusion. "The sea taught me to be humble," he says fervently. "I always wanted to learn what the sea is about - its force, its way. You mustn't do things against the sea, but be harmonious with it. This respect for the sea shapes your character so you can adapt to anything in life." He sometimes misses the ocean but has no regrets. "Never look back is my motto. It gives you a kink in the neck."[6]

Chapter 24

Fred Carpenter and Susie Sidney sell North Star

Throughout our ownership of North Star, there have been rumours of foul play in the sale of North Star to Sven Johansson from Susie Sidney and Fred Carpenter. The doubt in some peoples' minds has to do with a plane crash that Fred Carpenter was in that will be discussed in the next chapter. Some family members and other Northerners feel very strongly that Fred was taken advantage of by Sven after the accident and that Fred would never have sold the boat if he had been in his 'right mind'. There are others who feel just as strongly that the deal to sell North Star was made by Fred's wife, Agnes, and Susie Sidney when Fred was in hospital in a coma, perhaps because they felt that he would not recover and so Sven represented an opportunity to get rid of the boat and get some cash. Another story is that Sven 'sweet-talked and charmed' the women when Fred was injured and that is how he acquired North Star. Others, still, feel that the sale was made before Fred's accident. Despite the former of these being insulting accusations towards Agnes, Susie, Fred and Sven, these are very strong feelings held by very strong-minded people who have felt this way for generations now. Sven has been dogged by these rumours wherever he has travelled. "I was even down in Fort Good Hope and there was a government agent there and he came up to me and he said, "You fooled that Eskimo guy who was knocked in the head," so it's been kind of floating around," he says. Some stories have been passed down through generations. In order to get as close to the truth as possible, I began to chase the paper-trail, tracking down bills of sale, telegrams, reading old interviews and making my own interviews. This is what I found. One salient point was told to me by Fred and Ada's daughter, Mary Carpenter Frost. That is, that when the ship was being sold, the only family and friends who were aware were the ones who were still in the Arctic. The rest of the family had no opportunity to try and convince their father to keep the ship. "The family that lived on the island at the time did not think of the ship's rich history.

No one south of 60 was consulted," she says, the bitterness of the event still strong on her mind.

North Star as Sven first saw her, after she was six years on the beach.

In the early 1960's Sven Johansson and Fred Carpenter were aware of one another. Both were well known for their various exploits and word had got around that Sven was interested in perhaps purchasing North Star. Fred Carpenter knew that Sven was in the Western Arctic working with the reindeer industry, deciding where herds should be kept and streamlining the business to make it successful and profitable. Sven felt that he wanted to purchase her, provided that she was still sound. "I first met Fred in the early sixties. I was quite well known in the North and I met him a few times when he was down in Inuvik, for conferences and things. I had seen pictures of the North Star and I had immediately fallen in love with her." At one of the conferences Fred asked Sven if he planned on putting reindeer on Banks Island. It was a bit if a test of Sven's mettle and expertise since you cannot have caribou and reindeer herds in such a small place. Sven passed the test by assuring Fred that he would never consider mixing the herds.

Agnes Carpenter recalls that Fred had been trying to sell North Star for a long time before Sven came along. "Fred had tried for years to sell North Star, even to the government and it fell through. They wanted to change the boat name to North Star 3 or North Star 4. He also tried to sell North Star to the museum in Yellowknife as a heritage center and they wanted to buy it. He tried three or four times but they never got the money for it. He wanted the ship to be preserved. He was afraid that people might get into it and set fires or break the glass and that she would just end up rotting on the beach. The North Star is the last one left in the water. That ironbark needs to be in the water."

Another piece of evidence that shows that Fred Carpenter was planning to sell the ship appears in Richard Condon's book, The Northern Copper Inuit: a history. Condor started his research at Holmon Island in the 1970's and on page 29 he describes Fred Carpenter as having once been the top fur trapper in the western Canadian Arctic, but now his ship, the North Star, is for sale.

Sven had run another Arctic schooner with the Canadian Reindeer Project, Nanuk II, and saw the opportunities that a ship like that could provide in the North. In January of 1967, a chance came up for Sven to travel to Banksland. "I arranged to go to Sachs and to see the boat. Fred knew that I was interested in her. We delivered fuel up to the north tip of Banks Island in a Beaver airplane. I was working as a barrel handler. We had the equipment on the front of the plane so that we could easily roll out the drums of fuel. I was with the NorthWest Territories Game Service." After leaving the fuel cache on Northern Banks Island, Sven ended up stepping off the plane at Sachs Harbour and was greeted by Fred. "You've come to buy the boat! If you no buy boat, Sven, then we no more friends." Sven was taken aback by the greeting and replied, "Hold on there buddy. A boat is not worth a friendship". The two men laughed together and wandered down to see the ship. Later, back at Fred and Agnes's home, Fred pulled out a screwdriver and told Sven to go down to North Star on his own and poke around to make his own survey of her to satisfy himself that she was not rotten. "Fred was an extremely smart businessman - an aristocrat - he was a leader there. Fred gave me a screwdriver and said 'you go and poke around North Star and tell me if there is any rot or problems with the boat. You go by yourself and I will wait for you."

The two men trusted one another and Sven retired to North Star and spent the afternoon crawling through her bilges and combing her sides. Since the ship was leaning on her shoulder, drifting snow had collected and frozen into spaces in the bilges. If the wood was rotten, then this was the place it would be most evident. After chipping through the ice Sven was able to tap along the inner hull with the screwdriver and recognize that the hull was sound. This was truly a testament to her builders and to the people of Banksland who had maintained her over her lifetime, but the fact of the matter was that she had been lying out on her side for over 6 years, through all of the storms and wind as well as being baked in the hot days of summer. "I knew that the boat had been lying on her side and so any fresh water would have pooled and collected there and that is where the rot would be - but of course there was none, just snow and stuff - but she was sound because she had been kept in the freezer", remembers Sven.

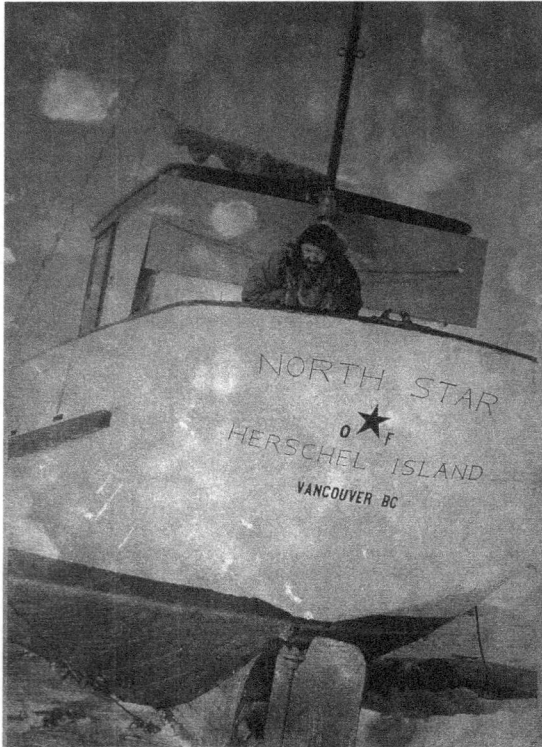

Sven surveying North Star prior to sale.

The engine was still installed but the magneto on it was broken beyond repair. Fred had tried to get a replacement but as this was the last of the Atlas gasoline engines built, there were none to be had. Sven calculated into his offer how much it would cost him to purchase a new engine and get it shipped up by barge. Just a year earlier Sven had replaced the gasoline engine aboard Nanuk II with a diesel and so he was aware of how much the venture would cost and how much work it would be. He also had to calculate the cost of the gear, caulking and paint to get her ready for sea.

Sven returned to the house. "Fred," he said. "I want to buy North Star but I don't have much money and I don't want to owe you anything. I want to make a cash offer and then no more payments. I don't want to be paying you a hundred dollars a month or something. I can scrape up $2,000. If I buy her, then I will have to use any more money I earn in order to replace the engine and electrical and propeller in order to get her up and running." Sven offered him this incredibly low price and Fred quickly accepted. "I just want to see the ship get used and out to sea. I don't want to see her lying on the beach where someone might start a fire in her or get wrecked some other way," replied Fred. Just a year earlier another schooner had been torched on the beach by children playing with matches. Fred Carpenter was more than aware of all of North Star's sister-ships and how no one seemed to be valuing the old workhorses. In fact, Sven's offer to buy North Star was the last time anyone offered to buy any of the Arctic schooners lying on the beach. Fred's wife Agnes told me, "I didn't want to see him sell it and he practically gave it away because he didn't want to see her sit and die. None of the sons could take it on the ocean. She had to be restored. He sold her for so little and afterwards we ordered a little speedboat and it cost more than what he got for North Star!"

After they struck the deal, Sven returned to Inuvik in order to arrange the money. In the mean time, Fred contacted his sister Susie Sidney, the co-owner of North Star. By all reports, Susie was unhappy with the amount that Fred had accepted. While in Inuvik Sven went to see Susie and she refused his offer. Sven was dumbfounded. He went to the post-office and wired Fred, asking him if he still accepted the offer. The telegram reads: PLEASE CONFORM (sic) RETURN WIRE THAT YOU STILL AGREE TO SELL NORTH STAR AT 2,000.00 DLRS HALF TO YOU ANF(sic) HALF TO SUSIE STOP IF SUSIE AGREES TODAY I WILL COME TO SACHS WEDNESDAY SKED(sic) TO PAY YOU. SVEN JOHANNSON. "I then just waited a few days and then got a phone call from Susie's new husband Peter Sidney, "Heard you had trouble with Susie - you ask again and no more trouble. Look she just like that - wants more" and he told her to take the money."Fred wired back that he was standing by his word" and so Sven returned to Susie's house. In his absence, Susie had invited in Fred's wife, Agnes, who was visiting on the mainland as well as Fred's son, Dr Noah Carpenter. Susie was reluctant to sign but Noah told her that in his opinion, she should. Susie said: "Fred want to sell North Star to Sven for "nothing" what you say?" Noah replied: "North Star has done all she can for Sachs - go ahead and sell". Sven remembers Noah saying, "Let her go, Susie," he said.

"She's done enough for Sachs Harbour. It's time for someone else to have her." When meeting Susie again with the original "contract of sale" - Noah Carpenter (the MD) just opened the door arriving from South. After that Susie signed and I gave her $1,000 in cash. Fred got his $1,000 and the purchase was fair and legal."

PAGE 3

(c) All costs incurred after the date of this Agreement of

Sale shall be the responsibility of the buyer Sven Johansson.

(d) The selling price agreed upon is the sum of $2000.00 in full.

(e) Upon signing this Agreement of Sale payment in cash shall

be made as follows:

$1000.00 paid to Fred Carpenter

$1000.00 paid to Susie Sydney

this being payment in full of the agreed selling price.

We certify that we are the rightful owners of the vessel "NORTH STAR"

at the time of this Agreement of Sale and hereby agree to the above

conditions of sale and upon signing also certify each receiving due

payment in full. Herewith the ownership is transferred to the buyer.

Fred Carpenter	_Sachs Harbour_	_May 10th/67_
(Fred Carpenter)	Place	Date
Mrs. A. E. Carpenter	_Sachs Harbour_	_May 10th/67_
Witness (1)	Place	Date
Mrs Agnes Nasogaluak	_Sachs Harbour_	_May 10th/67_
Witness (2)	Place	Date

Sale contract between Fred Carpenter, Susie Sidney and Sven Johansson.

Since the ship had never been registered, Sven now began the long red-tape process to register the vessel and to prove ownership. Sven explains that the importance of getting all of the paperwork is so that there is no question of ownership. "You can't steal a boat - it is like selling a farm, an acre of land. There is a clear agreement so that there is no funny business."

There is no disputing that Fred Carpenter and James Wolki purchased North Star from the Northern Whaling and Trading Company of Oakland California on August 16th,1936. The original builder's certificate says this as does an 'Agreement of Sale' receipt from the NWTC. The receipt also shows that there were 'Duties Paid' upon North Star's arrival into Canada. If that was not shown then Sven would have had to pay them to the Canadian Government. The next event in North Star's ownership was when James Wolki traded his half-interest in North Star to Susie Sidney for the Nanuk II.

"Then I had to trace back to when Susie had traded for the North Star with Jim Wolkie. When Susie's first husband had died she then owned the Nanuk II. She traded the Nanuk 11 for half ownership of the North Star. I had to go to Jim Wolki with an RCMP officer and have him read out what had happened with the trade. Jim signed with an X since he couldn't write and then the RCMP officer held his hand over Wolki's hand and helped him sign," remembers Sven. Two elders, Silas Kangegan and Sam Amihua signed as witnesses.

He continues, "Me becoming sole owner was all done "by the book" as required by the old act which changed in 2007. I had to legally prove the whole history of ownership of North Star. That was done by the "Builders Certificate" from Geo. W Kneass and the "Agreement of Sale" 1936 when Fred and Jim become owners. Fred gave me those 2 documents. The verbal agreement between Jim and Susie I had to legalize at Tuk - witnessed by RCMP. That was done - and Fred and Susie could then legally sell North Star to me. That was done with a signed Agreement of Sale.

The important regulation in Maritime Law is that a ship can only be a Registered Canadian Ship (with Blue Book) when the entire line of owner-ship can be legally documented. I registered North Star" 'anew' as it is called. To get Blue Book Registry I had to show legally documented the whole line of owners. The earliest is a "Builder Certificate" by Geo. W. Kneass, San Francisco. Next there are a Sale Document between Captain Pedersen and Fred Carpenter/Jim Wolki at Herschel Island 1936. Next I had to get the legal document of transfer of 1/2 ownership from Jim Wolki to Susie Sidney (widow of Fred Wolki) with the "schooner Nanuk II" as the "payment value". That document showed the legal ownership of 1/2 of North Star by Susie now married "Sidney" and 1/2 legal ownership by Fred Carpenter (the original 1/2 ownership from 1936). I then had to show a legal document that transferred full ownership of North Star to me. She was registered as North Star of Herschel Island. Before that "Blue Book" she was not a registered Canadian ship."

When you have the Blue Book in your name there cannot have been any other "owners" of North Star than what is at Ship Registry at Vancouver. Just as sure as no-one can steal or fool anyone to be legal owner of a farm - big or small. It is as clear and simple as that."

With all of the paperwork in order and everything legally signed and witnessed Sven got on with the big job of putting the old girl in shape to head back to sea. "After I bought the boat, I lived at Sachs with Fred and Agnes for a week or so while I got North Star ready. I stayed again with Fred and Agnes in 1968 when getting ready for sea (new engine) and Fred was there and we had great time. It is important that Frank Carpenter (the RCMP) lived in Sachs at that time and we were great friends. If there would have been anything wrong with me taking North Star off the beach he would not allow it. Fred's wife Agnes was very smart and a top notch "business person" and no-one could fool her about values and ownership. Joey Carpenter was aboard from Sachs to Tuk as a good friend - how could that be if I was such bad fellow?" Sven wonders.

Sven needed to return to the Delta to finish some work with Rocky Mountain House and so hired Fred Carpenter on to help get the ship painted. Fred in turn hired many of the Bankslanders and much later Agnes invoiced Sven for the work. Agnes also writes in the letter that she knows that the sale of the boat was before the accident but that Fred doesn't remember selling the boat. In January of 2012 Agnes Carpenter confirmed with me that the sale of the boat was before the plane accident. "Oh, for sure. They started talking about selling the boat back in 1966. North Star was sold way before the plane accident."

North Star's final launch from Sachs Harbour.

In order to launch the ship, Sven hired the DOT tractor to push her into the water. As she hit the water, after so many years of drying out, she rolled back and forth and the force of the launch shot water up between the ironbark and fir hulls. "The first sign of bad thinking was that I was laughed at openly: "What is that crazy Sven wanting to do with an old rotten boat"? When North Star was rolling from the force of the tractor, water came inside the ironbark and then came out as a spout when rolling the other way. Then it was said that "the boat was full of water sinking already". It was all a cynical chuckle - but who is laughing now? The boat had no value until I started working on her."

Sven recalls that "the style of boat everyone wanted then was the new plastic (fibreglass) ones with a big outboard on the back so that you could drive around fast (Sven feigns smoking and looking 'cool'). I wasn't worried because I knew why the water was spraying out," he says with a smile. "I took out the old Atlas by myself and dragged it into the hold. Then I put in my new little engine. Everyone thought I was crazy. The old engine had this huge, huge propeller and with the new engine the propeller couldn't turn very fast and when I went by people would yell at me of how stupid I was for buying this boat. Then I put the new propeller on and started to get charters and then everyone was saying 'hey, why didn't Fred give me the boat - you shouldn't have it'. It was just envy. When everyone saw that the boat was getting charters people started teasing Fred that he shouldn't have sold the boat."

The process of switching out the massive old Atlas engine and acquiring a new diesel engine was an enormous prospect. It is a big enough job to do in a major city center with equipment and the access to parts but to do this from hundreds of miles north of the Arctic Circle was very difficult. With the engine room measured and a decision made of how much power North Star would need, Sven began to telegraph to dealers and eventually settled on a GM 353 - a 'screaming Jimmy'. There was only one available that would fit North Star's requirements and there were two problems associated with it. The first was that the engine was built backwards, that is, the flywheel was at the front of the motor and the generator, filters and wiring had been mounted opposite to what was already set-up space wise aboard North Star. The second problem was that this motor was in Florida, USA.

The decision to switch North Star's power plant from the Atlas gasoline engine to a keel-cooled General Motors was made easier with the reality that there were no spare parts available to fix the Atlas. It would have been far easier to repair the Atlas than to remove it and then order and ship another motor up to the high Arctic as well as all of the problems associated with fitting a new engine to existing systems.

Sven arranged by telegram to have the motor trucked as far as Inuvik and then it was placed in the hands of the Northern Transportation Company and moved by barge to Sachs Harbour. The price for shipping it from Inuvik to Sachs was $37.00 on July 6, 1968. (It is a bitter irony that the barge service that helped end North Star's career was instrumental in breathing new life into her). A new propeller also had to be sought out as the large one that the Atlas used was much too big for the considerably smaller diesel engine. Until the new, smaller prop was delivered and installed the small diesel engine could barely move North Star and as noted, became a source of more ridicule of Sven by the locals. "My work on North Star before putting to sea was removing old Atlas engine and installing the Detroit. I had some funny time because the oil pump was installed the wrong way. I had a tractor pushing North Star sideways of the beach before working. They were building a school and all working there - I was all alone."

With the motor ashore Sven moved it next to North Star, lying alongside the shore. He built a ramp and then using a chain come-along sweated the huge, new motor up to the ship's side. There was still no one to help him as people were busy with building the school or finishing up their own fur shipments to get to market and so he carried on along. The engine was inched up to the gunwhales. As he was just figuring out how to get it over the railing safely a wave broke at the harbour's edge. The engine rocked back and then in one terrifying display of momentum rolled right over the three foot gunwhales then across the deck and fell right down the main hatch and eight feet later smashed down onto the keelson. Miraculously, the only damage was that the engine speed regulator had sheared off as did one of the engine mounts. When the engine was finally in place he was able to lash the broken leg of the mount down for the trip to the mainland and then jury-rigged the regulator so that once the engine was started it would be at a constant speed. North Star's luck continued.

With North Star back in the water, Fred showed Sven the ropes and one day they went on a trip around the harbour while Sven got used to his new command. "When first motoring with the new engine, just before leaving Sachs, Fred was aboard, and as a best friend. No sign of bad feelings." Work continued right up until the ship leaving Sachs Harbour for good, as reported by the premier edition of the Sachs Harbour newsletter with the headline:

"THE NORTH STAR SAILS AGAIN

Evening August 13 all people at Sachs were on the lookout as the old ship was launched once more under the supervision of Sven Johansen (sic), his new owner. There she is...floataing (sic) again. With a brand new engine she sailed out of the harbour and disappeared in the fog on her way to the Delta for a new career as a cruiser. Joe Carpenter and Roger Kuptana are on board for that adventurous trip."[1]

Still sporting her large, unwieldy, heavy propeller, North Star's new engine strained to turn it and the boat speed was negligible. Sven remembers many people jeering at him for changing motors and for buying such an old boat. In any case, North Star proceeded to sea. Joey Carpenter remembers the historic scene as the Queen of the Banksland Fleet left Sachs Harbour for the last time. "When North Star left with Sven - it was kind of an emotional thing. Sven was busy down in the engine room and I had to be in the pilothouse. A lot of men were following us in their boats and all the canoes. Everyone else was on board North Star for the last time. After three or four miles they all just jumped back into their boats and went back to Sachs. It was a very significant moment in the history of Sachs Harbour. Of all of the boats that had been part of the schooner era, part of the life-line between remote Banks Island and the Canadian mainland and as the symbol of Banksland prosperity and hard work, North Star 'the Queen of the Banksland Fleet' was arguably the most recognized and the boat that the community was most proud of was leaving - forever. The community's boats all swarmed around her as she left the harbour. On board Carpenters, Wolkis, Pokiaks, Elias', Thrashers and many other Inuvialuit all stood on deck each lost in their own thoughts of what the ship was, of what she represented. According to Sven most still thought that he was a fool for buying her but still resented that she had been sold out of the community. As North Star made her way further from shore the Bankslanders slowly disembarked onto the smaller craft, leaving a skeleton crew of Sven, Robert Kuptana and Joey Carpenter, the latter two came on as unpaid crew to help deliver North Star to Tuktoyaktuk.

The usual route was to follow the shores of Banks and Baillie Islands and then to anchor and wait for fair weather before making the open crossing. Sven struck out for Tuktoyaktuk, confident in his new ship and his navigation skills. The crossing was made in fog and so Sven relied a lot on checking the depths and the colour of the water.

For many of the Carpenters' friends and family, the first time that they heard that North Star had been sold was the same time that they heard the horrible news of Fred's accident. Without knowing the details or dates it was easy to draw conclusions that the events happened around the same time, even perhaps when Fred was lying in hospital in a coma. In fact, the sale of North Star to Sven Johansson occurred a full eighteen months before the airplane crash.

It was after Fred returned to Sachs Harbour, not remembering or believing that he had sold his beloved ship that a request was made to Sven to sell the ship back to Fred. When this was denied, legal avenues were looked into by some family members to have the sale annulled.

Joey Carpenter is happy that the ship was put back out to sea."I keep telling people that they made good use of it. It was good that Sven bought her and took her away. Better than just sitting on the beach, kids just smashing it." Fred's grandson Larry, Andy's son, adds in a letter to us, "We are so happy that you have the North Star and that it was sold out from Sachs. If it hadn't been, then she would just be a pile of boards on the beach. She would have been ruined." Another of Fred's sons, Stanley, adds, "All of the other boats ended up being destroyed. When Dad was selling North Star, I didn't think it was a good thing. My dad was wiser, though. He was a wise man. If he hadn't sold her then she would just be a pile of wood lying on the beach now. I know my dad knew it was right to sell the boat. My dad stood and watched her go."

Joey, Stanley and Larry and many of the Carpenter family have often mentioned how happy they are that the ship has been able to carry on and be cared for. The very real danger of a ship lying on the beach for too long is the same as that of an abandoned building. Trouble seems to find it. Some have been stripped of their metals and the hull used for firewood, others left to crumble in the elements. The saddest story I have ever heard was of the Kneass built, Tudlik, who was carried North aboard Patterson in 1929 to bring Steve Angulalik's furs to Herschel Island from his post at Perry River. Robin McGrath wrote in Up Here magazine that Tudlik's engineer was Morris Pokiak who besides his engineering skills also brought along the recipe for marmalade moonshine. Apparently Pokiak could keep the Atlas going with no more than a screwdriver and a hammer. Tudlik made the round trip each year until the end of the schooner era when she moved Angulalik to live in Cambridge Bay. Lying at anchor the incorrect news got out that she had a broken keel and so she was hauled ashore and sold. The new owner took a chainsaw to her side and cut a door into her hull in order to turn her into a coffee shop. To add insult to injury the once proud Arctic Schooner has subsequently been reviewed as 'the worst restaurant in the North, and that's saying something'.

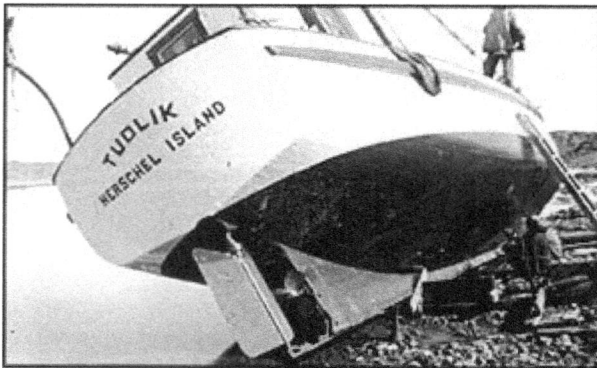

**Tudlik at Cambridge Bay, the worst restaurant in
the North, and that's saying something.**

Sven made the trip alone from Tuktoyaktuk to Inuvik and then went below to rest. "I slept a long time because I haven't slept in a long time. I had a little dinghy that I kept with the boat that I had taken up to the beach. Then I went up and slept in the cabin ashore. I got up and rowed to the boat and tied it up and went aboard. I went down in the hold and there was the old engine and all of the rap-trap that I had aboard since the last harbour and so then I said to myself, 'Okay guy, now you have a boat. So what in the hell are you gonna do now?' I had no plans for the future. Just wanted her. She was just so damned beautiful, I just wanted her. About the same time I heard a holler on the beach from the channel where we were anchored. So I poked up my head from the cargo hold and there were a bunch of guys waving and screaming so I rowed ashore. 'Is this your boat?' 'Yes.' 'Can we charter you?' And that was just an hour after I went aboard after having the sleep so I said, 'Sure what do you want to do?'

They wanted to do gravity metering in the Beaufort Sea for oil deposits. You put a bell right down on the bottom and from that you can get the gravity and you get the information. "So when do you want it?" "Well," they said "Right away!" So I said, "Give me ten days." I wired back to Vancouver and they wanted sleeping quarters for twelve people and cooking facilities. So, right where the Captain's bunk is now I put in a cook-stove oil stove and a chimney and all that stuff where the glass port is on deck was a fitting for a stove pipe. Then I had to go to a workshop in Inuvik to get the engine installed right. I got the right size coupling for the shaft and then I had to build a port-a-potty on the back of the pilothouse and all that stuff and then they put on freezers and stuff and I had a new prop because I wired down to Vancouver to get one and that turned out really good. They had to make a new end of the shaft since the old one wasn't standard and then of course we were ready to go. That first couple of months I got money back to pay for what I purchased the boat for and all the damned stuff that I put into her.

Then started the damned envy. I know that the drastic contrast between North Star on the beach for 6 years (engine not working) - and the apparent success I made after 1968 must have started envy and jealousy in persons devoid of any accomplishment in their lives that they cannot have any respect in themselves. I started to have people coming aboard or meeting me and saying 'why in the hell did Fred sell that boat to you? If he'd have selled it to me I would be making all the money.' Finally I got fed up with this one guy who was running around Inuvik saying this so I finally said, 'Listen Buddy - you have no clue as to what to do with that boat. If you had gotten that boat you would have wrecked her first thing you did.' That came with me here to Victoria, that envy. There was a bookshop here (Wells Books) with two ladies and they had been up in the Arctic and I invited them aboard North Star and we got talking and then the name came up - of a young girl she was probably twenty when I met her - they were wanting to mention her. So the ladies said, "but you seemed such a nice guy," and I said, "thank you," because the young girl had told those two ladies - she had been crying saying 'that goddamm Sven, he had stolen the boat from Fred' and all that sort of thing'.

Then one of Fred's kids started hounding me for me stealing the boat and he told it to the former commissioner of Iceland, Bent Sivertz, who lived here, a friend of me, and he starts asking me, 'How did you buy the boat?' And I said, 'We wrote a contract,' and then he said, 'What language did he communicate?' and I said 'English', because he had the idea that Fred didn't understand anything and I would fool him to get him to sell it to me, you see. I even got a phone call from this same son of Fred accusing me of stealing the boat and I knew that he had a lawyer listening in, recording, because he said 'You got to say that to be legal' (that the phone call was being recorded), so he said, 'Well, I record this stuff so I can figure out what you are saying.' So this lawyer, he starts babbling of how I fooled Fred and I said, 'Wait a minute, North Star is a Canadian ship - registered. You cannot get a boat registered in your name until you get the entire history of the ship and I had to go to Jim Wolki in Tuk with the RCMP and Jim Wolki didn't write so the RCMP asked questions of Fred and the ship and his half part in it and then he had to write down this on the paper and sign it. The RCMP held the pen and Jim made an X and then after that I went to the registry in Vancouver and registered her as my marine property with a bluebook and you Goddam is not going to say anything about me fooling anybody. Fred Carpenter was the smartest man I ever met - he was a businessman because he had the store - and you think that he didn't understand money?'"

SOME OF THE DOCUMENTS TO DO WITH SALE:

1. Statement of verbal transfer of ownership - NSHI

James Wolki hereby declares

-that I, on 16th of August 1935, purchased from the Northern Whaling and Trading company of Oakland California, USA, one half interest in North Star and that I, in 1944, transferred that half interest to Susie Sidney and Susie Sidney transferred to me the whole interest in Nanuk II

and that this verbal trade of interests also meant that I had no more interest in North Star and Susie Sidney had no more interest in Nanuk II since the year 1944.

Dated this February 26th, 1968 at Tuktoyaktuk, NWT, Canada

signed and witnessed

2. Letter from Agnes Carpenter to Sven Johannson Dated Dec. 5, 1967

Dear Sven,

Very happy to hear that you and Norma got married. And hope you both have a long life together.

Fred is still improving and gaining weight. Not like when he first came home. But he's not quite like he use (sic) to be. But maybe slowly he'll come back. There is hope. We're finally paying for the double tent, we owe you. It's $150.00 was it? We never got around in using it yet. Also I'm sending the time, when these guys worked on North Star last summer.

Workers on North Star

David Nasoqaluck hours - 37 - 74.00

Frank Kudlack hrs 25 - 50.00

Wallace Lucas - hrs 10 - 20.00

Noah Elias - hrs - 10 - 20.00

Moses Raddi - hrs - 3 -6.00

David Lucas - hrs - 5 - 10.00

Fred put in 29 hours (75.00) of Labour, also as forman (sic).

We had bad weather nearly all summer. That's the only reason why Fred got more guys to work, as soon as we had good weather for a day or two. Just only one side in the bottom is not painted, cause it was frozen in.

Fred has forgotten completely that he sold the "North Star". He can't believe it. I told him when he sold it, but he said he must have been out of his head, when he sold it. I told him this happen (sic) long before the accident. He was planning to fix it up next summer. It's part of his life. He has taken it hard. I sure hope it won't get him down, as there has been enough bad time this summer.

Sven, he wants to buy the boat back. I know it's hard. But it's for his own good in recovering. He says he'll pay you for the boat, also when you spend aside from it. I hate to say this, but it's like part of his flesh. So please let us know. Best regards.

Mrs Agnes Carpenter

In regard to Agnes's letter Sven wrote to me that, "I know that he wanted it back, but what would he have done with North Star after him being all busted up like that?"

3. Document: to Registrar of Shipping/Customs House/ Edmonton, dated July 5, 1967 in which Sven claims ownership in order to register ship. The following documents were included in his request:

4. Letter requesting approval by Minister of Transport

5. Certificate of Record signed by A.H. Clifford showing that the North Star was built for the Northern Whaling and Trading Company of Oakland California

6. Letter of sale dated August 16, 1935 at Herschel Island in which Northern Whaling and Trading Co. sold the North Star to James Wolki and Frederick (Fred) Carpenter

7. Agreement of Sale signed May 6th and May 10th, 1967 in which the sellers certify past ownership history. It is certified that in the summer of 1944, Susie Sidney obtained half ownership from James Wolki in exchange for the Nanuk II on a verbal agreement. ....Please note that twenty-three years have passed during which time Susie Sidney has been considered as owner by all persons in the area.

8. Document: signed by James Wolki on February 26, 1968 stating that he had purchased one half interest in North Star on August 16, 1935 and that in 1944 he transferred this half interest to Susie Sidney in exchange for ownership of Nanuk II (witnessed by Silas Kongegana and Sam Amakina).

9. Document: from Department of National Revenue Customs and Excise dated April 3, 1968 in regard to registering and naming North Star. "....the Minister of Transport has consented to the registry in Canada at the port of Edmonton of the undocumented ship North Star.... ...The name North Star is already in use, as is North Star 11 and North Star 111. However, you could obtain approval for North Star 1 or North Star IV. It is noted that our previous correspondence referred to North Star of Herschel Island and you may wish to seek approval of this full name, or to effect registry for an entirely different name. MORE FOLLOWS and signed W.L. Edwards/Registrar of Shipping.

10. Document: Northern Transportation Company invoice to Sven Johansson for transport of; I Marine Engine, GM

353, dated July 6, 1968. Price of transport from Inuvik to Sachs Harbour - $37.00

Sven concludes the whole sale by writing: "It is sad that the minds of two men, Fred and Sven 1967 - deciding the best for North Star based on knowledge of sea and ships - could be made so ugly as was done, based on envy and greed for money.

The price, $2,000. was right and it was an historic event. It was the very last exchange of real value in the 'Old Schooners' fleet. Since I bought North Star - NO ONE has been paid one red cent for any 'schooner'. They are all on the beach 'falling apart." The second last of the fleet was Nanuk that I repaired and put to sea. She was burned at Fort Franklin by kids."

Chapter 25
Fred's Plane Crash

In 1967, Fred and Agnes Carpenter were in Inuvik with some other family. Noticing North Star alongside the point, they walked down and spoke with Norma and Sven, asking how the boat was and how the business was going. At the end of the conversation Fred jokingly told Sven, "I think I should kill you so that I can get my boat back!" Since Sven and Norma had resurrected North Star, Fred had been teased by many people about selling his old love since she now looked as though she had some life in her and was back to making money. "If I had failed and the boat sunk or I couldn't make money with her then they wouldn't have been so rough on Fred," Sven says. "I really felt bad for him that this man who had started the Sachs Harbour community and who had used North Star to take care of so many people was now being joked at. It was really mean of them. I knew that Fred was joking about killing me. It was just an expression in the North. Everyone said it. It didn't mean anything." "Like most people, Eskimos hated being laughed at or teased. Usually this was not done cruelly, for it was important that the person be able to save face by laughing along with the joke."[1] The whole damned settlement of Sachs Harbour was built on his shoulders," adds Sven.

That evening or perhaps a week later - (the records are blurred on this as the records for plane crashes were not formally archived for another decade), Fred, five members of his family and a National Geographic photographer all boarded the plane back to Sachs Harbour. Fred had purchased yet another washing machine and this was stowed behind the passenger seats. The weather was unsettled and there was a thick bank of fog so there must have been some concern by both the pilot and the passengers that the flight should be postponed.

The flight across would have taken about an hour and half and when they arrived there was still fog at the entrance to the Sachs runway. The pilot made an attempt to land but with no visibility he banked around and took a second try at it. I have heard several accounts of what happened next. One was that Fred had undone his seatbelt in order to make sure that a child had his seatbelt done up. Another is that he had undone his seatbelt and had moved up to help the pilot in picking the landing strip out of the brume. In any case, the plane missed the runway by a few feet, caught the landing gear in a ditch and smashed into a rock wall. People were thrown from the plane and jet fuel was spilled all over the scene. Everyone was unconscious. The first to get his bearings was Fred's son, John Willy, just back from his first year in the Armed Forces. He quickly moved the baby to safer ground and then started pulling the rest of the passengers from the wreckage.

"I killed that plane." The crashed plane at Sachs
Harbour. Photo credit John Carpenter.

Fred was smashed up and looked dead. He had a huge head injury. An hour later a second plane arrived and on board was another of Fred's sons, Dr Noah Carpenter. This plane was loaded with the injured passengers and flown to hospital in Edmonton.

Fred regained consciousness 28 days later and a month after that he was released into Agnes' care. It was obvious to everyone that the accident had changed him. His memory was very, very poor and he required help with the most basic of tasks. Jack Grainge was a friend of Fred Carpenter's and visited him while Fred was recuperating. "Fred suffered a concussion while in a plane crash, while landing in a partial fog. He had disconnected his seatbelt in order to point out the place to land. An hour later, Dr Otto Schaefer and Noah Carpenter, a medical student and son of Fred arrived in another plane. I visited Carpenter in the Charles Camsell Hospital, but his mind had not then recovered. I believe he did not recognize me."[2] Agnes remembers very well the sad time. "There were five of his family members aboard. Fred hurt his head. It made him forget a lot of things in the present. He would sleep five minutes and then think that he had slept all night. He walked around all night. He had blood clots on three parts of his brain. Sometimes he would walk around outside and forget to put on his parka. He could remember everything from the past but he couldn't remember what he had just done."

After the horrific plane crash, Fred Carpenter's condition was so severe that he was not expected to live and the whole community entered a period of mourning. Here was the patriarch of their community, the man who had effectively settled what would become the Hamlet of Sachs Harbour, the man who had held the land for the Canadian government in order to prove Canadian Sovereignty over the western Arctic, the man who had negotiated for a school to be built, an airstrip to connect his people with the rest of the world and a man who throughout his life had shown by example that the true definition of an Inuvialuit, a true Canadian, was one of self-sufficiency - never asking for welfare yet still contributing financially to the country through paying taxes, buying war-bonds and by being one of the best fur trappers in the history of the western Arctic and setting records that would never be surpassed.

It was no surprise then, that one day when a plane landed on the gravel runway at Sachs that it was Fred Carpenter who stepped off and looked around at his community. Less sure on his feet and somewhat still confused from the massive head injury he had incurred; Fred still noticed right away that something was not right with what he was seeing. He walked down to his home and met his first born son, Frank. His family rushed around to greet him, with tears of joy in their eyes.

"Where's my boat? Where's the North Star?"There was an awkward silence. Agnes tried to distract him, tried bringing the grandchildren to see him. Frank turned away, unable to answer his father.

RCMP officer Cal Alexander based at Sachs Harbour remembers that Fred "wasn't able to do a whole lot after that, physically or mentally." One of Fred's daughters, Diane, adds that "he crashed in 1967. It was in the fall time 'cause it was really foggy. Maybe sometime in August. He was actually sitting on the doorway of the plane 'cause there was no room. When they crashed, it was so foggy the pilot couldn't see, so he landed on the side bank of the runway. The door flew open; it caught my Dad I guess." Another of Fred's sons, Stanley, recalls that the plane crash set his own life on a different trajectory. "I quit school after the plane crash to help my family out. Put food on the table. Caribou."

Taking care of Fred when Agnes was on the outside was shared between his children and grandchildren. Les Carpenter was at home at Sachs Harbour one time while his parents, Frank and Florence, were away. "My parents were on holidays. I was at home at Sachs looking after the house and one day Fred came over quite excited. I couldn't get a handle on what he was so excited about - because he was talking in broken Inuvialutuk. Finally, he got me to understand that he wanted me to turn the radio on. Geez, he had a few tears in his eyes and everything. I got the radio on and that's when I found out that Elvis had died. Fred was quite broken up about that. It was about 24 hours of everything to do with Elvis on CHED out of Edmonton; we could get it really good at Sachs."

Fred Carpenter in retirement.

Mary Frost remembers visiting her father at Sachs Harbour. "When I went home, Dad took me to where the plane crash had been. He said "I killed the plane!" He had such a positive attitude" Fred's son-in-law, Martin Goodliffe, remembers that "his short term memory came back slowly and I believe it was his enthusiasm for life that made it come back at all."

In 1984 Fred Carpenter passed away. He had lived an incredible life stepping from the life of a nomadic hunter to the leader of the white fox capital of the world, the owner of North Star - Queen of the Banksland Fleet - and a legendary trapper, trader and friend to all.

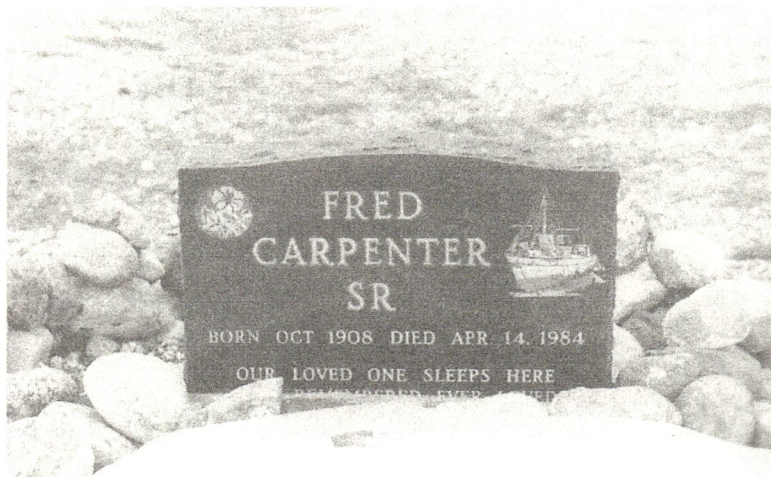

Fred Carpenter's gravestone with his beloved North Star etched into it.

Fred Carpenter's gravestone sits in the graveyard at Sachs Harbour overlooking the hamlet that he helped to create. The headstone has an etching of North Star on it and his Inuvialuit name, Ajgaliaq, that translates to 'big hand' - a person who is always willing to help others. An official flag was produced for the Hamlet of Sachs Harbour that features North Star. On the site of where Fred Carpenter's old house stood a community center has been built. It is named for him.

Chapter 26
Sven and Norma's North Star Adventures

North Star of Herschel Island began a few years of paying work, being chartered out primarily to businesses involved in the oil industry. "During the seventies Tuktoyaktuk became the center of activity and exploration once more. But this time it was exploration of another kind -oil and gas."[1] One charter was to take water samples at various depths right to the sea floor in order to find out if there were any naturally occurring organisms that feed on petroleum. The oil industry and the Federal Government were concerned even at this time in the early 1970's of what effect an oil spill would have on the environment. The organisms multiply in number in the presence of petroleum and then feed on it effectively cleaning the water. "Alcanivorax borkumensis is a rod-shaped bacteria that relies on oil to provide it with energy. Relatively rare in unpolluted seas it quickly comes to dominate the marine microbial ecosystem after an oil spill, and it can be found throughout the world's oceans."[2] Once the water samples had been brought up on to North Star of Herschel Island's deck a laboratory was set up with microscopes so that they could determine the amount of the A. borkumensis in each area.

In July of 1969, Sven received a letter from the Canadian Department of National Revenue inquiring if North Star of Herschel Island was available for participating in seismic surveys in the Arctic. The tone of the letter speaks to the desperation that both the government and the oil companies such as Dome Petroleum were feeling over the lack of boats available for hire. In fact, as North Star was the last of the 'Arctic schooners' still operating, she was the only vessel in Western Canadian Arctic waters that was up for the job. Sven wrote back immediately including the information that, "this vessel is suitable for offshore exploration, if small-sized instrumentation is used, and for transportation. A boatcrew and workcrew of 10-12 can be accommodated. Voyages exceeding 30 days can be made. A new diesel engine is installed and she can make seven knots. At present she is the only local vessel suitable for ocean navigation."[3]

Many other voyages included using airguns and dynamite to explore the depth of permafrost on the sea floor. This was primarily with the thought of running oil pipes which it had been determined must be laid at a forty foot depth. This work was primarily done aboard North Star of Herschel Island in 1971 making her one of the first, if not the first ship, to be involved in exploring the Arctic for oil deposits. Many trips were made by the oil industry aboard North Star using gravity metering. A gravity meter was lowered to the seabed and it would measure the amount of gravitational force on the bottom. If there was an air pocket found then there would be a lower gravitational pull which indicated that there was a greater likelihood of finding oil in that area.

A depth charge explodes astern of North Star of Herschel Island in an attempt to find oil.

North Star's cargo hold was turned into a scientific lab with a workbench bolted to the forward bulkhead with microscopes set up alongside tools such as dynamite charges and airguns.

On one of the trips North Star of Herschel Island was heading up to Inuvik. The ship was in mid-channel on a beautiful early summer (standard joke is late winter) day. The ship was carrying two crew, Mike and Sam, as well as Norma and Silva. Mike had the helm while Sven was below having some caribou steak when Mike hollered for Sven to come and take a look at something. Just off the bow was an upside down car, seemingly floating along the channel! Sven figured out that the car was in one or two feet of water just outside of the deep channel. It looked to have been abandoned during the winter when the driver was on this stretch of water when it was frozen and used as the ice road between Tuktoyaktuk and Inuvik. The crew decided that only in the MacKenzie Delta could there be a possible collision between a car and a ship.

Regular trips were made to supply the enormous oil drilling ships who drew too much water to enter many of the Canadian Arctic ports. North Star would be given a Latitude and Longitude position to meet a ship somewhere in the Beaufort Sea and they would set off and re-supply them with food and supplies to carry on. Sven installed a Kelvin-Hughes radar for this work since North Star was often working in fog. "I would be watching on the radar and then right out of the mist there would be one of these huge ships and we would go alongside them with their groceries and stuff," he said. The radar was also used when they were taking seabed samples or water samples and he would be given exact Latitude and Longitudinal positions where the scientists were to take each sample. Of most importance were the 'seismic shooting ranges' that these oil ships would then give to North Star to take back to Tuktoyaktuk for the oil companies to decipher.

"These seismic records were valued at millions and millions of dollars. They were held in these big boxes and we would stow these below and then get them back as soon as we could." On one trip in 1971 three men off of one of the ships accompanied the records. A storm was brewing and it was unsafe to carry on at sea and so Sven took the ship into North Star's old stomping grounds at Pauline Cove in Herschel Island. "The holding ground at Pauline Cove is so awful!" Sven recalls, "and we got a forecast of high winds. The anchoring bottom is just slimy, so we went over to the other side and couldn't get the anchor to hold there, so back to Pauline Cove and we put out the anchor again. The wind came up and started blowing fifty and then sixty knots. The anchor began dragging and we were pushed right up ashore on the beach. We had millions of dollars of records aboard." The storm kept raging and North Star was being pummelled by the wind and pushed beam on to the shore. She was in danger of losing her rudder and propeller if this continued.

North Star's decks covered with scientific equipment for the oil industry where dog teams, sleds and pelts once stood.

"So, I took a line and I brought it ashore and then back to the transom. I found someone there with a tractor and I had him ready to haul on the line to bring the stern back out to the sea so that I could back up. I yelled to the crew that when I scream that they had to let go the line and then to haul it in as fast as they could so that it wouldn't go into the propeller." With the wind shrieking through the rigging and the engine whining at full revs they completed the manoeuvre. Then, with the bow square-on to the beach, Sven drove the ship ashore. They ran out an anchor on each side and buried them in the beach. The ship was secure.

The three crew from the oil ship had had enough of an adventure and so the next day they chartered a plane to pick themselves and the records up and take them to Inuvik.

On the very last charter before leaving the Beaufort Sea North Star was hired once again by the Fisheries Department. The research was done and North Star was in the vicinity of Herschel Island when a huge thunder and lightning storm came up. This is very unusual for the Arctic but as the ship made passage the thunder and lightning crashed all around them. "Whaboom, Whaboom, Whaboom!!, it was very scary. I was worried about the mast and the radio antennae on top of it since we were the only target out there." Sven disconnected the antennae and carried on across the Beaufort Sea. Running all night he entered the MacKenzie River and arrived at the dock with the records intact. By carrying on to safe harbour he arrived a day earlier than the charter had specified and so was docked one day's pay.

Looking back at all of his Arctic adventures with Rocky Mountain House and aboard North Star of Herschel Island, Sven once remarked, "That was the happiest, most interesting time of my life."

Johansson had the business with North Star going and was still keeping busy with the big game hunting and so occasionally he would hire another man to skipper North Star for him. The man's name was Silus Kandigana who was half Alaskan Eskimo and half Alaskan Native-American. "He was the nicest, kindest person," remembers Sven. On one of the trips Kandigana nearly lost the ship to some charter guests who proved unscrupulous. "Kandigana had a group aboard and the engine broke down, "says Sven. "The ship was forcefully blown onto a beach at Nicholson Point. It was the same storm that broke up the Arctic schooner Omingmuk at Tuktoyaktuk. They weren't in any danger or anything (because of the configuration of the beach and North Star's stout construction). Silus got the engine going but they couldn't get off the beach so one of the guys who chartered us went and arranged for a tractor or something to push North Star back into the water. Once the trip was over he said that he was going to court and claim salvage rights on North Star - the one that chartered me. I told him about salvage law and he ended up backing down." In Canada when a boat is in distress the Captain will sometimes ask for assistance, usually in the form of a tow from another vessel. Before any lines are secured between the two vessels the Captain of the vessel being rescued must make it clear to the assist vessel whether or not it is a salvage action. There have been some unfortunate cases where novice mariners unschooled in maritime vernacular have unknowingly given up the rights to their vessel by agreeing to have their boat salvaged, rather than assisted.

Sven and Norma had a good business going with numerous charters keeping the ship busy for a few years. They would have been content to stay doing this but it seemed that just as when they first bought her, seeing the ship up and running had caused some jealousy. Word had got around that they were securing a lot of business. The grandson of the legendary writer, James Fenimore Cooper, was a man named Paul Fenimore 'Nick' Cooper and he and a man named Bob Ketching who was based on Herschel Island decided that local Inuit should be doing the work that Sven and Norma were getting. Nick bankrolled a project to bring a boat up for this purpose and they found one in Florida and had it trucked up to Seattle. From there they sailed it around to Tuktoyaktuk with the idea of having it chartered for scientific surveys. The wooden vessel had not been designed for use in the icy waters and began taking on water shortly after her arrival in the Beaufort Sea which was apparently the end of that venture.

The Canadian Government then decided to run their own vessel and learning that North Star was not for sale they purchased an old fishing seiner from British Columbia. This was at the time that the Federal Government was buying back fishing licenses in an effort to clamp down on the fishery and lower fishing quotas, so there were a lot of old fishing boats for sale. The boat was last seen on the shore at Tuktoyaktuk and apparently did not have the same success as North Star enjoyed. Len Pearson of SV Thane became involved in the project once North Star was back in Victoria. He picks up the story: "Sven had a most eclectic group of acquaintances and one of his acquaintances was Don McWatt who was a friend of Sven's from the Arctic. Don was a pretty hot to trot Scotsman who came out full of romance, married an Inuit girl in Aklavik and eventually became very wealthy. Had all kinds of ideas. He was an entrepreneur's entrepreneur and had all this money happening. The game was afoot in the Arctic with the oil industry and the oil industry had to come up with a certain amount of money spent on environmental studies too because of the EPA's in the States. So the EPA (Environmental Protection Agency) was forcing the oil companies to spend millions on stuff. And one of the stuff happened to be to study Bowhead whales, which happened to be in Canadian waters at the time and who wants to study them, even in the winter time? So the Americans came across with a 1.2 million dollar contract to study Bowhead Whales out of Aklavik and Tuktoyaktuk. A guy named Bob McKenzie who was friends with Feniman Cooper's grandson - he had moved to the Arctic sort of to get away from mother's apron strings and he and Bob McKenzie and Bob McKenzie's wife formed an interesting threesome out of Herschel Island, year after year. Then Bob McKenzie found that the Americans were looking for a boat so that they could go and study Bowhead Whales. There were no boats there. Sven had gone, so Bob says to Fenimore, 'Gosh I wish I had a boat'. Fenimore says, "I'll get you a boat", and Fenimore gets his agents - Fenimore was very rich, we're talking old money, so anyway's Fenimore Cooper's grandson, he finds a boat of Canadian registry built in Nova Scotia, lying in Florida, buys it, has it trucked to Tacoma and he flies down from Herschel Island to Tacoma, takes the 48 foot schooner north and renames it from Pressure Ridge to the

Unguluk and it must have been a hell of an adventure to go out around Bering and all around - so gets to Tuk and they get the charter. Big money - but Bob was unavailable to drive it most of the time. The whales were playing in Malluck Bay - they were right there and all they had to do was go out there but Bob would say ' Oh, bad sign.' Bad signs all the time – 'it's gonna blow.' He wastes the season up there and then realises he needs another boat. Don McWatt who was running environmental cleanups for the oil companies realises there is use for a boat here so he phones his friend Sven. Meanwhile Bob McKenzie's got the Unguluk. 'Sven', he says ' I need a boat up here, can you find me a boat to do this Bowhead whale research thing?" Sven went around and went around and I guess the Sequel was for sale at Fisherman's Wharf at the dock. Sven thought this boat will be perfect and that Don should buy this boat but it needed to be protected. It needed gumwood on the outside to protect it. It needed a lot of stuff for fitting out for a trip to the Arctic. So Don hired me to do this work and to deliver it up there. I tried to get it done here in Victoria and one screw up after another, ended up going to Nanaimo to Stones and lived on the boat while I put a gumwood sheath on her. I had very little experience in this area - just winging it. I put a steel bow on her and heaters, insulation, rigging - a whole lot of stuff and took it up to Skagway. The idea was to load it onto flatdecks. Meanwhile, while this was going on, Don had other irons in the fire and wanted a new boat to charter to Dome Petroleum as a patrol boat for oil spills and to carry pollution nets, so, anyway, Don and I went and got a company to design and build a steel hull, twin engines tunnel drive, wheel house forward, no bunks in her and a big hold and a big flatdeck. From six weeks from when we said, 'This is what we want,' it was designed and built in French Creek, Parksville B.C. area. By the time I got up to Skagway with it the boat was ready to launch. Instead of having only one boat to take to Tuk, suddenly I had two boats."

In any case, Sven and Norma had earlier seen the writing was on the wall though and recognised that their time in the Arctic had come to an end. They could sell North Star and stay north, finding employment as they had in the past or they could sell off their property, plane and equipment and then head south. This is just what they did and in 1973 they worked their last charters as they couldn't leave until mid-August when the ice cleared.

One of the last charters that they made was for an oil company who were making man-made islands. They wanted the area surveyed to the NorthWest of an island North of the MacKenzie River which involved sending down a large scoop which grabbed the gravelly seabed and took a sample. Once the sample was brought on deck they could determine if it would make good building material.

The charter was fairly straightforward and so they worked North Star in a straight line grabbing a sample, examining it and then moving to the next survey site. At each stop, gravel came up until they began to hit a solid surface and no gravel was available. What they were about to learn was that a year before a barge had broken free from its tug and sunk in this spot. North Star's bottom touched and astoundingly they found themselves aground. "We hit that damned barge!" says Sven. "There is so little tide there, maybe six inches, but it was ebbing and we just got more and more stuck until the tide changed. I remember I could touch it with a boathook"

After the charter, North Star returned to Inuvik and they arranged a sling which hoisted North Star's stern out of the water as the grounding had damaged the propeller. This was banged back into shape and the boat was re-launched ready to continue on her voyage south.

North Star wintered at Inuvik in 1973 and, as the ice broke up in 1974, Sven arranged for North Star to be launched by crane and then he quickly shifted her around into a safe basin clear of the ice. As spring turned to summer they motored down to Tuktoyaktuk and the Government Fisheries Observer, Roland Allen, came aboard. Other federal scientists came aboard and loaded up the main deck with seismic recorders. While the scientists were busy getting their gear ready, Sven worked board the Kneass built, Omingmuk and unstepped her mast right at the Tuktoyaktuk dock. Omingmuk was virtually a wreck at this point and Sven was given permission to take whatever he needed to outfit North Star of Herschel Island. Even at this time he had the idea of re-rigging North Star of Herschel as a fully-rigged ship with square sails on three masts.

Silva Johansson playing aboard wreck of Omingmuk at Tuktoyaktuk.

The scientific voyage took the ship across to Kughalit Bay where they set temperature probes on the sea bed. Seismic testing for the oil industry continued right through July. On July 15th, 1973, the ship returned to

Tuktoyaktuk and the deck was cleared of most of the scientific gear and then Omingmuk's mast was shipped aboard.

The next charter was from the Montreal Fisheries Board, an example of how diverse and from how far across Canada the interest in the Arctic was at that time. Before casting off they burned all of their garbage on the sandspits, which was the common way to get rid of trash at the time. The next month was spent readying North Star for her voyage south. They finalised cutting their ties with the Arctic on Monday, August 13th, 1973 when Sven sold his warehouse and cabin to Ray Anderson. The Northrop family came aboard for a last visit. Mr Gustavsen from the Boundary Commission heard through the Northern grape-vine that North Star was heading south and he dearly wanted the ship to stay so that he could charter her. He flew in by helicopter, kicking up all kinds of dust around and over the ship and then hurried aboard and asked about arranging a charter. He and Sven made plans for using the ship to survey the B.C./Alaska boundary at a later date since the Johansson's were firm in their decision to go south.

With the decks cleared away the Johansson took a walk around Tuktoyaktuk and on August 19th, 1973 they toured Our Lady of Lourdes, noticing the similarities between the two ships. Our Lady of Lourdes had long since been retired and was a bit of a sorry sight compared to North Star who was eagerly sitting at the dock ready to start the second part of her career. Jim Wolki came aboard and looked at his old ship and wished the family well on their voyage.

Our Lady of Lourdes in her permanent berth ashore at Tuktoyaktuk.

The Johansson's had one final bit of business to complete in Canadian Arctic waters that was indicative of how much Sven had learned about thoroughly doing his paperwork when dealing with government authorities. Jim Scott recalls how his first meeting with Sven Johansson went. "It was the spring of 1973. I was the RCMP Corporal at Tuktoyaktuk. One morning there was a knock on the office door and a gentleman asked whether I could provide an official list of the contents of his vessel for his intended trip to San Francisco! It was Sven Johansson, and the vessel was the S/V "North Star of Herschel Island". Sven explained that he would be stopping in at various ports in the United States, and then returning to Canada. He wanted any interested officials to be aware that whatever was on board was his personal property from Canada, and not items purchased in the US. He intended to sail to San Francisco, and the yard where she was originally built. With pad and pencil in hand, we headed for the ship, and were met by his wife and small daughter. After tea and small talk we began.

We crawled all over that ship from stem to stern and listed every piece of machinery, coil of rope, every wrench, hammer, and all manner of other hand tools, coils of wire, cable, as well as nails, bolts, washers, and various stacks of lumber. He showed me nooks and crannies in that hull that I would never have found. He insisted we climb in every one of them. Well, as you know, he's a bit smaller than I, and while he darted in and out, and around and about like a leprechaun, I was all twisted up like Gulliver in Lilliput most of the time. It took the best part of two days! When we were done, I sat down at the typewriter and completed the "official list" that Sven requested. (I believe I typed the list on the Canada Customs forms we had in the office.) That detailed list was so complete, that I remember typing the words, "And that's all!" above my signature. (I can't remember how many pages it filled.)

When I returned to the ship with his "official list", the pilothouse was filled with a number of local hunters, including "Big Jim" Wolki and his son Figueres. Sven brought out a small vial of spirits (rum, I believe), and we all shared a dram or two, while Sven and the others took turns telling hunting stories. It was a grand time.

The next morning, we watched the "North Star" sail west over the horizon. Years later, my wife and I retired in the Victoria, BC area. One day we received a telephone invitation from one of the organizers of the "Arctic Luncheon". (It's an annual event at a local restaurant in Victoria.) When we entered the dining room, there was Sven in his navy turtle neck sweater, smiling and chatting with everyone. When he spotted us, he came towards and exclaimed those words I'd typed at the bottom of his list; "And that's all!" while hugging my wife and I. In conclusion, I must tell you that Sven Johansson is one of the most irrepressible story tellers that I have ever met. And when he sets his mind to a purpose, he usually succeeds."

As a teetotaller, Sven denies supplying any liquor, but who knows what the other trappers may have had in their knapsacks. With the contents of North Star all registered the Johansson's cast off and headed down to the Arctic Ocean. One grey, cold and foggy day in the 24 hour daylight turned into another as the threesome carried on sailing west in the Beaufort Sea. Watching for ice, always on the look out for the flat black pans that could cause a lot of damage, if not sink them. It was in these waters that "Captain Cook in his last voyage of discovery had come to anchor as he searched for the NorthWest Passage. With him was Captain Bligh."[4]

The family set out into the Beaufort Sea and North Star of Herschel Island traced her old milk run back to Herschel Island where they dropped hook on August 23rd. They took their skiff ashore and stepped back in time. There were many families there enjoying the last rays of summer. They toured the grave sites, recognising some of the old timers' names. So many were of Hawaiian and South Pacific origin mixed in with those of the Inuvialuit. There were still dogs everywhere and children playing down at the beach. Seal skins stretched out on rocks to dry and campfires burning. One of the families gave them the hind quarter of a caribou and Silva enjoyed playing around the camps though it was noted in the logbook that by the end of the day she "was very seal-oil smelling".

After a few days at Herschel Island to re-group, the ship continued her western course and next stopped at Kakowik where they anchored at Bernard Harbour, Alaska. Sven rowed ashore to clear customs and was greeted warmly. There weren't many tourists that ever stopped here and the DEW line personnel sent Sven back to collect Silva and Norma to come ashore and visit with them. Tom Bailey gave them a piece of whale baleen as a souvenir of their stop. The customs agent looked at the nice family and their tidy ship riding proudly at anchor and waived the inspection which must have been a bit of an anti-climax for Sven after having spent those two days back in Tuk making North Star's inventory with Jim Scott. They spent a peaceful night at anchor and the next day headed back to sea.

North Star of Herschel Island rounded the north point of Point Barrow on September 2nd and the trip south started to become a reality. The Johansson travelled twenty-four hours a day and rounded out and south into the Bering Strait where they were met with heavy seas and gale force winds. The daily run average dropped from one hundred miles to twenty as North Star of Herschel Island was knocked side to side with waves breaking over the bow in regular succession. They stayed in the pilothouse, watching the weather deteriorate and their weather window to get south begin to close. Norma and Sven spelled each other off at the helm and on look-out and after a month since the voyage began the lack of sleep was starting to catch up with them.

The wind and seas had begun to subside and the ocean began to flatten out. Just after midnight on September 3rd Sven was catching a catnap when the ship drove hard aground onto Seahorse Island. He was up in a flash and threw the engine from full ahead to full astern. The wind had picked up and there was a fair sea running. North Star was lifted up and thrown down onto the rocky ledge again and again. This had been the death of many Arctic schooners before her and Sven and Norma hung on tight with the engine screaming and the ship not budging. The grounding had woken Silva and she was in the pilothouse, wide-eyed and hanging onto Norma. Each blow went right through them and it seemed like the ship would be pounded to pieces any instant. Fifteen times she was thrown onto the rocks. Sven recalls, "Backing up didn't work, because it draws the stern down and further aground. So I pictured North Star's underwater configuration. I figured that if I could turn her on a pivot point and face out from where we came we could get off." Sven put the helm hard over bore down on the throttle and then with a final thrust of the engine and at the top of a wave she was spat back out into the angry sea. "I don't really remember it being that bad," he says, with a twinkle in his eye. "The seas weren't that huge". Sven's modest appraisal of the situation is perhaps a nod to one of his fellow Arctic travellers, Vilhjalmur Stefansson, who once wrote, "An adventure is a sign of incompetence." A pet peeve of Sven's is when he hears what he believes to be exaggerations of people's adventures or the wind and sea state, but in this case the ship's log verifies that this had been a sticky situation.

Sven lowered the revs on the engine and pointed the ship away from Seahorse Island. Norma took the wheel again while Sven checked the bilges to see if she was taking on water. Incredibly, the tough little ship seemed to have survived the grounding but they wouldn't know until a few hours had passed if any water was leaking into the hull. With their nerves shattered and wanting to be near shore in case they had to abandon ship, they carried on and dropped anchor off of Wainright. No one would get any sleep but it was time to take stock of their situation, give the engine a rest and carry on with regular inspections of the bilges.

They stayed at anchor for the next two days, resting and planning their next move. The weather had deteriorated and now they were late in the season, anchored in a shallow bay on a lee shore. To weigh anchor now and head out into the huge swells was not an inviting option but their present position was not restful. The ship began to roll 22 degrees side to side and pitch with the bigger swells. The anchor rode pointed forward like an iron bar. Should it fail, North Star would be on the beach and broken up in minutes. As the swells grew they touched bottom twice. If this continued the ship would beat herself to death on the hook. On the second day four Eskimo came out in a small boat and visited the ship. They brought fresh moose meat with them which was a welcome change to the caribou they had been eating since Herschel Island. "The sea was a monster, with winds whipping up to 50 miles an hour and the ship pitching constantly at a 35 degree angle." Little Silva said the trip was fun, and laughed as her father told a story about the day North Star had visitors aboard. The winds were howling and the ship was riding the waves at anchor like a roller-coaster," Johansson said. "The men, all sailors were hanging on to the rails, looking green. Little Silva, dancing up and down and singing, 'row row row your boat, gently down the stream,"[5] reported the Vancouver Sun.

The Johansson's shifted into the harbour at Wainright whose entrance was so shallow and muddy that they had to burrow the keel to get into the harbour, much like the old whaling ships had done on their way to Herschel Island. Once in, they dropped hook but to leave would require ploughing their way back through the mud.

In the early light of September 6th the swells had come down enough that they weighed anchor and headed back out into the ocean. The next day they passed Point Hope and were immediately into heavy, rolling swells that pitched North Star around like a cork. There was no way to make headway into them and so they tried beating their way forward by taking the waves on first one bow and then the other. It was hard going as they tried to make it into Cape Prince of Wales. The log for that day simply reads "very rough time."

On the 8th of September they made it into the Bering Strait and by 0530 they were anchored off of Teller. The whole day was spent catching up on sleep, eating their first hot meal in days and cleaning up the mess of bedding, books and crockery that had spilled out during the rough passage. It wasn't until the next day that they finally made it ashore.

Their hope of making a fast passage from the Arctic to Vancouver had been dashed. The season was getting on and soon the days would be filled with more winter gales. Teller suddenly seemed like a good option for the winter. They caught a car ride into Nome and picked up some groceries and enjoyed being ashore. Back at Teller they toured the historic graveyard. Sven and Norma asked around and found a yellow house that was up for rent and quickly signed the agreement for it. On September 28th, Silva celebrated her fourth birthday aboard North Star.

The next day the winds punched their way into Teller with thirty knot gales, gusting to fifty. North Star dragged her way across the harbour until Sven got a second hook out. She lay out on two chains with Sven on anchor watch as the ship rolled away the day and night. With the plan for them to winter in Teller, Sven began to build a cradle for the ship to sit in ashore. By mid-October he was still working on this when the ice started forming in the harbour. He rigged cables to her bow and stern and pulled her next to the shore to try and haul her out the way that Fred Carpenter did but the cables broke and North Star was left sitting alongside the shore with ice now chafing the hull. He finally got the ship out with a crane and they settled in for the winter.

With the ship out of the water Norma and Sven made an inspection of the hull to see what damage had been done by the Seahorse Island incident. Norma wrote, "Bottom very scarred where caught on truck at Immerk Island. Sven says if it hadn't been for the ironbark we would have sunk." There was no obvious damage from the latest grounding and so they moved their belongings into the yellow house.

On November 10th the first major storm hit Teller with a vengeance. The combination of south-east winds funnelling the waves at high tide into the harbour made even walking ashore a dangerous affair. Sven checked on North Star and the cradle. All seemed secure. It was a good day to be ashore.

The waves came higher and pounded the front of the house. The storms kept raging and Sven and Norma were awakened one night to the sound of waves smashing up against their house. Beach pebbles were being whipped against the house. Sven bent on his hip waders and sloshed out onto what used to be their front yard and saw with horror that North Star was partially in danger of floating away. The stern was already afloat. "A month later a storm struck, pounding the house with six foot waves, which washed gravel from the beach onto the roof. Johansson fought his way to the boat. Before the storm, the North Star was beached four feet above sea level he said. Within minutes after the storm hit it was surrounded by water and in danger of drifting off. I threw out both anchors and it held, but it was a close call."[6] The following year a similar storm hit the house and tore it in half.

The Johansson's house at Teller was torn in half by a storm the following year.

As the harbour froze over for winter the Johansson's could finally relax. The break-up of ice in Teller harbour didn't happen until June 1st of 1974. The month of June had been spent painting the ship, overhauling the engine and packing North Star up again. The biggest job was repairing the keel that had been damaged in the Immerek grounding in MacKenzie Bay. Sven replaced a plank and caulked it in with a combination of MarineTex epoxy and cement. The ice in Teller had also damaged the rudder and steering gear and this was also repaired. He then built a floating dock for North Star to sit alongside and purchased 24 sacks of gravel for ballast so that the dock was steady. They then loaded "truckloads of boxes and gear aboard".

Sven fixing damaged North Star's damaged rudder at Teller.

In April of 1974, John Bockstoce was back in the north, doing research on whaling. He writes, "one day I drove to the town of Teller at Port Clarence and to my surprise saw the North Star of Herschel Island in a cradle on the beach there. I hadn't seen her since that awful storm in 1973, and I finally had a chance to meet her owner, Sven Johansson, who had been asleep when we first visited. He was on his way from the Canadian Arctic because his little daughter, Silva, was to begin school in the South, but the autumn passage from the Mackenzie Delta to Bering Strait proved to be unusually stormy and difficult, and when they reached Port Clarence, he decided to winter there, renting a small house near his boat. Later in the spring, Romayne, (John's wife) and I traveled on North Star to King Island in Bering Strait and then to Nome, where we collected our crew and then left for Barter Island."[7] An interesting tidbit of Nome history is that it was so named when a navigator aboard one of the early voyages of discovery wondered what the name of the point should be and messily wrote beside it the word Name. His a must have looked like an o for that is what ended up on the next official charts.

The Bocktoce's passage from Teller to Nome aboard North Star of Herschel Island had a secondary purpose. John was hoping to make a stop at Claire Point in Little Diamede Island to investigate Eskimo ruins but the sea was running very high and there is no protected harbour there. The ship drew a "crowd of Eskimos who I'm sure would very much like to have been picked up by North Star and taken to the mainland but there was no way to do that," remembers Bockstoce. He adds, "It was probably the last thing that Sven wanted anyway, to have all of these Eskimos climbing over the rail." Bockstoce was in those years still trying to make a NorthWest Passage by umiak, a voyage that he and Sven would later complete in Belvedere.

On the last day of June they cast off from their floating dock and headed back out to sea. It was like the ocean had been put on pause waiting for them. They were immediately back out into giant swells. Their course took them to King Island, Sledge Island and Nome where they put in for a couple of days. The ocean remained busy and the logbook for the passage has regular mention of "big swells". They threw the anchor out at Sledge Island to try and get some sleep.

On July 7th they made it to Kokcchik Bay at Nunivak Island where they pulled in to try and get a break from the constant rolling. At two in the morning they cast off and headed back out into growing south-east winds. The anemometer registered 37 knots and the seas were an average of twelve feet. North Star rolled 22 degrees to port and 24 degrees to starboard with each wave. The vents on deck had to be covered so that the breaking waves wouldn't fill the below decks. Hauling close to shore they anchored once again but there was no protection and the rolling and pitching continued. The log reads, "bilge water - crash, crash, crash". To break the monotony they tuned the SSB radio in to hear the news and heard that one of the men they had hired to help with work on North Star at Teller, had committed suicide.

They decided to wait out the weather system and stayed anchored at Platinum for several days. They would have stayed longer but on the third day the anchor began to drag. As they weighed anchor they saw that the one inch chain had become fouled from all of the pitching and had wrapped around the upper fluke. To clear it as the ship was being pushed astern by the wind required seizing off the chain and then taking the weight of the anchor with a handy-billy so that the foul could be lifted free. As North Star pitched and rolled astern Sven leaned over the side and muscled the 150 pound anchor into submission on deck and then cranked in the last few fathoms of chain so that it could be dogged down safely.

Once again they were underway and into the thick of things. Twenty foot waves surged towards them in unbroken lines across the horizon. The wind whipped the whitecaps forward and across North Star's deck and as she plunged into them her bow would be buried right to the focs'le hatch. It seemed like the Arctic had North Star in her icy grip and wasn't going to let her get south without a fight. By this time the Johansson's knew without measure that the ship could take whatever was thrown at her but the sleep deprivation, lack of hot meals, the cold and wet and constant rocking of their bruised and battered bodies was beginning to take its toll. Sven checked the chart and saw that they might be able to sneak into the small island, actually a spit called Hagemeister Spit to try and get some rest. Norma, who acted as first mate, spelled her husband at the wheel in all but the heaviest seas. "When things got really rough, I didn't try to cook," she said in an interview at its anchorage in Deep Cove, North Vancouver. "We would drink soup and hot chocolate and wait out the storm. Besides, she added no one feels like eating when you are bucking a forty knot gale and the waves are thirty feet high."[8]

At seven pm they anchored there and were finally able to turn off the engine after days and days of the constant 'Screaming Jimmy'. The seas still made their way in and they continued rolling now 35 degrees to port and 24 to starboard. To try and sleep was impossible without wedging oneself in and then hauling up the leeboards and pillows to try and stay in one place.

"At Valdez (Alaska), the skipper had a bad moment when the depthfinder picked up the ocean bottom where, according to the charts it was not supposed to be. The earthquake in Valdez in 1964 changed the ocean floor and they haven't yet amended the navigational charts...we discovered our hull was only in six feet of water."[9]

The next morning they inspected the ship. Sven found that the metal covering boards by the anchor hawsepipe had come adrift. The huge waves had found a small opening and ripped them asunder, an incredible force considering they had lasted through all of the ice and storms for the previous forty years. He went around and caulked and hammered them back into place with copper nails. The rudder indicator was jammed full of dried salt which needed attention and he also sealed off the aft and midship vents where waves were splashing through and filling the bilge with each roll. It was like trying to mend a moving roller coaster with always one hand for the ship and one for yourself.

They weighed anchor the next day and ploughed through dense fog using the depth sounder and a depth plot to find their way into the more protected cove of Point Moller. The log makes no mention of the conditions but exclaims, "Tuesday, July 30th - Sven had first bath since Teller!"

They continued to island hop, trying to make some progress south without having to spend days and nights at sea. The log continues to Deer Island, passed by King Cove, Dolgoi Harbour and then anchoring again at Humboldt Harbour. They stayed two days and would have stayed longer but the wind continued to build and they dragged anchor once more. To try and re-set in these conditions was more trouble and more dangerous than putting out to sea and so they drove back into 'big swells' to Jack Bay and on August 9th finally sighted Kodiak. The weather moderated some and they passed the next 72 hours steaming towards Homer where they set anchor under the watchful eyes of harbourmaster Dennis Oxford.

They were soon joined aboard by Ted Pedersen, C.T. Pedersen's son who had launched North Star at Herschel Island from his father's ship upon her arrival in the Arctic. "On the Alaskan Peninsula, North Star made a difficult crossing of a waterway called False Pass, to the islands off Sand Point. The ship then travelled to the west coast of Kodiak Island through the Shelikof Strait to Homer, where the family spent ten days while repairs were made to the vessel."[10]

The next day they weighed early and went through Montague Strait and made port in Yakutat where on August 29th they celebrated Sven's 50th birthday. For two weeks North Star lay at anchor as storm winds and seas pounded the North Pacific. It seemed like the season was almost over and they would be stuck on the hook at this tiny island until the spring.

On September 21st they had had enough and took off into the inky, black night. Their course was for the inappropriately named Cape Fairweather but the big swells crashing up against the shore made the entrance terrifying to consider. With faith in their ship they turned and drove straight up to the anchorage and by five thirty were riding to the hook again, this time at Flynn Cove. From this anchorage they made Juneau, celebrated Silva's fifth birthday near Ratz Harbour, carried on to Ketchikan and finally made Prince Rupert back in Canada on October 2nd. "'It was a relief after months of ice and wind to see dolphins and sea lions playing beside the boat and to watch sea birds flying overhead.' Mrs Johansson said."[11]

From here they were in fairly protected waters and racked up the miles as they steamed down the Inside Passage, arriving in Vancouver, B.C. on October 18th. After years in the Arctic their first observation was that the "pollution in the air was almost unbelievable." On October 26th they moored in the Fraser River and put some of their Arctic gear into storage at B.C. Packers. "Many fishermen make the same journey around Alaska but Johansson believes the North Star is the first pleasure craft to undertake the 4,000 mile voyage." I just wanted to see if it could be done," said the skipper. The main thing is to follow the patterns of the wind and ice currents and to never take chances. I am more nervous in city traffic than I am at sea."[12]Skippers who brag about hair-raising adventures at sea are generally poor navigators", he said" The rest of 1974 was kept busy moving North Star of Herschel Island around through southern B.C. waters as they decided what their next plan would be. There were some small charters with a wedding and taking friends out for small trips.

On January 1st of 1975 North Star of Herschel Island was in Vancouver and the Johanssons motored over to see the Annual Polar Bear Swim where hundreds of people line the beach and on a signal run into the cold waters for a swim. "We went right out through looking at the damn 'polar bears'", Sven says, laughing. One of the safety boats came by and hailed them. "Hey! Is that Fred's boat?" "I couldn't believe it. We had just arrived from the Arctic and someone recognised her!" says Sven. "It turns out she had been a nurse or something up there and knew of North Star. They came alongside and we had a nice chat and a giggle".

"When we had been up in Tuk we had taken out some VIP's for a charter and one of them said that I should call him if I ever needed anything. So, I called him up and asked him where to moor the ship in Vancouver. We ended up staying at the Royal Vancouver Yacht Club! It wasn't my style and so after a couple of days I found a government dock and we emptied out a lot of the salon into storage of all of our Arctic things."

Ted Pedersen giving Sven Henry Larsen's ditty bag to be donated to the St. Roch exhibit at the Vancouver Maritime Museum.

Sailing down the northern B.C. coast.

On their arrival in Vancouver On September 2nd, Sven officially presented Henry Larsen's ditty bag to the Vancouver Maritime Museum to be part of their permanent display with St. Roch. It was a nice reunion but sad as St. Roch, a government run ship and sister Arctic ship was apparently suffering from rot and lying in a museum while North Star of Herschel Island continued to voyage on. North Star arrived at Fisherman's Wharf and was boarded by the Coast Guard as someone had reported them overdue. "Apparently we were cause of concern and considered overdue. A misunderstanding in time to leave statement and arrival in Victoria!!! Good that people think of you".

With only one day to rest up, North Star carried on to the Port Townsend Wooden Boat Festival which Sven found to be "very disorganised, no moorings etc". His complaint over moorings is in the logbook but the adventure of their arrival isn't.

The ship had agreed to tow a couple of longboats - eighteen foot open boats with lug rigged sails and rowing stations down to the show. The tow went fine but as they rounded up past Port Townsend, an area of the coast with notoriously big currents and tides, North Star of Herschel Island's engine sent up a huge plume of white smoke. Sven shut down the engine. The ship was making close to eight knots and heading right for the port where every manner of classic yacht and boat, old schooners, cutters and fancy mahogany launches, whose brightwork was so glossy that they could be used as mirrors, were rafted to one another four and five deep. Along charges North Star making no noise but the swoosh of her bow wave. The longboats were trailed off of each quarter and so North Star of Herschel Island was presenting with approximately forty or fifty feet of surface area. The tide got a hold of her and so Sven radioed to the Wooden Boat Show organisers that he needed a tow. "They sent out this little tin boat with an outboard motor. There was no way it was big enough. The Coast Guard was in dry-dock and out of service, so we drifted with the tide and wound up on an island on the other side of the bay. The Kneass built ship did what she had done a hundred times and rested up against the shore. The longboats left and went to the show and we sat there. Another boat came and offered to take us off - for salvage - which means that they would then own the boat. I told the crew to never, ever utter the word emergency or they can do that.

That night, the Coast Guard launched and came over and towed us right into the show. It was quite an entrance. I thought that the engine was still broken though. Then I found out that the people in Sooke had sent a boat to tow the longboats back but not North Star. I got on the phone and told them that they can't just abandon North Star, so they towed us to Victoria. Len Pearson came out in Thane and he towed me close to my mooring but there was some problem in getting in. I decided to try the engine and 'boom' - it started right away. I could have brought North Star back on my own anyway. Very strange thing, that engine, running on only two cylinders."

Blaney Scott, who owned Scott Plastics which overlooked Fisherman's Wharf, let Sven haul North Star ashore there another time, made a personal loan of one thousand dollars to Sven so that he could get the engine parts. Johansson ended up replacing the cylinder head with a different type that gave North Star lower compression and she continued to be reliable. Sven figures that while sailing the ship some saltwater got in and corroded one of the pistons, making it stick, and the white plume was fuel being sprayed straight out and through the engine.

The ship was back in Victoria the following week and Silva started correspondence school, working away at the galley table. Len Pearson of Thane who had helped tow North Star in recalls how he and Sven first crossed paths. "I became aware of Sven when I saw North Star coming into the harbour. I was building Thane (a replica of Joshua Slocum's Spray - the first vessel to make a single-handed circumnavigation) over on Finger One at Fisherman's Wharf and this boat came into the harbour, obviously new to the bay. I was aware of her at that point - he went and cleared Customs and then came back to Fisherman's Wharf and tied up right across from me and sat there for a season and I got to know him there. That would have been around '73. I guess he had wintered in Alaska that year. He was several seasons in Victoria with Silva going to school. One interesting thing that happened with the Johansson's then was that Silva had all kinds of friends coming down to the boat and I'm building Thane right across the finger at finger one, and I'm working up on the foredeck and I hear all this whooping and screaming and pulling on ropes and the kids are yelling you know all the usual things that kids do on boats and I'm working away when all of a sudden I noticed that there was no more noise. Everything had gone silent. So I looked up from what I was building, the cabins, or something on Thane, and all the kids were standing on the dock looking down between the dock and North Star, so I wondered what's got their attention. So I put my tool down and walked down the length of Thane and across the dock and looked over them to see what they were looking at and there was bubbles coming up. What the hell? And without even thinking why there would be bubbles I dropped flat on the deck with my arm and head in the water and pulled up Silva - still making bubbles. And the kids hadn't made any alarm or I guess they just thought this was probably normal - that Silva went down and was down four or four and a half feet under water - so I dragged her out and put her on the deck all sputtering and went back to work!"

In 1976 they settled into a house in the quiet neighbourhood of James Bay in Victoria, leaving North Star of Herschel Island at Fisherman's Wharf. They ended up living with the famous boatbuilder Frank Fredette and Sven got a job working as a shipwright for Jenkin's Marine but was laid off after only 14 weeks. Work continued on North Star; burning the paint off of the decks; re-doing the pilothouse; working on interior layout; moving boiler from focs'le to cargo hold. He installed a new galley and built the salon in red cedar. "When Jim Shearer had been working aboard North Star up in the Arctic doing work for the Geographical Survey of Canada he had set up a huge work table right across the forward bulkhead in the cargo hold. All of that came out and I re-did the heating system since it was operated by a 32 volt pump to circulate the heating fluid in the copper pipe around the boat. I lowered the boiler right down onto the keelson so it was at the lowest point and then we didn't need the pump anymore."

On June 10th, 1977 the charter from the International Boundary Commission finally came together, years after Gustafson had inquired about it with Sven when the ship was in Inuvik. North Star of Herschel Island was badly missed in the North as her size and strength made her perfect for the type of work that was active in those years. The family cast off with Gerry Anderson and Bob Spelling aboard. They moved up to Deep Bay and anchored and on June 13th weighed anchor at 0700. At 0915 a Canadian Naval Squadron hove into view and Sven dipped North Star's Canadian ensign as a traditional sign of respect to them. The Squadron did not reply. Unbeknownst to Sven an Admiral was watching from ashore. He ordered the Squadron to turn to and steam back and return the salute and ordered them to always return North Star of Herschel Island's flag etiquette! Sven was later told that this is now in the standing orders - that all Royal Canadian Naval vessels are to return North Star of Herschel Island's salute.

The ship carried on through the Salish Sea, past Alert Bay, Bella Bella, Seaforth Channel, Grenville Channel and made a stop in Halibut Bay. Silva had been complaining of a wart on her foot so Sven rowed ashore and found a slug to put on it as he had heard that this cured them. The logbook does not record if this was a successful medical intervention. On July 6th they 'burned the old horse', a nautical expression meaning that from this point on in their voyage their debts were paid, in this case meaning that the fuel and supplies that they had invested in for the trip were now paid off. Crab pots were put down and a good 'crabbing' was had by all.

The point of the voyage was to re-survey the B.C./Alaska boundary that had been laid down in 1903. In 1793 George Vancouver sailed through the Portland Canal, a glacial fiord that is about thirty miles long. The Alaska Purchase of 1867 let the Canal be the dividing line between Canada and the United States; however, within that canal there are four small islands. On paper then, Canada received Pearce Island and Wales Island while the United States took ownership of the two much smaller islands Sitklan and Kanagunut. In 1896, however, when the details of the Purchase were still being negotiated, the United States Corps of Engineers sent Captain David D. Gaillard up to the canal and gave him $5,000 to survey the canal. By coincidence, his ship was the Patterson, later to be made famous by Captain C.T. Pedersen and, of course, the ship that delivered North Star to the Arctic.

Gaillard did not reach Portland Canal until September and with the weather already turning he was instructed to "make the necessary preliminary examination, and erect such quarters and storehouses as may be hereafter needed for the work of survey". Gaillard had brought along a crew of masons and labourers and went about following his instructions to build "the four storehouses to be constructed on the Alaska side of Portland Canal".

The first crew was put ashore in the pouring rain and built a small storehouse measuring about 3.5 x 5 metres with rubble masonry walls of 45 cm. On the Southeast corner a plaque was mounted stating, "U.S. Property. DO NOT INJURE". A flagpole was erected, the U.S. flag raised, hats were doffed, and a salute was made followed by three cheers. They then moved to the second U.S. Island, built a similar structure with identical plaque and the salute to their flag was made again. Things then took a strange turn as they then moved to the Canadian territory and built two more storehouses with U.S. Property plaques and once again raised their flag, saluted it and cheered.

Having completed all of this work in twenty-four days with no surveying, Gaillard turned south. He was next heard of when he was called upon to build the most difficult section of the Panama Canal that was subsequently named, Gaillard Cut.

It was not until 1901, five years later that Gaillaird's handiwork came to light when U.S. charts showed the islands as having changed nationalities.

The Canadian government immediately asked for an explanation of why the U.S. had built on Canadian soil. The Canadian Privy council advised Prime Minister Laurier that the U.S. may have built these structures "with the design of fortifying the claim of the United States to those islands." Governor General Lord Minto then asked the United States government why they had done this, his request coming straight from the Crown. Canada's stand was that the buildings meant nothing; however the Canadian government received the less than satisfactory answer that "the buildings were on a part of the Pacific Coast, the ownership of which is in dispute between the United States and Canada." Claiming sovereignty of the uninhabited islands by building on them and raising their country's flag might seem preposterous, but it is what might have happened to Banks Island, had Fred Carpenter under the request of the Canadian government not taken North Star there in 1953. In more recent times we have seen Norway attempt to claim Canada's Han's Island as their own by planting a flag on it or the ridiculous showboating of the Russian government using a submersible to plant their flag on the seabed of the North Pole.

At this point the argument began to get more notice as the Yukon Gold Rush began and Canada needed to be able to land on their own territory rather than crossing into U.S. waters. In 1903, both Canada and the United States sent representatives to London, England to review the historic Anglo-Russian treaty of 1825 under the eyes of Baron Alverstone, Lord Chief Justice of England. The trial lasted from September 3rd to October 20th, 1903. One of the sticking points of the case in the eyes of the British justice was that the flag raising and cheering would have been the actions of men taking the land for their country for the first time. The United States countered with the argument that it would have been un-American not to cheer and doff their hats when they raised their flag. In the end, the Canadian case won. Many Canadians, having studied the claim felt that the justice did not go far enough and that all four islands should have been ceded to Canada. The United States felt that they had lost out on two islands.

Only one of the four storehouses was ever used and that was storehouse number 4 that ironically was built right across the boundary line near Hyder, Alaska. It has been both a cobbler's shop and a jail.

On Canada's to-do list for many years was to survey the buildings and the border and it was not until 1977 that the Canadian office of the International Boundary Commission, under the direction of Carl J. Gustafson, chartered North Star of Herschel Island to do just that.

Sven was asked to locate the buildings as their positions were not exactly known as well as to describe what condition they were in and to photograph them. Sven noted in a follow-up letter to Gustafson that photography was very difficult as the buildings were shadowed by crab-apple trees and brush. Johansson noted that storehouse 4 was a well known landmark as it is on the road between Hyder, Alaska and Stewart B.C. and so the family set about finding the other three buildings.

North Star of Herschel Island cast off from Stewart on August 8th, 1977 and two days later felt that they were in a position to find the buildings. They were working from the report made by Gaillard in 1897 and after looking at the co-ordinates in his report realised that his navigation must have been off. Marching inland about a mile they found Storehouse 3 completely grown over with large trees and crab-apple trees. All that was left of the fifty foot flagpole was a two foot rotted stump with a ring of stones around its base. This discovery of Storehouse Number 3 was made on August 9th, 1977.

One of the storehouses hidden in the trees.

Weighing anchor they then moved to Lizard Point where Storehouse Two was supposed to be, however they could not find it. A search was made inland for a mile with no luck and so they returned to the ship, weighed anchor and shifted to another bay which was also bereft of storage buildings and so they anchored further away for the night. The next day they steamed around and found Storehouse Number One which they inspected. The mystery then, was, where was Number Two building? Re-reading the report Sven realised that no survey had been made by Gaillard and that the locations had been added later as likely spots. Knowing the steaming time for the Manzanita in 1896 he then calculated where the building should be. To make matters more interesting, the storehouse was described to have been south of Lizard Point. He and Norma discussed where they would have built storage houses and looked in those places.

The series of islands in the area were shown as being on one side of the boundary or the other depending upon which chart was looked at. North Star was taken into each cove and the search continued for boundary markers. "I discovered error in boundary report' was all that was written in the log but this was followed up with a thirty page report with photographs of the error. The confusion in finding Storehouse number 2 was that it was described as being south of Lizard Point. While studying the U.S. and Canadian charts Sven realised that there are Lizard Points on two different pieces of land in the canal as well as Lizard Cove and Lizard Point Light. They made a good assumption of where the storehouse would have been built and after moving the ship to a new anchorage found it immediately. Sven concludes his report by noting that in all of the storage houses "the stone walls are solidly intact and require little repair other than some chinking. Restoration of all woodwork and clearing of surrounding land could be done at little cost. New flag poles could be cut and raised at each site. A bronze plaque with appropriate inscription could be on or adjacent to each building. Such restoration and a ceremony with raising of the Canadian flag at Storehouses 1 and 2 would be in accordance with old traditions of asserting and maintaining sovereignty over land. I feel these storehouses are of definite historic value, the sites are most attractive and are quaint, historic sites which should be re-stored and preserved."[13] Once again North Star of Herschel Island had played an important part in asserting Canadian Arctic sovereignty!

The spring of 1978 was spent in coppering North Star of Herschel Island's hull. Murray Boy is a fisherman who has kicked around the docks of Victoria, B.C. for most of his life. He was living aboard his boat at Fisherman's Wharf when Sven hired him to help with coppering the ship's bottom, a huge undertaking and one that had probably not been done in these waters for over a century.

The new copper bottom for North Star of Herschel Island.

Copper plating a ship's bottom was once the regular way to protect any wooden ship from being eaten through by teredo worms and other invasive species. The teredo is like an underwater termite that attaches itself to a wooden hull and then chews its way through the hull. They can grow to be a foot or more in length and can quickly sink a boat if not dealt with immediately. Ships that did not have copper bottoms would regularly have to put in to dry-dock or be careened ashore. Workers would then apply torches to the hull to try and burn the worms out, a situation where the cure was almost as bad as the disease. Teredo are unheard of in the Arctic but in the southern oceans where Sven was planning on sailing, they are a common nuisance and danger. Murray recalls the summer well. "I first met Sven when I was running the Robertson II and he tied up alongside of me, before he had her rigged. That was in '72. Sven was giving slide talk shows. I was doing the same getting some interest for the ship, this was before SALTS (author's note - SALTS is the Sail and Life Training Society - a youth training program aboard tall ships). He wanted me to come and see his slide show. It was like looking at a blank piece of paper, there was so much snow." Robertson II was a Lunenburg built fishing schooner that upon her retirement from the fishery was brought around to Victoria to start a sail training program, based upon the successful tall ships adventure society run by Toronto Brigantine Incorporated - the organisation that gave me my start in traditional ships and where I eventually took command of STV Pathfinder. The marine community in Canada is a very well-knit one.

Murray continues, "He was an amenable guy, he got up every morning and did something, like we all did in those days. I enjoyed the story of how he found the boat upside down and going through the Bering Sea, Beaufort Sea and the Chuck-Chuck. He's always had a project on the go, never without a project. Like a lot of us. We were a pretty tight community, everybody pitched in for most jobs. It was in the mid 70's, in the late fall or in the winter. I knew Sven quite well then. We both had our families aboard with our kids. North Star had been hauled out in the vacant lot next to Scott Plastics. This was right across the street from Covenaugh House, which was the internment camp for the Japanese during the war.

We stripped off every strip of gumwood. The hull was in good shape. We had to refasten thousands of holes in the inner hull from the gumwood. We dipped thin wood (Len remarks that they were skewers) into epoxy and then went at it, plugging each hole.

A sheet of copper beside North Star, ready to be fastened.

We then laid down Stockholm tar over the whole area to be covered and put Irish ship's felt over this. By the end of each day when walked home we both looked like a couple of black men. We heated the tar in a cast iron pot and then used either a tiger torch or just lit a fire. It took a couple of weeks. Sheets and sheets of copper. We then put more tar on top of the felt. The copper sheeting was in big sections. Norma and Silva were involved. Anybody that was hanging around would lend a hand, but no one else but Sven and me were doing the tarring. It was hard to get off, that tar, but it smelled nice. I went off to work up the coast and didn't see Sven or North Star for years."

Fastening the ironbark back on was another big job. Each piece had been carefully removed, cleaned and numbered but re-attaching it was like constructing a jig-saw puzzle with pieces thirty or forty feet long and with minds of their own. They all had to line up perfectly and then hammered home into the rock hard quarter-sawn, edge grain fir.

The coppering drew a lot of attention from passers-by and from the locals at the dock. John MacFarlane was the President of the Maritime Museum of BC and wrote about the procedure and North Star's need for it. "Prior to the move, in anticipation of travelling to the South Seas, Sven had researched ways to keep the ship's bottom from being attacked by teredo worms, an invasive species that can chew its way into a wooden ship's bottom and destroy it in short order. The teredo is repelled by copper and most modern anti-fouling paint at the time contained some degree of ground copper, however Sven recognized that this would soon slough off and he would be forever re-painting North Star. As his nature, Sven looked to the past to see how clipper ships had controlled the problem and decided, as their owners had, that copper sheathing was the way to go. He hauled the ship ashore behind Fisherman's Wharf and set to coppering, a maintenance task that while once commonplace, had probably not been done more than a handful of times worldwide in the past century.

This plating extended to a level above the waterline and visually formed part of the boot-topping. On the voyage I took it had been on for about fifteen years and it was about three years since he had checked it. Copper sheet comes in different thicknesses and he had to buy about 1,000 square feet at about two dollars per square foot. Even at twenty-thousands of an inch thick it weighed about 1,000 pounds. He used pure copper nails. The hull was sheathed in GreenHeart (IronBark), a very hard and durable wood, so he had to drill each of the nail holes first, about 8,000 in all, and he tarred each of the nails. Surviving and even flourishing on a minimal income, Sven undertook all of the maintenance of North Star himself. It was not only cost-effective but there is no marine trade that he does not seem to have mastered independently. Doing big maintenance jobs himself was a real necessity."14

When Sheila and I first looked at purchasing North Star of Herschel Island we were amazed by the amount of books that he had aboard. Being biblio-philes, we appreciated his love of the written word but his collection was overwhelming. The two bunks in the focs'le were piled right up to the deck-head and there were stacks of books on every surface throughout the ship. Part of our deal with him was that he would leave the nautical books aboard and take the rest with him. On one hand, acquiring a huge library of sailing books was appealing, but on the other hand it would have left us no room for our own books. In the end Sven had a change of heart and took all of his books with him, though he has been very generous in loaning us any texts that we wanted to read.

Sven's library weighed a lot and as he acquired more and more books over the years, North Star settled lower and lower into the water to the point where the copper sheathing was no longer above the waterline. Rather than purge some of his collection, Sven's solution was simply to add more copper sheathing to the hull.

There was some concern from passers-by that the copper would form a gal-vanic charge by setting up an electrical current with the iron in the ship. It was after dark on the first trip out with the new copper sheathing when Sven looked overboard. "It was like a fire around the whole boat! Is the damn boat going to fall apart?" As it turns out, he was just passing through a large area of phosphorescence. Thirty-four years later the copper looks almost brand new.

Another major project was that Sven added to North Star's keel. The ship had been designed to have a short keel so that she could make it into the shallow harbours in the Arctic, be easily beached at season's end and that if she was caught in the ice, that she could be forced up and out without damaging the keel. A longer keel would break off and sink the ship. As a result, with her roundish hull, North Star of Herschel Island tended to roll in heavy seas, much more than other ships of her length and tonnage. Another two feet, six inches was added to her four foot draft, making her more stable. He also drilled and bolted the ribs right through to the planking, making North Star of Herschel Island even stronger.

Sven had a dream to sail the ship to the South Pacific Islands and then on around the world with a cargo hold full of replicas of western artwork and films and slides of statues and sculptures. He wanted to share with the world the beauty of western art and perhaps to trade for some local art treasures along the way. He knew that he would be making this trip alone or perhaps with one or two others and so needed a way to handle all of the rigging and sails. Looking at the clipper ships of old as his model he began a search for a proper ship's capstan - a proper vertical winch that could not only help in sailing the ship but could be used for launching small boats of which he now had four, as well as to take on or discharge cargo and to haul the ship ashore and to careen her if he wanted. His search took him to a shipyard where a large two speed capstan had been taken off of the wreck of an old rum-running ship named Fitzhugh. This ship had been a notorious thorn in the side of the U.S. Coast Guard when she used her capstan for loading cases and cases of alcohol in ports such as Vancouver and Victoria and then offloaded them to smaller vessels off of the western coast of the United States during prohibition.

With North Star of Herschel Island's re-fit complete, the ship cast off on June 1st, 1978 just before midnight to make best use of a flood tide. Aboard were Sven, Norma, Silva, Bob Spearing, Dave Garry, and Wayne and Hazel Goern. The weather was calm and clear and on June 2nd they docked at Nanaimo where Wayne and Hazel disembarked. The crew was kept busy putting the ship back to rights from the jumble left over from all of the work completed the previous winter. Jim Butterfield joined the ship in Campbell River and they carried on North to Port Hardy at the north end of Vancouver Island. At Prince Rupert more gear was loaded to help with the survey. These included Zodiac boats and gear for the helicopters that would be used in the survey. By June 25th they were well on their way to Ketchikan. Sven was very disappointed with the lack of discipline among the hands aboard and described the situation as a 'sorry state' when people living in a small space choose to not get along with one another.

North Star's capstan from old rum-runner FitzHugh.

The helicopter made daily runs between North Star who was acting as the mother ship and sending the boundary workers out into the bush to log a visible border between Canada and the USA. The zodiacs were used for ferrying crew and supplies back and forth including kerosene for the stove. By early July the rubber boats were already leaking from their hard use. Norma and Silva went ashore and up into the bush camp with the crew by helicopter and chose to live out on the land for several weeks. "North Star of Herschel Island acted as a joe-boat. We would go up the narrow fjords and land the survey crews at selected shallow beaches. Then the helicopters would take over. This work was finished in 1979."[15]

The Johansson's upon their arrival in Victoria, B.C.

Sven moved the ship up the coast as the trail blazing moved north, arriving in Wrangle, Alaska in mid-July. One of Sven's strictest rules aboard is that there was to be no alcohol which did not impress the survey crew. He complains in the log that some of the crew were drunk when handling the zodiacs and that when they came back aboard that they caused "quite a disturbance, all drunk and dishevelled. Damned this bloody booze." Due to being drunk on the job one of the crew was fired and became aggressive. With the fired man put ashore, Sven moved the ship up to Bradfield Canal to meet the next helicopter.

By September 1st the crew had finished for the season and made her way down to Prince Rupert where the surveys were shipped back to Ottawa for processing. With fall upon them the crew now were back into the familiar weather patterns of wind, waves, rain and fog. By the time that they made it back past Campbell River in mid-September Sven writes, 'it is a nice relaxing day with good food - Norma baked bread again - and nice (to) have (a) reunion (with) the family.' At Ganges Harbour in Saltspring Island Sven contacted a former crew member of the Patterson who sailed on her from 1927 - 29. The old salt's name was Gillar and he joined the ship for a small trip around the harbour. A few days later they rounded down into the lumpy seas of the Strait of Juan de Fuca but Sven notes that 'the ship is now all different with keel and some ballast'. With 580 nautical miles astern since leaving Prince Rupert the family was happy to be back at Fisherman's Wharf in Victoria.

On October 1st North Star of Herschel Island headed out to Vancouver, setting sail along the way and there they met up with legendary cruising authors Eric and Susan Hiscock aboard Wanderer IV. The log reads, 'Very nice people with experience including world cruising.' The Hiscocks and other friends Tau and Margo had dinner aboard and the conversation went on into the night. North Star needed to be back in Victoria for the meeting with the Thermopylae Club (of which Sven Johansson was Commodore) and HMCS Oriole - two tall ships in Victoria Harbour of suitable vintage. On October 2nd while making anchorage at Mudge Island North Star ran hard aground. The current had set them towards the shoal and the engine moving astern walked them right on top of the rocks. "We spent three hours of extreme discomfort and some worry on that rock. Ship heeled 35 degrees to port but was well supported by water and had a lot to go before danger of rubbing strake (becoming submerged - which would have had her lying flat in the water) and just a little water entering around engine exhaust pipe which was caulked by Sven (meaning that he plugged the exhaust pipe so that seawater couldn't reach engine). At 0037 cow hide was used (to protect hull from chafing) and still at 35 degrees crew rested half standing on port coamings. On rising tide ship quickly righten herself and before 0300 refloated."

Making up for lost time Sven motored back to Vancouver. Silva was very excited for the next day when Sven's mother, Silva's grandmother, Ester, was to visit the ship. Sven recalls that his mother spoke only Swedish and so he had sent her specific instructions of how to get to Vancouver airport and that they would meet her there. Sven, Norma and Silva watched as the passengers disembarked from the plane, but no Ester. They searched all around and then Sven saw his mother, surrounded by six security guards, on the other side of a plexi-glass window. He jumped over the security fence and knocked on the window. "There was no translator service in the international airport," says Sven. "When you think of what happened to Robert Dziekaᴥski just a few years later when he couldn't be understood and he was tasered and died, it is unbelievable. My mom couldn't speak any English and so she just kept on saying the same phrase louder and louder that meant my son is going to take me to Victoria. But it was in Swedish, so all they heard was Victoria and so they were going to put her on a plane to Victoria!" Once settled into the main salon in North Star of Herschel Island, Ester had a great time cruising through the Gulf Islands and visiting Victoria. "We were babbling Swedish like nobodies biz!" remembers Sven.

The ship moved to Pirate's Cove in the Gulf Islands, an anchorage in DeCourcey Island made famous by the cult leader, Brother X11, an English man named Wilson who claimed to be the reincarnation of the God Osiris. He and his wife, Madame Z, formed the Aquarian Foundation in 1927 and kept his many followers isolated in the islands while he accrued a fortune from their donations of savings and property. His yacht, Lady Royal, was kept in the well-hidden harbour. When one of his followers escaped in a rowboat and alerted the RCMP, Wilson scuttled his vessel and disappeared. His death was reportedly in Switzerland years later, though some feel that it was faked. His fortune has never been accounted for and is rumoured to be buried on DeCourcey or Valdez Island.

Leaving the anchorage North Star met up with tall ship Sagres II and back in Victoria had a "nice gam (chat) with Eric and Susan aboard Wanderer IV." On October 22 North Star participated in the annual Thermopylae Cruise Other ships included Messenger III, Thane, and Pathfinder III. Many members and guests of Thermopylae aboard. The trip took the small flotilla 32 miles up to Sidney where they anchored for the night. Sven later took the ship into Powell River and there they met up with Len Pearson aboard S.V. Thane. They anchored out with Thane alongside. The ship's log reads, "Fun and usual arguments".

North Star of Herschel Island set off bright and early in January 1979 for the practical exam cruise for seamanship training with the Inuit. Aboard were Tom Elanik, George Carpenter, Peter Elanik, Vichen Firth and Clarence Felix. Sven noticed that Fred's son, George, seemed to hang back from the other Inuit trainees and he perceived it to be bullying, something that he cannot stand. "It was that same old damned hatred. Just jealousy. The Carpenters had been sort of the family that everyone looked up to and they saw this as a way to get back at him or something. George was a very nice, polite guy but really uncomfortable because of the others."

The ship left again in October for a charter by Joel Cotten heading North of Tofino on the west coast of Vancouver Island. Aboard were Joel Cotten, Jim Butterfield, Len Pearson, Larry Grobraus and three of Joel's hands. Norma and Silva opted to stay ashore at Butterfield's until the charter was done. Out in the Pacific they met up with large swells and fog. The charter was to use North Star as a base camp while the crew cut alder branches in an old logging area to help lumber trees to grow back. After a long afternoon of back breaking work they had supper aboard and 'the usual discussion about the world - life and coming disaster in general.' The wind picked up the next day and they rode to two anchors with a stern line ashore. The next two days Sven minded the ship, keeping a roast in the oven while shifting to a different anchorage twice due to dragging. Three days later with the work in the wind and rain completed the crew moved the ship up to anchor off Hot Springs Cove where all went ashore for a bath in the natural pools. The return to Victoria by October 20th was uneventful. Len Pearson remembers the trip out to the west coast. "He got a contract with a guy named Joel who had a contract to release forty acres of Hemlock. Releasing means that it's been planted with small Hemlock trees but before the Hemlock grow big the Alder trees take over. If you leave it like that the Hemlocks will choke to death and Alder at that time didn't have any value and the Hemlock is what they wanted for pulp. So all the Alders had to go. There's two ways of doing this. One way is that you go along and slash and poison them which is not organic. Or you just go along and cut the Alders down and hope that they don't regrow before the Hemlocks have a chance to grow through.

So here's this forty acres up behind Tofino and off we went, a crowd of us. Mary Graham went with us on that one - that's another story from the coast. Mary eventually got assassinated in Costa Rica - a drug deal or something. That was another wacko drug case. But we had a lot of different adventures. So, Joel hired all us guys and off we went with the idea was to slash or get rid of all of the alder trees. Most of the alder trees were up to two inches in diameter and maybe 12 or 14' feet high - just cut em off. I had a Stihl (chainsaw), big with a very short blade, and I had immense power and I could just use it like a one handed scythe and I could catch the trees and then lay them behind me like I was cutting barley or something. I did 15 acres in 3 days. I was exhausted but it was sort of a macho challenge and we were to get a free day with pay if we could get it done on time, so that was the incentive. Then when we got the job done a day early he tried to welch on us but we went to Tofino and had a good piss-up anyway on Joel.

We were all living on North Star. It was a camp. Sven was anchored 20 feet from the beach. In those areas where a river comes down, it is very deep and then it is very shallow, so there is only a small transition. It's really hard to anchor and when you do anchor you tie to the shore and then at low tide you're on the bottom. Sven was nervous the whole time but he fed us good. So that was our releasing program. Logging in what is now Clayoquot Sound, which has now become an area of note to the hippies and tree-huggers."

Sven adds that there were some problems with some of the loggers because they all wore 'nail boots' for traction when they were in the woods. "I told them that there was no way they could wear them on deck but some of them kept on trying to sneak aboard with them on. You could hear the nails going into the paint and cracking it. One evening I was down below in the salon and I heard one guy come aboard with his boots on. He was trying to be really quiet and sneaky. I waited at the bottom of the ladder and as he started down I grabbed him by the ankles and yelled. He was gone up and over the side so fast!'

Sven's idea of converting North Star of Herschel Island into a three masted square rigger was beginning to come together. He had drawn up the plans and found a fellow ship's captain, to donate the wood for the spars. Len Pearson was there and adds, "He got this idea that he wanted to rig North Star as a model of the Thermopylae so that took years in the development before he finally decided that he needed to do this. So I had an old truck and Bill Walker who was an ex-captain of the Oriole, (a 31 metre sailing ketch - the oldest commissioned ship in the Royal Canadian Navy), he had some property over on North Pender Island. Sven and Bill had become friends I believe through the Thermopylae Club or perhaps the Maritime Museum and Bill had offered Sven a big tree to make spars out of and there's one lying in his backyard over on North Pender.

Sven got together a big power saw and an Alaska saw mill and a bunch of ropes, blocks and fenders, a big box of beef bones - I never saw so many beef bones, with some meat on them - for he and me to eat so we went over in my old 59 International Traveller - just a brute of a truck - I called it Lurch - so we went over there and looked at the tree that Sven had been given and it was about five feet in diameter and it was a windfall which means that it had fallen sick. When it fell it was rotten. So we cut into it, and I said that it was good for firewood, so I bucked up a whole bunch of it and left it for Bill for firewood, several cords.

Meanwhile, Sven now is looking for a tree. So he goes off. There was no power, no electricity, no water, no nothing in this old shack and we camped there, burning these beef bones over an open fire and gnawing on them. Damn they were good and looked like Northern fare. So anyway, Sven gets to a telephone, phones Bill and says that the tree that he said he could have was no good, so what to do? And so Bill says, 'pick out a standing one and chop her down'. We looked around and saw this brute of a tree and it was 500 feet or so south of the highway and up the hill. We're talking a steep mountain path, not even a path, a forest, with this bloody great big first growth Fir tree standing on it. I'd fallen a lot of trees but never anything quite this big. It was like five feet in diameter. Sven decided that was the one we wanted and so we fell her down and cut her off to a reasonable length, I don't know maybe forty feet or something or other and so we had this big tree now and it was about four and a half to five feet diameter at the cut. It was a huge tree and it was too big for the Alaska saw mill. So, I cut some big wedges and we had sledgehammers and by big wedges meaning the trunk of a ten inch diameter fir tree, cut as a wedge, then we sliced into the end of the tree with the end of the big power saw and then started driving these wedges. So I split forty feet of five foot diameter Douglas Fir in half. Then we propped the half up on its edge again and now we could run the Alaska saw mill down through it. We proceeded to cut it into the lengths and widths that Sven required to make his spars. He wanted ten inches, and eight inches, six inches and five inches and so forth to provide him with the size of the spars that he had calculated that the Thermopylae would have had, if the Thermopylae had been the size of the North Star.

Len Pearson cutting down the big fir tree that became part of the new rig.

So we had this humongous pile of planks way up in the woods, any one of them heavier than we could lift. He happened to have a 600 foot role of one inch poly-prop line which we strung from snatch blocks from tree to tree to tree to tree down to Lurch out on the highway. We had walkie-talkies and Sven has this peculiar voice that when he's excited you can't tell from screaming, yelling at me through the walkie-talkie. And I'm down on the road with old Lurch and I'm hooking onto the rope and then barrel-assing down the road 'til a plank on the other end would come chock-a-block with the first snatch block. We were ploughing a logging route down the hillside using this method. We made an awful mess down on the road, but we got all of the planks onto the road and then hauled them out onto Shark's Spit, which is the gap between North and South Pender and cold-decked them there or stocked them on the sand until we could get our act together on how to get them to Victoria. It was quite a pile of planks in a multitude of sizes. Some of them were probably 4-500 pounds apiece. This must have been wintertime; otherwise I would have been off sailing somewhere.

Elaine, my partner at the time, was back on Thane in Canoe Cove, which was convenient. Once we got the logs cold-decked on the beach, we got on the ferry and went back to Canoe Cove and brought Thane over to South Pender Island by the small boat gap under the bridge to Shark Point. With the rowboat, I only had a small skiff at that time, at high tide we got all the big planks into the water all roped together in a long, long trail and pulled them, with the tide, over to where Thane was. By this time it was pitch black and with this long trail of planks towing in the water we headed off with Thane. We hauled the anchor up and headed off to Tsehum Harbour in Sidney, hauling all these planks. It was an incredible trip. So we got to the planks to the Federal Dock at Fisherman's Wharf on Tsehum Harbour and there's a BB winch crane there for the use of people and I guess it was the next day we had all these logs in the water underneath the crane.

I went and got Sven. Sven and I had gone down to Victoria to get a boat trailer and we couldn't find a boat trailer anywhere until we found one that is normally used for hauling a herring skiff. It was a barge, four wheels, double axle trailers - big boat trailer. It must have been spring time because there was no herring skiff on it. I knew the guy who owned it but he was off herring skiffing, so we borrowed the thing, I don't think we had plates on it or anything and we got the trailer away from Ogden Point, I think that was where it was stashed, got it up to Sidney, got the logs and the planks out of the water and onto the skiff and heading back to Victoria we got a flat tire on the trailer.

If we had run the trailer (by keeping on going) we would have ruined the tire and it wasn't our trailer and we felt a bit obligated not to bugger up the equipment, so I came into the gas station with the tire flat and went to the pumps and talked to the guy who was running the pumps and I said, 'I've got a flat tire here and I don't think I can move this trailer and I'm stuck, stuck right here with my truck and my trailer right in front of your gas pump and we tried to get the wheel off the trailer and it wouldn't come off, it was rusted - seized, right on. So we jacked her right up high and they were tubeless tires but anyway we got the bead broken and reached into the tire and fixed it on the spot. The guy running the gas station wasn't particularly pleased but he didn't quite know how to get rid of us unless he helped us fix the tire.

We got the tire fixed and we pumped it up and headed for Victoria and brought them in at the old McKay Cormack shipyard where Sven by this time had berthed the North Star and he had use of one of the old warehouses there - it's where the Coast Hotel is now. The city waterfront has changed big time. So anyway Sven had an old warehouse there and we got all of the big planks inside and I left him there and the rest of it is Sven's history. That was my part in getting those spars that you have now, into the boat from a tree on Pender. I have used parts of that tree on Thane. Whenever I needed a piece of fir I would go and cut some of the cuttings from Sven making the spars. It was the toughest, gnarliest fir that I have ever come across. Seasoned standing, first growth. The heart of a first growth tree is hardened already - 65-100 years standing there. It was just the sapwood. Boy, that sapwood was something else. So tough and wouldn't split. You couldn't split it worth beans because the grain was so tangled."

During 1980, Sven worked building a pilothouse aboard the fishing boat, Pacific Gale, and in re-building the focs'le on North Star and installing double-acting worm gear steering. He had heard of the worm-gear up for sale in the United States and high-tailed it down there to get them. The worm gear is a very traditional method of connecting the helm to the rudder and has been used for centuries aboard traditionally rigged ships. This system was installed to replace North Star's original steering mechanism which was very basic and an accident waiting to happen. It involved a steel rod from the roof of the pilothouse that was attached to a wheel which then met another wheel in the house and then to a link that attached to cables running through blocks in the lazarette and on to the rudder head. Sven left the blocks in the lazarette which could be put back into service for emergency steering gear. He also stripped the decks again for re-painting and built a tabernacle for the mizzen mast.

Another project was installing electronics with the ship still in the water, a job that required a lot of nerve and a steady hand. Len recalls that "one time I was helping Sven install a sender for the depth sounder on North Star. I was down under the hull with scuba tanks and Sven was inside. He drilled a small hole where the wires would lead to the sender. I took a toilet plunger and covered the hole while he fished the wires through. Then it was just a case of fishing on the nut and tightening it to the inside flange that Sven was holding. Then I took a lot of caulking and mounted the sender. This was the way that we put some through hulls (pipes and valves to allow water in or out) in her, too.

One time, I was diving down under the hull waiting for Sven to get ready for the project. We were at Fisherman's Wharf. On the seabed there are tons and tons of coils of stainless steel rigging. When the fishermen would come in each year they would spool off the old gear and dump it right into the harbour. I was looking at all of these wires and touched one of them. This set off some action as some of the coils sprung up and I became caught in them. Visibility was down to zero from all of the sediment being stirred up and I was caught pretty good on the bottom. I nearly died that day. The only thing that got me out was just keeping my head and not panicking."

In July, North Star departed for the Boundary Survey project. The pace to get north was much slower and there were days spent at anchor writing letters, fishing and hiking ashore in the Gulf Islands. Back to Victoria and they made fast to the grid to inspect the copper sheathing at low tide. A grid is a flat base alongside a fixed pier in a tidal flat. A boat moors to the pier at high tide. When the tide ebbs the boat ends up sitting on the flat base and stays vertical since she is made fast to the pier. After the inspection and the tidal flood, North Star spent the next month going back and forth to Vancouver meeting with the Hiscocks again and travelling up to Chatterbox Falls.

Sven was keeping quite busy those days. Over the winter of 1980 and into the early months of 1981, he had secured a contract to train Inuit from the Western Arctic in sail training and seamanship so that they could secure jobs on oil rigs and supply ships in the Beaufort Sea. Essentially, he was training people to be doing the same sort of work that had been done aboard North Star prior to her leaving for the south. Canadian Marine Drilling out of Calgary, Alberta hired Sven and North Star of Herschel Island to "conduct and supervise a training course in basic seamanship and boat handling during January and February, 1981. The trainees, all Native Northerners from the western Arctic were split into groups of five men. Each group spent three weeks aboard. The government invested in the project and there was quite a media buzz whenever Sven and the Inuit made port up in the Gulf Islands."[16]

"The program, the only one of its kind in the country, is sponsored by private enterprise, involves Native Canadians and, for the Northerners taking part, it is a positive step in their taking a more active role in the development that has overtaken Canada's northern-most frontier within the past decade.

With the commencement of the drilling season this summer, what they have learned will be put to the test on Dome Petroleum's floating drilling rigs in the Beaufort Sea.

Five Northerners, three from Tuktoyaktuk and two from Aklavik are on board North Star. Another five are learning theory at Tuktoyaktuk. The two groups will switch places in three weeks....it is the brainchild of Peter Devenis of Dome Canmar's management team and Don MacWatt who heads Beaufort Environmental Support Services.

Johansson "considers it to be the perfect training vessel for the Northerners, who, through stories told by their parents, remember when native families travelled in groups aboard her. In the Western Arctic there is a good old tradition of boats and seamanship. The North Star was owned by Eskimo trappers. They know how to handle boats in high winds, ice conditions, the whole works. They don't have to step down to anybody in the Western Arctic."[17] In this interview Sven states that "from 1973 until 1982 she engaged in a variety of Arctic roles. One of these prepared young Alaskan Eskimos for work on Arctic oil ships."[18] "The trainees, all native Northerners from the western Arctic, were split into two groups of five men. Each group spent three weeks at the coast, learning basic seamanship, using North Star of Herschel Island as the training vessel."[19]

In addition to the sail-training, Sven had another interesting iron on the fire. Len Pearson recalls that "Sven had several contracts with a group wanting to go look for Sea-Monkies in the Aleutians and other adventures."Pearson's remark about 'Sea-Monkies' is right on the mark. One of the more interesting requests made for North Star of Herschel Island's services came in the spring of 1981. The request was made for her to be chartered up to the waters in and around the Aleutian Islands. This was of course, an entirely reasonable request considering the ship's construction and Arctic heritage, not to mention the skill of Captain Johansson, Norma and Sylva. What made the request somewhat unusual was that it was to go in search of actual mermaids.

When Clio Smeeton was twenty-three she was sailing those same waters with her parents and a friend, Henry, making a North Pacific crossing from Japan through the Aleutian Islands of Alaska to British Columbia. Her parents, Myles and Beryl Smeeton are highly regarded for their lifestyle and for pioneering the world cruising lifestyle. The Smeeton's books are highly encouraging to any armchair sailor who wants to cast off the shackles of land and head off on a small sailboat in search of adventure.

What Clio saw that day, as she sat on her parent's boat would set in motion a voyage aboard North Star of Herschel Island decades later. When Clio was making this Pacific passage she locked eyes with a mermaid. In fact, she recalls seeing many mermaids and mermen and this image, of course, stayed with her throughout her life.

Her father, Myles, recalls that day, "Look, look, "cried Clio, suddenly pointing close off the weather bow. "What is it, what is it?"

Close off the port bow an animal was lying in the water; it looked to be about the size of a sheep and had long yellow, pepper-and-salt hair like a cairn terrier, of a reddish yellow colour. As the bow approached, it made a slow, undulating dive and disappeared beneath the ship. What most impressed me was the length of its hair, about four to five inches long; and when I first saw it on the surface the hair was floating round the body like weed growing on a half-submerged rock. I never saw its head, but Clio, who also saw it come up on the other side of the ship and look at us, said that the head was more like the head of a dog than a seal, with the eyes close together, not set on the side of the head, like a seal's. Henry confirmed this impression, saying that it had a face like a Tibetan terrier, with drooping Chinese whiskers.

In Stellar's account of his exploration with Bering in the ships St Peter and St Paul, from Kamchatka to the North American coast in 1741, he writes of an animal he called the 'sea monkey', reddish yellow and about four feet long, which has never since been identified, so that naturalists have thought it never existed. Stellar, however, was a very acute and literal observer, unlikely to imagine anything that he did not see. They were observed several times on this voyage, which is described in the book ... called Where the Sea Breaks its Back, by Corey Ford. ...we all believe that the animal we saw was the same creature; neither sea lion, seal, nor sea otter, that Stellar describes in some detail."[20]

Georg Wilhem Stellar was a naturalist and he is credited with finding and describing hundreds of specimens in his voyages in the North Pacific and around the world. He is probably best known for the Stellar's Sea Cow, a mammal similar to the Manatee but very different than the creature that he and the crew found in 1741. "It was about two Russian ells (five feet) in length, the head was like a dog's, with pointed erect ears. From the upper and lower lips on both sides whiskers hung down which made it look almost like a Chinaman. The eyes were large; the body was longish, round and thick, tapering gradually towards the tail. The skin seeme thickly covered with hair, of a grey colour on the back, but reddish white on the belly; in the water however, the whole animal appeared red like a cow...(We were amazed by) its wonderful actions, jumps and gracefulness. For over two hours it swam around our ship, looking, as with admiration first at the one and then at the other of us. At times it came so near to the ship that it could be touched with a pole, but as soon as anybody stirred it moved a little further...After it had observed us for about half an hour, it shot like an arrow under our vessel and came up on the other side....in this way it dived perhaps thirty times. (At one point), it seized a seaweed in its mouth and swam toward the ship, making such motions and monkey tricks that nothing more laughable can be imagined...It was seen several times in other places of the sea."[21]

Sven recalls that when he met Clio she was living in a house on Vancouver Island. "She was such a nature lover that when a squirrel burrowed a hole into her house and made a nest behind her bookcase - eating up the backs of the books - that she just let it be!," he says.

When Miles Smeeton's Godson, Miles Clark, contacted Sven with the idea of looking for the sea monkeys or mermaids he met a kindred spirit. Sven is a romantic if ever one lived and he loved the idea of this search. The practical and experienced side of him though laid down the plan of when they would need to cast off in order to meet the best conditions under the banner of the British Aleutian Island Expedition of 1981. Miles had heard of Sven through Sven's friendship with the Smeetons and they had been writing back and forth for the whole winter to plan the trip. "I explained to him over and over again that we have to make a really early start if we are going to get to Sitka," says Sven. "The winds blow clockwise in the early part of the year so that we would have a following wind there. Later, it switches and so you have headwinds. I wanted to leave in early spring," he adds.

It is interesting to note that mermaid and merman sightings have historically been more common at the poles, usually on the Atlantic side. One theory for the pole related sightings particularly the Norse merman, was put forward "by Lehn and Schroeder. They consider that mediavel Norse descriptions depict a natural phenomenon. Atmospheric refraction distorted images of sea mammals. Even at close distances, ordinary objects are rendered unidentifiable." The theory basically says that light rays travel on nearly horizontal paths the closer that they get to the poles. This allows for a bounce or refraction, distorting, for instance, a walrus into a figure resembling a mer creature. In a related study, the scientist "Nordgard proposes that the hooded seal (Cysophora cristata) may have provided a source for visions of mermen."[22]

On May 29th, 1981 the British Aleutian Island Expedition began. Onboard at the start were Sven, Silva, Norma and Stuart Johansson. The ship's log reads, "This summer we were joined by the British Aleutian Island Expedition 1981. Miles Clark Expedition leader from Cambridge England. The expedition will board in Cook Inlet area and then will sail for Sitka Island where camp will be established ashore. We are hoping for an interesting summer. Installed auto-pilot which 'makes running a pleasure. 'We have now a total of ten tons ballast and will see if it makes motions more pleasant. Right away hit by a squall of 38 knots in strong opposing current and caused a most confusing sea. Roll to 25 degrees but I feel the ballast did a good job of stabilising the ship."

All depth sounders were broken during the night passage in Discovery Passage as the ship kept hitting drift logs which probably damaged or broke off the transducers. After a few days in Prince Rupert slipped lines and at 0600 were rammed by a small boat. The trip carried on north and they put in at Flynn Cove where they had last been in 1974 on their way south from Sachs Harbour. Launched gig and went ashore. Found gaff but not much else. The wind and wave predictions were all good and so they pushed on to make good use of the weather. A humpback whale came right up beside the ship. The entrance to the open ocean provided a big swell which soon combined with a head wind. The ship's log continues, "Not to the liking of good old North Star, nor its master. North Star's length filled just below crests and we dive into next wave with a bang and get some sea over the bow. First time in my running the ship (like this) excepting once in the Delta Channel out to Beaufort Sea. At 2100 hrs we had just enough of it with rolls to 24 degrees and heavy showering." At 9pm Sven made the decision to try and seek shelter at Liturga Bay. To do this they had to turn beam onto the ocean swells with the ship now rolling 28 degrees until they made port and finally anchored.

Sven had mentioned the previous morning that the fine weather that they first experienced was a reward for their living right. On this day they expected worse weather to which Sven wondered what they had done wrong yesterday. Made harbour with radar broken down and phoned Miles Smeeton to let him know of arrival. They set off once again for Yakatat and found themselves in the midst of the halibut fleet and had to dodge poles and buoys and fish boats all night. Realised at this point in voyage that all of the compasses would need swinging since loading the ten tons of ballast. Went up on the grid and replaced transducers and then met up with 87 year old Ted Pedersen who came aboard for dinner and a night of reminiscences of his Arctic life. Ted was described in the logbook as being "young and spry and happy to be living in a house he built by himself. After so much time alone in the Arctic he enjoys visits but is obviously happy to be heading back into his own thoughts and solitude existence."

Miles Clark had made some arrangements, perhaps due to his Godfather Miles Smeeton's influence that gave the expedition crew members a free ride with military aircraft from England to Alaska. They joined the ship with each member carrying aboard a lot of gear and a lot of provisions, also from the military.

North Star's log continues, "The Expedition crew all aboard and the ship weighed anchor on June 29th. Heavy seas and strong currents made the decision for them to re-anchor which they did three more times due to poor holding or shallow bottom. Rolling hard at anchor and water entering exhaust so that engine would not re-start. Made note in log to always run engine when rolling at anchor. Very uncomfortable conditions. The weather forecast continued to call for light winds while the ship rolled at anchor in a forty knot gale out of the south."

The next day, June 28, the weather forecast was calling for more wind and rain but time for the expedition was ticking away. Sven spoke with Miles about time and weather. "Warned about pointless delay to extent of failure. Now eight days behind schedule because of going to Anchorage. Suggested Homer all winter but expedition wanted Anchorage and we got it. Expedition decided to stay with ship. I asked for decision at Homer."

Next day headed back out into rolling seas. "Heavy going and had rough beat back to island. Hove to under engine for lunch and then continued to south-west of island. Sheltered from wind and sea but had tidal race. Anchored. The wind and seas dropped in the evening and so all ashore for a walk. Spoke with old-timers of Chedian (1942 crack boat crew). Back aboard and with conditions looking better, "decided to make attempt for Homer. Up anchor at 2350". The reader may have noticed at this point that Sven made his decisions about weighing anchor and heading out to sea based upon weather and tide, as they should be, though the rest and comfort of the crew must have taken its toll. Heading out into lumpy seas in the middle of the night again and again puts the miles astern but is very tiring.

The ship's log continues, "Fine weather until 0500 when eleven miles west of Anchor Point a twenty to twenty-five knot wind came up from the southwest, right on the nose. Lumpy seas. Started tacking under power to try and make some forward way in twelve foot seas." Sven remembers that they "were all sea-sick like dogs. I was yelling at them to hang on or get below. If you fall overboard, it will be hell of an awful thing to try and get you. Waves over bow at times. Heavy going."

By eight in the morning Sven altered course to get as close to Homer Spit as the wind and seas would let him. North Star of Herschel Island pitching and rolling with Expedition crew hanging on for dear life as the ship smashed through tons of water, waves breaking over the deck. Sven continued to alter course until they finally rounded the breakwater and a peace came over the ship. The feeling of being thrown around for hours and hours with the scream of the wind, the clanking of the anchor chains and the sails flogging out of their gaskets and then suddenly arriving into a calm oasis brought smiles to the crews faces as they wondered if they would ever dare putting back to sea again.

Alongside in Homer at last, after a week of wind and waves the British Aleutian Expedition crew members sat around the deckhouse table eating soup and crackers and drinking mug after mug of hot tea. The marine radio crackled out the updated forecast of predicted on-going gales. Crew morale dropped to an all time low.

After a sleep and a clean-up, all went ashore for showers, laundry, mail and groceries. The gales were still evident ashore and there were still some decisions to be made of what to do next. The crew living in the focs'le had noticed that the pounding of the bow into the waves had opened some small holes on deck and much of their gear was soaked with saltwater. The afternoon was spent trying to plug these holes and dry out bedding and clothes. The forecast remained grim and the crew's morale is noted in the log as being quite low. If the crew had known about the storm in 1961 back in the Beaufort Sea when there was concern that the pounding of the ship had caused a gap on the foredeck to open up, I am sure that the mood would have been untenable.

Still moored at the Homer Basin, the seas looked fine in the harbour and the temptation the next day to head out was strong. Radio reports came in with observations of sixteen foot waves outside of the harbour and thirty-five knot winds. The crew could not believe that there would be such a disparity and many complained that they should head back out. Sven writes, "Have been through that before. Will not take risks and knowingly go into bad weather." The ship was moved out to a mooring buoy to await a break in the weather which came at dawn on July 2nd.

Sven described the forecast as not being encouraging but that he had to "do something. Expeditions walking around and in Salty Dog Saloon and as always, few people see further than their nose. A prudent mariner must see ahead, 12-24-48 hours and decide by a long time ahead assessment of any situations."

They slipped lines at 0315 and had a relatively calm going until 0630 when the northwest wind started cranking up to twenty knots. Soon it was holding steady at twenty-five knots and a sea so bumpy that it indicated worse ahead. The observational reports from other ships ahead stated winds of forty knots heading their way. With this knowledge and having worked North Star through forty knot gales before, Sven made a course for Port Chatam. "Of course," he writes," not approved by some - but soon realised the decision was the right one." As they made harbour and dropped anchor the wind came screaming across the rocks at them punching forty knots and then some. Even at anchor in a sheltered harbour, North Star kneeled to the wind, rolling with the gusts while the spume was driven off of the top of the waves, quickly soaking anyone on deck." Sven adds, "I had a hell of a time with Miles Clark. He was contacting Miles Smeeton and saying that I was chicken for not carrying on."

North Star's log records: "Some of the crew ashore the next day and one member found what he was sure was the nest of a marbled murlet. If this could be confirmed then it would be the first one ever found. Salmon were jumping all around the ship and so rods and gear were rattled out and many hours were invested in catching one, but to no avail." On July 3rd, Sven writes into the logbook that "I am now sure that we will not reach Sitka in time to do any useful work on that island."

On July 4th, Sven explained the situation to the expedition from a Captain's perspective. So much time had been lost at the beginning of the venture in trying to get to Anchorage to pick up crew rather than taking off from Homer, that it seemed unlikely, considering the weather, that they could make it to Sitka. The crew respectfully disagreed. Then the wind came up. Miles went ashore to find out if a plane could take them to Sitka but wasn't able to resolve this. They weighed anchor and headed back out to sea. By late after-noon the wind was back up to forty knots and by evening they turned and ran with the wind to Bedfax Bay on Alligator Island. The maneuver required entering on a following sea with waves of twelve to fourteen feet which Sven described North Star as handling beautifully. With the wind holding steady the following day there was no question of going to sea so the crew all went ashore and went swimming in the lakes and rivers there.

The Expedition finally caught a break in the weather and with light winds and seas North Star made a run to Malka Bay where they were greeted at the entrance by one hundred or more sea otters. Silva caught a flounder and James a halibut. Smiles were all around until the next forecast of more gales came up. Thirty knot gales all across the North Pacific from Japan to Kodiak. Sven writes, "It is just not the right summer to go west. Expedition in low morale and apathetic about anything and very disappointed."

Gales were predicted the next day and Sven asked if anyone wanted to make a run for Kodiak but the vote was to stay on the hook. The next day, July 10th, the ship started off again to the west. The day started fairly calm but within hours they were 'slogging' into a twenty knot westerly with rain and a forecast of more gales. Anchored south of Point Bailey. Up early and 'poor prospects' for carrying on west. Ran towards Port Liam covering eighteen miles through Whale Passage. The expedition crew went ashore to make phone calls and then had a campfire by the edge of the small town. Norma found a First Nation's kitchen midden while hiking. A midden is basically a junk heap consisting of old bones, pottery, shells and anything else that might have been cast off from a First Nation's village.

They weighed anchor at 0645 and headed for Ousiche Narrows. Good trip to Kodiak after all that they had been through. There was no space in the small boat harbour which was fine with Sven, 'just as good because fee is $12.00 per day'. They found a solid anchorage and with the expedition safely in Kodiak they decided to follow Sven's earlier decision and made plans to fly to Sitka Island. "Too many miles in a small ship with people of differing ideas, egos and skills," wrote Sven in the logbook. "Just waiting. Getting tired of all stupidity in the whole undertaking of all the dirt and apathetic attitude of expedition. However, all bad things come to an end. Finally all expedition off the ship, three going to Sitka via Anchorage. Into unloading dock and finally everything off at 1630. Bad planning and poor executing of everything to the end. Ship happily to anchorage and cleaning up and enjoying our selfs (sic). So ends." Sven remembers saying to Miles Clark and the Expedition crew that, "this is the end of it. That's it. I'm giving up."

The day after the British Expedition left the ship Sven vented in the logbook and we get a more accurate look at what life was like aboard North Star during the adventure. "What a wonderful feeling of being private and not baby-sitting. Must say the British were a terrible disappointment in every respect from attitude to ability. I can only say, 'God Help the Queen!'"

Thirty years later Norma still remembers the mood of the whole charter party. She said that they "were the strangest group they had ever had before. They were obviously used to more posh surroundings and they were very, very snooty British types." She said that they had the whole voyage provisioned with army/navy rations. "This was in the days before freeze dried food and everything was in envelopes". What had started with the impressive name of the British Aleutian Expedition, Sven, in later years, referred to as the "sea cow UK expedition to Kodiak Island."

In his 447 page book, <u>High Endeavours</u>, a biography of the Smeetons, Miles Clark writes about the expedition aboard North Star of Herschel Island. "Like Clio and Henry, Miles (Smeeton) was so certain that the animal they had seen was the same creature (as that seen by Stellar), that in 1981 I took a Cambridge University expedition to Sitka to investigate - among other things - the possibility that this endearing creature may survive. The limited research we carried out provided neither proof of existence, nor any other plausible explanation of these sightings. And so for the moment the sea monkey must live in the realms of the Yetis, the Nessies and a score of other almost-animals, waiting to be rescued from sceptical smiles by true scientific discovery."[23]

The story doesn't stop there, though. Miles Clark was soon after awarded the Scientific Exploration Society's Bish Medal for "leading a Cambridge research expedition to Alaska's remote Aleutian Islands - seeking evidence for the existence of a marine mammal positively identified by the early explorers and two hundred years later by Miles and Beryl Smeeton."[23A]

The next couple of weeks Sven took his time and waited out weather as they harbour hopped and made many hikes ashore. On July 25th with the anchor set and the family all snugged down for the night in Juneau Harbour, Norma called Sven on deck. A very intoxicated fisherman was racing around the harbour narrowly avoiding collisions with other boats. As he kept on rounding closer to North Star Sven and Norma weighed anchor and moved out of the way to avoid trouble.

They finally did make it into Sitka Harbour at the end of July and enjoyed the living history of it from when Sitka was the capital city prior to the Alaska Purchase. Many museums and ice creams were enjoyed by the crew. By mid-August they were back in the Inside Passage and hailed Allen and Sharie Farrell aboard Native Girl. They came aboard North Star and then all went ashore in Native Girl's gig to look at a new boat Allen was building. This boat was Allen's last and ended up being christened China Doll. "An excellent job they are doing. Just delighted to see Allen working without any power tools. Some are very gifted," wrote Sven in the log. The quiet of the beautiful anchorage was broken by the sound of so many modern boats running their generators - a frequent complaint in the logbook this season.

The Farrells were famous for their cruising lifestyle and for the boats that Allen built. Living ashore at Lasqueti Island he would beach comb with each tide and then haul in whatever wood he wanted. British Columbia's Inside Passage beaches are often choked with telephone pole sized pieces of cedar, fir, and arbutus. Allen worked without power tools, cutting everything by hand and creating beautiful wooden boats that he and Sharie and their two daughters would then sail to the South Seas. The hull designs were in his head and his love of woodworking showed in details such as Native Girl's three hundred or so hand cut drawers in various sizes throughout the boat. An interesting coincidence is that years later my wife and I came very, very close to purchasing Native Girl prior to our involvement with North Star.

When Allen finished China Cloud he took down the tarpaulin that had been covering the project and made junk-rigged sails from the tarp. A few years later a man was admiring China Cloud and lamented that he would never be able to own a boat as beautiful as her. Allen looked up and said, "She's yours!" He immediately handed over ownership to the stunned fellow and kept his word. This was very indicative of Allen's character and spirit. A few years later Sharie passed away and Allen was feeling depressed. China Cloud's new owner had kept in touch with him and now returned the boat, knowing that Allen would no doubt like to get back sailing. Upon Allen's death China Cloud's ownership reverted back to the lucky man.

China Cloud.

After stopping in at Nanaimo, making Dodd's Narrows and back to Pirate's Cove at DeCourcey Island, North Star of Herschel Island met up with 'Manaia' - the Christensen's new boat just launched and out for a ten day shake-down. Sven was quite impressed with the vessel. On September 1st North Star of Herschel Island was involved in a colour ceremony at sunset with a cannon shot. The log reads, "Blowing ship's horn - North Star's horn best in fleet. Singing in pilothouse. The voyage to Sitka, Alaska ended back at Fisherman's Wharf on September 2nd. 4,255 miles logged. 'That will do, men!'"

The fall of 1981 and winter of 1982 were mainly spent improving the interior of North Star of Herschel Island while she was moored at Fisherman's Wharf. Sven had been working on a new program of seamanship training with the Inuit but this was cancelled and so he used his time building out the bunks in the salon and straightening out previous projects.

John Bockstoce contacted Sven and asked him to go to San Diego to investigate the sailboat, Pacifier, that he was considering purchasing for an attempt at becoming the first sailboat to make it through Canada's NorthWest Passage from west to east. Sven flew to California and as a result Bockstoce purchased the sixty foot cutter and hired Sven to convert her for 'Arctic Duty' in 1983. Sven felt that the name Pacifier was an insult to both the ship and the Ocean and so she was renamed 'Belvedere of New Bedford', a nod to the famous Arctic whaling ship of the same name and Bockstoce's home port. The initial plan was to sail her to Herschel Island in the summer of '83. Sven sailed the ship to Victoria and put her on the same dock as North Star at Fisherman's Wharf in July. Johansson cut the twin keels off of Belvedere and then had them re-welded with a 'weak weld.' "You see," he explains, "When the ice buckles between the keels it can rip them off and shatter the boat. I wanted the keels to shear off easily." Sven hired Ken Keith to work on Belvedere while he readied for a voyage to the Queen Charlotte Islands (now Haida Gw'ai).

On July 15th, North Star of Herschel Island was once again underway from Victoria with Sven, Norma, Silva, Allison Cuthill and Peter Tihus aboard. After camping ashore at Newcastle Island, the ship put Allison ashore and carried on north through the Inside Passage. After running night and day, Sven moored the ship to a log boom and caught some sleep. As they next rounded out past Port Hardy and into the open Pacific Sven sighted two sailing ships that "made some excitement in my mind. First I sighted to the west a sail that resembled a pirate Pelucca - made me think of old Josh Slocum and the Spray. Then to SW I saw a sail that made my heart pound - a square rigger!'" That evening they anchored, but dragged all night.

North Star of Herschel Island's logbook next reads, "Weighed anchor in the rain and were greeted by eight killer whales and one Pacific porpoise. The latter swam away from the killers at incredible speed. Never saw as fast a porpoise before. The whales followed the shore at six knots." The ship remained anchored at the top of Vancouver Island waiting for a break in the wind to cross to the Queen Charlottes Haida Gwai). Sven discovered some broken parts in the generator and so they decided to head to Prince Rupert to get parts. Weather continued to hamper their moves and so they made the most of it gunkholing around and eventually made the crossing in light air. Snagged the anchor on some rocks on Friday, August 13th and broke the 5/8" chain. The trip to Haida Gwai was a mix of beautiful anchorages and hikes ashore.

Crossing back they stopped at Port Hardy and then over to Predeaux Harbour at the entrance to Desolation sound. More whale sightings, swimming and a wonderful time. Sven spoke with some people from Sachs Harbour who knew Fred Carpenter. After a time at the resort at Roche Harbour they continued back and into Canada and secured at Fisherman's Wharf, Victoria.

In 1983 Sven turned his attention slightly away from North Star of Herschel Island in order to attempt to become the first Captain to sail through the NW Passage from west to east and also to replenish his cruising kitty for North Star. On May 5, 1983 he cast off with Belvedere and arrived in Tuktoyaktuk in late August. The summers of 1984, 85, 86, and 1987 Sven spent skippering Belvedere. Each of those seasons the ship was turned back by ice and each of those winters they returned to Tuktoyaktuk and hauled out. In 1985,

Sven and Norma began divorce proceedings and by 1986 Norma and Silva had moved ashore.

During the off-seasons, Sven continued work aboard North Star building the spars and re-rigging the ship. Finally, in 1988 Belvedere broke through to the Atlantic side arriving in Greenland in September of 1988. In 1989 Silva and Sven flew to Greenland and prepared the ship. When Bockstoce and more crew arrived they sailed her down to New York Harbour and then to her new home port in Camden, Maine where he left the ship. Sven had thought that Belvedere wasn't going to make it through the NorthWest Passage in 1988. "We thought we'd lost again. The stark, pure-white ice massed around us, grinding against the hull. We crept along and then anchored for four days until an east wind shifted the ice enough to let us sneak through and reach Baffin Bay, and later, Holsteinborg in Greenland."[24]

North Star of Herschel in her new rig as a fully rigged ship.

In 1989, after the delivery of Belvedere, Sven and Silva were back in Victoria and Sven was able to complete the rigging of North Star of Herschel Island.

She made her first appearance as a full-rigged ship when she took part in the Spanish Festival in Sooke. North Star was a highlight of the show, playing the part of the Spanish explorers while the Sooke longboat society ferried people around the harbour and the Sooke First Nations plied the waters in their war canoes. North Star was presented with a curved and pointed war canoe paddle as a thank you for her participation.

The ship careened to clean and work on her bottom.

In 1990 North Star of Herschel Island participated in the Victoria Classic Boat Festival. She then cast off on September 5th for a voyage North of Vancouver Island. Their first stop was to anchor in Montague Harbour; Galiano Island where they saw the Farrell's now completed China Cloud. Sven visited aboard their junk rigged ship in the evening. He wrote about the experience in the ship's log. "Rowing back was a beautiful experience. Completely silent tranquility, the water calm and the sky clear with an enormous moon. All this one miss in the city." The ship made it up to Port Hardy where they were joined by Peter McAllister and the Sierra Club/Raincoast Conservation Society for a voyage to the old growth watershed of Kaeye River.

Murray Boy, who had last seen North Star of Herschel Island when he helped Sven to copper the ship's bottom was working up the coast when he saw the ship approaching. "The next time I saw Sven was in Euchott Bay on the central coast. I was running a 160 foot tug that came out of the Arctic. We were doing helicopter logging. I had two big barges behind me with the Sikorsky gear on. I looked down from the bridge and around the corner comes Sven and North Star! I remember looking down and I was looking at the top of his mast. He had the protesters (the environmentalist group) with him. He had a whole lot of hippy chicks aboard and they were all hooting and hollering about stopping us from logging. I yelled down "Sven come on up for supper. We're having steak tonight!" I was able to build a bit of a bridge between the loggers and the protesters without any yelling and screaming going on. There was about twenty of them came aboard and of course the loggers loved it because the girls weren't wearing brassieres and we'd been in there about thirty or forty days. They had a tv camera crew with them and I was able to get them up in a helicopter, in the Bell JetStar, to show them - to explain to them how clean heli-logging is.

The next day their complaint was that with us doing the heli-logging that there would be no jobs for us and no jobs for our kids. So, I said okay - we're always looking for guys to work as set-chokers. It was good pay. Then they say we don't have the proper boots and I just said show up on the heli-deck at 5 am tomorrow. Next day we set out all of our extra cork boots on the heli-deck and waited for them. Not one showed up."

This voyage was the start of conservation groups proclaiming the area that North Star of Herschel Island voyaged to as 'The Great Bear Rainforest'. Publicity from the trip resulted in the area becoming a protected zone for wildlife and from logging and a magazine article, 'Making the jump into a Dark Fiord', and the book, The Great Bear Rainforest. Both feature photographs and descriptions of North Star. The success of taking the old Arctic ship in an eco-friendly way into British Columbia's wilderness made the decision for the eco-groups to eventually purchase their own ship and the publicity of that voyage helped secure the Great Bear Rainforest as a protected area - another proud achievement for the great ship.

In March of 1991 'Seafaring with Sven' came to life as the Maritime Museum of British Columbia chartered North Star of Herschel Island as a floating base for their school children program. The Museum brought aboard artifacts, ship models, knot boards, books, a sextant and lots of food and warm clothing. They sailed through the Gulf Islands and school groups came aboard. One evening, at Saturna Island, the program was moved to a community hall where Sven gave a lecture and slide presentation about North Star of Herschel Island's history. At Horton Bay on Mayne Island, a few days later, the children arrived on the dock with ukuleles and serenaded the crew with sea shanties before coming aboard to explore the floating Arctic museum.

In the spring of 1992, North Star of Herschel Island again teamed up with the Maritime Museum of British Columbia and provided a floating classroom for school groups to come aboard. The program started in Victoria, with a module being taught at the museum and then a tour of the ship that included hoisting the teachers up in the bosun's chair as the students sang sea chanteys. The program was so popular that North Star of Herschel Island then visited ports up the Salish Sea with stops at some of the Gulf Islands. By the end of the two week program Johansson estimated that over 800 children had been aboard the famous Arctic ship.

In February of 1993 Sven motored the ship west to Sooke and back for bottom work. On May 21st they left for the Longboat Festival at Penn Cove in the USA. They arrived back in Victoria on May 23rd. In June, the ship continued her involvement with the longboat and war canoes out of Sooke. The group boarded North Star in Victoria with some of their boats and canoes and aboard and others being towed astern. The voyage stopped at Port McNeill and the next day there was a flotilla and re-enactment of the European arrival at Bella-Bella with North Star of Herschel Island playing the part of the European voyagers once again.

In 1994 Silva was aboard for a March trip out to Malaspina College. They took the students out into the Strait of Juan de Fuca for a day sail. Silva came aboard again in the summer for a couple of days and they took the ship and anchored at Montague Harbour. The next day they arranged for a photographer to come out in a speedboat and photograph North Star of Herschel Island under sail. The wind picked up and the opposing current made the seas 'very rough'. As the ship was rolling with the engine off, water poured in through the exhaust pipe creating too much pressure for the motor to turn over. Sven and Silva anchored North Star under sail so that Sven could drain the engine and re-start it.

Sven received some criticism for his decision to re-rig North Star of Herschel Island as a fully-rigged ship but his plan was to use the vessel for trade wind sailing not in tacking or beating to weather. His response to critics has been to point to a carved wooden sign on the main bulkhead, "A gentleman never beats to windward." Besides, he adds, "Captain Vancouver and Captain Cook had the same rig and they sailed everywhere they wanted to."

The year of 1995 was mainly spent at anchor off of Fisherman's Wharf. One evening Sven was staring up at the rigging and he had an epiphany. He wasn't a reindeer herder, or a sailor. In his heart he was a choreographer. He envisioned dancers able to leap high above the stage. Using his sailing rig experience he designed a piece of equipment that allowed dancers, able bodied or not, to be able to do just that. He formed the Discovery Dance Society, built his dancing 'instrument' and shortly thereafter began to receive accolades from the dance communities in Prague and North Carolina, to name but two.

Sven Johansson, 2012.

In early 1996, after years of being asked by many people, including myself, to sell the ship, Sven finally relented and by the spring of that year we were her proud new owners.

Chapter 27
Sheila and Bruce's North Star Adventures

**Captain R. Bruce and Sheila Macdonald after taking
on a Northern Canadian treasure.**

After North Star of Herschel Island's adorning herself with the hanging flower basket (which was harder to remove than it was to spear in the first place) we enjoyed two days at the Saltwater Festival. Towards the end of the weekend we decided to cast off and head back down to Victoria. With the sounds of sea chantey groups serenading our departure we slowly headed south, minding the temperature of the transmission and revelling in the memories of the fine weekend.

In the late afternoon the wind began to pick up and menacing clouds started to fill the sky. We took the ship down through Baynes Channel and she began to pitch into a mounting swell. Unbeknownst to us, the wind had already picked up back at the Saltwater Festival, so much so that some of the tents had blown down and the finale had been cut short. We later learned that many of our friends were concerned about us sailing down into the storm.

By the time that we had made it down to the southern tip of Vancouver Island night was fast approaching. We could see large seas breaking over the rocks by Discovery shoals to leeward and the screaming of the wind blanketed the sound of our diesel engine. At this time the transmission began to belch smoke and the thought of taking the ship further out to sea to make the approach to Victoria was not appealing. Rolling waves were now ploughing towards us making North Star pitch heavily. I put the helm hard over and we tried to make an attempt into the protected harbour at Oak Bay Marina. Night was on us and the harbour unfamiliar. We recalled hearing that the holding ground in the anchorage was very bad and as this would be our first time anchoring the ship we carried on back up the strait and headed into Cordova Bay.

The lights of the Royal Victoria Yacht Club provided a way-point and we rolled our way over until we were abeam their clubhouse and then rounded up and let go the anchor. The lee shore at Cordova Bay is a sandy beach and there is a big playground there filled with large cement critters for children to play on, including a Cadborosorus, the local sea serpent who has been sighted for hundreds of years in these waters, akin to the Loch Ness monster or Lake Okanogan's Ogopogo. We took some bearings on the club to see if the anchor was holding. With my binoculars I could make out people sitting in the bar at the yacht club and Sheila and I joked that they were probably taking wagers on whether or not we would drag right up onto the beach. A few days later a man showed up at our dock and told me that he had been watching us from the club and that they had been betting on us.

Going forward to check the chain I laid my hand on the rode and it drew straight forward, bar tight but by the rumbling through the chain I knew that they were dragging. We laid out a second anchor, a 250 pounder on 5/8 inch chain and then let out extra chain on both of them. It appeared that they were holding for now and so we put an anchor light up and then took turns on anchor watch.

The next morning the wind had died down and we began the slow, back-breaking process of trying to unwind the anchor chains that had braided themselves around and around all night. As the first anchor cleared it brought up two abandoned crab traps, chock full of crabs who had been cannibalizing themselves since the float line to the trap had parted. We released the rest and cranked away on the storm anchor chain. It was heavy work, heavier than it should have been and the reason soon appeared - a heavy electrical cord running across the bay that we had snagged. The tension on the cord was enough to pull the bow of the ship down.

We rigged a slipping clove hitch to the cable, all the while wondering if we were going to get zapped by it, and then made that line fast to the capstan and hauled taut on that. We were then able to lower the anchor enough to clear it and then bring it a cock'a'bill, or right up to the hawse-hole. A quick tug on the clove hitch and North Star was underway once more.

The trip back in the bright sunshine reflecting off of the blue ocean was a nice finish to our first trip with the ship. We had coped with engine problems, attended a maritime event, survived a storm, dragged anchor, coped with a fouled anchor and all in all challenged our family to this new lifestyle....and loved it.

We were back out and underway to the Vancouver Wooden Boat Show as autumn drew near. It was North Star's first appearance at the event and she drew quite a crowd. Lots of people showed up and we let them tour the boat. As the weekend drew to a close the weather began to deteriorate and crossing Georgia Strait in the Salish Sea was not looking very tempting. A television station came down and made a newscast about the ship and her history. At the end of the segment the reporter asked our eldest daughter, Maida, who was about eight years old at the time what the best part of living on a boat, was. Maida piped up that "the best part of living on a boat is that you can pick your own neighbours. If you don't like the people at your marina you can just move to another one." We cast off early on the last day of the show and made it up and out of English Bay as the wind began to pick up. Our departure brought out quite a few boats who wanted to escort North Star and perhaps see us set some sail. She really is a beautiful ship.

A powerboat pulled up alongside with a radio station crew and wanted to have an interview about the ship's history. We were talking back and forth when Maida and Isabel reported that there was a strong smell of smoke coming from the engine room. As the questions from the radio station kept on coming I ran down and saw that our transmission was glowing red and there was thick black smoke coming off of it. We cut short the interview and radioed for assistance since we were now on a lee shore with building seas and wind and the engine was out of service. We set some sail and started heading back into port and were picked up by a boat called the 'Blue Flasher' who was shorter than our Whitehall dinghy but had two massive outboards on her. As Blue Flasher brought us back in we were greeted with the news that the docks that we had been on were temporary for the show and so there was limited docking now. We did find a spot and allowed the transmission to cool down.

The next day the storm had passed and we decided to head back to Victoria but very slowly. We stopped the engine several times and allowed her to cool down. We anchored out a couple of nights and had a very nice vacation with lots of swimming and hiking in the Gulf Islands. When we finally did make it back to the Canoe Club our neighbours told us that they had seen the newscast and wondered if we had decided not to come back because we didn't like them. We finished off the season by entering the Victoria Classic Boat Show where North Star won the Boater's Choice Award which is a people's choice honour for the best boat as voted on by the public that visited the show.

The highlight of our first winter aboard was the Great Snowstorm of '96. We were just getting used to living with minimal electricity, using a footpump for water and then heating it on the oil stove if we wanted hot water and using the fireplace for warmth. A record snowfall crippled the city partly because the city council had just sold off all of the snow removal equipment and we listened on the radio to reports of many people whose homes had no electricity, frozen pipes and no heat. We had the only home in Victoria that was built for the Arctic, a pantry with about two months food supplies, 450 gallons of fresh water, a generater, a wood stove and an oil stove! North Star was in her element and the snow insulated the hull which made for comfortable living. We noticed that when North Star has snow on the decks that she takes on a different sort of movement, almost as though she is enjoying it. We made snowmen on deck, had snowball fights and were sad to see it all melt away a week later.

The author after the big snowfall of '96.

Sheila in the snow.

Over the next few years we worked on re-finishing the ship outside and in. Summers were spent cruising the San Juan and Gulf Islands. We particularly liked anchoring in Montague Harbour where we often would stay a week. The small Davison dinghies would be launched so that we could do some small boat sailing and rowing and lots of swimming and berry picking. On SaltSpring Island we went horseback-riding and tried to time our arrival for the weekly market where the locals come out to sell their organic produce, fudge and tie-dyed clothing. The transmission continued to give us problems. We had it re-built twice and it continued to overheat despite all new parts. We got good at setting the Fisherman and headsails in order to keep steerage way while I checked the fluid levels and let the engine cool down.

Caption:Maida, Isabel and Sheila got to work sewing sails right after we bought the ship.

Maida and Isabel playing their bull kelp trumpets.

For the first few years we were still home-schooling Maida and Isabel and this brought lots of great opportunities for transferring standard curriculum into practical use. For instance, when we were underway, one or both girls would help with the navigation. They quickly learned how to identify light-houses and buoys, to check the serial numbers on them against the chart and then to mark an estimated position. It didn't take long for them to pick up on transferring Latitude and Longitude coordinates from the GPS onto the chart and into the logbook. When we were choosing a spot to anchor they could help with swinging or heaving the lead in order to determine the depth of water we were in.

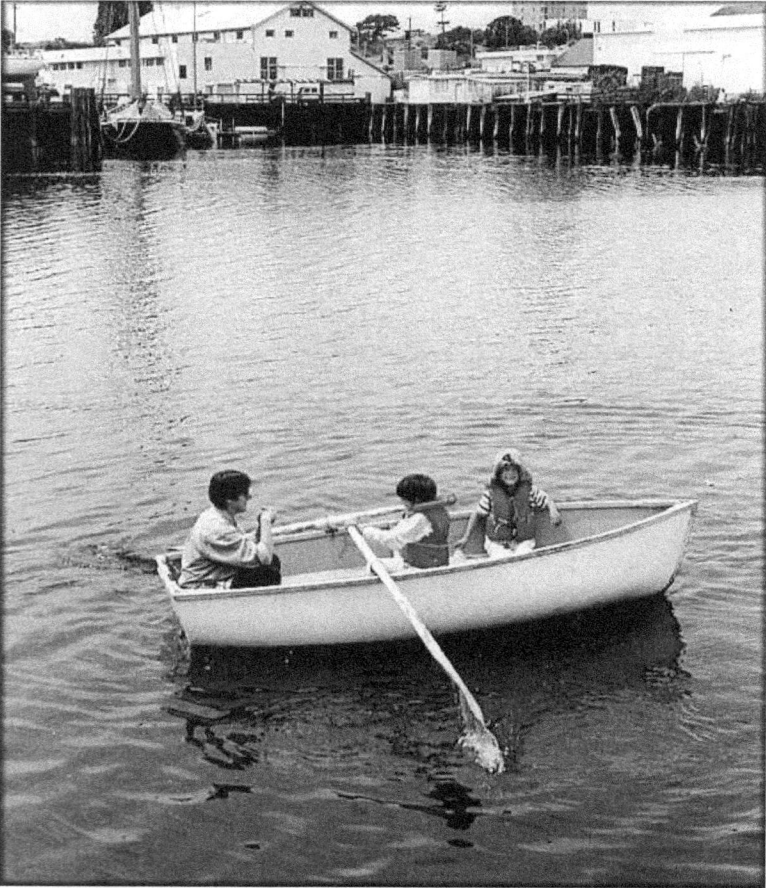

**We went rowing almost every day or evening and Maida
and Isabel were soon expert with the sweeps.**

Isabel scraping the deck.

The Macdonald family in second year aboard.

Maida varnishing the sweeps.

The ship came with crab traps and even though we are vegetarian it was fun to set the trap and then haul it up to see what we could catch. This is something that all of the children got into. After flipping the crabs over and determining their gender or maybe measuring them the girls got the idea of marking the crabs back with Sharpies or nail polish and then returning them to the sea and then trying to catch the same ones again. There were often Sea Stars to find on the pilings, shrimp and prawn cleaning off the hull and the occasional eel swimming by. People sometimes asked how it was raising kids without television and the honest answer was that there was no time for that. Even when we were alongside in the winter we had various skiffs or rowboats to be launched. Both girls became excellent at rowing. One winter we regularly rowed over to the SALTS shipyard and watched the construction of Pacific Grace, a large gaff-rigged schooner along the lines of Bluenose II. We were there for her launch and it was great that the children had been able to see her evolve from the keel up. On a much smaller scale we built our own rowing dinghy at the Victoria Classic Boat Show one year under the watchful eyes of master boatbuilder Quentin. It was like magic to see the pile of lumber transformed into something that the children had made and could be proud of. Sheila named her Twinkle and I believe that she is one of the most photographed dinghies in the harbour.

A few years into our life aboard we decided to invite a foster child into our family. It was something that Sheila and I had been thinking of doing for many years and we felt that this would be a good experience for Maida and Isabel as well as for the new child. We knew that there would be some challenges but thought that the experience of being in a loving home would be a good thing for our foster child. We worked with the Ministry for Children and Families and knew when our foster son, Evan, would be arriving. Sheila was making a quick trip to Ontario when I received a call from the Ministry telling me that Evan had a sister, Kayla, who also needed a home. I called Sheila and we quickly agreed that we would welcome her as well. Suddenly we were a family of six!

We converted the foc'sle by adding another bunk and lockers so that Kayla could live up forward with Maida and Isabel and we converted our bath/shower room into a nice cabin for Evan. We later ended up building a separate cabin for Kayla. One observation that we quickly made was how often people would talk to each and any of our four children (for we truly treated all of the children as our own) and tell them how lucky they were to be living on such a wonderful ship and in such a cool home. All of the kids grew up with a strong sense of pride in their home which was a wonderful thing to see.

One summer we headed back to the Vancouver Wooden Boat show. Aboard was Philippe MacLenahan, a French sailor who had spent most of the season with me aboard Pathfinder ten years earlier. During the show we saw our friend Pete 'Thor' Watson aboard Providence, his gaff-ketch that he had purchased and sailed back from Norway and then converted her to a fish packing boat. He needed a place to moor and so joined the wooden boat show. When it came to leave we fired up the engine and were in the process of casting off when we realised that we had no steerage way. I jumped on the dock and stuck my head in the drink. Our propeller was gone!

Pete volunteered to put on his diving gear and look for it. We lowered a small kedge with a line bent to it. He swam to the end of the line and then swam in a circle, slowly taking in the line with each circuit. After a thorough search he couldn't find it. On a hunch he made one last dive and looked directly below North Star where he found the prop – right under the kedge. He needed to cast off and get back to work after that and so once again we were on the temporary docks and broken down. Our problem now was that while we had the propeller we did not have the locking nut to keep it on.

We began scraping down North Star's hull as soon as we purchased her.

The ship sailing in more recent years.

Philippe put on his Speedo bathing suit and dove overboard with a chunk of plastercine which he used to make a mould of the threads on the shaft. With this pattern we could get a new nut made, if we could find a machine shop. We were about to go ashore to start our search when I looked up and there was another old mate from Toronto Brigantine, Phil Mansell. It was great to see him after many years and greater still when he told us that he owned his own machine shop and specialized in making things like nuts!

The next morning we had the new nut and a spare. We secured the propeller as best we could and then headed out once again. After a lovely trip sailing through the islands we participated in the Victoria Classic Boat Show again and then went back up to Saltspring Island in September, enjoying the freedom of being home-schooling parents who could sail in the off-season.

North Star of Herschel Island at anchor. Author photo.

In 2002 we were invited to participate in the American Sail Training Association's tall ship festival. The first port of call was Steveston, B.C., a fishing port on the Fraser River. We arrived the morning of the event and there were tall ships and small ships, yachts and tugs and vessels of every description off of the river mouth. The day wore on and we were told over the marine radio that the ships would enter as they were called. It was a very slow process. Finally, in the late afternoon Peter Watson on Providence got on the radio. He knows this port better than anyone and he announced that shortly, when the tide turned, that the strength of the flow coupled with the river would make entering impossible. He suggested that if anyone wanted to be alongside that night that they enter right away.

The next hour was a lesson in the International Collision Regulations as every skipper dropped the hammer on their gear box and tried to get in. It was very exciting and as we got closer we could see hundreds of thousands of people all standing ashore and waving. CBC Radio interviewed us and this was carried right across the country.

Three days later after we had given hundreds of tours to a very enthusiastic crowd we were underway again at first light. There was a strong westerly wind blowing which created large, standing waves at the shallow river mouth. After casting off we were committed to going since there was no room to turn around, especially as the whole fleet was around us. We met the first wave head on and buried our jib-boom which stands fifteen off of the water, right down to its heel. The second wave broke over our bow, roared down the deck and covered the deckhouse windows. As we rose up on the third wave using all of the power that we could muster, North Star shot off the top like a fifty ton board-sailor. The crew on the vessel abeam us said that they could see the whole bottom of our keel and our propeller.

The next ports of Anacortes, Everett and then locking up into Lake Washington and Seattle brought out more crowds and an opportunity for us to visit aboard other ships and make friends with sailors from other countries. Almost all of the fleet had made a side trip to Coos Bay, a deviation that we didn't think that our schedule would allow. Dusk was upon us when we arrived in Everett and after a very long day at sea we were ready to hit our bunks. There was a huge crowd of people lining the wharf and we assumed that they were waiting for a ferry. It turns out that the local newspaper had incorrectly reported that a whole fleet of tall ships would be pulling into their port. Many of these people had been standing on the dock all day to see a tall ship. We were it! After securing the ship we put on the smallest tall ship festival in the world as hundreds and hundreds of people queued up to tour North Star in the dark. We felt sorry for the Everett crowd at the size of the show but their enthusiasm for our Arctic ship was incredible. The tours went on for hours at which point a few other ships had pulled in and so we were able to finally get some dinner in and a bit of sleep before another early morning departure.

North Star sailing into Tacoma Harbour.

Generally, Sheila and I like an early start and we tend to let the kids sleep in while we put out to sea. It is a special time for us as we putter along, drinking our tea and enjoying the quiet of the dawn. This morning's quiet was broken by an enormous sea-lion who had slept on a large sea buoy and serenaded us as we passed him. We sold a lot of North Star tea and North Star t-shirts and later had an extra batch of them made by a street-kids association in Port Townsend and shipped down to us.

Isabel, Maida, and Kayla model the ship's sweatshirts.

Prior to the Tacoma show we were directed to an anchorage up a sheltered bay. The shallow bay had a good mud bottom and it was hard to believe that the major centers of Tacoma and Seattle were just around the corner.

In 2005, the tall ships festival began in Victoria and ended in Tacoma Washington for us. At Tacoma we brought aboard guests from that city including many dignitaries for the sail past. We put up a good spread of sail and held our position in the fleet until the wind began to pick up. With her round, copper bottom North Star of Herschel Island sails like a bat off of the wind. Once she starts slipping along and building momentum there is really no stopping her. We ended up having to turn the engine on and run it full astern in order to slow down and not get ahead of the fleet.

For the 2005 festival, North Star of Herschel Island was honoured to be named as the Official Canadian Goodwill Ambassador. This honour included the ship being led in to Tacoma harbour by members of the local First Nations band, who were wearing traditional dress, playing drums and paddling birch bark canoes. Right before we made port they came alongside of us and we exchanged goodwill gifts with them. It was a scene that could have taken place two hundred years ago and it was particularly fitting considering our ship's First Nation heritage.

As the Official Canadian Goodwill Ambassador we exchanged gifts with the local First Nations tribe as we entered Tacoma Harbour.

Over two and a half million people attended the Tacoma Festival and many of these people purchased weekend passes and returned every day. One woman whom we welcomed aboard had grown up at Sachs Harbour and remembered travelling aboard North Star as a child. She had read in the newspapers that we were bringing the ship in but couldn't believe that it was the same ship until she saw it with her own eyes. We don't often allow the general public below but this was obviously a special case. Once down below she burst into tears of happiness. Long lost memories of her childhood came rushing back to her and the experience was significant for all of us. We left her down there to go down memory lane. The next day she returned with her grandson so that he could learn another piece of his heritage, something that would have been lost had North Star never had new life breathed into her.

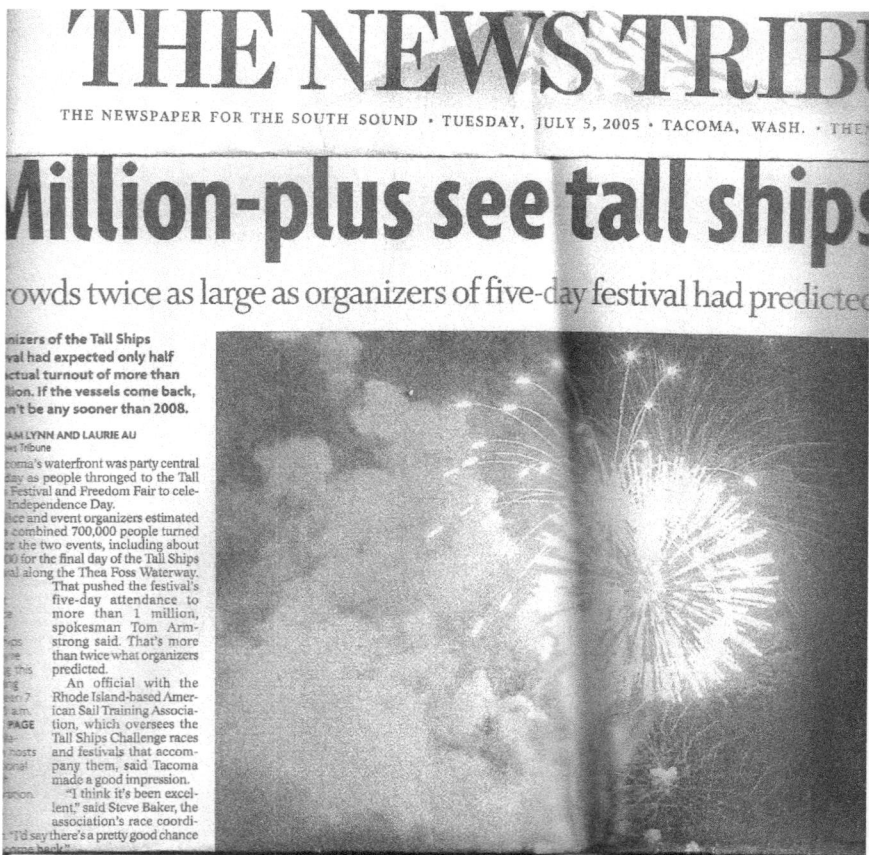

THE NEWS TRIB

THE NEWSPAPER FOR THE SOUTH SOUND · TUESDAY, JULY 5, 2005 · TACOMA, WASH. · THE

Million-plus see tall ships

Crowds twice as large as organizers of five-day festival had predicted

Organizers of the Tall Ships Festival had expected only half actual turnout of more than million. If the vessels come back, won't be any sooner than 2008.

BY ADAM LYNN AND LAURIE AU
The News Tribune

Tacoma's waterfront was party central day as people thronged to the Tall Ships Festival and Freedom Fair to celebrate Independence Day.

Police and event organizers estimated a combined 700,000 people turned out for the two events, including about 100,000 for the final day of the Tall Ships Festival along the Thea Foss Waterway.

That pushed the festival's five-day attendance to more than 1 million, spokesman Tom Armstrong said. That's more than twice what organizers predicted.

An official with the Rhode Island-based American Sail Training Association, which oversees the Tall Ships Challenge races and festivals that accompany them, said Tacoma made a good impression.

"I think it's been excellent," said Steve Baker, the association's race coordinator. "I'd say there's a pretty good chance they'll come back."

Tacoma newspaper during the Tall Ships Festival.

CANADIAN VISITOR

LUKE BOGUES/PENINSULA DAILY NEWS

Maida Macdonald, 15, of Victoria climbs the rigging of her family's tall ship, the North Star *of Herschel Island, on Thursday after it berthed at the Northwest Maritime Center dock in Port Townsend. The Macdonald family lives aboard the* North Star, *which was built in 1935 as a cargo ship for fur trading with Inuit tribes. The ship leaves today, but will return to Port Townsend for the Wooden Boat Festival on Sept. 10.*

Maida caught aloft by newspaper photographer.

North Star of Herschel Island with Bounty replica during Victoria Tall Ships Festival. Photo credit Doug Hankin.

The ship with Nina replica. By Doug Hankin.

In 2008 the ship participated in the Victoria Tall Ships Festival once again but upon leaving for Tacoma our propeller lost a blade. By the time we replaced the prop the fleet had gone and the weather had turned. We made the most of it, though, and continued to enjoy the ship. We replaced the propeller and continued to explore the San Juan and Gulf Islands with the ship. Our favourite times are when we find an anchorage and can swim off of her and just get away for awhile. As our children have grown into adults the necessity of their making money for post-secondary education combined with a severe injury that I incurred at work has meant that we have had to temporarily shorten our sailing season.

North Star of Herschel Island at anchor in Montague Harbour. Author photo.

Swimming off the ship. Author photo.

Every year or two we have entered the Victoria Classic Boat Festival. This gathering of hundreds of old powerboats and sailboats is an opportunity to meet other Captains and crews and to look at their wonderful boats. Some are immaculate, their brightwork so shiny that you can see your reflection in it. Many are works in progress but it is inspirational to see the amount of care and labour that are being injected into them. North Star of Herschel Island is always somewhere in between. As one of the oldest ships and as one who has probably been worked the hardest in her lifetime she carries her scars with Canadian pride. In 2008 she won the Peoples' Choice award for best in the festival as voted on by the general public. In 2010 she was awarded the Best Old Sailboat award as voted upon by the other participants and the festival judges. You might not be able to see your reflection in her brightwork but you can see her indomitable spirit.

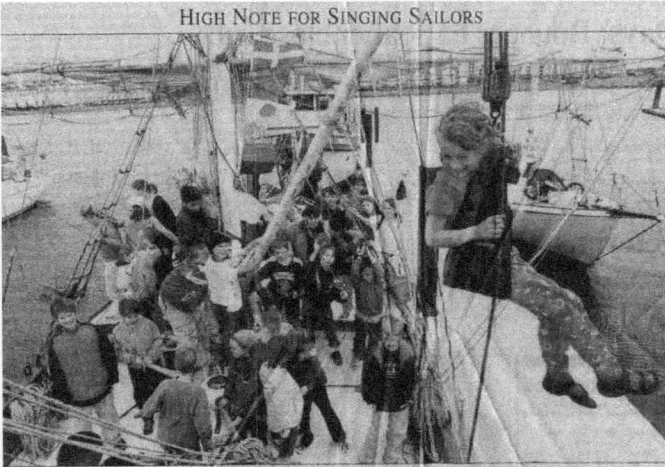

HIGH NOTE FOR SINGING SAILORS

ine-year-old Isabel MacDonald gets a bird's-eye view of the Inner Harbour from bosun's chair aboard the sailing vessel Northstar Wednesday afternoon. Macnald is a member of South Park School Intermediate choir under the direction of Marne St. Clair. The choir has been practising sea chanteys at school, and sang some of them aboard the Northstar during the year-end field trip, a B.C. sailing heritage tour. *Bruce Stotesbury/Victoria Times Colonist*

Isabel gets hauled aloft in a bosun's chair during a school tour.

Our family of six out rowing. Photo credit Diane Marsh.

It has all been worth it, though. We have sailed over 20,000 nautical miles up and down the coast and provided an interesting childhood for our two children and two foster children to grow up in. It has been a challenge at times but the values of chop wood and carry water are ones that have become a part of all of us. Living so close to nature has given us an appreciation for living in harmony with the environment that might not be so strong if we were shut off from it and being the caretakers of such a wonderful ship is a pleasant responsibility. An added bonus has been meeting many of the original owners' families and all of the other people who have stopped by the ship or written to us or joined us on the ship's website or FaceBook page.

Margaret (Carpenter) Hawkins at the helm of her Father's ship as we leave Victoria Harbour. Author photo.

Three generations of North Star of Herschel Island's owners were represented on this historic cruise.

In 2011 we were very happy to take out three generations of North Star of Herschel Islanders for a cruise off of Victoria in the Strait of Juan de Fuca. Margaret (Carpenter) Hawkins and her husband Lyle, along with their two sons and their families - Fred Carpenter's great grand-children, as well as Sven Johansson were all aboard for that historic cruise.

North Star's rigged to run with the wind.

North Star of Herschel Island under full sail. Photo credit Cindy Lee.

North Star of Herschel Island in the mist.

CONCLUSION

In conclusion, I am writing this in the warm, cozy pilot house of North Star of Herschel Island as she sits moored to the wharf in downtown Victoria, British Columbia. All around me are reminders of the stories that I have shared - small brass plaques of various tall ship festivals, classic boat shows and other adventures. There is a piece of baleen stuck above a depthsounder, a curved war paddle that was given to the ship in a First Nations ceremony and chisels made with caribou antler handles lying atop the table. Almost every day people stop and admire her strong lines and point out the heavy bronze fittings that secure the main cargo hatch or perhaps the original ship's bell or the well worn sails and hundreds of miles of rigging. Her story seems never complete as we still regularly meet people who have known her in at least one of her incarnations. She epitomises the harsh and rugged beauty of the North and the people who have sailed in her.

When Henry Larsen, the Captain of the RCMP's St. Roch was invited to the Maritime Museum to see his ship become a dry-docked exhibit he said that she "was the last vessel from an era that had lasted more then 400 years."(1) He no doubt believed that North Star, like St. Roch and all of the other "Arctic Schooners" had long since disappeared. My hope is that North Star of Herschel Island will continue to be an ambassador for the North, for Canada and as a strong symbol of Canadian Arctic Sovereignty and of the men and women who sailed in and cared for her for many years to come.

To keep abreast of North Star of Herschel Island's adventures and see even more pictures please visit her website at www.northstarofherschelisland.com or find her page on FaceBook.

Her e-mail address is northstarofherschelisland@gmail.com

ENDNOTES

A NOTE TO THE READER

1. McGhee

2. Smith Sinews of Survival p98-99

3. Page 173, Merchant Princes, Peter C. Newman

4. Taylor, People of Light and Dark, page 1

5. Corriveau, The Inuit of Canada, page 5

6. Ibid, page 16

7. Arctic Revolution

8. INUVIALUIT: A BRIEF HISTORY, page 4

9. Thrasher - Skid-Row Eskimo, page 155

10. - Mary Frost. Ottawa Citizen Correspondence

11. de Poncins, Kabloona, page ix

12. A History Original Peoples of Northern Canada, page 63

13. Thrasher - Skid-Row Eskimo, frontispiece

CHAPTER ONE

1. Nasogaluak, HERSCHEL ISLAND CULTURAL STUDY, pge 3

2. Arctic Revolution ,page 69

3. NTLGEO, May64

4. INUIT the North in Transition

5. Nasht, The Last Explorer, page 34

6. INUIT the North in Transition

7 A gentleman adventurer, page 163

8. NTLGEO, May64

9. Larsen, The Big Ship, 1967

10.Wolki, The toughest year of my life

11. Ibid, page 19

12. Ibid, page 20

13. Ibid, page 20

14. Ibid, page 25

15. Ibid, page 29

CHAPTER TWO

1. Oliver, page 4

2. Ibid, page 5

3. Iron Will and Arctic Ice page 28

4. Brown's Free Spirits, page 107

5. Herschel Island Cultural Study, page 9

6. Ibid, page 3

7. Op.Cit, Brown, page 107

8. Gruben, LIFE OF THE PIONEERS IN BANKS ISLAND. page 10

9. Ibid

10. Hunt, Rebels, Rascals & Royalty, page 134

11. Gillham, Raw North, page 136

12. OpCit, Brown, page 108

CHAPTER THREE

1. Buliard, INUK, page 38

2. Beaver Winter 1980

3. Ibid

4. Crowe, 2004

5. Erickson, True North, page 181

6. Hoskon, 2005

7. The Passing of Herschel Island, page 382

8. Bockstoce 1986:279 page 45

9. Hunt, Rebels, Rascals & Royalty

10. Canada's Arctic Sovereignty, page 100

11. Beaver Winter 1980

12. Yukon North Slope Cultural Survey, page 2

13. Red Hunters of the Snow, page 280

14. INUVIALUIT PITQUSIIT: THE CULTURE OF THE INUVIALUIT

15. Reindeer Herders of the MacKenzie Delta, page 9

16. Arctic Revolution, page 111

17. Thomas Edouget interviewed by William Hurst, page 285

18. Quotes from Yukon North Slope no 1 by Nagy, page 51

19. Merchant Princes, page 180

20. Beaver 1980

21. Across time and Tundra, page 88

22. Merchant Princes, page 190

23. A History Original Peoples of Northern Canada, page 104

24. Ibid, pge 104

25. de Poncins, KABLOONA, page 12

26. A History Original Peoples of Northern Canada, page 109

27. Bruemmer, Beaver, Herschel the Big Town, Winter 1980

28. Ibid

29. Beaver Winter 1980.

30. Cruickshank, READING VOICES, page 82

31. Passing of Herschel, page 366

32. Coccola and King, INCREDIBLE ESKIMO, page 72

33. Canada's Arctic Sovereignty, page 105

34. Ibid, page 105

35. Hudson's Bay Trader Lord Tweedsmuir, page 19

36. Burnham 1986:105

37. Cruickshank, READING VOICES, page 91

38. Arctic Revolution, page 16

39. Arctic Townsmen, page 43

40. LIFE OF THE PIONEERS IN BANKS ISLAND 1928-1929, page 13

41. Mountie on Mukluks, page 73

42. Prince of Wales Heritage Center Website

43. YUKON NORTH SLOPE CULTURAL RESOURCES SURVEY, page 9

44. TAPE 3A, 1991 YUKON NORTH SLOPE CULTURAL RESOURCES SURVEY

45. Across Time and Tundra, page 127

46. Ibid, pages 114-115

47. Nagy, Quotes from Yukon North Slope, page 50

48. I, NULIGAK, pge 143

49. Dora Malegana, page 6 of 13B

50. Fur trade posts of NWT, page 83

51. Stewart, Life in an Eskimo Village, page 44

52. Ibid, page 45

53. A History Original Peoples of Northern Canada, page 113

54. Life in an Eskimo Village, page 46

CHAPTER FOUR

1. Tale of the Lucin, page 69

2. Pacific Motor Boat, 1935

3. Brunot, 1991

CHAPTER FIVE

1. Quotes from Rough Passage by Commander Graham, page 93

1A. Hudson's Bay Trader Lord Tweedsmuir, page 15

2. A History Original Peoples of Northern Canada, page 170

3. Inuit jouney by boat, 1913, The Beaver, Winter, 1980

4. Bradbury, Ten Years in the Arctic, page 6

5. ledyard, eskimos now the world, page 115

6. INUVIALUIT PITQUSIIT: THE CULTURE OF THE INUVIALUIT, page 45

7. Paulayuuq Oral History Project, pge 243

8. INUVIALUIT PITQUSIIT: THE CULTURE OF THE INUVIALUIT, page 46

9. Arctic Townsmen, page 44

10. Op.Cit, ledyard, page 116

11.YUKON NORTH SLOPE CULTURAL RESOURCES SURVEY, page 27

12. Op.Cit, ledyard, page 119

13. Ibid, page 120

14. Paulayuuq Oral History Project, page 242

15. Ibid, page 243

16. Inuit jouney by boat, 1913, The Beaver, Winter, 1980

17. Kowichuk, A TYPICAL YEAR OF AN INUK, page 2

18. Price, THE HOWLING ARCTIC, pge 171

19. Gillham, Raw North page 121

20. Sophisticated Eskimos by R.N. Hourde and William Gibson, The Beaver, September 1952

21. Dictionary of Maritime Heritage

22. Paulayuuq Oral History Project, page 240

CHAPTER SIX

1. Madsen 1957
2. Letter, Stefansson to Desbarats, May 18 1913
3. Jenness 1991
4. Wood, Inspector RCMP, to Commissioner RCMP, Ottawa, 18 August 1931, National Archives of Canada
5. Usher, Bankslanders, Volume 1, page 37
6. Ibid, page 39
7. Jimmy Memorana Interview, September 2002,
8. Condon 1996
9. Elizabeth Banksland Interview, September 2002,
10. Raw North, page 113
11. Usher interview with Fred Carpenter
12. Ibid, page 2
13. Larsen Reports and other papers, page 76
14. Eddie Gruben interview, Tuktoyaktuk, 11/10

CHAPTER SEVEN

1. Usher, Volume 1 Bankslanders, page 6,
2. NTLGEOMay64
3. Canada's Western Arctic
4. Ibid, page 157 (Canada's Western Arctic)
5. Ibid, page 155
6. Op. Cit Volume 1 Bankslanders/ Usher
7. Volume 1 Bankslanders/ Usher, page 40
8. A History Original Peoples of Northern Canada, page 114
9. Inuvialuit, A Brief History, page 13
10. Banksland Story
11. Herschel Island Cultural Study, pge 2
12. Ibid, page 3
13. INUIT the North in Transition
14. My Name Is Masak, page 90
15. Toronto Star Weekly, Feb 19, 1927 page 28 Volume 1 Bankslanders/ Usher
16. A History Original Peoples of Northern Canada, page 113

17. Charlie and Persis Gruben, page 1

18. Ibid, page 2

19. Life of the Pioneers in Banksland, 1928-1929, pp,6,7,9

20. Ibid, page 9

21. Usher, Volume 1 Bankslanders, page 53

22. Banksland story

23. Ibid

24. Op.Cit, Usher, page 29

25. Ibid, page 29

26. Usher, Bankslanders, Volume 3

27. Macdonald, Canadian North, page 156

28. NTLGEO May64

CHAPTER EIGHT

1. Usher, Bankslanders, Volume 1, page 66

2. Life of the Pioneers in Banks Island, page 15

3. T.H. Manning an attempt to circumnavigate Banks by canoe

4. The Changing North, page 53

5. Usher, Use of Snowmobiles

6. Inuktitut 1989, 70:37 from Sinews of Survival p 109

7. Herschel Island Cultural Study, page 2

8. The Changing North page 53

9. NTLGEOMay64

10. Ibid

11. Op.Cit, Usher, page 21

12. Arctic Visions, page 15

13. Inuvialuit Final Agreement

14. NTLGEOMay64

15. Ibid

16. INUIT the North in Transition

17. Op.Cit, Usher, Volume 1, page 67

CHAPTER NINE

1. Remote outpost rolls out

2. Ibid

3. Edmonton Journal newspaper, taudette@thejournal.canwest.com

CHAPTER TEN

1. Buliard, Inuk, page 220P220,
2. Yukon North Slope Cultural Survey, page 2
3. Fred Carpenter/Goodliffe
4. Usher, Volume 1 Bankslanders, page 75
5. Ibid, pge 48
6. NTLGEOMay64
7. Settlements of the NorthWest Volume 4, 1966
8. NTLGEOMay64
9. Op.Cit, Usher, page 49Volume 1 Bankslanders/ Usher
10. Ibid, pge 49
11. Bessie Wolki Tape 4B
12. Rokeby-Thomas, Arctic Darkness
13. Red Hunters of the snow, page 280
14. Father Emile Petitot Among the Chiglit Eskimos, page 27
15. My Name Is Masak, page 90
16. NTLGEO May64
17. Among the Chiglit Eskimos, page 18
18. NTLGEO May64
19. Brown, Arctic Journal, page 210
20. Usher, Bankslanders Volume 2, page 76
21. Op.Cit, Buliard, page 189
22. Land of the Long Day, page 41
23. Inuit glimpses of an Arctic past page 66
24. McIntyre, Quiet and Reserved Splendor, page 38
25. Arctic Visions, page 15
26. Ibid, page 15
27. Bertram Pokiak, Tuktoyaktuk. page 78
28. INUK by Buliard, page 216
29. HUNTERS OF THE NORTHERN ICE, page 182
30. Usher interview with Fred Carpenter, July 18TH, 1967, page 12
31. LeMeur, Banksland Story, page 6
32. Yukon North Slope Cultural Resources Survey, page 8
33. Ibid, page 4
34. Op.Cit, Usher Volume 1,, page 51
35. Usher, The Inuk as Trapper, Volume 2 pp. 207-216.

36. Hunters of the Northern Ice, page xiv

37. Nagy, Quotes from Yukon North Slope no 1, pge 84

38. Forget veggies - get vitamins from blubber

39. Ibid

40. Encounters with Arctic Animals, page 108

41. Op.Cit, Buliard, page 213

42. Thomas Edouget interviewed by William Hurst, page 284

43. HUNTERS OF THE NORTHERN ICE, page xiv

44. Op.Cit, Usher Volume 2, page 1

45. Irniq, preface to Sacred Hunt by David F. Pelly,

46. NTLGEO May64

47. I was no lady, page 130

48. Carpenter, UNESCO, page 15

49. Encounters with Arctic Animals, page 107

50. Op.Cit, Buliard, page 214

51. Pat Barry from the singing of Al Cox . As found on Digital Tradition.

CHAPTER TWELVE

1. Banksland Story p28

2. LIFE OF THE PIONEERS IN BANKS ISLAND 1928-1929, page 23

3. YUKON NORTH SLOPE CULTURAL RESOURCES SURVEY, page 5

4. Usher, Volume 1 Bankslanders, page 50

5. LIFE OF THE PIONEERS IN BANKS ISLAND 1928-1929 page 10

6. Hohn, Arctic Schooner Voyage

7. HUNTERS OF THE NORTHERN ICE, page 33

8. LIFE OF THE PIONEERS IN BANKS ISLAND 1928-1929, page 9-10

9. Arctic Crossing, page 66

10. Ibid page 67

11. My Name Is Masak, page 67

12. Ibid, page 95

13. Arctic Schooner Voyage/Hohn

14. Arctic Passage, Bockstoce, page 212

15. Arctic Schooner Voyage/Hohn

16. My Name Is Masak, page 94

17. Usher, Volume 1 Bankslanders

18. Gillham, Raw North, p. 120

19. Arctic Schooner Voyage

20. Kasteltein, Relic of Arctic Transportation, page 4

21. Op.Cit, Hahn, , p 27

22. Ibid page 27

23. Noah Piugaattuk 1983 p.. 117

24. Kroetsch, The oral tradition is like the Mackenzie Delta

25. VOL.VI NO.3 THE ARCTIC CIRCULAR 27

26. Herschel Island Cultural Study, page 8

27. Bruemmer, Arctic Memories, page 27

28. Op.Cit, Usher, page 45

29. Ibid pge 46

30. Ibidpage 46

3 Op.Cit, Usher

32. YUKON NORTH SLOPE CULTURAL RESOURCES SURVEY, page 2

33 Op.Cit, Usher, page 54

34. Ibid, page 54

35. Ibid, page 55

36. Ibid, pge 55

37. Lopez, Arctic Dreams, page 43

38. Op.Cit, Usher, page 47

39. Op.Cit, Hunt, pge 122

CHAPTER THIRTEEN

1. Stewart, Life in an Eskimo Village, page 27

2. The Eskimo of North Atlantic, page 73

3. INUVIALUIT PITQUSIIT: THE CULTURE OF THE INUVIALUIT, page 11

4. Op.Cit. Stewart, page 27

5. File 11458

6. Across Time and Tundra

7. Plowing the Arctic, page 123

8. Inuit: Glimpses of an Arctic Past .

9. Sophisticated Eskimo, page 36

10. The Dictionary of Arctic Maritime Heritage, page 76

11. Heroes: Canadian Champions, Dark Horses & Icons, page 2

12. NATIVES AND OUTSIDERS, page 54

13. Stewart, Life in an Eskimo Village, page 28

14. Merchant Princes, page 175

15. Report 11458, Sept, 12, 1941

16. leMeur, from the introduction to True Experiences - Men of the North

17. Mowat, High Latitudes, pp. 240-41

18. Berton, The Mysterious North.275-76, 373

19. A History Original Peoples of Northern Canada, page 23

CHAPTER FOURTEEN

1. INUK by Buliard, page 39

2. The Big Thaw, page 8

3. Herschel Island Cultural Study, page 7 of 10b

4. LeMeur, OUR LADY OF LOURDES, page 16

5. Op.Cit., Buliard, pge 40

6. Ibid, page 40

7. Herchel Island Cultural Survey, page 24

8. Ibid, page 24

9. I, NULIGAK, page 149

10. Father Deheurvent, page 106

11. Cockney footnote page 106

12. p. 94 I, NULIGAK

13. Gruben Interviews, page 2

14. Ibid, page 4

15. Ibid, page 5

16. Ibid, page 5

17. Ibid, page 6

18. Aulavik Oral History Project Tape Number N92-007-894A, page 1

19. Op.Cit, Gruben, page 7

20. Op.Cit , Aulavik, page 2.

21.Op.Cit., Gruben, page 8

22. Ibid , page 9

23. Aulavik Oral history Project, page 2

24. Op.Cit., Gruben, page 11

25. Ibid, page 11

26. Op.Cit, Aulavik

27. Herschel Study tape 24B, page 3

28. Arctic Passage by Bockstoce, page 92-93

29. Herschel Island Cultural Study

30. Ibid

31. Ibid

32. Yukon North Slope Cultural Resources Survey, page 8

33. Herschel Island Cultural study, page 8 of 10A

34. Kowichuk, A Typical Year of an Innuk

35. The Big Thaw by Ed Struzik p 144

36. Confessions of an Igloo Dweller, page 29

37. Nuyaviak, Mangilalik Adrift on the ice, page 4

38. Learmonth, Interrupted Journey, page 24

39. Brown, Free Spirits, page 97

40. ledyard, eskimos now the world, page 121

41. Ibid page 197

42. Ibid, page 200

43. Op.Cit, Kowichuk, page 5

44. Tranter, Plowing the Arctic

45. I,NULIGAK, page 95

46. Op.Cit, Buliard, page 40

47. Bessie Andreason, page 2

48. Confessions of an Igloo Dweller, page 29

49. Struzik, The Big Thaw, p. 145

50. White, MOUNTIE IN MUKLUK, page 45/6

51. Dobrin/Saga of St. Roch p 43

52. Op.Cit, Kowichuk, page 5

53. Dueck, Voyage Through the NorthWest Passage

CHAPTER FIFTEEN

1. Thrasher - Skid-Row Eskimo page 31

2. Tranter, Plowing the Arctic, page 104

3. Larsen's reports, page 70

4. Op.Cit, Tranter, page 115

5. Ibid, page 116

6. Ibid, page 117

7. Usher 4A, page 7

8. Op.Cit, Tranter, page 118

9. Ibid, page 119

10. Larsen's reports, page 72

11. Op.Cit, Tranter, page 119

12. Ibid, page 120

13. Ibid, page 120

14. Ibid, page 120

15. Larsen's reports, page 73

16. Op.Cit, Tranter, page 122

17. Ibid, page 123

18. Ibid, page 123

19. Ibid, page 124

CHAPTER SIXTEEN

1. Nagy, Quotes from Yukon North Slope no 1, page 105

2. Thrasher - Skid-Row Eskimo, page 57

3. THE INUIT WAY - A GUIDETO INUIT CULTURE, page 12

4. Op.Cit, Nagy, page 105

5. THE INUIT WAY - A GUIDETO INUIT CULTURE, page 13

6. Stewart, Life in an Eskimo Village, page 26

7. Op.Cit, Nagy, page 101

8. The Changing North, page 50

9. INUVIALUIT PITQUSIIT: THE CULTURE OF THE INUVIALUIT, page 20

10. Ibid, page 21

11. Hunt, Rebels, Rascals & Royalty

12. THE INUIT WAY - A GUIDETO INUIT CULTURE, page 13

13. Op.Cit. Hunt

14. Op.Cit, Nagy, page 101

15. Leechman, Beauty's only skin deep, page 38

16. Ibid, page 38

17. Op.Cit, Nagy, page 3

18. Herschel Island Cultural Survey, page 3

19. A History Original Peoples of Northern Canada, page 57

20. Op.Cit, Herschel Island, 9 of 9A

21. Ibid, page 9 of 8A

22. Op.Cit, Gruben page 18

23. Emma Malegana Edwards, page 8 of 22A

24. Sir Hubert Wilkins, Enigma of Exploration, page 45

25. Buliard, INUK, page 50

26. Op.Cit, Gruben, page 18

27. Encounters with Arctic Animals, page 108

28. I was no lady, page 130

29. Hunt, Rebels, Rascals & Royalty, ppp 120/121

30. de Poncins, KABLOONA page 48

31. THE INUIT WAY - A GUIDETO INUIT CULTURE, page 17

32. Ibid, page 17

33. Ibid, page 17

34. Op.Cit, White p. 63/64

35. NATIVES AND OUTSIDERS, page 54

36. NTLGEO, May64

37. NATIVES AND OUTSIDERS, page 55

38. Ibid, page 59

39. Father dehurtevent

40. Arctic Crossing, page 119

41. Ibid, page 119

42. Herschel Island Cultural Survey, page 6.

43. NTLGEO, May64

44. Ibid

45. Ibid

46. Ibid

47. Ibid

48. Ibid

49. Ibid

50. Ibid

51. Ibid

52. INUVIALUIT PITQUSIIT: THE CULTURE OF THE INUVIALUIT, page 14

CHAPTER SEVENTEEN

1. Gordon Pinsent radio show Late Show onFlorence Carpenter

2. Les Carpenter from Gordon Pinsent show)

3. Canadian North, page 162

4. Arctic Revolution, page 10

5. Arctic Revolution, page 11

6. Op.Cit, Pinsent

7. Op.Cit, Pinsent

8. Op.Cit, Pinsent

9. Op.Cit, Pinsent

10. Op.Cit, Pinsent

11. Op.Cit, Pinsent

12. Op.Cit, Pinsent

CHAPTER EIGHTEEN

1. Gruben, Life of the Pioneers in Banks Island, 1928-1929, page 12

2. My Name Is Masak, page 56

3. Thrasher, Herschel Island cultural Study, page 4 of 10B

4. Within the Circle, page 140

5. Inuvialuit Pitquisit: the culture of the inuvialuit, page 61

6. Thrasher, Skid-Row Eskimo, page 68

7. Ibid, page 68

8. Gillham, Raw North, page 115

9. Ibid, page 71

10. Within the Circle, page 140

11. Usher, Volume 1 Bankslanders, page 51

12. Pioneer of the North The Stan Peffer Story, page 32

13. Ibid, page 37

14. Vyvyan 1961 57-75

15. Arctic Townsmen, page 49

16. Berton, The Mysterious North, pp. 275-76

17. Cf Kennicott, page110

18. Macdonald, Arctic Townsmen, pp 139/40

19. Canadian North page 158

20. Livingstone of the Arctic, page 130

21. Ibid, page 159

22. WITHIN THE CIRCLE, page 139

23. Livingstone of the Arctic, page 129

24. Ibid, page 130

25. Canadian North

26. Livingstone of the Arctic, page 130

27. Macdonald, Canadian North page 155

28. LeMeur, Aulavik Oral History Project, page N92

29. Op.Cit, Macdonald, page 155

30. Livingstone of the Arctic. page 130

31. Thrasher, Skid-Row Eskimo Eskimo page 44

32. Persis and Charlie Gruben, tape 2a

33. Ibid, tape 2a,

34. Op.Cit, Thrasher, page 66

35. Mary Frost Carpenter memory

36. Nagy, Yukon North Slope Cultural Resources Survey, page 5

37. WITHIN THE CIRCLE page 136

38. Mary Frost Carpenter memory

39. Bruemmer, Arctic Memories, page 118

40. Stan Peffer story, page 21

41. Ibid, page 22

42. Ibid, page 22

43. Encounters with Arctic Animals, page 107

44. Pioneer of the North, Story pge 48

45. Ibid, page 49

46. Ibid, page 54

47. Ibid, page 54

48. Usher, Volume 1 Bankslanders, page 51

CHAPTER NINETEEN

1. Usher, Volume 1 Bankslanders, page 63

2. My Name Is Masak page 51

3. Mowat, High Latitudes, p 242

4. Frost, UNESCO, page 18

5. Inuvialuit Pitquisit: the culture of the Inuvialuit page 58

6. My Name Is Masak page 19

7. Life in an Eskimo Village page 54

8. Among the Chiglit Eskimos xi

9. Thomas Edouget interviewed by William Hurst page 29

10. Life in an Eskimo Village page 53

11. Inuvialuit Final Agreement

12. NTLGEOMay64

13. My Name Is Masak page 44

14. Arctic Townsmen page 38

15. Bruemmer, Arctic Memories, page 15

16. NTLGEOMay64

CHAPTER TWENTY

1. Lemeur, OUR LADY OF LOURDES, page 1

2. Ibid, page 1

3. Ibid, page 2

4. Thomas Edouget interviewed by William Hurst

5. Coccola and King, Incredible Eskimo, page 36

6. Thrasher, Herschel Island Cultural Study page 9

7. Dehurtevent, Paulatuuq Oral History Project

8. Op.Cit, Lemeur, page 8

9. Ibid, page 8

10. Ibid, page 10

11. Ibid, page 12

CHAPTER TWENTY-ONE

1. Usher's The Bankslanders, Volume 3

2. Price, The Howling Arctic, page 151

3. Ibid, page 150

4. Canada's Arctic Sovereignty page 113

5. Hunt, Rebels, Rascals & Royalty page 106

6. Ibid, page 107

7. memo Sept 6, 1951

8. Op.Cit, Hunt, page 107

9. Usher, Volume 1 Bankslanders, page 56

10. Op Cit, Usher, page 54

11. Ibid, page 54

12. Changing North page 239

13. Royal Tour of Canada Schedule

14. Ibid

15. Livingstone of the Arctic page 159

16. Gilham Raw North page 241

17. Arctic Circular

18. Ibid

19. Op.Cit, Hunt, page 198

20. Pierre Trudeau, January 1, 1970 from preface (the Howling Arctic by Ray Price)

21. Thrasher - Skid-Row Eskimo page 162

22. de Poncins, KABLOONA, page 43

23. Robert Kuptana, born 1943 from the IRC 25th anniversary book page 91

24. Land of the Long Day, page 29

CHAPTER TWENTY-TWO

1. Rebels, Rascals & Royalty

2. Stan Rogers

CHAPTER TWENTY-THREE

1. Salt of all trades

2. Adventurer finds life

3. Inglis, Back to Victoria

4. Ibid

5. Salt Of All Trades

6. Ibid

CHAPTER TWENTY-FOUR

Sachs Harbour Newsletter

CHAPTER TWENTY-FIVE

1. Stewart, Life in an Eskimo Village, page 29

2. The Changing North, page 51

CHAPTER TWENTY-SIX

1. MacKenzie Yesterday and Beyond, pae 154

2. Scientific American Magazine, July 31, 2006

3. Sven Johansson, personal correspondance

4. Sea of Bear, page 55

5. Robinson, The Vancouver Sun, January 10, 1975: Family Sailors Blow in on Star by page C21

6. Ibid

7. Arctic Passage Bockstoce page 99

8. Op.Cit, Robinson, page C21

9. Op.Cit, Robinson, page C21

10. Op.Cit, Robinson, page C21

11. Op.Cit, Robinson, page C21

12. Op.Cit, Robinson, page C21

13. Report, page 4

14. www.nauticapedia.ca

15. Back to Victoria/Inglis

16. Cowichan News, January 28, 1981, Inuit Boat Crew Hones Skills For North at Cowichan Bay, page A15

17. Gulf Islands Driftwood "School Children get a taste of roguish sailing culture"

18. Sven interview, Gulf Islands Driftwood - undated

19. Document dated March 16, 1981 from Canadian Marine Drilling Ltd, Calgary Alberta - a reference letter stating that SJ "did conduct and supervise a training course in basic seamanship and boat handling for Canadian Marine Drilling Ltd at Vancouver Island, BC during January and February 1981.

20. Smeeton, The Misty Islands

21. Golder/Berings Voyage Volume II

22. ARCTIC: ENIGMAS & MYTHS, page 63

23. High Endeavours, page 347

23A Ibid, page 347

24. Salt of all Trades

CONCLUSION

1. Dobrin, Saga of the St. Roch, p 43

Bibliography

Advisory Committee Northwest Territories (as prepared for, Settlements of theNorthwest Territories Volume 4 Ottawa, 1966.

Alexander, Bryan and Cherry. What Do We Know About the Inuit? Peter Bedrick Books, New York, 1995.

Allen, Dennis (writer & director). CBQM. A National Film Board of Canada Production. Ottawa.

Allen, Dennis (writer & director). DVD: The Hunt and the Walk. MacKenzie Delta Films.

Allen, Dennis (writer & director). DVD: my father my teacher. MacKenzie Delta Films/Big Barn Entertainment in co-production with the National Film Board of Canada. 2005.

Alunik, Ishmael & Eddie d. Kolausok & David Morrison. Across Time and Tundra: The Inuvialuit of the Western Arctic. Raincoast Books, Vancouver. 2003.

Alunik Ishmael, Call Me Ishmael: Memories of an Inuvialuk Elder Kolausok Ublaaq Enterprises, Inuvik, 1998.

An officer of the Viewforth of Killarney, Sufferings of the Ice-Bound Whalers William Whyte and Co., Edinburgh, 1776.

Anderson, Alun, AFTER THE ICE: Life, Death, and GeoPolitics in the New Arctic. Smithsonian Books, New York, 2009.

Andreason, Bessie. "Time of Trial and Sorrow". from True Experiences - Men of the North, self-published - undated.

Anon, Alaska Boundary. Vancouver Province, Vancouver. September 23, 1912.

Anon. Arctic Schooners. Vancouver Province, Vancouver. March 19, 1913.

Anon. Arctic Schooners 'Moras' & ' Kittiwack'. Vancouver Province, Vancouver. March 22, 1913.

Anon. Elvira. Vancouver Province, Vancouver, November 12, 1913.

Anon. "George Kneass. S.F. Boat Builder", Pacific Motor Boat Magazine, February, 1932

Anon. Mary Sachs. Vancouver Province, Vancouver. February 24, 1914.

Anon. New Gasoline Schooner for Hudson's Bay Company. Vancouver Province, Vancouver, September 17, 1913.

Anon. NWT Dog Sledding Association, Mushers' Manual, NWT Dog Sledding Association, 1999.

Anon. 'Schooner Our Lady of Lourdes Safe', CatholicHerals.co.uk, page 7, 5th December 1941.

Anon. "The Metropolis of the Pacific Coast - A History", Bay of San Francisco - a History Volume 1, Lewis Publishing Company, Chicago, 1892.

Anon. The Northern Schooners (Transit, Mary Sachs, Alaska, North Star, Belvedere). Vancouver Province, Vancouver, September 26, 1913.

Anon. The Northern Schooners (Hettie B, Mary Sachs, Alaska, Polar Bear, Elvira, North Star), Vancouver Province, Vancouver, September 27, 1913.

Anon. "Yacht was first to travel Arctic west to east under sail", Times-Colonist (newspaper) page D15, Victoria, Friday November 25, 1988

Apakark, Anthony. THRASHER: Skid-Row Eskimo Thrasher, Griffin House, Toronto, 1976.

Aquilina Alfred P. MacKenzie Yesterday and Beyond, The Hancock House, North Vancouver, 1981.

Arthur, James, Allen. A Whaler & Trader in the Arctic 1885-1944: my life with the bowhead , Alaska Northwest Publishing Company, Anchorage, 1978.

Atwood, Margaret. Strange Things: The Malevolent North in Canadian Literature. Clarendon Press, Oxford. 1995.

Aurora Research Institute. Doing Research in the Northwest Territories: A guide for researchers Aurora College, 1998.

Ayles, G. Burton and Norman B. Snow. Canadian Beaufort Sea 2000: The Environmental and Social Setting, ARCTIC Magazine, 2001, VOL. 55, SUPP. 1 (2002) P. 4–17

Baker, Peter. Memoirs of an Arctic Arab: the story of a free-trader in Northern Canada Yellowknife Publishing Company, Yellowknife, 1976

Balikci, Asen. The Netsilik Eskimo Natural History Press, Garden City, 1970.

Banerjee, Subhankar (Ed.) Arctic Voices: Resistance at the Tipping Point. Seven Stories Press, New York, 2012.

Banks Island Newsletter. THE NORTH STAR SAILS AGAIN..., Sachs Harbour, NWT, Issue #1, August 1968

Banting, Erinn. Canadian Aboriginal Art and Culture : the Inuit Weigl, Calgary, 2008

Barr, William. Red Serge and Polar Bear Pants: the biography of Harry Stallworthy, RCMP. University of Alberta Press, Edmonton, 2004.

Bartlett, Captain 'Bob'. Sails Over Ice Charles Scribner's Sons New York, 1934.

Bartlett, Robert A. THE KARLUK'S LAST VOYAGE: an epic of death and survival in the Arctic. Cooper Square Press, New York, 2001.

Basque, Garnet (ed). Frontier Days in the Yukon Sunfire Publications, Langley. 1991.

Bastedo, Jamie. Reaching North: a celebration of the subarctic Red Deer College Press, Red Deer, 1998.

Beaver,The. 'News of the Fur Trade' Dispatches, June, 1934.

Beaver, The. 'News of the fur Trade' Dispatches, December, 1939.

Bennett, John and Susan Rowley. Uqalurait (compiled and edited by) : An Oral History of Nunavut, McGill-Queen's University Press, Monteal, 2005.

Bennett, Paul. Her Lines and Her Name Hint of a Romantic Past. The Daily Colonist, Victoria, 1978.

Berton, Pierre. The Mysterious North, McLelland and Stewart, Toronto, 1956.

Berton, Pierre. WHY WE ACT LIKE CANADIANS: a personal exploration of our national character. McClelland & Stewart, Toronto, 1984.

Bertram, Colin. Arctic & Antarctica: a Prospect of the Polar Regions. W. Heffer & Sons Ltd, Cambridge, 1958.

Bial, Raymond. The Inuit Benchmark Books, New York, 2002.

Billington, Keith. COLD LAND, WARM HEARTS: more memories of an Arctic Medical Outpost, Lost Moose - an imprint of Harbour Publishing, Madeira Park, 2010.

Blohm, Hans-Ludwig, (The) Voice of the Natives: the Canadian North and Alaska Penumbra Press, Ottawa, 2001.

Bockstoce, John R., ARCTIC DISCOVERIES: images from voyages of four decades in the north, University of Washington Press, Seattle, 2000.

Bockstoce, John. Arctic Passage : a unique small boat voyage in the great Northern waterway, Hearst Marine Books, 1991.

Bockstoce, John R., Steam Whaling in the Western Arctic Old Darmouth Historical Society, New Bedford. 1977.

Bockstoce, John R., Whales, Ice, & Men University of Washington Press, Seattle, 1986.

Boult, David. The Inuit Way: a guide to Inuit Culture Pauktuutit, no publishing data.

Bradbury, Cecil E. Ten Years in the High Canadian Arctic Books, St John's. 1994.

Briggs, Jean L. Never in Anger: Portrait of an Eskimo Family Harvard University Press, Cambridge, 1970.

Brody, Hugh. Living Arctic - Hunters of the Canadian North Douglas & McIntyre, Vancouver, 1987.

Brody, Hugh. The Other Side of Eden : Hunters, Farmers, and the Shaping of the World, North Point Press, New York, 2001.

Brown, Bern Will A Time in the Arctic, Friesens, Altona, 2007.

Brown, Bern Will. The Aklavik Journal: a reprint of the community newspaper of Aklavik NorthWest Territories 1955-57. Bern Will Brown, Colville Lake, 1996.

Brown, Bern Will. Arctic Journal Novalis, Ottawa, 1988.

Brown, Bern Will. Arctic Journal (Volumes 1 & 2): A Fifty- Year Adventure in Canada's North, Novalis, Ottawa, 2003.

Brown, Bern Will. Free Spirits: Portraits from the North, Novalis, Toronto, 2007.

Bruce, Donald. Yukon Calling. Self Published, Vancouver, 1973.

Bruemmer, Fred. Arctic Memories: Living with the Inuit Key Porter Books, Toronto, 1993.

Bruemmer, Fred. Arctic Visions: Pictures From A Vanished World. Key Porter Books, Toronto, 2008.

Bruemmer, Fred. Canadian Arctic "This Is Your Home" Victoria Daily Times Weekend Magazine, Vol. 20 No. 7 - Feb 14, 1970. Victoria, B.C. 1970.

Bruemmer, Fred. Encounters with Arctic Animals McGraw-Hill Ryerson Limited, Toronto, 1972.

Bruemmer, Fred. 'Herschel! the Big Town' The Beaver Magazine, Winnipeg, Winter 1980.

Bruemmer, Fred. Seasons of the Eskimo - A Vanishing Way of Life McClelland and Stewart, Toronto, 1971.

Bruemmer, Fred. (principal writer & photographer), Dr W.E. Taylor General Editor. THE ARCTIC WORLD. Century Publishing, London, 1985.

Buliard, Roger P. INUK, Farrar, Strauss and Young, New York, 1951.

Burn, C.R. "After Whom Is Herschel Island Named?", Arctic Journal, Arctic Institute of North America, Vol. 62, No 3, 2009.

Burnham, George H. The White Road: A True Story, Interlake Graphics, 1986.

Butters, Tom. Personal Correspondance, June 2011.

Byers, Michael. 'Every Arctic Voyage is a Potential Disaster', Ottawa Citizen, September 3, 2010.

Canadian Broadcasting Company (CBC): DVD: The Northerners, Ottawa. March 8, 1978.

Cantwell, Sister Margaret. SSA in collaboration with Sister Mary George Edmmond SSA, North to Share: the Sisters of Saint Ann in Alaska and the Yukon Territory Sisters of Saint Ann, Victoria, 1992.

Carpenter, David. Welcome to Canada. Porcupine's Quill, Erin, 2009.

Carpenter, Edmund (ed). COMOCK - the true story of an Eskimo hunter as told to & by Robert Flaherty, David R. Godine, Boston, 2003.

Carrighar, Sally. Icebound Summer. Alfred A. Knopf, New York, 1953.

Carrighar, Sally. MOONLIGHT AT MIDDAY. Penguin Books, London, 1961.

Carter, Karla and Audrey Simser, (editors). Tuktyaktuk/Tuktuuyaqtuq 1997.

Cavell, Janice & Jeff Noakes. ACTS OF OCCUPATION: Canada and Arctic Sovereignty, 1918-25. UBC Press, Vancouver, 2010.

Chance, Norman A. The Eskimo of North Alaska. Holt, Rinehart and Winston, New York, 1966.

Clark, Miles. High Endeavours: The extraordinary life and adventures of Miles & Beryl Smeeton. Greystone Books, Vancouver, 1991.

Coates, Kenneth. Best Left As Indians: Native-White Relations in the Yukon Territory, 1840-1973. McGill-Queens University Press, Montreal, 1991.

Coates, Kenneth and Judith Powell. The Modern North: People, Politics and the Rejection of Colonialism James Lorimer & Company, Toronto, 1989.

Cockney, Catherine. Paulatuuq Oral History Project: Interview Transcripts of Father Leonce DeHurtevent Parks Canada, Inuvik, 2002.

Conaty, Gerald T. with LLoyd Binder. Reindeer Herders of the MacKenzie Delta Key Porter Books, Toronto, 2003.

Cole, Bryan Gunner (Ed). DVD: Arctic Son. Docurama Films - a film by Andrew Walton, 2007.

Condon, Richard G with Julia Ogina and the Holman Elders, Foreword by the Honorable Nellie Cournoyea. The Northern Copper Inuit : A History, University of Press, Toronto, 1996.

Conibear, Kenneth. Arctic Adventures with Lady Greenbelly Trafford Publishing, 2000.

Cook, John A. PURSUING THE WHALE: a quarter-century of whaling in the Arctic. Houghton Mifflin Company, Boston, 1926.

Copland, Dudley. Livingstone of the Arctic: first resident physician to the Inuit - first Arctic milkman. with a foreword by A.Y. Jackson. Canadian Century Publishers, Lancaster, 1978.

Corley-Smith, Peter. 10,000 Hours: A Helicopter Pilot in the North, Sono Nis Press, Victoria, 2002.

Corriveau, Danielle. THE INUIT OF CANADA, Lerner Publications, Minneapolis, 2002.

Cotter, H.M.S., 'A Fur Trade Glossary', The Beaver Magazine, September, 1941.

Cowan, Susan (editor). We Don't Live in Snow Houses Now Canadian Arctic Producers Limited, Arctic Bay, 1976.

Cowell, Doug with Graham Osborne (photos). 'Making the Jump into a Dark Fiord', Beautiful British Columbia Magazine, Vancouver, Winter, 1994, Vol 36 #4.

Cox, Lynne. South With the sun: Roald Amundsen, his polar explorations, & the quest for discovery. Alfred A. Knopf, New York, 2011.

Crisp, W.G., The Casual Kogmoliks, The Beaver, pages 50-53, Winter 1963.

Crowe, Keith. J. A HISTORY OF THE ORIGINAL PEOPLES OF NORTHERN CANADA . Arctic Institute of North America, McGill-Queens University Press, Montreal 1974.

Crowe, M.J., A Calendar of the Correspondence of Sir John Herschel. Cambridge, Cambridge University Press, 1998.

Cruikshank, Julie. Life Lived Like a Story - life stories of three Yukon Elders University of Nebraska Press, 1990.

Cruiksjank, Julie. Reading Voices - Dan Dha Ts'edenintth'e: Oral and Written Interpretations of the Yukon's Past Douglas & McIntyre, Vancouver, 1991.

Dahl, Jens. Saqqaq: an Inuit Hunting Community in the Modern World University of Toronto Press, Toronto, 2000.

Dalton, Anthony. THE FUR-TRADE FLEET:Shipwrecks of the Hudson's Bay Company. Heritage House, Victoria, 2011.

Daly, Tom with Colin Low (Director) and Wolf Koenig (Producer). DVD: YUKON GOLD, National Film Board of Canada, Ottawa, 1955.

Davis, Richard C. (Ed). Lobsticks and Stone Cairns: Human Landmarks in the Arctic, University of Calgary Press, Calgary, 1997.

de Coccola Raymond and Paul King. The Incredible Eskimo: Life Among the Barren Land Eskimo Hancock House Publishers, Surrey, 1986.

Dehurtevent, Father Leonce. Paulatuuq Oral History Project, Interview Transcripts of Father Dehurtevent. Catherine Cockney, Parks Canada, Inuvik, 2002.

Delgado, James P. ACROSS THE TOP OF THE WORLD: the quest for the northwest passage. Douglas & McIntyre, Vancouver, 1999.

Devillier Donegan. The Living Edens: Arctic Oasis DVD, PBS.

Dick, Lyle. Muskox Land University of Calgary Press, Calgary. 2001.

Dickson, Frances Jewel. The DEW Line Years: Voices from the coldest war Pottersfield Press, Lawrencetown Beach 2007.

Dignard, Martin J. and William Reeve (directors). DVD: Great North (Mother Earth), Hydro-Quebec, 2006.

Dobrin, Michael. "Iron Will and Arctic Ice: the last of the whaling men", Up Here magazine, Yellowknife, September, 1992.

Dobrin, Michael. "Saga of the St. Roch", Up Here Magazine, Yellowknife, March, 1992.

Donrin, Michael. "She Sailed Into History", Up Here Magazine, Yellowknife, Nov./Dec, 1990.

Dobrowolsky, Helen. A History of the Tr'ondek Hwech'in.

Dobrowolsky, Helen. Law of the Yukon Lost Moose, Whitehorse, 1995.

Douglas, William O. Banks Island: Eskimo Life on the Polar Sea National Geographic Magazine, Washington, May 1964.

Down, Susan. "North Star is Their Home", Islander Magazine, Times Colonist Newspaper, Victoria, Aug. 9, 1998.

Down, Susan. 'Square Dance', Pacific Yachting, Vancouver, October, 1996.

Dueck, Cameron. The New NorthWest Passage, Great Plains Publications, Winnipeg, 2012.

Duffy, R. Quinn. The Road to Nunavut: the progress of the eastern Arctic Inuit since the second world war. McGill Queen's University Press, Montreal, 1988.

Duke, Warren. Sailing Out of the North: full-rigged Inuit ship tours coast. On the Docks, 1990.

Duncan, Allan. introduction by Pierre Berton. Medicine, Madams & Mounties : Stories of a Yukon Doctor 1933-1947 Raincoast Books, Vancouver, 1989.

Edmonton Journal Service. 'Remote outpost rolls out welcome mat for RCMP', Canada.com, 8/21/2010

Elliot. Nan. "I'd Swap My Old Skidoo For You" Sammamish Press, Issaquah. 1989.

Emmerson, Charles. The Future History of the Arctic. Public Affairs, New York, 2010.

Erickson, George. True North: exploring the great Canadian Wilderness by Bush Plane Thomas Allen Publishers, Toronto, 2000.

Feagan, Robert. NAPACHEE Sandcastle Book, Vancouver, 1999.

Finnie, Richard. Lure of the North. David McKay Company, Philadelphia, 1940.

Fitzhugh, William W. & Susan A. Kaplan, innua: spirit world of the bering sea eskimo. Smithsonian Institution Press, Washington, 1982.

Flannigan, Bennett and M. Hladun. Inuit of the North Fitzhenry & Whiteside, Canada.

Fobes, Natalie. I DREAM ALASKA, Alaska Northwest Books, Anchorage, 1998.

Ford, Corey. WHERE THE SEA BREAKS ITS BACK: the epic story of a pioneer naturalist and the discovery of Alaska. Little Brown & Company, Toronto, 1966.

Fossett, Renee. In Order to Live Untroubled: Inuit of the Central Arctic, 1550 to 1940 University of Manitoba Press, 2001.

Foster, John & Janet. DVD: JOURNEY TO THE SEA OF ICE. Discovery Channel, Canada.

Fournier, Suzanne and Ernie Crey. Stolen From Our Embrace Douglas & McIntyre, Vancouver. 1997.

French, Alice. My Name is Masak Portage and Main, Winnipeg, 1992.

Freres, Revillon. 1992, Eskimo Life of Yesterday Hancock House, Saanichton, 1977.

Frison-Roche, Roger. Hunters of the Arctic J.M. Dent & Sons Ltd, Toronto 1969

Freuchen, Peter. Ice Floes & Flaming Waters: a true adventure in Melville Bay. Victor Gollancz Ltd, London, 1955.

Freuchen, Peter. Peter Freuchen's Book of the Eskimos. Worls Publishing Company, Cleveland, 1961.

Frost, Mary Carpenter. Inuit Cultural Survival In the Face of Change. UNESCO Cultural Conference, Calgary, 1989.

Geller, Peter. Northern Exposures: photographing and filming the Canadian north , UBC Press, Vancouver, 2004.

Gibson, James R. Otter Skins, Boston Ships, & China Goods: the maritime fur trade of the northwest coast 1785-1841 University of Washington Press, Seattle, 1999.

Gillham, Charles (illust. Bob Hines), E. RAW NORTH, Herbert Jenkins Ltd, London, 1947.

Gillingham, D.W. UMIAK! museum Press Ltd, London, 1955.

Godsell, Jean W. I Was No Lady ...I Followed the Call of the Wild Ryerson Press, Toronto, 1959.

Godsell, Philip H. Red Hunters of the Snow Ryerson Press, Toronto, 1938.

Godsell, Philip H. "The Passing of Herschel Island", R.C.M.P. Quarterly, Volume 9, Number 4, April 1942.

Golder, F.A. Bering's Voyage Volume II. American Geographical Society, 1925.

Goodliffe, Jason. FRED CARPENTER. School report for Miss Branch, Samuel Hearne Secondary School. Unpublished. 1997.

Grace, Sherrill E., Canada and the Idea of North. McGill-Queen's University Press, Montreal, 2001.

Graham, Angus. The Golden Grindstone: One Man's Adventures in the Yukon with an introduction by Lawrence Millman. The Lyons Press/Globe Pequot Press, Guilford, 2006.

Graham, Commander R.D. Rough Passage Rupert Hart-Davis, London. 1952.

Grainge, Jack. The Changing North: Recollections of an Early Environmentalist. Occasional Publication No. 47, Canadian Circumpolar Institute, University of Alberta, 1999.

Greekas, John. Pioneer of the North: the Stan Peffer Story - Aklavik, Inuvik, North West Territory as seen by John Greekas, Biggar to Begger, Peachland, 2000.

Grenfell, Sir Wilfred with and introduction by Ronald Rompkey. Adrift on an Ice Pan. Creative Publishers, St John's, 1992.

Grierson, John and Sir Hubert Wilkins: Enigma of Exploration Robert Hale Ltd, London, 1960.

Gruben, Charlie. "Summer Crossing - Life & Trip from Banksland". from True Experiences - Men of the North, self-published - undated.

Gruben, Helen. Amos, Beverly., Glowach, Sue. Siglitun Basic Language Lessons. Inuvialuit Cultural Resource Centre, Inuvik, 2009.

Gruben, Persis. "Life of the Pioneers in Banks Island 1929-1930". from True Experiences - Men of the North, self-published - undated.

Grygier, Pat Sandiford. A Long Way From Home: the tuberculosis Epidemic among the Inuit, McGill-Queens University Press, Montreal, 1994.

Hall, Captain Charles Francis. Life With the Esquimaux M.G. Hurtig, Edmonton, 1970.

Hall, Ed Editor,A Way of Life Department of Renewable Resources, Yellowknife, 1986.

Hall, Sam. The Fourth World : the heritage of the Arctic and its destruction Knopf, New York, 1987.

Hamilton, Gordon. Inuit Boat Crew Hones Skills for North at Cowichan Bay., Cowichan News, page A15, January 28th, 1981.

Hamilton,John David. Arctic Revolution: Social Change in the Northwest Territories 1935-1994 Dundurn Press, Toronto, 1994.

Hamilton, R.A. (ed). Venture to the Arctic, Pelican Books/Penguin, New York, 1958.

Hancock, Lyn. The Mighty Mackenzie, Hancock House, Saanichton, 1974.

Hancock, Lyn. There's a Seal in my Sleeping Bag Harper Collins, Toronto, 2000.

Hancock, Lyn. Winging it in the North Oolichan Books, Lantzville, 1996.

Harper's Magazine, The Great North, Gallery Books, New York, 1990.

Harrington, Richard. Northern Exposures, Thomas Nelson & Sons, Toronto, 1953.

Harrington, Richard. The Inuit: Life as it Was, Hurtig Publishers, Edmonton. 1981.

Hartman, Roberta (editor), Paulatuuq Oral History Project: Inuvialuit Elders Share Their Stories Parks Canada, Inuvik, 2004.

Harry, David G., Banks Island: Gem of the Western Arctic from Canadian Geographic Oct/Nov 1982, Vol. 102, #5,pages 54-61.

Haycock, Maurice. On Site With MAURICE HAYCOCK: Artist of the Arctic: paintings and drawings of historical sites in the Canadian Arctic Edgar Kent, Campbellville, 2007.

Hayes, Bob. Wolves of the Yukon, Druckerei Fritz Kriechbauer, Germany, 2010.

Henderson, Ailsa. Nunavut: rethinking political culture UBC Press, Vancouver, 2007.

Hendry, Charles E. Beyond Traplines ; towards an assessment of the work of the Anglican Church of Canada with Canada's Native Peoples Ryerson Press, Toronto, 1969.

Herbert, Wally. Hunters of the Polar North Time Life Books, Amsterdam, 1981.

Hess, Bill. Gift of the Whale: the Inupiat Bowhead Hunt, A Sacred Tradition. Sasquatch Books, Seattle, 1999.

Hickey, Clifford G. (ed). The Western Canadian Journal of Anthropology Volume 4, Number 3: Contemporary Eskimo Studies. Western Canadian Journal of Anthropology, Edmonton, 1975.

Hill, Dick. INUVIK - a History, 1958-2008 Trafford Publishing, Victoria. 2008.

Hill, Leslie C. and Scott A. Simpson, Yukon Numismatica, Friesen Printers, Altona, 1990.

Ho, Zoe (ed). Tusaayaksat presents The Inuvialuit Year: a showcase of contemporary Inuvialuit life and culture, Inuvialuit Communications Society, Edmonton, 2009.

Hohn, E.O. ARCTIC SCHOONER VOYAGE, The Beaver Magazine, pp24-27, Summer 1955.

Hohn, E.O. In the Home of the Snow Goose. The Beaver Magazine, pp 8-10.

Holland, Clive. Arctic Exploration & Development c. 500 BC to 1915. Graland Publishing Inc., New York, 1994.

Holmlund, Mona and Gail Youngberg, Inspiring Women: a Celebration of Herstory. Coteau Books, Regina, 2003.

Honigmann,John J. and Irma . Arctic Townsmen Canadian Research Centre for Anthropology, Saint Paul University, Ottawa, 1970.

Honigmann, John J. and Irma, Eskimo Townsmen Canadian Research Centre for Anthropology, Ottawa, 1965.

Hoskin, M. "Caroline Herschel - the Unquiet Heart", Endeavour, 2005.

Hourde, R.N., Sophisticated Eskimos, The Beaver Magazine, September 1952.

Houston, James. Confessions of an Igloo Dweller McClelland & Stewart, Toronto, 1995.

Howerd, Gareth, Dew Line Doctor Trinity Press, Worcester, 1960.

Hunt, Barbara (editor). Rebels, Rascals & Royalty: the Colourful North of LACO Hunt Outcrop, Yellowknife, 1983.

Hutchison, Isobel W. NORTH TO THE RIME-RINGED SUN: being the record of an Alaskan-Canadian journey made in 1933-34. Blackie & Son Ltd, London & Glasgow, 1934.

Igloliorte John. An Inuk Boy Becomes A Hunter Nimbus Publishing, Halifax, 1994.

Inglis, Alex. Northern Vagabond: The life and career of J.B. Tyrell - the man who conquered the Canadian North. McClelland & Stewart, Toronto, 1978.

Inglis, George., Back to Victoria. The Islander, Victoria, November 16th, 1980.

Ingram, Rob and Helene Dobrowolsky. Herschel Island: An Annotated Bibliography Yukon Archives, 1989.

Innis, Harold A. Fur Trade in Canada (the), University of Toronto Press, Toronto, 1962 &1999.

International Arctic Science Committe. Climate change impacts on Canadian Western Arctic: the Inuvialuit of Sachs Harbour www.eoearth.org, 2010.

Inuit Tapirisat of Canada Inuit of Canada, Hull, 1998.

IRC Inuvialuit Final Agreement- Celebrating 25 Years, Inuvik, 2009.

Inuvialuit Social Development Program, Qikiqtaqruk (Herschel Island) Cultural Study English translations and transcriptions of interviews 17 to 35 Inuvik, 1994.

Irvine, T.A. The Ice Was All Between. Longmans, Green & Company, Toronto, 1959.

Irwin, R. Stephen. Hunters of the Ice, Hancock House, Surrey, 1984.

Isaac, Elisapie. If the Weather Permits (DVD) a film , National Film Board of Canada, Ottawa, 2003.

Issenman, Betty Kobayashi. Sinews of Survival - the living legacy of Inuit clothing UBC Press, Vancouver. 1997.

Jackson, Susan (editor), Yellowknife NWT - an illustrated history Nor'West Publishing, Yellowknife 1990.

Jackman, Philip. "Forget veggies - get vitamins from blubber", Collected Wisdom, The Globe and Mail, Toronto, May 20, 2011.

Jaine,Linda (editor). Residential Schools: the Stolen Years University Extension Press, Saskatoon, 1995.

Jaine, Linda & Drew Taylor (editors). VOICES: the Native in Canada. University of Saskatchewan, Saskatoon, 1992.

James, William C. A fur Trader's Photographs : A.A. Chesterfield in the District of Ungava, McGill Queens universit Press Kingston and Montreal, 1985.

Jenness, Stuart E. (ed). Arctic Odyssey: the Diary of Diamond Jenness 1913-1916 Canadian Museum of Civilization, Hull, 1991.

Jenness, Stuart E., The Making of an Explorer: George Hubert Wilkins and the Canadian Arctic Expedition 1913-1916, McGill-Queen's University Press, Montreal, 2004.

Johansson, Sven. Cruising the Arctic Seas, unpublished manuscript.

Johansson, Sven. DVD: 8mm films North Star of Herschel Island Scientific Work in Beaufort Sea, Inuvik, undated.

Johansson, Sven. Location of Storehouses 1, 2, 3 Built by the US Corps of Engineers 1896, Portland Canal/Canada and U.S. Boundary. Unpublished. 1977.

Johansson, Sven., Personal Correspondence to Noah Carpenter, May 4, 1990 (from Maritime Museum of British Columbia Archives).

Jones, Mary Jay (ed). MacKenzie Delta Bibliography. Queen's Printer, Ottawa, 1969.

Kalluak, Mark. UNIPKAAQTUAT ARVIANIT: traditional Inuit stories from Arviat Volume two Inhabit Media Inc., Nunavut, 2010.

Kastelein, Richard. Relic of Arctic Transportation Provides Floating Museum. Slave River Journal, Slave River, 1992.

Keith, D. Stephen Angulalik: Kitikmeot Fur Trader. Kitikmeot Heritage Center (npd).

Keithahn, Edward L. Eskimo Adventure Bonanza Books, New York, 1961.

Kendall, Laura and Barbara Mathe and Thomas Ross Miller. DRAWING SHADOWS TO STONE: THE PHOTOGRAPHY OF THE JESUP NORTH PACIFIC EXPEDITION, 1897-1902. American Museum of Natural History, New York. 1997.

Khun, Edgar A. Ellesmere Land : A Mountie in the High Arctic Northwest Printing, Calgary. 2002.

King, J.C.H. & Birgit Pauksztat & Robert Storrie (Eds). ARCTIC CLOTHING of North America - Alaska, Canada, Greenland. McGill-Queen's University Press, Montreal, 2005.

King, JCH and Lidchi, Henriette (editors). Imaging the Arctic, UBC Press, Vancouver, 1998.

Kolbert, Elizabeth (ed). THE ENDS OF THE EARTH: THE ARCTIC. Bloomsbury, New York, 2007.

Kowichuk, Raddi. "A Typical Year of an Inuk." from True Experiences - Men of the North, self-published - undated.

Kowichuk, Raddi. " Murder & Vengeance in the Husky Lakes". Kowichuk, Raddi. "The Inuktuyut, The Cannibals of the North". from True Experiences - Men of the North, self-published - undated.

Kowichuk, Raddi. "The Inuktuyut, The Cannibals of the North". from True Experiences - Men of the North, self-published - undated.

Kroetsch, R. "The Oral Tradition is like the MacKenzie Delta" Northern review (Whitehorse), no. 28, Winter 2008, p. 181-186).

Kulchyski, Peter and Don McCaskill, and David Newhouse (editors). In the Words of Elders: Aboriginal Cultures in Transition. University of Toronto Press, Toronto. 1999.

Laid, Charles. DVD: Through These Eyes, National Film Board of Canada, 2004.

Larsen, Henry A. North-West Passage, The 1940-1942 and 1944 : City Archives, Vancouver Canada, 1954.

Larsen, Henry A. Reports and Other Papers Relating To The Two Voyages of the R.C.M. Police Schooner 'St. Roch' Through The North West Passage. PierWay Inc., Vancouver, 2000.

Larsen, Thor and Magnar Norderhaug. The Arctic, North Sea Press, Oslo, 1979.

Lassieur. Allison. THE INUIT, Bridgestone Books, Minnesota, npd.

Last Trapper, The (DVD), National Film Board of Canada, 2006.

Learmonth, L.A. "Interrupted Journey", The Beaver Magazine, September, 1951.

LeBourdais, D.M. STEFANSSON Ambassador of the North Harvest House, Montreal, 1963.

Leden, Christian. translation by Leslie H. Neatby Inuit Journey by Boat, 1913, from the diary of : The Beaver Magazine, Winnipeg, Winter 1980.

Ledyard, Gleason H. ESKIMOS - now the world (orig. pub. as And to the Eskimos, 1958) Christian Literature International, Canby, 1977.

Leechman, Douglas. "Beauty's Only Skin Deep", The Beaver Magazine, September, 1951.

Lemer O.M.I., Father with introduction by Diamond Jenness. Banksland Story, self-published, Sachs Harbour, February 1970.

LeMeur, Father. Our Lady of Lourdes, self-published, Tuktoyaktuk.

LeMeur, Father. True Experiences - Men of the North, self-published, undated.

Leong, Leslie. Our Forgotten North: a glimpse of the SubArctic in Canada's North, Leslie Leong Ent,, Fort Smith, 1997.

Lindsay, Debra. Science in the Sub-Arctic: Trappers, Traders and the Smithsonian Institute, Smithsonian Institute Press, Washington, 1993.

Lloyd Kyi, Tani and Richard Hartmier (photos). YUKON. Whitecap Books, Vancouver, 2001.

Lopez, Barry. Arctic Dreams: Imagination and Desire in a Northern Landscape MacMillan Publishing, New York, 1987.

Lotz, Jim. The Best Journey in the World: Adventure's in Canada's High Arctic, Pottersfield Press, Lawrencetown Beach, 2006.

Lovelace, John. Wings Over Canada (DVD) Season 4 ATV Productions. 2005.

Lowe, Ronald. Siglit Inuvialuit Eskimo Dictionary. Laval University, Quebec, 2001.

Lowe, Ronald Basic Siglit Inuvialuit Eskimo Dictionary COPE, Inuvik, 1984.

Lowenstein,Tom. Ancient Land : Sacred Whale - the Inuit Hunt and its Rituals Farrar, Straus and Giroux, New York.1993.

Loxley, John. Aboriginal, Northern, and Community Economic Development Arbeiter Ring Publishing, Winnipeg, 2011.

Lynch, Daniel M. Google Your Family Tree, Family Link.com, Provo, 2008.

MacDonald, Malcolm. Canadian North, Oxford University Press, London, 1945.

MacFarlane, John M. 'Careening Creates Character.' Resolution Magazine, Victoria, Spring 1994.

MacFarlane, John M., CAREENING THE NORTH STAR OF HERSCHEL ISLAND. www.nauticapedia.ca, 2011.

MacFarlane, John M. and Sven Johansson. The North Star, Resolution Magazine, Victoria, Summer, 1991.

MacFarlane, John M. and Sven B. Johansson. The North Star of Herschel Island: Last of the Western Arctic Trading Schooners. Unpublished.

MacKay, Douglas. Honourable Company : A History of the Hudson's Bay Company. Misson Book Co. Toronto, 1938.

Malaurie, Jean. Hummocks: Journeys and Inquiries among the Canadian Inuit. McGill-Queens University Press, Montreal, 2007.

MacNutt, Allan. Canada's Arctic Sovereignty or this land is our land, self-published, dist. by Heritage House, 2004.

Madsen, Charles with John Scott Douglas. Arctic Trader Dodd, Mead & Company, New York, 1957.

Mailhot, Jose (translated by Axel Harvey). THE PEOPLE OF SHESHATSHIT IN THE LAND OF THE INNU, Institute of Social and Economic Research, St. John's, 1997.

Manley, Seon and Gogo Lewis, (editors). Polar Secrets: A Treasury of the Arctic and Antarctic Doubleday & Co, Garden City, New York, 1968.

Manning, T.H., NARRATIVE OF AN UNSUCCESFUL ATTEMPT TO CIRCUMNAVIGATE BANKS ISLAND BY CANOE IN 1952, pages 171-197, Arctic Journal, Arctic Institute of North America, Ottawa. npd.

Marsh, Winnifred (ed). Echoes From A Frozen Island by Donald B. Marsh, Hurtig Publishers, Edmonton. 1987.

Martin, Lawrence. CHRETIEN Volume 1: the will to win. Lester Publishing, Toronto, 1995.

Mason, Bill. DVD: Cry of the Wild, National Film Board, Ottawa, 1972.

Maurice, Edward Beauclerk. The Last of the Gentlemen Adventurers: Coming of Age in the Arctic. Fourth Estate, London, 2004.

May, B.M. 'WALRUS HUNT' The Beaver magazine, September, 1942.

May, Katie. 'Saying Goodbye to Andy Carpenter', Northern News Service, February 24, 2010.

McAllister, Bruce. WINGS ABOVE THE ARCTIC: a photographic history of Arctic Aviation.Roundup Press, Boulder, 2002.

McAllister, Bruce. WINGS OVER THE YUKON: a photographic history of Yukon Aviation, Roundup Press, Boulder, 2008.

McEwen, Alec. "American Military Storehouses and the Alaska Boundary Dispute", North magazine, Volume 31, Number 1, Ottawa, 1985.

McGoogan, Ken. Fatal Passage Harper/Perennial, Toronto, 2001.

McGrath, Melanie. The Long Exile - a true story of deception and survival amongst the Inuit of the Canadian Arctic

Harper-Collins, London, 1986.

McGrath, Robin. 'Schooners of the Western Arctic', Up Here Magazine, Yellowknife, July/August 1989.

McKittrick, Erin. A Long Trek Home: 4,000 miles by boot, raft and ski, Mountaineers Books, Seattle, 2009.

McClellan, Catherine. My Old People Say: an ethnographic survey of Southern Yukon Territory, Part Two. Canadian Museum of Civilization, Ottawa, 2001.

McClellan, Catherine. Part of the Land, Part of the Water Douglas & McIntyre, Vancouver, 1987.

Mesler, Dorothy with Ray Woollam. KUUJJUAQ - Memories and Musings. Unica Publishing Co. Ltd., Duncan, 1995.

Metayer, Maurice (editor and translater). I Nuligak. PocketBooks, New York. 1972.

Mirsky, Jeanette. To the Arctic University of Chicago Press, 1970.

Mitchell, Marybelle. From Talking Chiefs to a Native Corporate Elite: the birth of class and nationalism among Canadian Inuit. McGill-Queens Native and Northern Series, Montreal/Kingston. 1996.

Monarchist. Royal Tour of Canada 1959: Tour of Canada by Her Majesty Queen Elizabeth II & His Royal Highness The Prince Philip, Duke of Edinburgh. self-published, 1959.

Moneo, Shannon. 'Adventurer Finds Life Is Not Always Smooth Sailing', SERENDIPITY, Victoria News, June 16, 1993.

Moody M.D., Joseph P. Medicine Man to the Inuit Arctic Memories Press, Denver, 1995.

Morris, Rob., North Star of Herschel Island. The Westcoast Mariner Magazine, pp16-21, Vancouver, April 1994.

Morrison, David A. Caribou Hunters in the Western Arctic Canadian Museum of Civilization, Ottawa. 1997.

Morrison, David and Georges-Hebert Germain. INUIT: GLIMPSES OF AN ARCTIC PAST Canadian Museum of Civilization, Hull, 1995.

Morrison, Neil F. & Herbert Heaton and James Charles Bonar. The Dominion of Canada, Ryerson Press, Toronto, 1937.

Morrison, William. The Mounted Police and Canadian Sovereignty in the Western Arctic 1903-1924. 1985.

Morse, Eric W. Fur Trade Routes of Canada/Then and Now. National and Historic Parks Branch, Ottawa, 1971.

Moss, John (ed), Echoing Silence: Essays on Arctic Narrative University of Ottawa Press, Ottawa, 1997.

Mowat, Farley. Coppermine Journey, McClelland & Stewart, Toronto, 1990.

Mowat, Farley. Canada North McClelland & Stewart, Toronto, 1967.

Mowat, Farley. Canada North Now: the Great Betrayal McClelland & Stewart, Toronto, 1976.

Mowat, Farley. Ordeal on Ice McClelland and Stewart, Toronto, 1973.

Mowat, Farley. People of the Deer Pyramid Books, New York, 1971.

Mowat, Farley. The New-Founde-Land. McClelland & Stewart, Toronto, 1989.

Mowat, Farley. Tundra McClelland and Stewart, Toronto, 1977.

Mukti, God's Man From Banks Island, self published, 2012

Nadasdy, Paul. Hunters and Bureacrats: Power, Knowledge and Aboriginal-State Relations in the Southwest Yukon UBC Press, Vancouver, 2003.

Nagy, Murielle. Qikiqtaqruk (Herschel Island) Cultural Study: English Translations and Transcriptions of Interviews 1-16. Inuviauluit Social Development Program, Inuvik. 1994.

Nagy, Murielle. Qikiqtaqruk (Herschel Island) Cultural Study: English Translations and Transcriptions of Interviews 17-35. Inuviauluit Social Development Program, Inuvik. 1994.

Nagy, Murielle. Yukon North Slope Cultural Resources Survey: English Translations and Transcriptions of Interviews

1-18. Inuvialuit Social Development Program, Inuvik, 1994.

Nagy, Murielle. Yukon North Slope Cultural Resources Survey: English Translations and Transcriptions of Interviews 19-29. Inuvialuit Social Development Program, Inuvik, 1994.

Nasht, Simon. THE LAST EXPLORER: Hubert Wilkins, Hero of the Great Age of Polar Exploration. Arcade Publishing, New York, 2006.

National Archives Vault. DVD: The Year of the Hunter/The Story of Nanuk. Gatineau, Quebec.

National Film Board of Canada, DVD: Arctic Mission - the Great Adventure: People of the Ice, www.nfb.ca, St. Laurent, Quebec.

Nault, Jennifer Canadian Fur Trade: Hudson's Bay Company, Calgary, 2007.

Nayanguaq, Georgia. An Arctic Diary. Hurting Publishers, Edmonton, 1982.

Nelson, Richard K. Hunters of the Northern Ice University of Chicago Press, Chicago. 1975.

Nelso, Richard K. Shadow of the Hunter: Stories of Eskimo Life, University of Toronto Press, Toronto, 1980.

Newman, Peter C. HEROES: Canadian Champions, Dark Horses and Icons HarperCollins, Toronto, 2010.

Newman, Peter C., An Illustrated History of the Hudson's Bay Company Viking Studio/Madison Press, Toronto, 1989.

Newman, Peter C. Empire of the Bay Viking Studio/Madison Press, Toronto, 1989.

Newman, Peter C. Merchant Princes Viking, Toronto, 1991.

Newman, Shirlee P. The Inuits Franklin Watts, New York, 1993.

Nichols, Theresa & F. Berkes & D. Jolly & N.B. Snow. "Climate Change & Sea Ice: Local Observations from the Canadian Western Arctic", Arctic Journal, Arctic Institute of North America, Vol. 57, No. !, March 2004.

Niven, Jennifer. Ada Blackjack: a true story of survival in the Arctic . Hyperion, New York, 2003.

Nollman, Jim. The Beluga Cafe: my strange adventure with art, music and whales in the far north Key Porter, Toronto, 2002.

North, Dick. The Lost Patrol: the Mounties' Yukon Tragedy. Raincoast Books, Vancouver, 1978.

Northwest Territories Education, Inuvialuit Pitqusiit: the culture of the Inuvialuit 1991.

Nova/PBS Arctic Passage (DVD) Nova/PBS, 2006.

Nuyavjak, Felix. Mangilalik Adrift on the Ice. Self-published, Tuktoyaktuk, 1971.

Nutell, Mark (ed). Encyclopedia of the Arctic, Volume 1, Routledge, 2005.

Nuyaviak, Felix. "Golden Memories of the Past", from True Experiences - Men of the North, self-published - undated.

Ootes, Jake. NorthWest Explorer Vol 3 #3, NorthWest Territorial Airways, Yellowknife, 1984.

Orchard, Imbert. Martin: The Story of a Young Fur Trader Queen's Printer for British Columbia, Victoria. 1981.

Osborn, Kevin. The Peoples of the Arctic, Chelsea House Publishers, New York, 1990.

Oswalt, Wendell H. ESKIMOS AND EXPLORERS, Chandler & Sharp Publishers, Inc, Novato, 1979.

Palsson, Gisli (editor). Writing on Ice: The Ethnographic Notebooks of Vilhjalmur Stefansson. University Press of New England, Hanover, 2001.

Paschen, Elizabeth. Moosehide Jackets: Mackenzie's Journey Retraced University of Alberta Printing Services, Edmonton 1989.

Peake, Frank A. The Bishop Who Ate His Boots: a biography of Isaac O. Stringer, Anglican Church of Canada, Don Mills, 1966.

Penlington, Norman. The Alaska Boundary Dispute: A Critical Reappraisal. McGraw-Hill Ryerson Limited, Toronto, 1972.

Peterson, David. Tale of the LUCIN: a boat, a railroad and the Great Salt Lake Old Waterfront Publishing, Trinidad, 2001.

Petitot, Father Emile Among the Chiglit Eskimos Occasional Publication No 10, Canadian Circumpolar Institure, University of Alberta, Edmonton, 1999.

Pigott, Peter. From Far and Wide: A Complete History of Canada's Arctic Sovereignty. Dundurn, Toronto, 2011.

Pinsent, Gordon. 'Florence Carpenter - a language keeper', The Late Show, CBC Radio.

Pitseolak, Peter. Peter Pitseolak (1902-1973) Inuit Historian of Seekooseelak, McGill, Montreal, 1980.

Pitt, Michael D. Beyond the End of the Road: A winter of contentment North of the Arctic Circle Agio Publishing, Victoria, 2009.

Pokiak, Bertram. Tuktoyaktuk Memories from Inuktitut Magazine, #70, Ottawa, 1989.

Pokiak, James and Mindy Willett. Proud to be Inuvialuit Fifth House Publishing, Markham, 2010.

Pokiak-Fenton, Margaret & Christy Jordan-Fenton. a stranger at home, Annick Press, Toronto, 2011.

Pokiak-Fenton, Margaret & Christy Jordan-Fenton. fatty legs, Annick Press, Toronto, 2010 poncins, gontran de. Kabloona Time-Life Books, Alexandria, 1980.

Price, Ray. The Howling Arctic, Peter Martin Associates Ltd, Toronto, 1970.

Pryde, Duncan. NUNAGA: Ten Years of Eskimo Life. Walker and Company, New York, 1971.

Pryde, Duncan. NUNAGA: My Land, My Country M.G. Hurtig Ltd, Edmonton, 1972.

Ransom, M.A. with Eloise Katherine Eagle. Sea of the Bear: Journal of a Voyage to Alaska and the Arctic 1921, United States Naval Institute, Annapolis, 1964.

Rasmussen, Knud. Across Arctic America: narrative of the fifth Thule expedition University of Alaska Press, Fairbanks, 1999.

Ray, Arthur J. I Have Lived Here Since the World Began - an illustrated history of Canada's Native People Key Porter Books, Toronto, 1996.

Reiss, Bob. The Eskimo and the Oil Man. Business Plus/Grand Central Publishing, New York, 2012.

Robertson, Heather. A Gentleman Adventurer: The Arctic Diaries of Richard Bonnycastle. Lester & Orpen Dennys, Toronto, 1984.

Robinson, Martha. Family Sailors Blow Into Town With Dreams On A Star. The Vancouver Sun, Vancouver B.C., 1975.

Rokeby-Thomas, Mrs Anna E., Arctic Darkness, from North Magazine, undated.

Rubin, Dan. Salt on the Wind. Horsdal & Schubart, Victoria, 1996.

Rudolf, Claire & Jane G. Haigh. Gold Rush Dogs Alaska Northwest Books Portland, 2001.

Sandiford, Mark. DVD: Qallunaat: Why White People Are Funny. Beachwalker Films/National Film Board of Canada, 2006.

Sandlos, John. Hunters at the Margin: Native People and Wildlife Conservation in the Northwest Territories UBC Press, Vancouver, 2007.

Schledermann, Peter. Voices in Stone: A Personal Jouney into the Arctic Past. Arctic Institute of North America c/o University of Calgary. 1966.

Schultz-Lorentzen, Finn. arctic. McClelland and Stewart, Toronto, 1976.

Schwarz, Herbert T. ELIK and other stories of the MacKenzie Eskimos McClelland & Stewart, Toronto 1970.

Schwarz, Herbert T. Tuktoyaktuk 2-3 M.F.Feheley, Toronto, 1975.

Scott, Marianne. "Salt of all Trades", Pacific Yachting Magazine, Vancouver, October, 2000.

Sharp, Anne Wallace. The Inuit: Indigenous Peoples of North America, Lucent Books, San Diego, 2002.

Shibasaki, Takashi & Atsushi Nishida & Wally Longul, directors. DVD: Arctic Circle: On Thin Ice & Battle for the Pole, National Film Board of Canada and NHK.

Shomon, Joseph James. BEYOND THE NORTH WIND: The Arctic Tundra. A.S. Barnes and Co., Inc., Cranbury, 1974.

Simpson-Housley, Paul. Arctic, (the) - Enigmas and Myths Dundurn Press, Toronto. 1996.

Smeeton, Miles. The Misty Islands. Grafton Books, London, 1969.

Smith, Anne. INUIT - people of the world Wayland, East Sussex, 1989.

Smith, Derek G., Natives and Outsiders: Pluralism in the MacKenzie River Delta, Northwest Territories, Department of Indian Affairs and Northern Development, Ottawa, 1975.

Smith, J.H. Greg. ESKIMOS: the Inuit of the Arctic Rourke Publications, Vero Beach, 1987.

Smith, I. Norman. (ed) The Unbelievable Land: 29 experts bring us closer to the Arctic. Foreword by General Georges Vanier. Queen's Printer for the Department of Northern Affairs, Ottawa, 1964.

Sperry, John R. Igloo Dwellers Were My Church, Bayeux Arts, Calgary, 2001.

Steele, Samuel B., FORTY YEARS IN CANADA: reminiscences of the great NorthWest with some account of his service on South Africa. McGraw-Hill Ryerson, toronto, 1972.

Stefansson, Evelyn. Within the Circle : Portrait of the Arctic Charles Scriberner's Sons New York, 1945.

Stefansson, Vilhjalmur. HUNTERS OF THE GREAT NORTH Paragon House, New York, 1990.

Stefansson, Vihjalmur. The Friendly Arctic. MacMillan & Co., New York, 1927.

Stellman, Louis J., Boat to Attempt Trappers' Rescue: New Effort to Save Marooned Families Begun, The Bulletin, San Francisco, April 9, 1919.

Steltzer, Ulli. INUIT: the North in Transition Douglas & McIntyre Ltd, Vancouver, 1982.

Stern, Pamela. "Upside-Down and Backwards in a Canadian Inuit Town", Anthropoligica, Canadian Anthroplogy Society, Volume 45, Number 1, 2003.

Stewart, Gail B. Life Lived In An Eskimo Village Lucent Books, San Diego, 1995.

Stone-Man-McNichol, Jane. On Blue Ice: the Inuvik Adventure, Outcrop, Yellowknife, 1983.

Struzik, Ed. Big Thaw, The: Travels in the melting North John Wiley and Sons, Mississauga, 2009.

Taylor, Hugh A. (ed) Arctic Images: The Frontier Photographed, 1860-1911. Public Archives Canada, Ottawa, 1977.

Templeton, Major P., Command Ranger Liaison Officer, Personal Correspondence to Fred Carpenter, Montreal, April 5, 1956.

Tetso, John. Trapping is my Life. Peter Martin Associates, Toronto, 1970.

Thibert, Arthur. English-Eskimo Dictionary, Canadian Research Centre for Anthropology, Ottawa, 1970.

Thibert, Arthur. Eskimo-English/English-Eskimo Dictionary Laurier Books, Ottawa, 1997.

Thomson, David. People of the Sea: A journey in Search of the Seal Legend World Publishing Company, Cleveland and New York, 1965.

Thompson, John Beswarick. The More Northerly Route: A photographic study of the 1944 voyage of the St. Roch through the Northwest Passage, Parks Canada, Ottawa, 1974.

Tichenor, Harold. The Blanket : An Illustrated History of the Hudson's Bay Point Blanket. Quantum Book, Toronto, 2002.

Tippett, Maria (photography by Charles Gimpel). Between Two Cultures: A Photographer Among the Inuit. Viking/Penguin, Toronto, 1994.

Tompkins, John Barr. A Voyage of Pleasure: the log of Bernard Gilboy's Trans-Pacific Cruise in the Boat 'Pacific' 1882-1883, Cornell Maritime Press, Cambridge, 1957.

Towriss, R. Wayne. YUKON by Northern Light. Studio North, Whithouse, 1992.

Tranter, G.J., Plowing the Arctic: being an account of the voyage of the R.C.M.P. 'St. Roch' through the North West Passage from West to East, Longmans, Green and Co.. Toronto, 1945.

Troubetzkoy, Alexis S. Arctic Obsession: The Lure of the Far North, Dundurn Press, Toronto, 2011.

Tweedsmuir, Lord. Hudson's Bay Trader Robert Hale, London. 1978.

Tyrell, J.W., Across the Sub-Arctics of Canada. Coles Publishing Company, Toronto, 1973.

Usher, Peter J. Aulavik Oral History Project, Tape 4A & 4B. Interview with Fred Carpenter, Sachs Harbour, 18th July, 1967.

Usher, Peter J. Fur Trade Posts of the Northwest Territories 1870-1970 Northern Science Research Group, 1971.

Usher, Peter J. The Bankslanders , Economy and Ecology of a Frontier Trapping Community - Volume 1: History Information Canada, Ottawa, 1970.

Usher, Peter J. The Bankslanders, Economy and Ecology of a Frontier Trapping Community - Volume 2: Economy and Ecology by Information Canada, Ottawa, 1970.

Usher, Peter J. The Bankslanders, Economy and Ecology of a Frontier Trapping Community - Volume 3: The Community Information Canada, Ottawa, 1971.

van Steensel, Maja (ed). People of Light and Dark. Spalding Printing Company, Ottawa, 1974.

von Hlatkey, Christina (Producer/Director), The Rapidly Changing Arctic (tv video), CBC.ca/nature of things.

Wachowich, Nancy. SAQIYUQ : stories from the lives of three Inuit women McGill-Queens University, Montreal 1999.

Walden, Arthur T. A Dog Puncher on the Yukon, Wolf Creek Books, Whitehorse, reprint from 1928.

Walker, John. DVD: PASSAGE, PTV Productions/John Walker Productions/ National Film Board of Canada, 2008.

Waterman, Jonathan. Arctic Crossing - A Jouney through the Northwest Passage and Inuit Culture Random House, Toronto. 2001.

Webster, Liz. Seafaring with Sven: Maritime Museum visits 900 children in the Gulf Islands - under sail. Resolution Magazine, Number 22, Spring 1991.

Western Arctic Handbook Committee Canada's Western Arctic including the Dempster Highway , Inuvik, 2002.

Wheeler, Sara. The Magnetic North: Notes From The Arctic Circle. Farrar, Straus & Giroux, New York. 2009.

Whelan, Dianne. DVD: This Land. National Film Board, 2009.

Wiebe, Rudy. Playing Dead: a contemplation concerning the Arctic NeWest Publishers, Edmonton, 1989.

Wild, Roland. ARCTIC COMMAND: the story of Smellie of the Nascopie. Ryerson Press, Toronto, 1955.

Wilder, Edna. Secrets of Eskimo Skin Sewing Alaska Northwest Publishing Company, Anchorage, 1976.

Wilkins, Charles. The Wild Ride: A History of the North West Mounted Police 1873-1904 Stanton Atkins & Dosil, Vancouver, 2010.

Wilkinson, Doug. Land of the Long Day Clarke, Irwin & Company, Toronto, 1955.

Wilson, Clifford. North of 55 Ryerson Press, Toronto, 1954.

Winchell, Mary E., HOME by the BERING SEA. Caxton Publishers, Caldwell, 1951.

Wolki, Bessie and Ivy Pannigak. "Life in Banksland During that Crossing." from True Experiences - Men of the North, self-published - undated.

Wolkie, Geddes. "The Trials & Ordeals of a Young Boy." from True Experiences - Men of the North, self-published - undated.

Wolkie, Jim. "The Toughest Year of My Life", from True Experiences - Men of the North, self-published - undated.

Wonders, William C. Canada's Changing North: revised edition McGill-Queens University Press, Montreal, 2003.

Worek, Michael (ed). The Arctic Coast, Natural Science of Canada Ltd, Toronto, 1970.

Wuttunee, Wanda A. In Business for Ourselves: Northern Entrepeneurs.

Yip, Mike. INUVIK self-published, Inuvik, 1974.

Zak, Nancy Carpenter. "A Personal Journey" from Earthwalking Sky Dancers, edited by Leila Castle. Frog Ltd, Berkeley, California, 1996.

Zaslow, Morris. ed. A Century of Canada's Arctic Islands 1880-1980, 1981 The Royal Society of Canada.

APPENDIX

AN INCOMPLETE LIST OF SCHOONERS AND OWNERS AND DATES

Please note that some of these vessels might be listed more than once. For instance in the case of Nanuk there are several vessels that share that name, but with different spellings and I cannot say with certainty whether it is one ship whose name has been spelled differently by different writers or owners of several vessels sharing a similar name. This list is a compilation of what I have seen written in texts or on the vessels that I have seen in photographs.

VESSEL NAME	OWNER(S)	YEARS	ADDT'L
Adanac	C. Rowan		
Admac			
Aklavik	H.B.C		Coppermine (Kugluktuk)
Alaska			
Alclavik			
Amingmuk	Jim Wolki		
Anderson River			Cape Bathurst/ Delta Area
An'ngugaaluk (Tar)	Persis Gruben's Grandfather		
Anna Olga	Slim Semmler also Ole Andreasen		
Annie			
Arctic	C.G.S. Captain J.E. Bernier		
Arctic Bluenose	Allen Okpik/ Anaqtuk (see also Saucy Jane)		
Arctic Trader			
Argo	Ernest Leffingwell	1909-10	Gasoline yawl whaler

Audrey B	Traders: Watson/ Purcell/Storr		Blt Vancouver, former rumrun- ner, fish-packer
Banalopy	Inuit owned		
Bay Chimo	HBC Cargo Ship	1930	
Bear Lake	Harrisons	1929-30	
Beluga	Stringer	1930's	Grandfather of Sarak Meyook
Beriuga			Delta Area
Bill Day	Bill Day		Only ever known as owner's name
Blue Fox	Fred Wolki		Andy Carpenter born aboard
Bluenose	Mabel & Alec Steffanson		
Bonanza			
Bonnie Belle	Bob Cockney (Nuligak)	Until mid 50's	
Brock River			King William Island area
Challenge	C.T. Pedersen	1908-09	
Charles D. Brower	Liebes & Co.		
Charles Edward	Arctic Transportation Co.	Built 1918	Wedgeport, Nova Scotia
Charles Hanson	Jim Hill		
Chinook	Leonard & McDonough	1932	Blt 1900 Vancouver, Reblt 1924, Victoria
Columbia	Levys & Palayak	1929-30	Fishing boat
Coppermine			
C.S. Holmes	Captain Blackland	1914	3 masted schooner
Delta			
Duchess of Bedford			
Eagle	Piqtuqan/Johny Norberg		Coppermine (Kugluktuk
Ebiktaorak		1930's	Picture from Finni Collection at Herschel I.
Ellen			
Elsie			
El Sveno	McIntyre, Lauritzen, Allan	Early 1900s	
Emma J.	H.B.C		Scotty Gall was a Captain

EmmaJane			Drifted ashore, frozen, Amundsen Gulf
Fort Ross	H.B.C.		Schooner
Fort St. James			Lunenburg built
Gladiator	Olle Andreason		Worked with Steffanson
Golden Hind			Delta area
Guy	Mission schooner		
Hayokhok		1920's	
Hazel	Johny 'one-arm' Togluk		
Henry Ford			Aklavik
Immaculata	Roman Catholic Church		Schooner
Jennings	R.C.M.P.	1960's	Schooner
Kaligraq	Isaac Alunik		Bought from Qikiqtaqruk (Ole Andreasen)
Karluk	Stefansson		
Kee			
Kigvalukmik	Inuayuuyaq		
Kingalik	Billy Joss		
Kotsik			
Krochik			Sunk in storm, Beaufort Sea, 1947
Kusseriuoak	Raddi Kowichuk		
Lady Richardson			Sunk in storm, Beaufort Sea, 1947
Margaret A			
Mary	R.C. Mission		Began as open boat, later decked in.
Mary Sachs	Captain Peter Bernard		30 ton, twin screw gas schooner
Messenger	All Saints Anglican Mission		
Nanok			
Nanook			
Nanuk (Polar Bear)	Ambrose Andreason		Ol Adam ½ owner, daughter Bessie)
Nanuk II	Jim Wolki		
Negik			

Nera	Herbert Guisler		Wrecked at Sunrock Beach, Alaska, 1913.
Nigek	Angik Ruben	1922	
Nigilik			Lost with all hands, Cape Serge, 1913.
Nipailuk	Sarah Meyook's family		
North Star	Andreasen (orig.) Billy Banksland		Gas schooner.
North Star (of Herschel Island)	Fred Carpenter/Jim Wolki/Susie Sidney	1935	
Nutik	Garrett Nutik		Kathleen Hansen's Dad, went to Banks Island
Ogmigmuk	Susie Sidney then Jim Wolki		
Okavik		1930's	
Okevik			Photographed at Herschel Island, 1930, Finnie Coll.
Okeevik	Harry Inukuqliq		
Old Maid No. 2	Klengenberg	1919	Originally Maid of Orleans
Olga	Old Man Tumma	Blt 1890	Sold to Capt. Mogg 1906, Wrecked Nome Alaska 1909
Olga			Sunk in storm, Beaufort Sea, 1944.
Omingmuk	Old Adam		Later owned by Jim Wolki/Inuathuyak.
Only Way	Kalinuk/Thrashers		
Okpik	David Bernhardt		
Ookpik	Adams/Pirtokranas/ Allens?		
Opegek	Old Adams family	1929-30	
Oriol			Shipwrecked in storm, 1946.
Ottawa			
Our Lady of Lourdes	Roman Catholic Mission		Aklavik
Pelly Lake			Arctic Red River
Penelope		1906	Lost at Shingle Pt. 1907

Pokiak	Pokiak		
Polar Bear	Louis Lane		Also Jorgan/ Klengenberg
Princess	Charles Green/ Martin Bramble		Wrecked Cape Prince of Wales, 1913
Ptarmigan			
Reindeer (Qun'niqaluk)	Charlie Gruben		Delivered by Patterson, 1929
Rob Roy			
Rosie H.	Fritz Wolki	1909/10	Whaling Ship
Saucy Jane	Old Dennis Anaqtuq also Henry Inukikyak/ Frank Cockney		Broke up around Tuktoyaktuk.
Scout			Herschel Island
Sea Otter	David Pintokra (Pirktuqann)	Blt in 1930's	Originally Japanese, captured by C.C.G. while poaching, then sold to D.P.
Sea Wolf		Early 1900s	Gasoline schooner, Kugluktuk
St. Roch	R.C.M.P., Henry Larsen		Built Vancouver
Sea Otter	David Pirtokrana/ Pirtaranun'	1930	
Shamrock	Old Fred Bennett/ Ningarsek	1922	
Silver Wave			Ada Blackjack was seamstress aboard.
Star			
Tadjok			2 masted schooner.
Teddy Bear	Joseph Bernard		
Tudlik	Angulalik	1929	Purchased from CanAlaska
Ugiyuk	Ningarsek/Akkayak	1922	
Ukkivik	Old Adams family	1929-30	
Ukpigualuk (Okpek)	Inualuugaq		
Ukpik	Inualuugaq		
Unguluk	Bob MacKenzie/ Nick Cooper		
Utuqasualungnik	Inualuugaq		
Uvakpauraq	Oliver Qikiqtaq		First steamboat

Viking	Kiasuk & Billy Thrasher	1929-30	
Wingmuk (Musk-ox)	Jim Wolki		

Index

Y

CPSIA information can be obtained
at www.ICGtesting.com
Printed in the USA
LVHW091129070419
R14677900001B/R146779PG612603LVX1B/1/P

9 781460 205570